FUTURE STATE

FUTURE STATE

Directions for Public Management
in New Zealand

Edited by Bill Ryan and Derek Gill

VICTORIA UNIVERSITY PRESS

VICTORIA UNIVERSITY PRESS
Victoria University of Wellington
PO Box 600 Wellington
vuw.ac.nz/vup

Copyright © contributors and editors 2011
First published 2011

This book is copyright. Apart from any fair
dealing for the purpose of private study, research, criticism
or review, as permitted under the Copyright Act, no part
may be reproduced by any process without the
permission of the publishers

National Library of New Zealand Cataloguing-in-Publication Data

Future state : directions for public management in New Zealand /
edited by Bill Ryan and Derek Gill.
Includes bibliographical references and index.
ISBN 978-0-86473-820-2
1. Public administration—New Zealand.
I. Ryan, Bill, 1946- II. Gill, Derek, 1956- III. Title.
351.93—dc 22

Printed by PrintStop, Wellington

Contents

Contributors

Jonathan Boston is a Professor of Public Policy in the School of Government at Victoria University of Wellington. He served as Director of the Institute of Policy Studies during 2008–11. Jonathan was one of the authors of *Public Management: The New Zealand Model* (Oxford University Press, 1996) that is still regarded as a seminal work in the study of public sector reform.

Michael Di Francesco is a Senior Lecturer in Public Sector Management at the Australia and New Zealand School of Government (ANZSOG) and an Honorary Senior Fellow in the School of Social and Political Sciences, University of Melbourne.

Elizabeth Eppel has been researching complex policy processes in public policy since 2006 at the School of Government, Victoria University of Wellington, where she recently completed her doctorate. Prior to 2006 she was a public management practitioner working in policy and senior levels of the New Zealand Ministry of Education and the Department of Prime Minister and Cabinet.

Helen Gilbert was, at the time of writing, an independent consultant. She is now the Policy Manager, Community and Strategy at the Taupō District Council.

Derek Gill is a Senior Associate at the Institute of Policy Studies, School of Government, Victoria University of Wellington and Principal Economist at the New Zealand Institute of Economic Research.

Evert Lindquist is Professor and Director of the School of Public Administration at the University of Victoria (British Columbia, Canada), has held the ANU–ANZSOG Chair in Applied Public Management Research (2010–11), and is Editor-Elect of the journal *Canadian Public Administration*.

Alec Mladenovic was, at the time of writing, a Research Assistant at the Institute of Policy Studies at Victoria University of Wellington.

Richard Norman is a Senior Lecturer with Victoria University's School of Management and co-director for the case programme of the Australia and New Zealand School of Government. His book *Obedient Servants?* (Victoria University Press, 2003) examined tensions of the New Zealand public management model of 'letting and making managers manage'.

Geoff Plimmer lectures and researches human resource management in the Victoria Management School, Victoria University of Wellington.

Stephanie Pride is a Strategic Foresight consultant.

Bill Ryan is an Associate Professor in the School of Government, Victoria University of Wellington, where he specialises in public management in both teaching and research. He was the Programmes Director for the first five years of the School of Government.

David Turner is currently a Chief Advisor in the Department of Building and Housing, responsible for evaluation of housing policy and programmes. At the time of writing he was an independent contractor in evaluation.

Amanda Wolf is Director, Graduate Research Programmes in the School of Government, Victoria University of Wellington. Her interests centre on methodology in policy-relevant research and analysis.

Abbreviations

ANZSOG	Australia and New Zealand School of Government
APS	Australian Public Service
APSC	Australian Public Service Commission
BASS	Better Administrative and Support Services (New Zealand)
CAP	Capability, Accountability and Performance (New Zealand)
CCNZ	Cancer Control New Zealand
CE	chief executive
COAG	Council of Australian Governments
CIU	Cabinet Implementation Unit (Australia)
DEG	digital-era governance
DHB	District Health Board (New Zealand)
DoL	Department of Labour (New Zealand)
DPMC	Department of the Prime Minister and Cabinet (New Zealand)
EIP	Emerging Issues Programme (New Zealand)
FACS	Family and Community Services (New Zealand)
FMIP	financial management improvement program (Australia)
FSNAC	Family Services National Advisory Council (New Zealand)
GDP	gross domestic product
GOAT	government of all the talents (UK)
HRM	human resource management
ICANN	Internet Corporation for Assigned Names and Numbers
ICT	information and communication technologies
IDC	inter-departmental committee
IPS	Institute of Policy Studies (New Zealand)
IS	information systems
JCPAA	Joint Committee of Public Accounts and Audit (Australia)

KRAs	Key Result Areas (New Zealand)
MAF	Management Accountability Framework (Canada)
MFAT	Ministry of Foreign Affairs and Trade (New Zealand)
MFO	managing for outcomes
MMP	Mixed Member Proportional electoral system (New Zealand)
MSD	Ministry of Social Development (New Zealand)
NED	non-executive director
NESTA	National Endowment for Science, Technology and the Arts (UK)
NGOs	non-government organisations
NPM	New Public Management
NZCTU	New Zealand Council of Trade Unions
NZIER	New Zealand Institute of Economic Research
OECD	Organisation of Economic Cooperation and Development
PFI	private finance initiative
PIF	performance improvement framework
PMB	program management and budgeting (Australia)
PPP	public–private partnership
PSA	Public Service Association (New Zealand)
RLGs	Regional Leadership Groups (New Zealand)
RoC	Review of the Centre (New Zealand)
SSC	State Services Commission (New Zealand)
SEMO	Strengthening Education in Mangere and Otara (New Zealand)
SRAs	Strategic Result Areas (New Zealand)
TBS	Treasury Board of Canada Secretariat

Figures and Tables

Figures

Tables

Preface

For those of us working in the New Zealand Public Service two decades ago, the reforms of the early 90s came as a liberation. We welcomed and embraced them, some of us with the fervour of religious converts. The previous system was preoccupied with due process, rules and equity of treatment, often for good reasons but, equally, when applied severely without good reason, the bureaucratic system as a whole could be very frustrating. It limited human potential and certainly limited the results it delivered for citizens.

And yet our public servant forebears a century earlier would have said exactly the same about the system of government, with its patronage, corruption and idiosyncrasy, that the bureaucratic system replaced. Clear consistent rules, due process and equity of treatment were an advance on what had gone before. As bureaucracy replaced patronage, so the 'new public management' reforms of the 1980s and 1990s replaced the bureaucratic era.

Now, in the first decades of the twenty-first century, we find ourselves straining against the constraints of the most recent reforms. They had considerable potential and much of that promise has been realised. We now have better public services, better customer service, and better value for money. We also make better use of the skills, talents and experience of the public servants who are critical to the functioning of the public sector. But we have not necessarily seen better results.

Like the contributors to this book, I believe that the system again needs to change. In the same way that, in the 1980s and 1990s, process, rules and standardisation had to give way to outputs, efficiency and managerialism, the focus now and into the future must be outcomes, effectiveness and leadership. These are the principles that must guide developments as the public sector moves ahead.

Not that the pathways forward are or will be easy to navigate. The issues are complex and much learning lies ahead – as the chapters in this book reveal. But there is little doubt in my mind that the ideas they cover will necessarily be part of the future, a future where the public sector gets better at achieving the policy outcomes sought and deserved by New Zealanders.

Professor Peter Hughes
Head of the School of Government
Victoria University of Wellington

Acknowledgements

The initiative for the Future State Project came from public service chief executives. As part of the Emerging Issues Programme (EIP) – a partnership between the public service and the School of Government through the Institute of Policy Studies (IPS) at Victoria University of Wellington – chief executives challenged the IPS researchers to look beyond the immediate issues confronting policy makers (such as the recession) and identify the next generation of longer-term issues likely to affect New Zealand.

In the first phase of the Future State project, the IPS commissioned a series of issues papers. We would like to acknowledge the contribution of experts who provided issues papers for this phase of the Future State project: Dr Lance Beath, Dr Paul Callister, Lindsay Gow, Dr Gary Hawke, Dr Richard Norman, Dr Katherine Silvester and Dorothy Wilson. We would also like to thank the New Zealanders who gave up their time to take part in workshops in Auckland, Marton, Napier and Wellington to help make sense of the themes that emerged from the issues papers.

While the particular concern of Stage 1 of the Future State was to identify the strategic cross-cutting public policy issues for the EIP work programme, the project also reviewed the ability of the public management system to respond to these challenges. The general concern among the chief executives was that, although the New Zealand public management model was ground-breaking when it was introduced in early 1990, it is no longer fit for the issues facing the state of the 21st century. The current New Zealand public management system was designed in earlier, simpler times but the times have changed. Recognising this imperative, Stage 2 of the Future State project looked at the changes required to the public management system to support the new ways of working in response to the challenges identified in Stage 1.

The members of the Stage 2 team are listed in the contributors section of this book but many others made it possible and the team members want to acknowledge and thank them. We are particularly grateful to the significant numbers of senior officials who participated in the various departmental reference groups, discussions and workshops, and to the Public Service Association, who helped with identifying PSA delegates to attend them.

The project would not have been possible had it not been commissioned and supported by the public service chief executives. Several also contributed their own time to attend workshops and all made their staff available to participate in workshops and discussions.

Throughout the project, the IPS staff provided support with events and logistics. In the last stage of the research, Dr Nestar Russell provided research assistance. Jenny Heine and Dr Emma Martin undertook the pre-submission editing and Aleck Yee created the graphics. On behalf of Victoria University Press, Dr Ginny Sullivan did the production editing, Greg Simpson created the cover, Kyleigh Hodgson did the typesetting and proofreading, and Fergus Barrowman watched over the whole thing.

We are profoundly grateful to all these people. Without their talents and cooperation, this project would not have been possible.

Introduction

For many years, New Zealand's public sector performance has been consistently rated in the top tier of countries on a variety of measures of comparative government performance. New Zealand achieved a step change in public sector reform in the 1980s when it introduced a distinctive and widely applauded model of public management. Despite attempts at continuing improvement, however, New Zealand has struggled over the past decade to keep developing that model, and to supplement and improve the frameworks and tools that public managers require to manage efficiently and effectively in the public sector in the changing circumstances of the twenty-first century.

The aftermath of the global financial crisis provides an imperative that was previously missing. Opportunities are now appearing for governments, ministers and public officials to strike out in new directions. A spirit is emerging within central government to take ideas that have been developing in public management internationally and to make them happen in ways that benefit New Zealand society. Public sector managers and staff are being encouraged by government to innovate so as to improve the efficiency and effectiveness of policies and management. In central agencies, work is well advanced on a project known as 'Better Public Services',[1] and, while this is still in its early days in terms of changes to formal systems and enacted practices, the promise is there. The major public sector union, the Public Service Association, is also adding to the mix with its 'Modern Public Services' project.[2] Equally interesting, in many pockets throughout the public sector, sometimes at the coal-face, sometimes in the middle and sometimes close to the top, individuals and small groups of public officials are doing interesting and innovative things in response to the circumstances confronting them, often working closely with others from the non-government sector. Frequently, they create these innovations by working around any constraints in the system.

Signs of this renewed enthusiasm surfaced in 2009 when the chief executives of several public sector organisations commissioned a group of researchers in and around the School of Government at Victoria University of Wellington to undertake a project looking at the 'future state'. They asked us to consider present trends that would impact on public management in coming years and wanted ideas on how those might play out. This book pulls together the results of that work.

1   See <http://www.dpmc.govt.nz/better_public_services/case_studies.htm>.
2   See <http://www.psa.org.nz/CampaignsAndIssues/ModernPublicServices.aspx>.

The project was completed in two stages. Future State 1 was an exploratory project that identified the longer-term public policy and management challenges facing New Zealand (a summary of the subsequent report is included as the first chapter in this book). A key conclusion was that the significant challenges facing New Zealand will inevitably cut across individual organisational boundaries. Therefore, a focus on bottom-line performance of individual public organisations (a feature of the New Zealand approach to public management) will not generate the step changes required to address the challenges identified in the report. Greater focus will be needed on whole-of-system performance in addition to initiatives designed to improve performance of the component parts. Some of the new approaches required were already emerging in practice but were operating at the margins and were yet to be recognised and reinforced. The second stage of the project focused on the implications for the public management system of the policy challenges identified in Stage 1. This work has been undertaken by a group of academic researchers with an interest in practice and who have advised and consulted government. Others in the team are experienced practitioners who have moved – permanently or periodically – into the academic world. In this way, collectively, we have tried to bring a combination of theory and practice to our work. The resulting essays comprise the bulk of this book.

Future State 2 began with the project team surveying the state of knowledge and the issues identified as problematic and in need of further investigation. This was done by systematically sieving the existing evidence, identifying gaps in knowledge and areas demanding more focused investigation. The result was seven work streams. They were:

- an exploration of emerging trends in governance;
- an international perspective on trends in governance;
- joint or shared accountability: issues, options and policy implications;
- experimentation and learning in policy implementation;
- agency restructuring;
- skills and capability; and
- the authorising environment.

An additional stream – on e-government – was commissioned for this book.[3]

The Future State project was able to build on evidence-based knowledge that has been accumulated in recent years, containing insights into how New Zealand's state sector actually operates. This included doctoral research

---

3   A further work stream was later developed looking at the public management implications of the Treaty of Waitangi. Unfortunately, this work did not reach fruition. It is clearly, however, a line of research that should be picked up again.

completed in the School of Government[4] that examined accountability, regulation, policy processes, information and communication technologies in public management, and service delivery. In addition to Future State 1, ongoing research into key aspects of public management known as the 'Emerging Issues' project contributed as well, also funded by the public service chief executives and undertaken through the Institute of Policy Studies as part of the School of Government. This included projects on:

- organisational performance measurement and management;
- the relationship between parliament, ministers, officials and judges;
- what enabled and what hindered joined-up government working; and
- information-sharing across government agencies to support more joined-up government.

So what emerged out of this research?

The Future State 1 report was written in the same spirit and identified similar issues and trends as the OECD's *Government of the Future* (2000) and *Governance in the 21st Century* (2001a). Its contents also resonate with ideas in the recent Moran Report (Advisory Group on Reform of Australian Public Administration, 2010) in Australia, and work of a similar nature emanating from think tanks such as Demos and the Work Foundation in Britain and the 'New Synthesis' project in Canada. Among them, there is considerable agreement on the most significant signs of the future, particularly the shift towards greater emphasis on 'governance' and the sense that a new era of public management is upon us. Inevitably, in discussing such trends, a work of this kind seems to imply that they have already arrived, fully formed and impacting on everything. Future State, however, should not be read in this way. The patterns it identified are still taking shape. As a result, the report itself and the chapters in this book should be understood as akin to scenario analyses. Trends are explored in order to visualise – all things considered – how the future might look if they were to mature.

The public management reforms of the late 1980s and early 1990s were a response to the economic, fiscal and political concerns of the time. They dramatically changed the manner in which New Zealand was governed and brought significant benefits in doing so, particularly in relation to budgetary and financial management, accountability and transparency (e.g., Schick, 1996). Subsequent reviews (e.g., Ministerial Advisory Group for the Review of the Centre, 2001) added new components (like 'managing for outcomes'), but the essential features of 'the New Zealand model of public management' (Boston, Martin, Pallot and Walsh, 1996) are still in place today (as shown, for

---

4   Including Judy Whitcombe (2008), Rose O'Neill (2009), Elizabeth Eppel (2009) and Peter Mumford (2010).

example, in the case studies and analysis in *The Iron Cage Recreated* collection; Gill, 2011). Some aspects of this model, however – e.g., its hierarchical, vertical, control-oriented framework, and its exclusive focus on single-organisation budgeting and management – are not necessarily appropriate for some of the circumstances confronting government now.

Future State 1 canvassed a range of ideas for the future and these are summarised in the first chapter of this book by Derek Gill, Stephanie Pride, Helen Gilbert, Richard Norman and Alec Mladenovic. Even before the global financial crisis of 2007–9 and the uncertainties created by the Christchurch earthquakes, the world in which New Zealanders live had become more globalised, more complex, faster moving, uncertain and subject to change. As the twentieth century flowed into the twenty-first, partly because of international inflows and outflows of people, money, goods and services, and the possibilities created by new information and communication technologies (ICT), New Zealanders were becoming increasingly diverse in their needs and ethnicities, varied in their lifestyles, demanding in their expectations and more ready to use their influence. The weight of these expectations increasingly impacts on government. In the world of the future, what will be needed are governments, ministers and public officials capable of recognising critical and decisive changes in society and seeing the implications for ways and means of governing. They will have to grasp where, when and how something needs to be done differently, where 'business as usual' no longer suffices.

What is needed now to achieve this is another step change. Step change for the future state – or certain key parts of it, anyway – cannot be achieved by working entirely within a single organisation and managing in risk-averse and routine ways. It demands working collaboratively with a wide range of partners in networks that may stretch out into the economy and civil society. Rather than delivering pre-determined responses or services to clients defined by eligibility assessed against standardised criteria, the search will be on for differentiated and customised responses that may include using new technologies in innovative ways to extend and deepen the range of options. Further, the users of government services will frequently be engaged no longer as 'consumers' but as 'producers' of the services and outcomes they need. Increasingly they will be involved as co-designers and co-producers in ways that bring citizens directly back into policy processes that affect them. Enabling these conditions demands that governments act in ways that build trust and share authority, negotiating new kinds of relationships with citizens. To be effective, new kinds of skills and competencies will be required of public officials, both ministers and public servants. These will include the capacity to scan society for key changes, the ability to make sense of ambiguity and uncertainty, a talent to mobilise organisational capability to adapt, and the skills and confidence to learn the way forward to an uncertain future, rapidly, and without losing sight of the desired outcomes. And, of course, it will need to be done affordably and sustainably.

These are exacting demands but, as the Future State Stage 1 report pointed out, there is more. Singular, universally applied approaches to public management throughout a jurisdiction will no longer suffice. The future is likely to be one of 'both–and', not 'either–or'. Performance will still be expected of public officials in efficient production of core output tasks (that is, 'bottom-line' individual and organisational performance) but also on their 'top-line' capacity to respond effectively to emerging problems and to achieve the goals and objectives of government.

Some of the new approaches required are already becoming apparent in practice, but have not yet been recognised and reinforced. Moreover, the frameworks supporting ongoing adaptations in the twenty-first century are likely to be different to the reforms of the late 1980s. They relied on changes to the 'hardware' of the architecture of government, the structural and system components of public management systems. The changes ahead, however, will depend more on subtle and multi-faceted modifications to the 'software' or mental models and practices used in the public sector. The future state must involve applying and integrating a wider range of values and approaches in order to respond to the twenty-first century environments. Doing so will require new types of multi-dimensional approaches to system coherence.

The question of system coherence in the face of the diversity and multiplicity of approaches to delivering policy and services is Evert Lindquist's starting point in chapter 2 of this book. In the past, theory and practice in public administration and management would have looked for and been based on some kind of integrating framework. A good example is *Government Management* (Treasury, 1987), which elaborated the framework upon which the new model of public management would be constructed. Writing today and from an 'outside–in' perspective, Lindquist (a Canadian academic presently associated with the Australia and New Zealand School of Government) surveys what is sometimes called 'post-NPM' thinking ('NPM is dead'), with NPM being the acronym for new public management. He concludes, firstly, that there is little point in asking whether NPM is dead, since many of those ideas – along with new ones (many of which are not really new) – will continue to animate dialogue inside and outside New Zealand on public sector reform; and, secondly, that the future will be one wherein 'no reform will be left behind'. What has changed, though, is that fiscal and other pressures have introduced a greater urgency, along with new technological possibilities for realising policy and service delivery objectives. Lindquist goes on to explore the potential of recent integrating frameworks such as the 'competing values framework' and the 'new synthesis' to capture the unique combinations for delivery policy and services, old and new, that will emerge in New Zealand and variously across different policy sectors. Indeed, the government and its central agencies need to develop such frameworks in order to anticipate the future challenges confronting these sectors, to assess the state of capabilities inside and outside government for addressing those challenges, to inform engagement with citizens and stakeholders about strategic directions and choices, and to monitor the performance of those choices.

In chapter 3, Bill Ryan argues that the future will be best served by multiple approaches to public management, not a singular model applied across a whole public sector, and that an additional model is currently taking shape. He explores a range of ideas presently featuring in the international public management literature (networks and governance, partnership and collaboration, participation and co-production) and suggests that, together, they represent a 'community-like' approach to governing that is coming more and more to the fore in some areas of state activity. Generally speaking, these ideas are not discussed in official public management documentation in New Zealand. Notwithstanding, they are starting to emerge in some examples of practice. Public managers confronted with new realities in their interactions with citizens are adapting to those pressures in ways consistent with what is also occurring in comparable jurisdictions. These 'community' approaches to public management are signs of the future and should be recognised, explicated and authorised. Public management across New Zealand government in the future is likely to be a context-dependent mixture of three approaches. Some government activities will be best conducted along bureaucratic lines, some in terms of a market, and others as a community. The formal public management system must enable each approach to be applied as each context demands. Shifting in this direction, however, will require a consideration of how Westminster-based conventions regarding relationships between ministers and officials will need to keep evolving.

Talking of ministers, in chapter 4, Michael Di Francesco and Elizabeth Eppel tackle what some might regard as a 'heresy' within public management. The NPM reforms adopted in New Zealand proposed – in fact, expected – that ministers would play an important role in the new ways of governing. In particular, ministers endorsed a framework of management and performance accountabilities that to be effective not only demanded new behaviours from public officials but also required ministers to adapt their own practices, for example, by taking a more 'managerial' approach to interacting with officials, and by making policy decisions based on evidence arising from a range of sources including (but not restricted to) monitoring and evaluation. Within the NPM context it was also assumed that ministers would assess the performance of the public sector in those terms. The role of ministers in public management is not often discussed by either academics or practitioners, and is a fundamental issue that Di Francesco and Eppel take up. They suggest that few ministers have developed the 'managerial' side of their job and argue that public management cannot progress further until ministers learn to do so (or that failed expectations of the model are revisited). The authors compare practice in New Zealand and Australia, including ministerial role designations, and expectations of ministers and parliament in responding to and using performance information provided by public servants. They suggest that we can no longer afford to 'sanctify' the role of ministers within Westminster conventions and that ministers should be expected to carry out their executive and parliamentary work in accordance with the expectations they themselves have set, as well as being made accountable for this. Di Francesco and Eppel's chapter concludes by canvassing various options to encourage greater 'professionalism' among ministers in these respects, including training and standards setting, ministerial appointments from outside parliament to inject external experience, using governance structures as 'choice architecture' to impose leadership and managerial responsibilities on ministers, and chipping away at the inherent adversarialism of Westminster-based parliaments by experimenting with consensus-based accountability structures.

The Future State 1 report emphasised the context of fiscal constraint in which public management will need to be conducted in the immediate years ahead but it also suggested that tweaking existing approaches may no longer be sufficient for the scale of the task required. What then needs to be done to ensure the affordability and sustainability of the public sector in the future? Bill Ryan confronts this question in chapter 5 by first casting a sceptical eye over the usual methods of achieving savings such as cutbacks, prioritisation and efficiency drives. There is little evidence that these methods lead to major savings; the cost of government on a number of measures, including total expenditure relative to GDP, has remained relatively stable in countries like New Zealand for many years. More radical innovation may be needed. To illustrate the measure of new thinking required, Ryan discusses the 'radical efficiency' agenda being discussed in Britain – an approach to public management that is predicated not on a market failure/tax-and-spend conception of government relative to society and the economy but one of 'social investment'. This kind of approach would recognise all the social and human capital brought to bear in achieving government policy goals. Under such an approach, the call on the public purse may in itself be reduced as a proportion of the aggregate volume of resources brought to outcome production; but, more importantly, the whole notion of the public value and governance produced might take on a deeper meaning, and hence affordability and sustainability could be thought of in new ways. Whatever the merits of such an approach, 'radical efficiency' thinking is a reminder of the importance of breaking away from unreflective repetition of the past and entertaining the types of radical innovation required for the future.

Radical rethinking as a requirement for the future is also addressed in chapter 6, which deals with experimentation and learning in implementation, written by Elizabeth Eppel, David Turner and Amanda Wolf. Too often, implementation and delivery have been treated in public administration and management as either a simple step in a linear, rule-guided sequence, located as a series of planned activities between policy design and the eventual results detected by evaluation, or more blithely entrusted to third-party delivery agents. Either way, the goals, objectives and strategies are designed in advance and the task of implementation is to operationalise the plan or achieve the pre-ordained targets nominated by the funder. Eppel, Turner and Wolf theorise an alternative interpretation of the nature of implementation, and draw out the management implications. Picking up on the Future State Stage 1 pointers to complexity, they show that implementation is, indeed, often complex. In consequence, implementation needs to be reconceptualised as a continual process of experimentation and learning. 'Experimentation' is understood in an everyday sense as describing an orientation that allows policy managers to make use of a full range of information and expertise gained in the process of implementing policy. They note that implementation refers to an evolving and emerging set of activities and behaviours in the 'real world'. The authors' research finds that successful organisational and individual practices are built upon identifying and working with observations that appear only when a policy is tested. Given a consistent strategic view of end goals, such learning enables redirecting efforts to build up a successful policy. Implementation practice requires appropriate permission and the ability to conduct design and implementation activities outside the responsible agencies at an early stage. Making use of learning as you go requires the continuous application of a habit of mind that asks not 'what are the facts?', but 'what does not seem right?' and 'what is the next question?'

Accountability is important in the public management system; it is even more so with joined-up government. As Future State 1 pointed out, a system wedded solely to vertical accountability will not work well in the future. Jonathan Boston and Derek Gill (chapter 7) explore directions for thinking about accountability. Joined-up government can take several forms, two examples of which are co-ordination and collaboration. The choice of form depends on the policy context, the intensity and scope of joint working, options regarding 'hard' and 'soft' factors, and the separability and interdependence of the task. How best to proceed with a joined-up task is often uncertain and views may conflict. In determining how to work together, argue the authors, a number of points need to be underscored. Participants must feel a sense of 'ownership' to generate a strong sense of shared responsibility; this is essential whatever the formal accountability regime. In the context of joint working, a concentrated approach to accountability is likely to be more effective where the policy problems are relatively 'tame', the tasks are clearly separable, levels of interdependence are low and there is minimal sole-person risk. Shared or diffuse accountability will be preferable when tasks are inseparable, and there is high interdependence and much collective wisdom. Boston and Gill go on to suggest that, given the importance of joined-up government, creative thinking is needed about how best to encourage new and successful forms of joint working. This requires central agency leadership, as well as a willingness to place more emphasis on horizontal accountability mechanisms to sit alongside hierarchical and vertical accountabilities. Joint working will be essential in the future – but so will be delivering 'results', fiscal constraint and meeting the challenges of 'wicked' problems. Innovative practices will be required with a new openness to collaborative arrangements and alternative accountability arrangements.

Quite rightly, the Future State report noted that the new information and communication technologies are playing a major role in what we are coming to understand as the 'twenty-first century'. These are also contributing to how we rethink government of the future. At one stage the field was given its own name: 'e-government'. Some think that 'digital-era governance' defines the future. In chapter 8, Miriam Lips argues, however, that much of the complexity surrounding electronic applications in government comes about because of narrow perspectives on e-government and misleading expectations about the transformational potential of technology in public sector reform. Recommendations for future models are not usually aligned with the managerial, governmental and democratic realities. Another problem arises with 'technological determinism'. Technologies do not drive change but public managers can use them to enable it. Lips continues by arguing that we need more research into the actual application of ICTs so governments in the future can make the best use of the opportunities and work in appropriate ways. They need to move away from a government-centric approach towards public service development and delivery, and shift towards new ICT-enabled citizen-centric service models such as networked governance. Lips concludes her chapter by noting a few 'system errors' that need to be fixed in the current public management system in New Zealand in order to make any progress with the design of an effective and efficient ICT-enabled future state.

New Zealand stands out for the extent to which chief executives have used structures as a lever for strategic change. Richard Norman and Derek Gill explore in chapter 9 what triggers organisational restructuring, how restructurings are undertaken and some of the consequences of restucturing.

They find that pressures from the formal system to initiate change (and to be seen to initiate change) encourage the use of structural change by new chief executives who in many cases are under pressure to demonstrate results within a five-year contract period. Restructuring provides a symbolic action visible to central agency reviewers and political leaders. Norman and Gill suggest that restructuring results in not easily observable losses in capability, and invariably takes longer to deliver improvements than anticipated. Restructuring initiatives are largely regarded as a 'freedom to manage' operational decision for a chief executive. The authors argue that, given the potential impact of the loss of organisational capability and relationship capital, as agencies become less able to collaborate with other agencies, this area of change needs scrutiny in a manner similar to a case for a budget bid for capital investment.

As Future State 1 and several chapters in this volume emphasise, new ways of working will be required across many aspects of governance. In the penultimate chapter, Geoff Plimmer, Richard Norman and Derek Gill discuss how, in turn, these new ways will require new skills and capabilities in public sector organisations. Their research found that a focus on building skills and capabilities provides a means of managing the inherent tensions between an authorising environment that emphasises control and risk aversion, and increasing demand for flexibility and innovation. A 'strategic human resource management' approach can be effective in building the skills and capabilities required. However, there are a number of barriers to taking this approach – ministers' specific and immediate demands, the struggle for management attention, weak central leadership and under-skilled line managers – all of which act as either distractions or impediments to capability.

In the final chapter, Ryan and Gill discuss the need to reignite the spirit of reform in public management in New Zealand. This spirit soared in the 1990s and again, briefly, in the early years of the twenty-first century but then faded. Future State 1 called for a step change in the means and methods of governing, a view that is supported in various ways by the contributors to the collection of essays in this book. Ministers in the present government say they are looking for innovation. If recent views emanating from Treasury are any indication, the leadership of the public service recognises that the conditions of governing have changed significantly in recent years. In response it appears that they want to address this fact by making continuing modifications to the existing public management system but not to considering fundamental change. On the other hand, in pockets throughout the public sector, confronted by circumstances where normal operating practice does not help them to achieve the policy outcomes sought by government, officials are creating new ways of ensuring they can. In doing so they are showing the way towards creating approaches to public management that point to the future. The authors argue that it is these individuals and networks that are reviving the spirit of reform and their work should be supported, applauded and taken forward. Ryan and Gill finish by identifying a selection of principles distilled and combined from the chapters in this book that could and perhaps should be adopted as part of the future state, as the directions for continuing reform by practitioners of public management in New Zealand.

Bill Ryan
Derek Gill

October 2011

1

The Future State Project: Meeting the Challenges of the Twenty-first Century[1]

Derek Gill, Stephanie Pride, Helen Gilbert, Richard Norman and Alex Mladenovic

The world we have made, as a result of the level of thinking we have done thus far, creates problems we cannot solve at the same level of thinking at which we created them.

Albert Einstein (quoted in Des MacHale, Wisdom, London, 2002)

Introduction

Powerful global forces will reshape the context for New Zealand over the next few decades. They include increasing international connectedness, geopolitical power shifts, rapid technological developments, demographic changes, climate change, growing resource scarcity and changing values. Some of these changes have been in train for several decades; others have come to the fore more recently. Together they are creating a world that is fast-paced, heterogeneous, complex and unpredictable. Within this context, New Zealand also faces some policy choices that are both unique and significant (e.g., maintaining and protecting the recently extended exclusive economic zone and completing the Treaty of Waitangi claims settlement process).

The current New Zealand public management system was designed in earlier, simpler times but those times have changed. Recognising this imperative, in July 2009 the steering committee of the Emerging Issues Programme (EIP)[2]

---

1   This chapter is a revised version of an article that appeared in the August 2010 edition of *Policy Quarterly* (Gill, Pride, Gilbert, Norman and Mladenovic, 2010). A fuller version of the arguments in this chapter is contained in IPS Working Paper 10/08 (Gill, Pride, Gilbert and Norman, 2010).

2   The EIP was an initiative established in 2006 between public service chief executives and the School of Government at Victoria University of Wellington to carry out research into significant policy and management issues relevant across a range of public service agencies.

commissioned the Institute of Policy Studies (IPS) to undertake an exploratory study known as the Future State project. This project had three primary objectives, namely, to:

- identify major public policy issues of relevance to New Zealand over the next two decades;
- consider the current public management system[3] and its capacity to perform in a much more dynamic world and an increasingly complex policy environment; and
- identify related research projects that could be pursued by the IPS under the EIP (which included Stage 2 of Future State).

The Stage 1 final report (Gill, Pride, Gilbert and Norman, 2010) can be accessed at <http://ips.ac.nz/publications/publications/show/295>. This chapter summarises some of the main points arising from that report.

The Future State (Stage 1) brief was to look beyond the immediate issues confronting policy makers (e.g., the consequences of the global financial crisis, including the tightening fiscal position) and to identify the next generation of longer-term issues likely to affect New Zealand. The project was to be exploratory: to capture and synthesise existing knowledge and information. The scope of the project was also limited to the main institutions of central government (i.e., public service departments and other non-trading entities, including statutory Crown entities).[4] Although local government was not part of the project (as the formal management framework under which it operates is different from the public management system in central government), almost all of the issues identified for central government are equally relevant to local government.

In order to identify future policy issues, the IPS commissioned overview papers from various experts on seven areas relevant to policy-making and the public sector. These covered New Zealand's evolving social structure and demography, technological developments, the economic context, environmental considerations, political and geo-political shifts, and public management issues. The experts were asked to provide a stock-take of the current state of knowledge in their specialist areas on likely global and national developments over the next 20 years, drawing upon recent futures work in New Zealand and overseas. Several structured discussions building on these papers were held to explore

---

3   For the purposes of this chapter, the public management system comprises the arrangements for governing a country, including the means by which policies are developed and implemented by public sector organisations and the processes for funding, managing and monitoring those organisations.

4   This recognises that New Zealand's democracy is highly centralised, with over 90 per cent of public expenditure being allocated through central government.

cross-cutting themes and possibilities. In addition to the expert academic contributions, the project team captured tacit and emergent knowledge from a range of participants, including Māori, business leaders, older people and younger people, migrants, rural dwellers and regional public sector managers.

The Future State Findings

New Zealand, rated 123 out of 223 countries by population size and twenty-seventh by gross domestic product per capita, is largely a 'future taker' rather than a 'future maker' on the global stage. The Future State project (Stage 1) identified powerful global forces that even the largest nations can do little more than react to over the next 20 years. These forces relate to:

- the shifting of economic and political influence from west to east, in particular the rise of China and India relative to the United States;
- continuing and maturing globalisation;
- greater internationalisation of policy as domestic policy settings are increasingly shaped by international agreements;
- increasing migration and urbanisation;
- increasing diversity in most societies;
- the ageing of most developed societies, but a swathe of (mostly) developing countries remaining 'juvenescent';
- changing values and world views as the 'digital generation' moves into management and leadership roles;
- continuing heterogeneity of family structures;
- continuing rapid technological development in information and communication technologies (ICT), biotechnology, nanotechnology and robotics, with the noteworthy consequences of:
  - ICT-enabled customisation, personalisation and participation;
  - ICT-driven challenges to privacy (due to increased availability of personalised data), authority and authorship; and
- transitioning to low-carbon economies, including the adoption of higher environmental standards.

Some fundamental forces that will shape New Zealand's future can be seen as local manifestations of globally occurring phenomena. Such forces include:

- high inward and outward migration, together with increasing population diversity;
- the continuing concentration of populations in urban centres, in particular in the Auckland region, and the coastal and peri-urban areas;
- climate change; and
- threats to biodiversity.

Other influences that will contribute to determine New Zealand's future are unique to its heritage and geography. These influences include:

- New Zealand's extensive exclusive economic zone and continental shelf; and
- completion of the Treaty of Waitangi claims settlement process and the opportunities and challenges that will arise in the post-settlement era.

New Zealand cannot affect the global forces of change in any significant way. It can, however, choose how it responds to both global and local forces of change. How the drivers and changes will play out in the future is obviously unknowable – it will depend on the policy choices New Zealand makes and will vary significantly across different sectors. The four challenges – affordability, complexity, diversity and predictability – that emerged consistently from our scan would stretch the most capable public sectors, even in the absence of tight fiscal restraint.

The forces of change confronting New Zealand, both globally and locally, and the challenges presented by those forces, will almost certainly require a major rethinking of policy settings and public sector practices. In this chapter, we have used the term 'step change' to describe the changes in policy settings required to alter the current trends in spending and policy results. Without such step changes, New Zealand will be limited in its ability to maintain the delivery of public services at levels that are achieved by similar countries. Step change requires public sector entities to reconfigure how they work internally and how they relate to each other and interact with society. Further, such changes will not be achieved by altering the 'hardware' of the architecture of government. Achieving change will require modifying the 'software' – the mental models or the conceptual architecture applied to policy problems. The important question then is, 'How is New Zealand's public sector positioned to cope with the challenges of the twenty-first century?'

The Public Management System: A Need for Change

The current New Zealand public management system is largely the legacy of major state sector reforms in the mid-1980s. These reforms, bold and ground-breaking at the time, replaced the unified, lifetime career service and monolithic sector-based departments with the apparatus of 'new public management', including employment contracts, single-purpose organisations, and an output-based approach to budgeting and management. This model of public management served the country well in the latter part of the twentieth century, lifting the performance of the state sector to a level that consistently earned high international ratings across a range of criteria. According to Boston and Eichbaum (2007: 136), the benefits of the reforms included:

> greater productive efficiency (especially in the commercial parts of the public sector), improvements in the quality of certain services (e.g. the time taken to process applications for passports and welfare benefits has been drastically reduced), better expenditure control, better management of departmental budgets, greater managerial accountability, and major improvements in the quality of information available to policy makers.

With minor modifications, the New Zealand public management model is still in place today, but accumulating evidence suggests it will be less fit to meet the challenges of the twenty-first century, in which conditions are less stable and predictable than previously. Globally and locally, the priorities, preferences and values of populations are more diverse yet the issues on which they want action are more complex and interconnected than in the past and more difficult to actualise. Citizens expect the modern state to grapple with a wider range of more complex issues. This complexity makes gaining and maintaining consensus on policy directions over the long haul more demanding. The same applies to the governance and management arrangements, including ways of organising implementation and service delivery. For many of the challenges (e.g., water management and governance, growing obesity levels, educational underachievement in some population segments), there are no simple answers, widely agreed and proven solutions, or obvious means to achieve them. In some areas (e.g., climate change), even problem definitions are contested. At the same time, the public increasingly expects speed, accessibility, customisation, transparency and user engagement in public services. If the public sector is to respond effectively, the public management system will need to be revised so that it supports a broader range of approaches and practices than currently.

Challenges and Required Responses

Future State (Stage 1) identified four key challenges for public policy and management development over the coming decades:

* affordability, which requires the ability to achieve step change in policy design and delivery;
* more complex problems involving many players, which requires the capability for leadership of issues, co-design and co-production;[5]

---

5 'Co-design' harnesses the knowledge of citizens and staff in creating solutions. Co-production occurs where both public organisations and citizens/clients must perform tasks if results are to be achieved, such as revenue collection.

- a more diverse and differentiated population, which requires the capability for differentiated responses; and
- a world of faster, less predictable change, which requires the capability for constant scanning and learning the way forward.[6]

Affordability

Compounding the immediate fiscal pressures generated by the global recession during 2008–9, New Zealand, like many other countries, faces significant longer-term pressures on both the demand for, and the cost of, publicly funded services. These will exacerbate the government's fiscal difficulties. The cost pressures will arise because government services are generally labour-intensive and, in particular, are high users of skilled labour and the cost of that labour is likely to continue to rise. On the demand side, the ageing population will provide the key driver, with expenditure on health and aged care projected to increase dramatically. Responding to these challenges simply by 'doing more with less' will not be sufficient – the gap is too large to be bridged by efficiencies alone.

The public policy challenge is to develop the step changes in policy design and delivery that succeed in achieving long-sought outcomes (e.g., reducing frailty levels in an ageing population, increasing levels of educational success and stepping up the productivity ladder), whilst minimising the effects of the underlying drivers on aggregate expenditure. Take, for example, spending on law and order (e.g., prisons, police and courts), where public expenditure relative to nominal gross domestic product (GDP) increased from 0.5 per cent in 1971/72 to 1.1 per cent in 1988/89, to 1.6 per cent in 2009/10. The number of people in prison or on probation has relentlessly increased while the overall level of crime has been dropping or stable since 1997. New Zealand now has the fourth-highest incarceration rate in the OECD after the United States, Mexico and the Czech Republic, yet a relatively small percentage of the population generates most criminal activity. Achieving a step change would require response at two levels. The first would be breaking the cycles of dysfunction among a relatively small number of families. This will require changes in how services are delivered by a range of government and non-government organisations, both inside and outside the law-and-order sector. At the policy level it will require replacing, for example, a 'race to the bottom' – with political parties competing to be 'tough on crime' – with a more durable policy bargain about a responsible and efficacious approach to sentencing policy driven less by a focus on punishment.

6   Learning the way forward is a response to complex problems involving acting, learning and then responding.

Complex 'Multi-actor' Policy Problems Requiring Partnerships, and New Types of Skills

Many of the policy outcomes that will be front-of-mind for government (e.g., reducing obesity levels in the general population) cannot be achieved through the provision of public services alone, but require the active contribution of citizen and business service users (co-production). For some complex issues (e.g., breaking the cycles of dysfunction mentioned previously), no one actor, including government, has all the knowledge, resources or capability to effect change independently.

In the past, government doing things *for* or *to* citizens may have been sufficient. Achieving outcomes in the face of twenty-first-century challenges will depend on the actions of many players and will therefore increasingly require governments to do things *with* citizens (or even to enable citizens to do things for themselves). Bourgon et al. (2009: 11) have described this challenge as follows:

> This context also pushes governments *beyond hierarchy* as a broad dispersion of responsibilities in society and the coordination of complex operations constitute the trademark of government activities. It challenges governments to experiment *beyond direct service delivery* with indirect means of delivery. It pushes governments *beyond the provision of services to citizens* as an increasing number of public policy issues require the active contribution of citizens in creating common public goods. It pushes governments *beyond borders of the traditional concept of the state* towards a dynamic open system where organizations, services and users interact.

This will require forming various types of partnerships with other actors and working with them in relatively open networks that stretch beyond government into the economy and civil society. In these networks, government will be only one partner among many although it may have superior access to resources and so may need to facilitate the participation of others.

Government will need to go beyond a 'delivery of services' model to an approach that encompasses co-production and co-design. These methods harness the knowledge and creativity of citizens and staff in identifying problems and in generating and implementing solutions. It offers the opportunity to uncover the real barriers to, and accelerate, solutions that will be genuinely effective.

Government currently works with citizens and businesses but often in prescribed and controlling ways. For example, under existing models of consultation, one party (government) often determines the timeframe, ambit of discussion, range of options to be discussed, process to be used and the purposes to which the fruits of consultation are put. If, in the future, government requires the co-operation and contribution of New Zealanders in order to achieve results, public agencies may need to cede control in some areas (e.g., timeframes, processes used) in order to harness the contributions they seek. If government organisations are to solve problems jointly with communities and business groups, the public sector will need to understand better how different groups experience the world, develop more trusting relationships and take on additional roles in working with them (e.g., moderator, facilitator, enabler, partner, listener and leader) (Pride, 2009).

Current processes for policy development, service design and service delivery do not necessarily allow for working in these less controlling, more deeply engaged ways with citizens, communities and businesses, so they will need to be adjusted or augmented.

Leading but not controlling will increasingly require public employees to engage with the public in different ways. Public employees working in partnerships and networks will need a range of 'soft' skills to build trust and negotiate relationships, help with sense-making, and assist and sometimes 'nudge' participants towards solutions. Developing the way forward will often involve learning to work with uncertainty and ambiguity, forging consensus and agreement, and creating a shared understanding of performance. Trustful behaviour is needed to motivate and maintain these kinds of interactions.

Diverse Society and Differentiated Responses

As is the case in many other countries, New Zealand's population is becoming more diverse. This plurality is increasing across a variety of dimensions, including ethnicity, family structures, geographical mobility and acknowledged sexual orientation. Heterogeneity is the new 'normal'. This increases pressure for services that are able to meet this increasingly wide range of needs. At the same time, citizens are getting used to technology-enabled, real-time, customised provision in the private sector so they come to expect flexible access to customised public services. The 'one size fits all' Fordist state prevalent in the twentieth century (Dunleavy, Margetts, Bastow and Tinkler, 2006a) will no longer suffice to meet expectations or necessarily provide the most effective outcomes in the twenty-first century.

The challenge for public services is to move to differentiated responses as the norm rather than the exception and to work in more diverse ways as a matter of course. One approach is enabling citizens to engage in co-design and co-production to create initiatives and solutions tailored to the needs of a particular sector, community group or individual. Another approach is to introduce alternative models of service delivery that 'mix 'n' match'. These will harness the full range of choices available through the chosen funding mechanism, allowing a mix of providers and services to match the client need in order to create the best fit that might achieve the outcomes sought.

Other options include making more use of information and communication technology to develop a more profound understanding of the citizens and their needs. The private sector has developed 'business intelligence systems' that use sophisticated data-mining and risk-screening techniques to understand service users' experience and behaviour. The information is then used to match customers' preferences to existing products and to shape the development of new products. In the public sector, these types of techniques could be used to improve, for example, government understanding both of clients at risk of poor life outcomes, and the development and design of individualised interventions that can help them.

ICTs can also be harnessed at a system and service level. Expert decision tools have the potential to transform policy, service design and service delivery by utilising the richness of the data that is available and the increasingly powerful tools for interrogating it. These can be used to support professional decisions with real-time, relevant, on-the-spot information. The extent of transformation will depend crucially on how professional providers (government and non-government) respond to the use of these tools.

A World of Fast, Unpredictable Change

The twenty-first century will be characterised by fast-paced change, growing complexity and unpredictability. New technologies are being developed and applied more quickly than ever, transforming what is possible, and doing so faster than legislative and regulatory processes can respond. In addition, changing conditions combine to increase and accelerate the unpredictability and rapidity of change. More diverse populations and denser global interconnections, for example, contribute to making the world more unpredictable.

In this context, governments still need to make decisions and act. However, the public management system that supports those decision-making processes has been predicated on relatively stable, predictable conditions. Existing processes, therefore, need to be supplemented by approaches and methods more suited to managing under uncertainty, e.g., scanning, sense-making and learning the way forward.

Working under uncertainty requires constant attention to what is emergent, scanning widely, recognising emerging change, making sense of it and imagining how it could unfold. In particular, it means listening beyond the 'noise' in order to pick out the important signals. Scanning allows organisations to better detect adverse conditions, guide policy, shape strategy, and explore the need for new products and services. Scanning helps provide a greater ability to anticipate future changes. To quote Bourgon (2009a: 9) again:

> Countries with the best ability to anticipate and to take corrective actions will have significant comparative advantage. They will best be able to innovate,

adapt and prosper in unforeseen circumstances and they will be better able to shift the course of events in their favour.

Some countries, such as Singapore, Britain and Finland, have well-established organisations and programmes that are dedicated to scanning the future.

Responding to complex problems, where the exact problem is unclear and the solution cannot be known in advance, requires different ways of working based on learning the way forward. Chapter 6 in this volume discusses in more detail the issues of policy implementation in the face of complexity. Current service design approaches aim to operationalise the policy decision and take it through to implementation. They assume that the solution can be known in advance. This assumption cannot hold when matters are complex. As shown in Figure 1.1, learning the way forward is required; that is, acting, sensing and learning then responding.

Figure 1.1. Sense-making in a Complex World

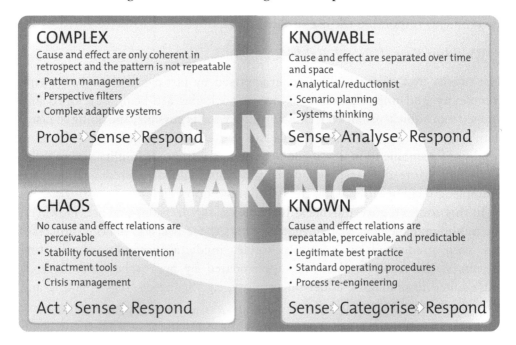

Source: Kurtz and Snowden (2003: 462–83).

The private sector has already developed techniques that involve learning the way forward. 'Agile development' is specifically constructed for situations where the problem is known but the solution is not, while the 'build to learn' approach is developed for situations where neither the problem nor the solution is easily evident. This later approach, for example, starts with small batches of 'minimum viable product' and then works iteratively with real user experience. This requires systems that are set up to allow fast iterations and to minimise the total time through each micro-development loop. It also requires quick response times to fix problems for customers, as well as monitoring the metrics that stakeholders care about. This in turn creates an ability to tell 'good' change from 'bad' change and to reverse 'bad' change early. Public sectors need to take up such methods as they learn to manage in the future.

Public Management: Twenty-first-century Demands

The present and future are therefore making new demands on public managers. They must be able to:

- recognise the need for step change when required and do what is necessary to make it happen;
- work collaboratively with a wide range of others as partners and to work with them in networks;
- enable co-design and co-production with service users and providers;
- lead by sharing authority rather than controlling;
- respond to diversity and plurality, providing differentiated and customised responses including harnessing new technologies to do so;
- deal with fast and unpredictable change, constantly scanning, making sense of what they see and learning the way forward; and
- do so effectively, affordably and sustainably.

A public management system fit for the twenty-first century needs to support all these approaches whilst preserving existing system strengths. The Future State project identified how changes under way will require 'both–and' rather than 'either–or' approaches. Public organisations will need to improve their performance on core output tasks (that is, 'bottom-line' individual organisational performance) as well as to build their 'top-line' capability to respond to emerging problems. They also need to shift from an environment that has been generally stable, and has emphasised control, linear accountability and outputs, to one that is more adaptable and at ease with ambiguity.

Some of the new approaches required might already be emerging in practice, but have not yet been recognised and reinforced. This suggests that the changes that need to be made (and, in a minority of cases, already have been made) to the public management system to support twenty-first-century public services may be different from the changes of the late 1980s. Rather than altering the 'hardware' of the architecture of government, or discrete formal and structural components of public management systems, the changes will be subtle and multi-faceted modifications to the 'software' or mental models used in the public sector.

The Public Management System in New Zealand: Facing Up to the Twenty-first Century – Key Areas for Change

New Zealand created a high-quality public management system but one that was appropriate for the conditions of the late twentieth century. The preceding section outlined some major twenty-first-century challenges and the nature of the responses they require. The Future State project identified two overarching system adjustments that will be required if the public sector is to respond appropriately. They involve moving towards:

- greater system coherence to support a whole-of-government focus; and
- applying and integrating a wider range of system values and approaches in order to support a broader range of responses.

Moving Towards a Whole-of-government Focus

From a Focus on Single Public Organisations . . .

A major formula of the New Zealand public management reforms in the late 1980s was to subdivide conglomerate departments into single-purpose organisations with clear roles and accountabilities, and to shift the locus of control for output delivery to chief executives and boards of public organisations. This principle enabled a focus on known and knowable problems within the particular field of policy defined by the organisation.

Recent initiatives by central agencies have focused on improving the efficiency of individual public organisations. Good reasons exist for this emphasis. There is no direct counterpart in the public sector to the market signals available to the private sector through competitive product markets, share prices on stock markets or company takeovers. The core non-market public sector needs comparable mechanisms to identify poor performers and to raise their performance. Central agency initiatives, such as the State Services Commission-led Performance Improvement Framework (PIF), can make a useful contribution by helping to lift bottom-line organisational performance and to realise additional efficiency gains. A focus on organisational performance alone, however, is unlikely to generate the step change in capability required. What are needed are methods and systems that support and drive holistic, all-of-government responses.

. . . to a Focus on Organisations and Sector-wide System Performance

One consequence of creating single-purpose organisations with clear roles and accountabilities has been tunnel vision that hinders cross-cutting solutions to complex problems. A model that emphasises specialisation and *ex-ante* specification of targets and accountabilities struggles to respond to emerging issues that demand systems thinking, interconnected responses, flexibility and innovation. The challenge is to continue focusing on 'bottom-line' organisational efficiency, while at the same time increasing the focus on 'top-line' policy effectiveness by harnessing the collective capability of the public sector in addressing problems chosen for action by ministers. In this rebalancing, a greater focus will be needed on understanding, managing and assessing whole-of-system performance.

The barriers in the New Zealand system start at the top with a fragmented structure of ministerial portfolios. Fewer and wider ministerial portfolios would simplify accountabilities and reduce the barriers to collaboration on cross-cutting issues. Similarly, making ministers formally accountable to the public for achieving specified outcomes for their portfolio – in the same way that bureaucrats are accountable for delivering agreed outputs against their appropriation – would strike a better balance between outputs and outcomes. Another possibility is to strengthen a collective, horizontal, senior leadership cadre with cross-agency obligations as a counterbalance to the vertical accountabilities dominated by expectations of chief executive performance. Relaunching circuit-breaker-type initiatives[7] to create cross-agency and sectoral forms of service delivery might also broaden the performance focus.

Other jurisdictions have systems that promote greater shared accountability in relation to shared outcomes and measure system progress in terms of movement towards outcomes. In Western Australia, for example, senior leaders in public organisations are assigned responsibility for integrating the 'value chains' (the flow of value-adding activities in an organisation) around particular outcome areas. This could be augmented by the Canadian approach, in which senior staff members are assigned a 'champion role' (an expressive, energetic public advocate) for cross-cutting functions such as collaboration, evaluation and learning.

Formal changes to the system alone will not, however, be sufficient to generate the step change in the level of system coherence that is needed. Working across organisational boundaries, for example, is not currently precluded by the current New Zealand public management model, but nor is it enabled or encouraged by the system settings. Earlier IPS research under the Emerging Issues Programme (*Better Connected Services for Kiwis*, see Eppel, Gill, Lips and Ryan, 2008) found that working collaboratively across the public sector requires a specific set of skills and dispositions. Hard-system factors, such as structures, appropriations, differences in pay terms and conditions, and formal mandates, while they had an impact, were less important than soft-

---

7   Circuit-breaker teams were developed in response to the Review of the Centre to address complex cross-cutting issues. Although the approach showed initial promise, efforts were not sustained and the initiative withered and died.

system factors, such as a sense of urgency (a 'burning platform'), leadership (public entrepreneurs, guardian angels and fellow travellers), learning by doing, and working from an outside–in client perspective. Respecting and valuing the world views, competencies, knowledge and contribution of those from different teams, agencies and sectors are fundamental pre-conditions for learning together about what will work. These ways of working are linked to a whole-of-system and solutions-focused approach, where the agendas and interests of individual contributors are subsumed within the collective endeavour of problem-solving. This suggests that the nature of the changes to the public management system to support twenty-first-century public services may need to be different from the changes of the late 1980s. Rather than major alterations to the 'hardware' of the architecture of government (e.g., organisational structures and systems), the majority of the changes will need to be subtle and multifaceted modifications to the 'software' of the mental models and everyday practices used in the public sector.

Supporting a Broader Range of Responses

From a Few Default Modes . . .

New Zealand's public management system was historically based on clan and hierarchy, as were most traditional, career-for-life public services. The reforms of the 1980s and 1990s used market values and methods to reshape structures and systems and increase freedom to manage and innovate. During the past decade this has been overlaid with a different form of control based on constant system reproduction and the internalisation of system values (Gill, 2011), driven by the desire to monitor performance and minimise risk. As a result, the current system relies heavily on a limited range of practices associated with the 'market' and 'hierarchy' quadrants shown in Figure 1.2. Yet these limits are not readily apparent to public managers in their everyday work. These 'default' modes appear to them as the normal and natural way of conducting the business of the public service. If New Zealand's prescribed public management system is considered in terms of a competing values framework, it becomes apparent that it is predicated on and supports values in the bottom two quadrants (Figure 1.2).

The Future State project found that effective responses to twenty-first-century challenges will require collaboration, trust, agility, creativity and innovation; in other words, values associated with the upper 'clan' and 'network' quadrants in Figure 1.2. The skills needed to operate in these ways are currently underdeveloped compared to the skills needed to operate in 'hierarchy' and 'market' modes, and will thus need to be augmented. However, substituting an operating style based on the values of the lower 'hierarchy' and 'market' quadrants with one based on those of the upper 'clan' and 'network' quadrants is not what is required. Across the range of public sector activities and obligations, some will be best run on hierarchical principles and others on those of market, network and clan. The challenge therefore is to build new strengths and capabilities so that the context-dependent application of each is enabled and an integrated approach to management flows throughout the whole public sector is achieved.

Figure 1.2. The Competing Values Framework

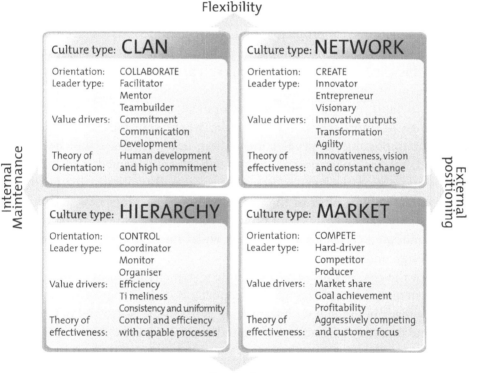

Source: Cameron, Quinn, Degraff and Thakor (2006: 66).

Public sector work is already multifaceted, but increasingly difficult and variegated challenges arising from a diverse and complex society will call for even more differentiated responses to achieving outcomes. Hence, the public management system will need to support multiple modes and approaches to managing organisations, resources and people, drawing on values from all four quadrants of the competing values framework.

. . . to Matching Form to Context

Looking ahead, individually and collectively, agencies and managers will need to apply a range of models and approaches to issues and have the knowledge and skills to adopt the best combination in each case to generate productive solutions. This will require a sophisticated understanding of context involving a conscious choice of modes, taking into account the underlying values they embody. Command and control approaches will not be a good choice in some circumstances, for example, where achieving desired outcomes depends on co-production. In the future, no one standard operating procedure will be fit for all purposes, and the capacity to make the right choices will be central to the overall performance of the public sector.

Current approaches to policy development are built around the idea of expert solutions to problems that were assumed to be technical and tractable. While suitable for simple or technical problems, this approach will not be sufficient for emerging challenges. These require not a technical fix but engagement, behaviour change or other kinds of co-contribution. The accepted, default mode for policy development needs to be augmented by a wider range of approaches. For example, where solutions to problems are unclear or impossible to predict and where new responses will need to be developed, the task of a policy analyst will be transformed from top-down analysis and option-designer to being a broker and facilitator for bottom-up learning. The public sector of the future will need to adopt new and multiple approaches to service design and policy. Policy practices need to be reframed to accommodate explicit choices about a wider range of approaches to policy, service design and service delivery.

As with the changes needed to generate a step change in overall coherence, formal system 'hardware' changes to support a broader range of responses will need to be made in tandem with significant shifts in the 'software' of the mental models and everyday practices used in and about the public sector.

Some responses to these challenges require greater shared understandings among politicians, public servants and the public as a basis for more durable policy and governance bargains. These ways of working should enrich rather than undermine democracy, although they may require some adjustments in the nature of the interactions between ministers and public officials, particularly their mutual expectations and obligations. They will also require public officials to take a strong leadership role in articulating a shared vision in their interactions with ministers, but this must be done in a constitutionally appropriate way. This in turn must be reciprocated with a significant shift in the role and conduct of ministers relative to public officials.

Conclusion

New Zealand is part of an increasingly fast-paced, heterogeneous, complex and unpredictable global environment. How this country responds to the new environment will determine its future prosperity and the well-being of its citizens. The capability and capacity of New Zealand's public sector will have a significant bearing on the country's ability to adapt and flourish.

The current public management system has served New Zealand well over the last 20 years. The evidence suggests, however, that it will not provide the optimal platform for addressing the challenges of the twenty-first century. The Future State project identified the need for rebalancing public management settings to strengthen overall system coherence. At the same time, there is a need to broaden the range of policy and delivery approaches supported, whilst retaining current system strengths. Analysis is required of how the public management system needs to change in order to enable the step change to occur that will help improve its contribution to governance in New Zealand. The subsequent research into selected issues and the chapters in this book (Stage 2 of the Future State project) are the result of that work.

2

No Reform Left Behind: Multiplicity, Integrating Frameworks and Implications for New Zealand's Centre-of-Government and Public Sector Improvement[1]

Evert Lindquist

Introduction and Overview

The Future State project is a collaborative research and dialogue process between top executives in the New Zealand public service and scholars associated with the Institute of Policy Studies to take stock of the state of the public sector, to get a sense of the challenges and possibilities for New Zealand, and to develop bearings and strategic perspectives to inform the next round of reform of public sector institutions. This dialogue has been proceeding as the Key government seeks to re-position the New Zealand economy and government spending, which involves making tough choices and thinking about how policy and public management should be calibrated for the longer term. Most recently, the government has announced its 'best-sourcing' approach to improving service delivery.[2]

Many of the ideas animating dialogue inside and outside New Zealand on public sector reform are not new, but such reflection is proceeding at an interesting time: many OECD countries have had two decades worth of reform informed by the new public management (NPM) and almost all have a daunting set of governance and budgetary challenges to grapple with. There has been considerable learning across time and jurisdictions about the impact

---

1   This chapter was commissioned as part of the Future State project under the Emerging Issues Programme. Presentations based on an early draft were made to several audiences in August 2010 in Wellington courtesy of the Australia and New Zealand School of Government, Victoria University of Wellington's Institute of Policy Studies, the New Zealand Treasury, and the New Zealand State Services Commission. I would like to thank Derek Gill, Bryan Evans, Bill Ryan, John Wanna and several helpful anonymous reviewers for thoughtful comments. The views contained in this paper are those of the author alone.
2   English (2010) outlines the general approach of the Key government; the 'best-sourcing' approach is outlined in State Sector Reform Secretariat (2011).

of NPM-inspired reforms, as well as new approaches to delivering policy and programmes, including taking advantage of ever-expanding technological possibilities. However, the NPM approach is now considered by many scholars and governments as insufficient for taking up new challenges, supplanted by a similarly diverse set of post-NPM approaches. Moreover, there have been significant shifts in government priorities induced by the new security environment flowing from the 9/11 bombings and the effects of and responses to the global financial crisis. The result is that dialogue on public sector reform is infused with greater urgency and more scrutiny of workability and effectiveness.

Chapter 1 tapped into several integrative frameworks to capture the great diversity of ideas swirling around on matters of public sector reform. It sets out some comprehensive possibilities for reform, arguing that the New Zealand government and its public sector should become more flexible, integrated and outcome-oriented. The purpose of this chapter is to provide an outside-looking-in perspective on New Zealand's reform challenges and the thinking animating the Future State project, and to consider the implications for New Zealand's centre-of-government. It scrutinises and builds on the first Future State working paper by putting in context post-NPM thinking and the growing interest in integrated frameworks for understanding public management challenges. By doing so, this chapter seeks to pave the way for more strategic dialogue, especially for central agencies considering how to better support governments and improve public sector systems in rapidly evolving external environments.

This chapter has six sections. The first identifies new themes and trajectories of reform in the post-NPM environment, recognising that integrated and digital themes may be gathering steam but NPM themes have no less salience. It concludes that, while there is an active search for the themes to animate the next wave of reform, all of the previous reforms remain important and very much in play. This creates difficulties for leaders and scholars seeking to move public sector systems in useful and productive directions as expectations for public sector leadership and organisational performance continue to elevate. Bearing in mind that contemporary reform directions are necessarily diverse and multi-faceted, the second section reviews examples of encompassing or integrating frameworks that governments and observers use to make sense of the diverse array of values and goals that should guide public sector leadership and reform. It considers the strengths and messages of these frameworks, and how they differ from each other. The third section examines the limitations and potential of the integrating frameworks for developing strategic perspectives on improving and reforming public sector systems. Although recent users (including myself) are well aware of Westminster and complex public organisational systems, the frameworks do not model important features of systems in different jurisdictions. The frameworks are useful for sense-making, and for assessing the directions and interventions for public sector improvement and reform, but they need to be better situated and used carefully.

The next two sections shift gears, considering the implications for reform. The fourth outlines some assumptions and New Zealand's reform advantages. It makes distinctions between government priorities versus public sector institutional development priorities, the goals of securing sustained 'improvement' in public sector systems versus 'reform', taking a public-sector-wide versus a policy-sector perspective, and how technology can lead to structural versus other kinds of change (*ex ante* and *ex post*). Without ruling out structural change as a way forward, it suggests that many improvements are emergent, taking place over longer periods of time. The fifth section considers the strategic implications for New Zealand's central agencies dealing with the country's fragmented state sector and comparatively weak centre. I suggest that the centre needs to develop, initially, a comprehensive perspective to inform state-sector-wide institutional development, and, subsequently, a broader approach to capability reviews that would assess state sector organisations in the context of broader networks and the trajectory of those policy sectors, while also considering the capabilities they collectively need to address future challenges. This requires adding new repertoires and capabilities in the State Services Commission and other central agencies, perhaps levering expertise in the new Productivity Commission. This would inform strategising on how to re-position New Zealand's state sector to deal with challenges in the context of a significantly constrained fiscal environment for the foreseeable future. In an era where 'no reform is left behind', governments must enhance their ability to anticipate needs and identify promising approaches tailored for each policy and administrative sector.

The chapter concludes by summarising key arguments, but goes on to observe that, even if modified capability reviews and monitoring systems are instituted by central agencies, sector leaders will need to find better ways to convey the complexity and diversity of policy challenges and government responses in order to advise governments and engage citizens and communities. Although there is a concerted search for a new post-NPM paradigm to guide improvement and reform, in the more likely scenario of 'no reform left behind', every jurisdiction will have different mixes of approaches, old and new, for delivering policy and services, and this will vary sector by sector. A key challenge for central institutions will be to recognise and convey the unique mix that will emerge in New Zealand.

1. Getting Bearings in the Post-NPM Environment

As governments around the world consider how to re-position and reform public sector institutions, there has been wide-ranging dialogue about what should constitute the core features of a new model for public sector reform. This inevitably gets intertwined with a critique of previous guiding frameworks for public sector reform and broader debate about directions in government and governance. This section briefly identifies the features of the NPM approach to public sector reform and the emerging themes of post-NPM thinking, but notes that little has been taken off the reform table. This has created a strong interest in and recourse to integrating frameworks for locating and strategising about reform.

The New Public Management in Perspective

Let's first acknowledge that the term 'new public management' was an *ex post* description of waves of diverse reforms that proceeded across several jurisdictions with different mixes and varying degrees of commitment to its precepts. On the one hand, there can be no doubt that the reforms that proceeded as part of the re-inventing government movement in the United States, the revolution in New Zealand, the United Kingdom Next Steps initiative of the 1980s and early 1990s, and the Australian reforms at the Commonwealth and state levels during the 1990s fall squarely into what became the NPM movement. Not only were government leaders in these jurisdictions closely monitoring each other, among OECD countries these four jurisdictions were also considered exemplars for new approaches to public sector reform.[3] On the other hand, the reforms that came to be known internationally in the scholarly literature as the new public management by the mid-1990s (terminology not recognised by most practitioners until the mid-2000s), have been assessed and re-interpreted in the scholarly literature and ascribed more coherence than they had in practice. Interestingly, ideas that were fellow travelling companions during the 1990s – such as alternative service delivery, collaborative governance, co-production, engagement and integrated service delivery – are emerging as 'post-new public management' reforms.[4]

Informed by the collections of Christensen and Laegreid (2002, 2006, 2007a) assessing the new public management reforms, Jun (2009: 162–3) has identified the new public management reforms as generally comprising:

---

3   On US reforms, see Gore (1993); and Osborne and Gaebler (1992); on the New Zealand reforms, see Boston, Martin, Pallot and Walsh (1996); on the Next Steps initiative in the UK, see James (2003); and for comparative perspectives, see Aucoin (1995); and Pollitt and Bouckaert (2004).
4   On nomenclature and methodology for studying reform, see Barzelay (2001). See Lindquist and Wanna (2010a) on different but parallel streams of initiatives.

- structural devolution and decentralisation;
- vertical co-ordination and autonomy within single agencies;
- managerialism and management techniques;
- contractualism, privatisation and entrepreneurship;
- market-driven techniques, competition and citizens as customers;
- rejection of the Weberian theory of public bureaucracy;
- deregulation and market transactions; and
- a focus on performance management and outputs.

Informed by the United Kingdom experience, Dunleavy and his colleagues earlier provided a more detailed itemisation of NPM reforms:

- disaggregation;
- purchaser-provider separation;
- agencification;
- decoupling policy systems;
- growth of quasi-government agencies;
- separation out of micro-local agencies;
- chunking up privatised industries;
- corporatisation and strong single organisation management;
- de-professionalisation;
- competition by comparison;
- improved performance measurement;
- league tables of agency performance;
- competition;
- quasi-markets;
- voucher schemes;
- outsourcing;
- compulsory market testing;
- intragovernment contracting;
- public–private sectoral polarisation;
- product market liberalisation;
- deregulation;
- consumer-tagged financing;
- user control;
- incentivisation;
- respecifying property rights;
- light-touch regulation;
- capital market involvement in projects;
- privatising asset ownership;
- anti-rent-seeking measures;
- de-privileging professions;

- performance-related pay;
- PFI (private finance initiative);
- public–private partnerships;
- unified rate of return and discounting;
- development of charging technologies;
- valuing public sector equity;
- mandatory efficiency dividends.

However, Dunleavy and his colleagues (2006a) did not attempt to capture the extent to which different jurisdictions embraced and implemented NPM reforms, although they venture assessments of where progress was made in particular areas they identified. Pollitt and Bouckaert (2004: 98–99) suggest that the United States, New Zealand and the United Kingdom can be considered 'NPM marketisers' and several of the northern European governments can be considered 'modernisers', adopting some NPM ideas along with already decentralised agency environments.

There have always been critics of the NPM, particularly so in New Zealand where there was a concerted and radical approach to introducing and anchoring the reforms in the 1980s.[5] Many jurisdictions, such as Canada, closely monitored these developments but did not adopt them, disconcerted by the amount of structural change and sharp delineation of roles and responsibilities for individuals and organisations alike. There has also emerged a critique of the NPM model both in light of experience and its ability to address the governance challenges of the 2000s. Jun has summarised the broad critique of NPM reforms as follows:

- too much fragmentation of roles and role ambiguity as a result of structural devolution;
- too many single-purpose organisations and too much vertical specialisation;
- insufficient co-operation and neglect of co-operation across agencies;
- too much managerial autonomy;
- too many discontinuities and non-linearities;
- undermining of political control and fostering of mistrust; and
- the creation of role ambiguity among political leaders, public servants and service providers.

He also argues that NPM thinking has presumed that citizens are passive and has not made room for them to have input into reform and policy and service design, has relied heavily on structural change as a way to modify behaviour and has been overly rational in its pursuit of achieving intended goals (Jun, 2009: 162–3).

---

5   See, for example, Boston, Martin, Pallot and Walsh (1996); and Kelsey (1995).

One could have a good debate about the extent to which NPM initiatives were comprehensively taken up and went beyond rhetoric in many OECD jurisdictions, whether the loss of public trust has anything to do with NPM reforms at all, and whether the NPM undermined or represented an assertion of political control in many jurisdictions. However, regardless of what ills we attribute to NPM logic, there seems to be growing agreement that the NPM approaches *on their own* will be inadequate for dealing with new governance challenges. Universally described as manifold and 'wicked' in nature, they will require comprehensive and co-ordinated approaches to governance, often engaging many stakeholders, and new capabilities and sensibilities in public sector institutions. Moreover, there is no doubt that many observers have been seeking a post-NPM approach under different labels for some time, such as joined-up, holistic, connected, whole-of-government approaches; integrated performance; and digital governance.[6]

Post-New Public Management Thinking: Differing Perspectives

Like the NPM, the post-NPM discourse on public sector reform is comprised of several over-lapping themes. In exploring the possibilities presented by digital technologies, Dunleavy and his colleagues (2006a: 480) identify three defining strands:

- reintegration of the delivery of services for citizens and communities;
- needs-based holism that organises government to more directly, efficiently and quickly address and respond to these needs; and
- more aggressive adoption of digital technology in front-end and back-end operations, as well as its web presence for citizens and other stakeholders.

With less focus on digitalisation, Jun (2009: 162–3) delineates key themes animating post-NPM thinking:

- reducing fragmentation through structural integration;
- asserting recentralisation and re-regulation;
- moving forward with whole-of-government or joined-up government initiatives;
- eliminating role ambiguity and creating clear role relationships;
- relying on private–public partnerships;
- increased centralisation, capacity-building and co-ordination;

---

6   On cross-government approaches, see 6 et al. (2002); Bogdanor (2005); Caiden and Su (2007); and Management Advisory Committee (2004); on integrated performance governance, see Bouckaert and Halligan (2008); and Halligan (2007); and on digital governance, see Borins et al. (2007); Dunleavy et al. (2006a); and Roy (2008).

- strengthening central political and administrative capacity; and
- recognising and factoring in the environmental, historical and cultural dimensions of institutions and communities.

Interestingly, though, Jun argues that NPM and post-NPM thinking share a top-down and rational posture, both seeking to reduce role ambiguity of key players and presuming citizens are passive consumers of government services.[7] He is wary of 'management-driven' approaches that may conflict with government and citizen preferences, particularly those evinced at the local and community level. He argues that top-down approaches will not be effective in a 'complex, turbulent organizational environment in which the government is constantly faced with unanticipated domestic and global challenges', and when citizens and communities are interpreting these events differentially; Jun calls for more public–private partnerships, and democratic, community and NGO engagement (2009: 163–4). These are interesting views, but these approaches have been widely discussed in the literature on public administration and governance for well over a decade, including redundancy and overlap.[8]

Several streams of literature and contributions have critiqued the NPM approach and supported increased engagement with citizens, communities and other stakeholders to address difficult challenges, drawing on effective practice. If anything, there appears to be an international consensus that new balances need to be struck, where public sector institutions must respond to the top-down priorities of governments, and the bottom-up preferences and potential of citizens, communities and other stakeholders.[9] The call in the first chapter of this volume for the New Zealand government and public sector to embrace more delivery flexibility and engagement approaches with stakeholders reflects this broader consensus.

---

7   Jun (2009: 163) argues that NPM and post-NPM assume 'that people's behaviour and actions can be changed by introducing structural, functional, and regulatory strategies designed by political executives and top agency management; that organizational members act rationally in the pursuit of central policy and management initiatives; that organizational roles need to be clearly understood and that ambiguity is detrimental to the functioning of the organization; that citizens are passive "customers" of public services and that they are satisfied as long as they receive efficient service; and that accountability and public trust can be ensured through efficient administration and the smooth coordination of the governing process'.

8   See Lindquist and Wanna (2010a) for a broad review. The literature has recognised the existence and functionality of overlap and duplication, as well as other writing that has long recognised informal, non-structural and ad hoc responses to organisational and governance challenges. See Chisholm (1992); Landau (1969); Lerner (1986); and Lindquist (1999).

9   See, for example, 6 et al. (2002); Bogdanor (2005); Denhardt and Denhardt (2007); Nabatchi (2010); OECD (2009a); and Turnbull and Aucoin (2006).

Conclusion: From NPM to Post-NPM – No Reform Left Behind

An intriguing feature of post-NPM discourse is that, despite the putative inadequacy of NPM approaches addressing future governance challenges, the checklist for assessing performance and the menu for reform are not shrinking. Lodge and Gill (2011: 160) recently found little evidence of a 'megatrend from NPM to post NPM governance' in the New Zealand context after reviewing changes in public service bargains, the machinery of government and reform of arm's length government. Elsewhere, few if any observers seem to suggest that good management of agencies, appropriate incentives, monitoring, alternative delivery of services and results should be dropped for whole-of-government, integrated service delivery and performance, citizen engagement and co-production (working with non-profit, community and private sectors as well as citizens) initiatives. Indeed, quite the reverse appears to be true, tantamount to a 'no reform left behind' movement: across jurisdictions the public sector reform agenda has been steadily broadened and deepened in the scholarly and professional domains.

The expanding management and reform agenda can be thought of as a widening set of aspirational values and increasing expectations for public sector leadership and organisational performance, reflecting the complexity and diversity of governance challenges. Moreover, it is commonplace in any jurisdiction to find a succession of reform initiatives over many years; new ones are announced before previous ones have been completed or assessed. In the face of this multiplicity of aspirations and reforms, often overwhelming executives and staff (or at least creating a degree of cynicism), some governments have developed more comprehensive frameworks that itemise factors that ought to be addressed when undertaking reviews of organisational capability and performance. There have also been recent efforts to develop encompassing frameworks to capture these diverse factors across public sector institutions, and to inform strategic dialogue, reflection and planning. Such frameworks are tacit acknowledgement that to focus only on the 'latest' sub-set of values or reforms would be to miss the larger strategic context, not to mention previous initiatives. The next section takes a closer look at these frameworks and explores why scholars and practitioners are taking greater interest in them.

2. Frameworks for Performance and Reform: Embracing Multiplicity and Diversity in Aspirational Values

The number of desired values and capabilities that public sector organisations should have in order to deal with governance and management challenges in future has grown. Governments and observers alike have sought more encompassing ways to capture these desired values and capabilities, to assess the performance of leaders and their organisations in relation to them, and to inform reform deliberations.

What follows briefly reviews examples of such efforts, without attempting to be exhaustive. First, we consider two comprehensive frameworks developed by central agencies in Canada and the United Kingdom to assess the performance of public organisations, and another framework developed in Australia to guide the comprehensive agenda of the Advisory Group on Reform of Australian Government Administration. Second, two theoretical frameworks are introduced: the Competing Values framework and the New Synthesis framework emerging from a six-country research-and-dialogue process, both of which have attracted the interest of public administration scholars because of their potential for analysing the diverse and often competing expectations associated with public organisations and reform initiatives. These latter two frameworks are assessed more closely in the following section of this chapter.

Central Governments: Capturing Capabilities in Assessment Frameworks

Central authorities in the Canadian and United Kingdom governments have developed distinct approaches to reviewing the organisational capabilities and performance of departments and agencies. In doing so, they have evolved comprehensive perspectives on capabilities of their core public service systems as a whole. The Treasury Board of Canada's Management Accountability Framework and the UK Cabinet Office's Capability Review framework have received international attention, but are distinct and complementary approaches. More recently, New Zealand has introduced a Performance Improvement Framework (PIF) drawing upon United Kingdom capability reviews, and the Australian Commonwealth government has introduced a 'blueprint' for reform, explicitly driven by a comprehensive reform framework, which will inform future capability reviews of agencies.

In Canada, the Management Accountability Framework (MAF) was developed by the Treasury Board of Canada Secretariat (TBS) for use by deputy ministers to engage executive teams by assessing the state of management of departments and agencies in ten areas: governance and strategic direction; policy and programmes; people; citizen-focused service; risk management; stewardship; accountability; public service values; learning, innovation and change management; and results and performance.[10] The MAF quickly became the basis on which the TBS sought data to inform indicators of progress relying on departments and agencies, as well as secretariats spanning Ottawa's central agencies. These assessments informed the annual reviews of deputy minister performance by the Committee of Senior Officials, and summary reports were

10 For more detail, see Fonberg (2006); and Lindquist (2009b).

eventually published, sometimes with deputy minister responses.

In the United Kingdom, the Capability Reviews were launched in 2005, providing independent reviews of a rolling group of departments, supported by Capability Review Teams (Cabinet Office, 2009), similar to the ways in which academic departments and programmes are traditionally reviewed. Anchored by a broader three-part framework (leadership, strategy, delivery), the assessment categories included: setting direction; igniting passion, pace and drive; taking responsibility for leading delivery and change; building capability; focusing on outcomes; basing choices on evidence; building common purpose; planning, resourcing and prioritising; developing clear roles, responsibilities and delivery model(s); and evaluating management performance.[11] The Capability Reviews differed from the MAF in three ways. First, they were more selective, focusing on a few entities each year; 22 departments had been reviewed by the end of 2009, 16 twice. Second, the Cabinet Office has always been more public about the implications of the reviews for the state of the public sector, showing aggregate scores over time. Third, the reviews more explicitly recognised the strategic challenges of specific departments, whereas the MAF assessments constitute more of a general systems check (Lindquist, 2009b).

Australia's Rudd government launched the Moran Review in 2009, which involved appointing an expert Advisory Group and a process of engaging public servants and the public, eventually leading to the report *Ahead of the Game*. The report was organised around the broad categories of: meeting the needs of citizens, encouraging strong leadership and direction, developing a highly capable workforce, and operating efficiently and to a consistently high standard.[12] For our purposes, the Blueprint was interesting because the Advisory Group and, later, the Rudd government took a comprehensive approach, seeing specific reforms as an integrated package, where one reform was linked to and would

---

11 These were recently modified and the notable changes are: develop people, set strategy and focus on outcomes, base choices on evidence and customer insight, collaborate and build common purpose, innovate and improve delivery, and manage performance and value for money (Cabinet Office, 2009: 32). Overarching reasons for the changes were to emphasise achieving value for money; linking capability to results and outcomes; sharpening focus on delivery; challenging the department to innovate; and encouraging them to collaborate with other departments, partners, stakeholders and citizens.

12 See Advisory Group on Reform of Australian Government Administration (2010). More specific themes and initiatives include: delivering better services informed by feedback from frontline staff and citizens; more open government, including making data more accessible and citizen engagement; enhancing policy capacity across the public service and with citizens and outside experts; reinvigorating strategic leadership through renewed values, clarification of Secretary roles, strengthened leadership and talent management; clarifying and aligning employment conditions across departments; strengthening the Australian Public Service workforce through recruitment, learning and development initiatives; encouraging more agency agility, capability and effectiveness, along with managing shared outcomes; improving agency efficiency and governance; and strengthening the APS Commission.

lever others.[13] A lynchpin of the implementation strategy was a more capable and potent Australian Public Service Commission (APSC), which would initiate capability reviews of departments and agencies informed by the broader reform agenda, which in turn would inform assessments of public service secretaries.

These examples show that governments have been developing comprehensive perspectives and governance frameworks for assessment based on notions of what might constitute 'well-performing' departments and agencies, and, in some cases, invoke such broad perspectives as a basis for considering reform. Any review of OECD publications on public management over the last few years – or of the documents of member countries outlining their priorities for public sector reform improvement – would show reliance on similar themes and language, whether the announced reforms were more selective or comprehensive in nature.

Integrating Frameworks: Competing Values and the New Synthesis

The ever-broadening set of pertinent values invoked to assess and motivate reform in public service systems has not gone unnoticed by observers. Some scholars have found Cameron and Quinn's Competing Values framework and Bourgon's New Synthesis framework as useful points of departure for capturing the values and contingencies at play in public sector systems and their implications for strategy and reform.[14] What follows provides a brief description of the frameworks and how they differ in terms of levels of analysis.

The challenge of identifying and balancing desirable organisational goals and values is well recognised in the leadership and management literature. Quinn's (1988) seminal work *Beyond Rational Management: Mastering the Paradoxes and Competing Demands of High Performance*, argues that top executives must have the ability to navigate competing and sometimes contradictory values to ensure that organisations can realise their potential. The Competing Values framework he developed and later elaborated with others revolves around four distinct traditions (see Figure 2.1 below) in leadership and organisational analysis: fostering *clan or collaborative culture*, with a focus on employee engagement; *managing hierarchy or control culture*, emphasising efficiency, routines, rules and systems; developing a *market or competitive culture*, with a focus on achieving goals and meeting customer needs; and *adhocracy or creative culture*, monitoring evolving environments, identifying new opportunities and seeking innovation. These traditions vary with respect to two dimensions: from having an inward focus to having an outward orientation, and from having a

---

13 For more detail on this perspective, see Lindquist (2010).
14 See Bourgon (2009a); Gill, Pride, Gilbert and Norman (2010); Lindquist (2010); and Norman (2008a, 2008b).

drive towards stability to fully embracing change. Each tradition has differing clusters of values, styles of leadership, management competencies, cultures and notions of effectiveness.[15]

Figure 2.1. The Competing Values Framework

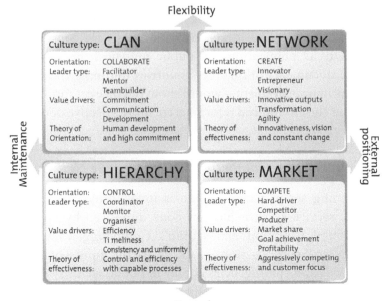

Source: Gill, Pride, Gilbert and Norman (2010: 28), as adapted by the authors from Cameron and Quinn (2006: 46).

Several key insights flow from this approach. First, all of these values and competencies can and should be found in all organisations, but high-performing organisations achieve unique and evolving balances at different points in their evolution that do not require *fully* trading-off those values or, in other words, their leaders achieve different mixes and balances. Second, the tensions between the opposite traditions – clan versus market cultures, and hierarchy versus adhocracy cultures – can be sources of insight. Third, transformative leaders reject trade-offs, confront duality, and begin to see new balances and sometimes innovation from them (Quinn, 2004). Indeed, in this view the best executives are Janus-like: they can see diametrically opposed values and approaches at play, identify possibilities and creative new balances for addressing the challenges of their organisations, doing so by recognising there are multiple levels of analysis and different ways of sequencing concrete actions (Cameron and Quinn, 2006: 53).

15   See Cameron and Quinn (2006); and Cameron and Quinn et al. (2006).

The Competing Values framework has been used primarily to educate executives and would-be managers about different aspects of organisation leadership and culture, and to inform change interventions. However, in recent years, public management scholars have found it useful for capturing the range of values and tensions inherent in public sector reform. Several New Zealand public administration scholars have used the competing values framework to argue that the pre-1988 New Zealand public sector reflected hierarchy and clan values, and that the 1988 reforms ushered in market and performance-oriented values by changing incentives, bringing in expertise from outside networks, and relying on contractualism and devolution to agencies.[16] Norman (2008a) suggests that the New Zealand government has moved back towards more clan-style approaches in the areas of health and housing, while Gill and his colleagues (Gill, Pride, Gilbert and Norman, 2010) argue that New Zealand needs a more whole-of-government and integrated approach to the mix of public management values, including greater reliance on collaboration and networks. Quite independently, Lindquist (2010) shows how the Moran Review's Blueprint framework acknowledged several streams of worthy and contending values, and that it is impossible to consider one aspect of public sector reform without directly or indirectly implying others. He argues that Australian Public Service (APS) leaders should understand the implicit logic behind the creativity in the Blueprint's design, and how recognising and working with contending values is important for executive development, addressing policy and management challenges, and fostering innovation.

The New Synthesis framework emerged out of an initiative led by Jocelyne Bourgon, former Head of the Canadian Public Service and Clerk of the Privy Council, to develop a modern and integrating theory of public administration, one that captures contemporary governance realities of the twenty-first century.[17] Sponsored largely by a network of government organisations from different countries, the initiative has tapped into the insights of practitioners and scholars from different disciplines to explore the implications of a typology through literature reviews, case studies and dialogue. The typology (see Figures 2.2 and 2.3 below) emerges from two dimensions: one ranging from public policy (government) results to civic results, and another from government (authority) to governance (collective) power. These lead to a typology identifying four modes of governance with different postures for governments and officials: performance (*exploit*), compliance (*conserve*), resilience (*adapt*) and emergence (*explore*).

16 See Gill, Pride, Gilbert and Norman (2010); and Norman (2008a, 2008b and 2009).
17 For various statements on and iterations of the project, see Bourgon (2007, 2008, 2009a, 2009b, 2010).

Figure 2.2 The New Synthesis Framework

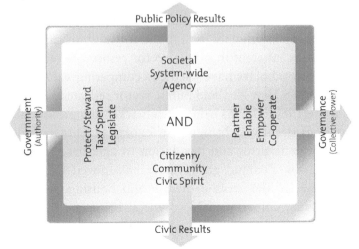

Source: Bourgon with Milley (2010: 205).

Figure 2.3 Modes of Governance

Source: Bourgon with Milley (2010: 209).

There is not the space here to analyse the framework's logical underpinnings and coherence, but these characteristics point to the dynamic quality of governance and to the rich connections between governments and civil society in different circumstances. Bourgon acknowledges that public service institutions (composed of many organisations) change slowly, protecting key values and traditions, and yet governments and specific organisations also anticipate and adapt to evolving circumstances (sometimes crises) and public expectations.

Moreover, even when governments are prepared to share governance and rely on or learn from non-government actors, they retain the important roles of monitoring, facilitating and supporting the development of capabilities in civil society and they participate in a range of co-creation and co-production activities with citizens and a variety of organisations.

The New Synthesis project follows in the time-honoured systems perspective of government and public sector organisations,[18] but offers a new twist. To varying degrees, all governments and public sector institutions (as complex organisations) are simultaneously in the modes of performance, compliance, resilience and emergence. Moreover, this mix varies by jurisdiction and over time. The project and its approach has gained widespread attention from practitioners and applied public management scholars, even if it conflates the idea of an integrating framework and normative ideal-types with models and theories of public administration. In contrast, Quinn's Competing Values framework works at a different level of analysis, considering the mix of different leadership, skills, norms and culture for organisations in societies. Gill and his colleagues (Gill, Pride, Gilbert and Norman, 2010: 36–41) rightly use these frameworks and trend analysis (demographics, internationalisation, technology, globalisation, etc.) to probe future directions for the New Zealand government and its public sector with respect to affordability, complicated problems, a more diverse population, and faster and less predictable change.

Conclusion: From Frameworks to Strategy

Governments and observers acknowledge that there is a long list of challenges, attributes and potential postures for public sector institutions when dealing with twenty-first-century governance challenges in the post-NPM environment. The number of aspirational values and expectations motivating governments and public sector institutions has not been pared back but, rather, expanded. Moreover, they are all viewed as potentially important depending on context, and there is an expanding menu of ways to achieve them, through a variety of government and non-government structures and partnerships, financial arrangements and technological possibilities.

Governments have acknowledged this multiplicity by adopting comprehensive frameworks for monitoring public organisations and guiding public sector reform, and there has been increasing interest among some scholars and practitioners in frameworks that organise and synthesise the expectations increasing in number and diversity. Such frameworks are useful because they can stimulate broad dialogue and reflection on the current postures of governments and public sector organisations to ascertain whether they anticipate emerging and future challenges.

18 For example, see Boulding (1956); von Bertalanffy (1972).

The critical issue, however, is whether these frameworks can be used for finer-grained analysis and arrive at useful advice for the central institutions of government. It is not enough to say that organisations and/or organisational systems are multifaceted when it comes to values, and that they might find themselves, along with governments and societies, in new circumstances such as crises, catching up with and realising the possibilities of digital technologies, and meeting the demands for integrated and tailored services for citizens and governments alike. The next section takes a closer look at limitations of these frameworks – and points to how to ground them in the reality of public sector institutions and increase the potential for truly strategic advice.

3. Integrating Frameworks in Perspective: Can We Move Beyond Sense-making?

Increasing awareness of the breadth and intractability of challenges and problems, and building and tapping into comprehensive and integrating frameworks will undoubtedly broaden our horizons about the directions and possibilities for public sector reform. Having reviewed the Competing Values and New Synthesis frameworks, and some implications for moving beyond traditional public management approaches, Gill and his colleagues (Gill, Pride, Gilbert and Norman, 2010: 51) observe that:

> Collectively, these responses add up to a subtle but significant whole-of-system change. Much of the change will be in culture, ethos, and the performance of roles rather than in the hard-wiring of the system. The overall effect will be a fundamental shift in how public services work and what they achieve. This system change will need to be effected in a context of fiscal constraint, so both change processes and the new state have to be characterised as achieving more with less. How do you best drive predominantly 'soft' change across a whole system? Can you simply scale up the same principles that work for organisational change? If not, what more will be needed to lead and drive the change to public service for the 21st century?

While embracing the horizon-broadening potential of these comprehensive frameworks, as well as the normative directions proponents call for (such as soft change and co-production), these colleagues ask important questions about the applicability and workability of the insights and arguments. And, even as a long-time user of both frameworks for analysis and teaching, I agree that more questions should first be asked about the assumptions, normative use, silences and limitations of these frameworks before we can more confidently have a strategic dialogue on public sector reform, particularly with respect to the implications for central agencies.

What follows identifies several issues, tensions and limitations. Recognising them provides firmer footing for considering the strategic implications of these integrating frameworks for Westminster governments and public sector institutions working in particular contexts.

The Frameworks Say Little About the Public Sector's Special Character...

When applied to public sector institutions, the New Synthesis and the Competing Values frameworks are not elaborated so as to acknowledge that the 'organisations' under study are large-scale, multi-organisation systems. These systems include core public sector organisations and agencies serving governments and the public, often working in federal and/or parliamentary governance frameworks, and usually in significantly different sectors or policy and service delivery domains. Both frameworks produce insights for single public organisations, but more needs to be done with respect to modelling explicitly the levels and differentiated roles of government organisations, whether they might be central agencies, policy departments, service agencies or different levels of government.

Ideas about engaging citizens or shifting away from hierarchy or compliance postures might have less relevance and resonance depending on specific organisational contexts. Moreover, despite emerging trends and shifting contexts, public sector organisations directly or indirectly serve governments and ministers, and are inevitably enmeshed in external fields of play conditioned and constrained by Westminster parliamentary principles, practices and authorities. Not only do these organisations advise on and implement government priorities, they must also respond to stakeholder and citizen preferences and attend to their own institutional needs. To lever frameworks properly requires fully modelling the organisations and their contexts and, as discussed below, this should bring to the surface more tensions and competing values, and potentially more opportunities for creativity and innovation.

The Frameworks Do Not Directly Deal with Overload and Scarcity ...

Those who develop comprehensive frameworks to guide and analyse public sector reform understand that governments have a bewildering and overwhelming multitude of challenges to address. However, while the frameworks point to the competing priorities and values, they do not properly acknowledge that governments are overloaded with tough challenges and problems, and, as is the case with New Zealand, do not seek to address them in the context of difficult fiscal circumstances. Indeed, the challenge for governments as part of complex government systems is to allot time, allocate scarce resources, make trade-offs and ensure system sustainability even when it is under significant stress.

While labelling governance challenges as 'wicked' has become another throw-away tag, governments *are* expected to address multiple streams of problems requiring years and decades to resolve (typically well beyond the terms of governments). If making progress on challenges is iterative, difficult, long-term, and involving multiple partners inside and outside government, how can the public sector be organised and reformed so as to deal with the coming and going of governments, wild-card events and shifting priorities?

Short of becoming fatalistic in the face of these realities, how should governments and societies establish reasonable expectations (whether achievable or by stretching goals) about making progress in addressing challenges and monitoring performance? Comprehensive frameworks have to be used in such a way that they highlight key trade-offs across challenges and over time.

The Frameworks Say Little about Critical Variables . . .

In her recent work, Bourgon with Milley (2010) indicates that choices about policy instruments and investments in co-creation arrangements depend heavily on the specific context of a jurisdiction. This is crucial when it comes to acknowledging exigencies, requirements, and possibilities across jurisdictions and policy sectors.

At one level, we can see that critical variables to consider include the geographical size and variability of countries and regions, the size and diversity of populations, the proximity of a jurisdiction to others, the wealth and education of citizens, and the relative size of the public sector to populations. For these reasons, addressing similar challenges in Canada, the United Kingdom and New Zealand may naturally lead to different strategic possibilities.

Likewise, the degree of advancement and availability of technology (software and hardware) in different jurisdictions, government organisations, sectors and communities will condition possibilities for collaboration, delivering services and monitoring performance in the digital era. The Future State project has undertaken trend analysis, but further use of more encompassing frameworks should be directed to collecting finer-grained information about the special character and potential of jurisdictions in order to produce useful strategic dialogue.

The Frameworks Should Address Specific Sector and Organisation Contexts . . .

Comprehensive and integrating frameworks provide pictures of the 'whole', but gaining traction for strategic purposes often requires closer looks at specific departments and agencies handling unique sector challenges, as well as the relevant constellations of organisations inside and outside government, communities and citizen groups. Notions like resilience and performance will vary considerably across policy and service delivery domains, as will opportunities for decentralisation and centralisation. So too will the number and capability of stakeholders and other governments, the extent and predictability of change, the degree to which the public believes it is an important domain, how the ways of working stack up against best practice in other jurisdictions, and the history and geography of interactions and choices that have been made over the years.

While general needs and reform directions can be identified at the system level, there can be distinct priorities, needs and directions for reform and building capability across domains. More importantly, understanding these differences will inform prioritising, balancing and sequencing choices at the system level.

The Frameworks Must Recognise Evolving Challenges and New Value Mixes . . .

When applying the frameworks to complex organisational systems, the opportunity for insight expands. However, analysis requires carefully assessing how such systems evolve, how their sub-systems differ, and how the values associated with one quadrant do not necessarily diminish as a system or sub-system moves in one direction, but may take on different shape and meaning.

The New Synthesis lenses of resilience, emergence, performance and compliance are attractive. They resonate as we think about examples like the readiness and response of Haiti after the 2009 earthquake, how Australia responded to the 2008 global financial crisis, and how the foundation sector and civil society in the United States generate demonstration projects and social innovation that may lead to government programmes. But how does one think about the conglomeration of issues in New Zealand, when the governance system is composed of policy domains in varying states of maturity and challenge? How can 'resilience' and social capital in different communities get assessed when it is difficult to assemble information across policy and administrative domains?

The Competing Values framework – which can help us to understand the appropriate and evolving relative mix of values, culture and leadership style for organisations over time (e.g., start-up, growth, consolidation, re-orientation) – is similarly challenged. How should this framework get applied to a complex, multi-level governance system, with every organisation and sector in varying states of evolution and 'fit' with their domestic and external environments?

Finally, even if an entire government or sector can be squarely located in a New Synthesis or Competing Values framework quadrant, the lenses associated with the other quadrants should be recursively applied to assess how arrangements are working. For example, the relief efforts of the Haiti government and aid agencies after the earthquake there might be assessed not only with respect to the values of resilience, but also of performance, compliance and emergence!

Sense-making is Distinct From Building Strategy and Coherence . . .

Good conceptual frameworks expand awareness of interconnections and complexity, and in this regard they are sense-making. Such sense-making broadens horizons, but may fall short of framing strategic choices, or generating and narrowing down strategic possibilities. Indeed, broad conceptual frameworks attune us to a larger circle of forces, actors and lead times, capturing and showing greater complexity than we initially thought. However, greater awareness of complexity can lead to unwarranted over-reaction, defeatism and even denial in the sense that the rendering of such complexity can be seen as encouraging complex as opposed to simple solutions. It may also result in insufficient acknowledgement that governments and societies have wrestled with 'wicked' problems, overload, technological change, globalisation and resource scarcity for many generations.

The point here is not to diminish current and future challenges but, rather, to acknowledge that good sense-making and strategic planning should be retrospective and forward looking (Mintzberg and Jorgensen, 1987). It can provide a basis for (but is not the same thing as) developing informed, grounded and useful narratives about how the past links to today's circumstances as well as different potential futures. Moreover, as is discussed later, sense-making is critical for governments and central agencies seeking to monitor progress and build coherence in the face of incomplete information, great diversity in policy and service delivery arrangements within and across sectors, and making sense of experimental and emergent approaches to grappling with societal challenges.

The Frameworks Create Possibilities by Focusing on Tensions and Constraints . . .

The Competing Values and New Synthesis frameworks have been used to explore new directions for organisations given new priorities and environmental challenges. They both remind us that *all* values and capabilities are important for well-performing organisations and well-functioning societies, even if some have been previously privileged and deserve less emphasis in the future. Strategic analysis not only requires identifying sources of tension and trade-offs across values, but also confronting them and striking new and sometimes difficult balances among them. At times, innovations and potentially superior outcomes can arise.

Chapter 1 of the Future State report identifies the four challenges of 'affordability, complicated problems involving many players, more diverse and differentiated population, and a world of faster, less-predictable change' (Gill, Pride, Gilbert and Norman, 2010: 37–41). But these should not be seen as distinct challenges: the key is to explore how affordability and sometimes significant constraint can lead to shrewd innovation, how co-production can move forward when trust and leadership may not be in great supply, how co-design might proceed with certain communities and demographic groups, how Web 2.0 strategies might proceed with younger demographic or professional communities on selected issues, how on selective issues social networking and citizen engagement might expedite scanning and futures work, and so on.

The Frameworks Do Not Inherently Point to Non-structural Change . . .

As noted above, both frameworks have been used to justify the need to (a) move from traditional and NPM approaches, echoing the views of proponents of post-NPM themes; and (b) increase reliance activities associated with 'governance' and 'emergence' such as co-production and citizen engagement. Chapter 1 in this volume suggests there should be less focus on hardware and structural change in public sector institutions, and more reliance on software or non-structural change, such as adopting new values, pilot projects, adhocracies such as 'circuit-breaker' teams, shared budgeting and new portfolio arrangements.[19] Although exploring non-structural approaches can be productive, structural change should not be ruled out.

Dunleavy and his colleagues (2006a) suggest that adoption of some digital technologies may lead to significant 'disintermediation' – or bypassing of existing state bureaucracies – and new ways to deliver programmes. This, in turn, may lead to structural change and oversight repertoires associated with compliance and performance. Even if governments want to give more scope to NGO and community sectors to innovate, this may require top-down leadership, new capacities, and alternative and workable performance regimes that will prod or enable the non-profit and voluntary sector and other delivery agents to experiment and avoid functioning as 'bureaucracies' at a slight remove. In

---

19 From Gill, Pride, Gilbert and Norman (2010: 50): 'Other responses identified included: reframing public policy development from controlling to leading; co-designing and co-producing to harness the knowledge and cooperation of citizens and business; tailoring service delivery to a more diverse population; using ICT to deepen understanding of clients' needs; scanning what is emerging – listening to the noise to react to signals earlier; learning the way forward – building knowledge about the problem and the right solutions on the go. This paper started by asking what the future state might need to do over the next two decades and what might need adjusting in the public management system as a consequence. The answer was that many of the necessary changes are to *how* systems are operated rather than to the hard-wiring of component parts.'

doing so, new kinds of hierarchies and quality assurance models may have to be adopted. This returns us to the observation that innovation in the public sector may arise from squarely addressing trade-offs.

Conclusion: From Sense-making to Strategic Integrating Frameworks

This section has sought to understand the virtues and limitations of comprehensive, integrating frameworks. By doing so, it has endeavoured to build out the foundation for identifying strategic possibilities that acknowledge specific institutional and societal contexts. This should lead to a more productive strategic dialogue about how to re-shape and position government.

After setting out the New Synthesis framework in a progress report, Bourgon with Milley (2010: 37) identifies, among others, the need to 'reposition the role of the centre of government to provide leadership and ensure coherence in the interagency and intergovernmental space of modern governance where multiple actors and several levels of government are involved'; and the need to 'reposition the role of line departments as the hubs of vast networks of organizations, some in government and some outside, contributing to common public policy results'. These are not new ideas,[20] but they invite the question of why such strategic positioning has not taken root and deepened much sooner. The causes that come to mind include the very real constraints and drags of Westminster governance systems, ingrained bureaucratic cultures, non-trivial resource investments, and political worry about unevenness in service delivery across regions and localities.

Surmounting these and other constraints to govern and manage the public sector in new ways requires careful acknowledgement of the specific and differentiated roles of organisations inside and outside government. It also requires acknowledging the manifold challenges and complexity that await governments seeking to modernise governance for the twenty-first century. The next part of this chapter seeks, in a high-level way, to put these challenges squarely on the table.

4. Exploring Implications for Public Sector Improvement (and Reform) in New Zealand

This section seeks to lay the groundwork for a strategic dialogue in New Zealand that explores the implications of the Competing Values and New Synthesis frameworks for considering future directions for public sector systems and central agencies. This is not a comparative study (for recent attempts, see Halligan, forthcoming; and Kelly et al., 2010) but nevertheless it seeks

---

20 Lindquist (1992) is just one example.

to provide an outside-looking-in perspective. Based on the reflections in the previous section, my working assumptions are as follows:

- The number of 'wicked' problems outstrip the capabilities of governments and therefore governments can focus on only a limited number of whole-of-government priorities.
- Public service institutions must serve governments of the day, fulfil existing statutory obligations, serve citizens and communities, and monitor their own capabilities as a corporate institution or collection of public sector organisations to handle emerging challenges.
- Many reform challenges require step-wise investments and non-trivial political and bureaucratic engagement, which together constrain the development of public sector institutions, particularly in non-government-priority areas.
- New Zealand's Westminster governance system has a unique character – including the organisation of central public sector institutions – which in combination with its geographical, cultural and economic attributes creates distinct opportunities for dealing with governance challenges.
- Many challenges are best addressed away from central government in some sectors, or at the local or regional level, where more innovative approaches may emerge – this requires flexibility from central institutions but not relinquishing the monitoring of progress.
- When confronted with significant fiscal constraint, governments have to reduce the extent of their direction and responsibility for regulating activity and delivering services or funding programmes, unless they can find truly innovative ways to do things differently.
- Administrative reform can proceed in non-structural ways with new perspectives, quick wins, pilots, collaboration, momentum from government policy priorities and steady progress in non-government-priority areas, while also invoking traditional values and structural change (efficiency, effectiveness, performance and accountability).

What follows reviews New Zealand's governance and reform advantage, governance challenges and public sector capabilities, multi-level governance and public sector reform, technology and structural reform of the public sector, and the role of central agencies and institutional reform.

New Zealand's Reform Advantage: Size and Proximity

New Zealand is a small country in a big world, geographically isolated with a relatively modest population, open to the vicissitudes of global markets, and with significant turnover in certain skill areas. While New Zealand's borders are controlled, it has an open and modern economy, it is nationally coherent with strong Māori and other cultural traditions, and it has an international reputation for public sector and democratic innovation. Indeed, New Zealand may be well placed to move forward with collaborative governance and devolution initiatives. Its national and local governments and Crown sector do not have provinces or states to navigate as part of a federal system. Moreover, Jun (2009: 164) notes that:

> Both the NPM and post-NPM writings underestimate the participatory process of democratic governance, particularly in local communities, where interpersonal relationships between public managers and local citizens are more likely to include non-hierarchical collaboration and a horizontal dialogue than in organizations, in which functionally focused horizontal coordination and vertical dialogue underlie centralization and integration.

Many of the most interesting and successful examples of collaborative and alternative service delivery reforms tend to happen at the local or community level. This, in combination with New Zealand's size and defined boundaries, suggests that ascertaining what works and does not work should be relatively easy compared to doing so in much larger jurisdictions.

Finally, we must acknowledge that the term 'public sector reform' is evocative in New Zealand, given the public sector and policy reforms of the 1980s, followed by the electoral reforms of the 1990s. For many citizens, these reforms, and the resulting debate and upheaval, remain fresh. However, an appeal to think comprehensively about governance challenges and alternative ways to approach the delivery of public services should *not* be interpreted as calling for a 'big bang' and/or one-size-fits-all approach across the range of government services. Rather, it can take the form of wide-ranging and ongoing reflection on challenges confronting the country, a commitment to consider steadily and to monitor progress and developments in other jurisdictions, and possibly to adopt new approaches and improvements in areas and sectors where it makes sense. Such reforms could be selective, incremental and consistent with government priorities, as well as public sector needs and community capabilities.

Critical Distinction: Governance Challenges vs Public Sector Capabilities

Public sector reform is intimately related to, but not the same thing as, addressing the priorities of duly elected governments and seeking new approaches to governance. Public sector organisations and their leaders should always have a responsibility for and strong interest in advising governments and should commit to implementing faithfully the decisions of democratically elected governments. However, the institutions of the public sector should be prepared to deal with emerging challenges in order to provide good advice to current and future governments and be willing to work in different ways to deal with those priorities.

Duly elected governments have varying degrees of interest in the nuts-and-bolts of public sector reform. Many countries have differing styles in this regard: in Canada and Australia, for example, the tradition is that public service leaders 'self-reform' with the endorsement and consent of the government of the day; and, in other jurisdictions, such as the United Kingdom under Thatcher and Blair, governments took direct interest in the performance and structure of government. The New Zealand experience, aside from the 1980s, has been more like the Canadian and Australian experience. But a key difference is that Canada has had a more integrated public sector with a core public service, whereas Australia and New Zealand have more de-concentrated public service and public sector structures, with the latter further along the continuum with greater reliance on agency and special-purpose entities.

If one views the core public sector (meaning the public service in the Canadian sense) as somewhat autonomous from the government of the day (in the sense of having to serve future governments), then it should intermittently consider its readiness as a *collection* of public sector entities, emerging practices and different models from around the world, and capabilities for dealing with future challenges and perhaps new ways to deliver services.[21] In addition to government, opposition party and public perceptions of the weaknesses and strengths of any institution, core public sector leaders should have their own views in this regard, which requires that chief executives work together to consider the needs of the public sector as a coherent institution with requirements that transcend those of particular departments and agencies.

This implies that, in addition to working on government priorities and administering programmes in place, public sector leaders need to keep one eye on the longer-term institutional ball and ways in which the public sector as a whole can be improved or reformed. They should try to develop a collective and comprehensive framework – even if departments and agencies will naturally contest elements and priorities within it – to recognise and anticipate the future challenges that not only confront the country but also may point to strengths and weaknesses of the public sector as an institution.

From this vantage point – that of the core public sector as institution – the arrival of governments with specific policy priorities can be seen as opportunities to address some institutional administrative priorities in more concerted ways. However, public service leaders should also think about ways in which institutional needs can be addressed without direct government engagement, given that ministers will have only a limited number of priorities at any given time.

---

21 Savoie (2006) provides a legal perspective on the 'constitutional personality' of the public service in the Canadian context with some comparative considerations.

Multi-level Governance and Differentiated Public Sector Improvement

When we think of whether and how to reform the public service sector, we naturally gravitate to institution-wide approaches and use integrative frameworks to make sense of complexity and to get our bearings for different directions. However, all public sectors – regardless of the larger governance system – can be analysed through the lenses of distinct levels of analysis, where some elements lead reform and others resist it. In choosing strategic pathways for reform, we must have a finer-grained appreciation of dynamics and possibilities.

In complex national governance systems, every department and agency has different core goals, tasks and cultures, and therefore different mixes of values, repertoires and future challenges to deal with. Indeed, the opportunities and often the imperatives for policy *and* administrative reform are usually found in specific policy sectors, consistent with the priorities of governments. Likewise, each region and community has a unique set of challenges, first-hand experience with the cumulative and horizontal impact of policy and administrative approaches across policy domains, and often ideas about alternative ways to deliver services. In short, different sectors and communities may have varying degrees of readiness for moving forward with reform initiatives and alternative ways to design policy and deliver services.

This suggests that, in parallel to assessing the health of the public sector as an institution, it is essential to gauge the trajectory, capabilities and challenges of departments, agencies and the larger network of government, for-profit and non-profit organisations associated with that sector (Atkinson and Coleman, 1989; Lindquist, 1992). What are the challenges confronting policy sectors and associated networks? Are they in decline or ascendency? Do the organisations that comprise the network have access to the right talent and emerging technology to address new challenges? Do they need to organise and strategise according to a new mix of values and opportunities? Do they co-ordinate and mobilise sufficiently in order to meet those challenges? Do core public service departments have sufficient talent to appraise these sectors and associated networks?

Similar questions could be asked (and more likely are) about regional and local economic, social and cultural development. Critical questions concern whether there are unique challenges at the local and regional level that require a different mix of public services, how the mix of current public services is performing, and whether alternative bottom-up ways of delivering regional and local services might provide better value for money and lead to innovation.

By undertaking systematic monitoring and asking these questions, it would become clearer in which directions public policy should move and whether services ordinarily delivered in certain ways by the public sector need to change. Do services need to be devolved? Put on a market footing? Is it time to encourage public–private partnerships or co-operative approaches? Should certain services be brought back into the hands of central government? Does the core public sector have the right information to provide answers to these questions and then to manage the transitions? Rather than have categorical responses to these questions, and the directions that public sector reform should take more generally, it is better to have differentiated and finer-grained views.

Technology, Structural Change and Potential for Improvement

This chapter noted earlier that Dunleavy and his colleagues itemise the potential of digital technologies to integrate better the delivery of services for citizens and communities; to allow governments to address the needs of citizens more holistically, directly and efficiently; and to improve the front-end and back-end operations and external web presence of governments. In doing so, there is potential for such technology to significantly reduce the size of traditional bureaucracies inside and outside government that are currently responsible for delivering services – what Dunleavy and his colleagues call 'disintermediation'. What follows seeks to contextualise those observations briefly for the purposes of thinking about the possibilities for reform in New Zealand, recognising that it has an e-government strategy (SSC, 2006).

On the one hand, a narrow focus on digital technology may under-estimate the potential for improving the relationship and expanding the possibilities between governments and citizens, communities and other actors. In addition to allowing for more speed, integration and tailoring of services, it may also allow communities and citizens to see more co-production and self-governance possibilities, thereby increasing their willingness to take on more responsibility and to experiment with co-production and network-based arrangements with regional and central government. Such technologies – insofar as they allow for better data collection and closer-to-real-time monitoring – may also give government and citizens more confidence in experimenting with alternative approaches to service delivery. Particularly in local contexts, the potential for digital technology to inform and enhance upstream dialogue may also serve to increase quality and trust when designing policy and services with citizens and other stakeholders.

On the other hand, we must acknowledge that securing benefits of digital technology has been long imagined but relatively slow to come for many advocates. Such delays flow primarily from the significant step-wise investments required as well as different ways of seeing how the public sector might work, not to mention new skill requirements, data inputs and so on. The notion of single windows has long been talked about, and some of these windows have opened, but there is greater awareness that multiple windows will be required

investments required, the needs to be served, and the very real costs
ienges of broader integration of services and associated technologies.

Finally, technological change is often not associated with structural change,
but as Dunleavy and others have noted, adopting new digital technology can
through disintermediation lead to the elimination of bureaus, which is a form
of restructuring. But other possibilities might emerge: the character, repertoires
and priorities of existing bureaus might change following the adoption of new
technology – staff may be liberated to add value in different ways or have better
ability to collect data and monitor progress. Moreover, we should recall that
hardware and software technologies are built on hierarchy and routines, and,
like bureaucracy, may constitute alternative ways of structuring information
and relationships.

Conclusion: The Challenge for Central Agencies

After recognising the limitations of the New Synthesis and Competing Values
frameworks for situating analysis and strategising about reform directions
in complex public sector organisation systems, this section has attempted to
provide more definition and considerations as a platform for considering the
implications for central agencies. It has suggested that geographical size is an
important factor underpinning reform possibilities, particularly with respect to
engaging citizens and communities, and experimenting with and monitoring
alternative service delivery arrangements. The section also made a distinction
between reforming the public sector according to further government priorities
and considering how the public sector as a constellation of departments and
agencies might 'self-assess', and set about ascertaining what their priorities for
reform might be as institutions in order to serve better in the present and the
future.

This latter point may seem pedestrian or radical depending on one's point of
view, and its meaning takes on a different resonance in different jurisdictions:
in Canada, there is a core public service composed of central agencies and
departments, and executives think of themselves as part of a cadre throughout
the public service that is responsible for the vitality of a broader institution (this
gets attenuated as one moves out to agencies and other independent authorities);
in other jurisdictions, like New Zealand,[22] where the centre is relatively weak and
the state sector is so distributed and fragmented, it is certainly more difficult to
think of it as an 'institution'. *This chapter argues that, notwithstanding the strong
incentive system and unique way of organising the state sector in New Zealand,
the leaders of state sector organisations need to develop more of a corporate
understanding and approach to capability.* On the other hand, one way to focus

22 See Gregory (2003a); and Lodge and Gill (2011).

for strategic purposes is to take an approach based on the policy sector to sizing up governance challenges and implications for public sector capability.

Finally, this section brought together earlier observations about the possibilities presented by digital technology for developing policy, delivering services and monitoring performance in different ways. It has suggested that structural 'reform' and new mixes of work may follow new ways of doing business engendered by technology, but this will likely be emergent and *ex post* in nature. This also links to the challenge of looking across public sector agencies to develop a sense of progress that takes in the entire public sector as well as horizontal synergies and institutional-level possibilities for investments, particularly when government finances promise to be very tight. Taken together, this suggests that New Zealand's central agencies may have to expand their repertoires.

5. No Reform Left Behind: Proposal for Improving Central Agencies and Public Sector Institutions

With the assumptions and possibilities explored above, as well as a better understanding of the integrating frameworks used to capture the many possibilities for reform and improvement, we can consider the implications for New Zealand's central agencies and what capabilities they might need to build in order to serve governments better and to move the public sector forward in the future state. Before setting out a modest proposal to expand the scope and strategic yield of capability reviews and monitoring of departments and agencies, it is useful to remind ourselves of the multi-faceted nature of central agency work and the particular character of central agencies and governance challenges in New Zealand. After setting out the proposal, this section considers the manifold purposes for which the information could be utilised and how an enhanced regime could be built on existing repertoires and emerging capabilities.

Central Agencies and Cross-pressures: Implications for Public Sector Improvement

There has recently emerged a literature on assessing the strategic capabilities of central agencies informed by Australian and New Zealand national, state-level and international comparisons (Halligan 2010a; Kelly et al., 2010; Norman 2008a). It considers the many demands and cross-pressures on central agencies of government, as well as the shifting roles and competition among these agencies to influence governments. These roles include:

- identifying government priorities (policy and administrative) and monitoring the quality of their implementation;

- serving the government of the day, including managing transitions and the normal work of government decision-making and oversight activities;
- scanning for and anticipating issues and trends, as well as the state of practice in other jurisdictions, and assessing the opportunities for learning and transfer; and
- developing and conveying a corporate perspective on public sector capability and preparing public sector institutions to serve future governments as well as the current government – referred to as a 'stewardship' role (Advisory Group on Reform of Australian Government Administration, 2010).

Much has been made about the shifting roles, complexities and rivalries inherent in the central provision of advice to governments, but for our purposes the most helpful perspective is the lens provided by Davis (1995), who locates central agencies at the nexus of political, policy and operational domains of government. Each domain has its own logics and imperatives, with central agencies having different mixes of responsibilities and relationships with governments when discharging their responsibilities. This perspective also implies that central agencies are constantly dealing with a never-ending stream of multi-faceted demands from governments.

In my view, the challenge of public sector improvement (and even 'reform') is best situated in the strategic domain of operational strategy, recognising that central agencies must always be alert and responsive to the strategic imperatives emerging from the political and policy domains reflecting the priorities of sitting governments. *Recognising that central agencies are constantly in overload mode in their ongoing efforts to serve governments and manage the broader public sector, a key implication flowing from this broader view of central responsibilities is that any proposals for change must fit into and build on existing repertoires.* Consistent with our earlier discussion about the merits of reform versus improvement, this suggests that modest proposals for improvement, rather than structural change and new capacities, might have far greater chances of take-up and institutionalisation. Ideally, the putative yields from such improvements would inform not only the specific need in question but also other streams of activities of central agencies.

The Character and Context of New Zealand's Central Agencies

The international literature has ventured assessments of how New Zealand's central institutions compare to those of other jurisdictions. Despite the central-ising tendencies of Westminster systems, and the relative 'comprehensibility' of governing and managing a relatively small jurisdiction, the centre of New Zealand's government capabilities has been viewed as comparatively small and weak when compared to other national and state-level jurisdictions, particularly with respect to policy co-ordination and leadership functions.[23]

Such observations are interesting because the New Zealand model of Westminster government and public sector is distinctive in several regards. First, even before the reforms of the 1980s and early 1990s, New Zealand had a persistent state tradition of many relatively autonomous and specialised agencies, which have been relatively cohesive in a small jurisdiction.[24] Second, the Treasury had a pivotal role in conceiving, launching and implementing the reforms of the 1980s, and continues that strong advisory role to this day. Third, the reform era led to the creation of a well-defined, independent and strong role for the State Services Commission with respect to hiring and monitoring the performance of chief executives in the New Zealand public sector, which is unique and has been internationally recognised. Fourth, notwithstanding the power of prime ministers, in the New Zealand context the Department of the Prime Minister and Cabinet (DPMC) has played the role of 'honest broker' and policy co-ordinator for the cabinet process rather than being an active participant in public sector management reform.[25] A virtue of New Zealand's central institutions is that there is relatively little overlap in their roles and responsibilities.

The main challenge confronting the public sector and central agencies in particular is that the Key government has announced a programme of significant budget restraint and rationalisation to deal with the effects of the global financial crisis on public finances. It is seeking to re-position the public sector to deal with future challenges in a fiscal environment that will be significantly constrained for the foreseeable future.[26] Central agencies – particularly the Treasury – will work with the government to identify targets, undertake strategic reviews and announce cuts, as well as monitor progress in meeting targets and how departments and agencies propose to rationalise programmes and operations.

The Proposal: Enhanced Capability Reviews and Monitoring

Recent developments and plans in New Zealand suggest that central agencies, beyond working with the government to set the framework within which to make cuts, will also have to assess the risks of alternative service delivery decisions, and monitor the performance of the new range of arrangements in the broader public and community sectors. In an era where 'no reform is left behind'

23 See Halligan (forthcoming); and Kelly et al (2010).
24 See Gill (2008a).
25 See Norman (2008a).
26 See English (2010).

because different configurations and mixes may apply in particular contexts, it is imperative that governments enhance their ability to anticipate needs and identify promising approaches tailored for each policy and administrative sector. Since central agencies will get further overloaded if they attempt to take on this responsibility directly, they need to encourage and prod lead departments and agencies to do so, and ensure that they are doing so in a credible way. From an operational and corporate perspective, this suggests that continuing to rely on department- and agency-specific capability reviews – even with the enhanced Performance Improvement Framework[27] – will be insufficient.

Recognising the ongoing work demands on central agencies, I suggest that the repertoires for monitoring capability and performance should be expanded to include:

- capability reviews of departments and agencies taking into account their emerging sector challenges and the state of broader policy/ administration networks to ascertain whether recruitment and learning repertoires will attract and develop good talent for future needs;
- best practice reviews of international procedures in designated sectors as well as in cognate policy and administrative domains;
- good monitoring and frank assessments of the state of institutional capacity across core departments, agencies and the broader public sector to inform sensible cross-agency rationalisation and investments; and
- analysis of where significant investments can be made in back-room and front-room information technology capabilities of portfolios of departments and agencies, and/or with departments, agencies, and specific communities and sectors.

The annual report of the State Service Commissioner does not provide assessments across departments and agencies, which is understandable given the bilateral relationship between the State Services Commission (SSC) and chief executives, ministers, and departments and agencies. Enhanced reporting could take the form of an annual report to the prime minister or a document developed by and circulated to all chief executives.[28] The capability reviews proceeding under the Performance Improvement Framework do not provide for forward-looking assessments of sector challenges or detailed information-gathering and assessment of overall capabilities across a policy/administrative network and the role of the focal department or agency in that network,

27 The first full round of assessments, released in September 2010, can be found on the SSC web site at <http://www.ssc.govt.nz/pif> (accessed 1 September 2011).
28 Examples include Canada's Annual Report of the Clerk on the Public Service of Canada versus Australia Public Service Commission's Annual *State of the Service* Report.

particularly with respect to preparing for future challenges. Addressing these gaps could be handled with an expanded set of questions under the 'Leadership, Direction and Delivery' and 'External Relationships' processes (SSC, Treasury, and Department of the Prime Minister and Cabinet, 2009). Undertaking assessments of sector challenges could be done in collaboration with entities like the new Productivity Commission.

The goal would be to raise the awareness of sitting governments of the state of the New Zealand public sector but also, and more importantly, to have chief executives develop a shared understanding of challenges and possibilities. Even the detailed annual *State of the Service* report produced by the Australian Public Service Commission does not currently have the envisioned reach – particularly with respect to assessing the capability of networks – so this would constitute an innovation. It would be a complement, of sorts, to the Kiwis Count initiative.

Enhanced Monitoring and Reporting: Potential Yields and By-products

Even in the context of significant restraint, such assessments could inform government decision-making and the development of the public sector as an institution in a variety of ways:

- as new priorities are identified by governments, advice on design and implementation possibilities would be informed by sound understanding of the readiness of public sector agencies and partners to deliver on those priorities;
- inform risk assessments on existing policy and programmes in light of evolving external environments as well as state and network capabilities;
- identify institutional priorities for strengthening and reforming public sector departments and agencies, particularly with respect to cross-organisational collaboration and working with broader networks;
- pinpoint opportunities to use government priority policy initiatives to address institutional development priorities consciously because of political attention and resource infusions, even if they might constitute de facto pilots;
- reduce the probability that chief executives will make unilateral restructuring decisions for their organisations that may not be prudent in terms of effects on the activities and outcomes of cognate departments and agencies, or may miss opportunities for collaborative solutions and investments;
- identify strategies for addressing institutional priorities for the public sector that are not top government priorities but can be steadily advanced through administrative means, such as re-allocation and leverage,

different recruitment and socialisation patterns, targeted training and development, technology advances, efficiency and more coherence;

- inform advice on the mandate and expectations when appointing chief executives who not only have led departments and agencies, but also work within and enable networks, and, of course, condition and inform assessments of their performance; and
- convey important strategic contextual information to change agents in the middle of public organisations and related networks about the possibilities for innovation.[29]

Such assessments could proceed on a staggered basis, with some form of regular reporting at the corporate level and a rotating set of strategic reviews of different policy sectors. In addition to contributions from the Productivity Commission, assessments could be informed by data and analysis from central and line departments and agencies, as well as university, think tank, associational, community and other expertise, perhaps assembled by means of task forces.

Making the Proposal Happen: Building from Existing Repertoires

Central agencies' responsibilities, of course, go beyond reporting, such as those associated with the political and policy spheres identified by Davis. Moreover, central agencies have other means – aside from more comprehensive reporting – for influencing the behaviour of line departments and agencies. These include effecting structural change, revising the mandates of departments and agencies, altering the conditions and incentives for executive engagement, appointing individuals to boards and leadership positions, resourcing, alternating administrative policy frameworks, and centralising policy development and oversight in specific policy domains by building central units (adhocracies) if the government believes there is insufficient co-ordination or capability. An improved capability review and monitoring regime is only one central avenue for exerting influence on New Zealand's public sector.

Given current mandates and capabilities, the SSC would be best positioned to take on the responsibility for an expanded system of reporting on capabilities because of its independence, its department/agency-based monitoring repertoires and its monitoring of other jurisdictions. However, information from secretariats across all of the central agencies – most notably the Treasury – would inform department and sector assessments. But moving in the proposed direction requires developing whole-of-government and sector-based data-gathering and review capabilities, including tapping into assessments from

---

29 See Floyd and Wooldridge (2000); Kelman (2005).

the Productivity Commission and other organisations, which would require altering the SSC's recruitment strategies and possibly its structure in certain areas. In addition to informing assessments, the Treasury would have strong views on sectors from an economics and policy perspective, and the Department of the Prime Minister and Cabinet would be able to lever them as it manages cabinet business, informs government priorities, and co-ordinates and monitors implementation in priority areas. But a key virtue of the proposed expanded review and monitoring regime is that it would build on repertoires already in place for the Performance Improvement Framework, and this includes input from all three primary central agencies.

This approach would allow for complementary and deepening specialisation by the DPMC. It could ensure that the DPMC could, as required, create design and co-ordination secretariats around the top priorities of governments. It could also focus the limited attention of the government and central agencies to ensure appropriate joint performance and accountability regimes for selected whole-of-government priorities, including dedicated central reserves, incentives for chief executives as individuals and as a collective, and performance-monitoring systems (with, given the attribution challenge, appropriate expectations). Indeed, to ensure collaboration and performance across entities, there is no substitute for the focused attention of the prime minister, key ministers and central agencies. Finally, while Kelly et al. (2010) point to the importance of establishing whole-of-government visions and plans (including priority areas and performance indicators) and selective policy reviews, it is critical to acknowledge that there can be too many priorities and reviews, which can foster confusion and un-strategic behaviour.

Reprise: A Modest Proposal for Informing Broader Strategic Perspectives

Given the breadth of New Zealand's public sector and the challenges that governments must deal with, the modest proposal set out in this section may seem insubstantial. However, governments must better anticipate governance challenges, and public sector leaders must better prepare their departments and agencies – individually and collectively – to provide strategic advice, to explore and monitor different ways to deliver services, and to ensure necessary capabilities are emerging in respective policy/administrative sectors beyond their immediate organisational boundaries.

Indeed, public sector leaders should have well-informed and shared views on public-sector-wide and sector challenges and capability considerations, even if these determinations are contested or not the highest priority of elected governments. Navigating and thriving in continually evolving governance environments, and making the most of scarce resources, requires public sector leaders to focus on current government priorities *and* have forward-looking, cross-cutting sensibilities.

6. Conclusion: Can Governments Go Beyond Integrating Frameworks and Enhanced Capability Reviews/Reporting?

This chapter has built on the call in the first chapter for new perspectives on governance in New Zealand's future state in an era of constraint. It has argued that, although there seems to be a concerted search for a new post-NPM paradigm to guide improvement and reform, what is more likely is that no reform will be left behind: every jurisdiction will have different mixes of approaches, old and new, for delivering policy and services. Given the multi-faceted challenges of leading and sometimes reforming public sector organisations, this chapter noted that more governments and scholars have been turning to integrating frameworks as guides for assessment. Although critiquing the ability of the New Synthesis and Competing Values frameworks to capture such complexity, as well as the possibilities confronting government, I have sought to elaborate on and extend the frameworks in order to understand better their application to the unique, complex and highly differentiated public sector context, and then to explore how governments and central agencies can more appropriately anticipate and make difficult decisions in every sector.

This chapter has argued that the New Zealand government should further encourage cross-cutting perspectives on the state of the public sector and within specific policy/administrative domains, particularly with respect to future challenges, and that public sector chief executives as a group have a special responsibility in developing such corporate and sector strategic perspectives. In this connection, and recognising the multiple demands on central agencies, a modest proposal to enhance the existing system of capability reviews and state-of-the-service reporting is set out, one that would lift the focus of assessment beyond the performance of individual departments and agencies. Indeed, as we move into an era of increased experimentation with policy and service delivery models, elected governments and citizens alike should have a sense of capability gaps across the public sector – within and across agencies – and what might be entailed in moving from the current state to a future state in different policy sectors, and whether expectations for performance inside and outside government are reasonable given the resources available to affected outcomes in desired directions. None of this presumes that improving how the public sector works should necessarily be radical or require structural reform or significant investments in new systems – although this might be called for in some sectors. Indeed, we might agree that achieving improvements of 20–30 per cent on a sustained basis over several years might be more productive and cause less upheaval.

The rationale for investing in an expanded, forward-looking and cross-cutting assessment regime by central agencies emerges from the very experimentation – in the form of alternative delivery models, some collaborative and some otherwise – that will likely emerge due to advances in technology, fiscal constraint, and the preferences of citizens and communities in New Zealand and other jurisdictions. However uneasily, governments will increasingly experiment with and rely on innovative partnerships, community-based approaches and individualisation, all of which may be enabled through technology and more subtle policy design. Such change will not necessarily be achieved by moving a large number of organisations in the public sector into the 'emergent' zone of the New Synthesis framework or the more outward-looking quadrant of the Competing Values framework; nor will such innovation always be preceded by citizen and community engagement. Indeed, these myriad solutions – which may evolve considerably in light of experience – will likely need a combination of assertive leadership inside and outside government, attention to developing new notions of performance and control, and establishing sufficient and sometimes new hierarchical capabilities and monitoring repertoires, to ensure that broader outcomes and choices are achieved at reasonable costs and with the minimum risk. Inevitably, how such choices and innovation emerge will differ significantly across policy/administrative domains. Moving further in these new directions may seem challenging, and public sector leaders may be sceptical about the merits of taking up an 'enhanced' capability review and monitoring system, but this chapter has argued that New Zealand, given its size and governance tradition, is well positioned to do so.

There is a final challenge, one not delved into here. Regardless of the precise paths chosen for improvements in diverse sectors, governments need to find better ways to convey to citizens and other stakeholders what has been achieved and whether these improvements are sufficient for addressing future challenges. Enhanced capability review and monitoring repertoires should not be confused with the need to communicate how public sector capabilities and new models for delivering services are evolving and performing. As governments around the world experiment with new approaches to delivering policy frameworks and services to the public, they need to find more effective, rich and succinct ways to convey how public sector contours, repertoires and capabilities have changed in doing so, particularly with respect to working with non-profit, community and private sector organisations to deliver services.[30] Next-generation reporting must move well beyond the current 'performance' approach, which has reduced external understanding of governments due to

---

30 See Lindquist (2011a; 2011b) respectively on various visualisation techniques and the possibilities for their use in various kinds of policy work.

its focus on outputs and outcomes, to show the nature of complex challenges, government responses (including the full range of collaboration and non-government activity), and how different the responses are across sectors. This suggests that, along with enhanced capability reviews and monitoring regimes, New Zealand's public sector leaders should invest in innovative ways to convey the evolving nature of public sector work and emerging challenges to governments and citizens alike.

3

The Signs are Everywhere: 'Community' Approaches to Public Management[1]

Bill Ryan

'Oh people, look around you, the signs are everywhere'

Jackson Browne, 'Rock Me On the Water'

At an early stage in the Future State project, some senior public officials expressed concerns that parts of the public management system no longer seem to work as well as they once believed, and are holding back developments. The question these officials asked is where to from here? In what directions should public management in New Zealand be headed? This chapter presents some answers to those questions. The discussion is both conceptual and practical, in the sense of the general implications arising. Part of the issue confronting public management in New Zealand is that, despite the high quality of today's public service in many respects, some of the fundamentals of the politico-administrative system need to be rethought for tomorrow. The task ahead is not easy. This chapter tries to identify some of those concerns. It should be noted that where public management thinking in Australasia is usually based on economics, management and organisational theories alone, this analysis brings to bear a perspective that also draws from history, sociology, and the study of power and the state.

Actually, the international public management literature contains a wide range of possibilities for the future. This chapter presents a selection of them: ideas that have not emerged as models or methods derived from theory, but as conceptual attempts to make sense of changes in practice that have emerged in some places. In fact, practice is well in advance of the theory. Practical adaptations are showing the way forward and this is where we must look to work out where to go. These developments are being actively debated and promoted in countries such as Australia, Britain, Canada and the United States

1   I would like to thank Elizabeth Eppel, Derek Gill and Miriam Lips for discussions on this topic stretching over some time. They are not to blame for what follows.

but have very little presence in discussion in New Zealand. I argue that we too should be seriously considering them partly because they deal with some problematic aspects of the economic underpinnings of the New Zealand model of public management and the way it has been implemented.

Paradoxically, whilst these ideas are absent in professional discourse, they are, in fact, emerging in practice in some well-known New Zealand initiatives. There are signs everywhere of public officials adapting to their societal environment, sometimes despite the constraints of the system in which they are working. A selection of illustrations is presented to demonstrate the point. The question then becomes, if these new ways of working are already emerging but only in some places, are there conditions applying in the New Zealand state sector that prevent them from becoming more widespread? I argue that this is the case. Some of these are due to certain features of the existing public management system that therefore need to be revised or replaced. Others barriers are created by conditions under which ministers and officials work that have little to do with the public management model *per se* and more to do with other aspects of our political system but which equally need to change. If public management in New Zealand is to accept the challenges of the future, attention has to be paid to these wider issues and not just the public management system itself. They demand socio-political understanding of governing and community-like (as opposed to market-like or bureaucratic) approaches to public management that are different from anything offered by the prescribed model. That said, this chapter also cautions against thinking that a single model of public management prescribed for universal application to replace the existing one is an appropriate way forward. Intentionally or unintentionally, this kind of mistake was made in the past. The future is more likely to be one wherein managing in the public sector comprises several different approaches maintained in balance, some based on hierarchy, rule and control; others on goods and services, self-interest and free exchange; and still others based on citizens, common interests and collective action. Which approach is appropriate when and where will depend on the societal purpose and the policy and management context.

Public Management Present and Future

Since the 1970s and 1980s, New Zealand, Australia, Britain, Canada and the United States have devoted enormous resources to reforming their public sectors and the creation of new systems of governing. This wave of reform was labelled 'new public management' (NPM), a collection of various more-or-less related ideas, based largely on economic and private sector management theories (Hood, 1991). Famously, New Zealand was regarded as a world leader in constructing NPM, although in truth it was not quite the 'pure' NPM model most assumed

(Lodge and Gill, 2011). Internationally, as the first decade of the twenty-first century has come to a close, there is a growing sense among observers and some practitioners that the NPM approach has reached its limits. Some say it is dead (e.g., Dunleavy, Margetts, Bastow and Tinkler, 2006a). Others say it is being transcended (e.g., Christensen and Lægreid, 2007a). Others talk about 'postmodern' public administration (e.g., Bogason, 2007). Several are talking about a 'post-NPM' stage although, like Lodge and Gill (2011), I am sceptical and would rather not arrive at such linear or totalising conclusions. It can be argued that 'the New Zealand model of public management' (Boston, Martin, Pallot and Walsh, 1996) did bring several benefits that could and should be retained. In other respects I argue that public management in this country needs to move in different directions, some of which are discussed in this chapter (see also Gill and Hitchener, 2011a; Norman, 2003; Ryan, 2004). The question then arises as to which directions of change and why?

As the Future State 1 project suggests, there are powerful global economic forces that will shape the politico-administrative systems of many countries including New Zealand over coming decades. These include peaks and troughs in international economic activity and the performance of particular countries; geopolitical shifts in power and the spread of democracy; rapid developments in technology, particularly in information and communication technologies; increasing resource scarcities and climate change; and changing values and the diffusion of ideas (for an American view of the impacts, see the special edition of *Public Administration Review*, December 2010, on 'The Future of Public Administration in 2020'). Other changes occurring *inside* societies such as New Zealand, Australia, Britain, some northern and western European countries, Canada and the United States, particularly socio-political changes, are less remarked in the public management literature. These are the focus of this chapter since it is clear that they are pivotal to the ongoing development of public management in this and probably other similar countries.

Of course, the practices of governing and public management that are constituted in any jurisdiction are a product of the particular mix of conditions and factors applying at the time (Pollitt and Bouckaert, 2004). One example is the dynamic relationship between politics and public management. There is no better illustration than the impact on the latter of the introduction in New Zealand from 1996 of the Mixed Member Proportional (MMP) electoral system. It followed a series of voter referenda in which the first-past-the-post electoral system and the 'elected dictatorship' it always seemed to generate (Held, 2006) were resoundingly banished. MMP led instead to minority governments supported by various forms of alliances and multiple-party cabinets and ministries. Previously used to dealing with single ministers, public officials needed to find new ways of dealing with increased levels of complexity and ambiguity in their relationships with the political arm of the executive (e.g., James, 2002). Economics too can have a major influence. As widely noted (e.g., Boston, 1991), the radical public sector reforms of the 1980s and 1990s in New Zealand were driven not only by ministerial desires to control the bureaucracy but also as part of a solution to high fiscal deficits, significant debt (including substantial unfunded liabilities) and a highly protectionist economy with a long history of slow economic growth (Scott, Bushnell and Sallee, 1990). In a very real sense – and without making any comment on the particular economic paradigms that were adopted – the so-called 'New Zealand model of public management' (Boston, Martin, Pallot and Walsh, 1996), and its strong marketisation agenda with a heavy reliance on privatisation, corporatisation and contracting out, was shaped by the economic forces that were impacting on New Zealand at the time. Some managerial components were also included,[2] but the model was largely derived from public choice and principal/agent theories (Boston, Martin, Pallot and Walsh, 1996; cf. Scott, 2001). Sociologically, the determination is entirely explicable, and the same kind of structural determination is important in the following argument.

However, there are multiple social, civic, economic and political forces that shape the form and content of public management in any polity. Pollitt and Bouckaert have created a model identifying the proximate sources of influence on public sector reform (2004: 25). It is a basic model, stripped to its core. A more complex picture of influence emerges in their analysis and, for the purposes of this discussion, I have adapted their figure and added an additional sphere of influence (equally skeletal) labelled 'civil society',[3] comprising 'providers and clients', 'civic associations and interest groups' and 'public and private media' and 'organisations and spaces for public discussion' (Cohen and Arato, 1994) (see Figure 3.1 below).

2　Jurisdictions such as Australia made a clearer distinction in the 1980s between a 'managerial' reform agenda and an 'economic' one. Indeed, during the 1980s, the managerial agenda dominated in the Australian Commonwealth (Keating and Holmes, 1990). In New Zealand, the economic agenda dominated and provided its distinctive components.

3　This analysis is underpinned by a conception of society as built on three distinctive spheres of activity: the polity, the economy and civil society. The conception of civil society I take from the seminal contribution of Cohen and Arato (1994). It is a combination of the domestic sphere, the realm of public association (especially voluntary associations), social movements and forms of public communication. The political and economic spheres arise out of civil society and share some of its forms of organisation. The political role of civil society is not given over to control or power but the expression of rights and influence through democratic association and unconstrained discussion in the public sphere (Cohen and Arato, 1994: ix–x).

Figure 3.1. Governance and the Influences on Public Management

A. Socio-Economic Forces		E. Political System		O. Civil Society
B. Global economic forces	C. Socio-demographic change	F. New management ideas	G. Pressure from citizens	P. Civic associations and interest groups
C. Socio-economic policies		H. Party political ideas		Q. Clients and providers

J. Cabinet and Ministerial Decision-making

I. Chance events e.g. scandals, disasters

R. Public and private media, organisations and spaces for discussion

K. Administrative System

L. Roles and practices

M. Structures and resources

N. Model and system

Adapted from Pollitt and Bouckaert (2004: 25).

For the purposes of this discussion, elite decision-making (J in Figure 3.1) is defined in terms of ministers, cabinet and the government of the day. Forces arising from the socio-economic sphere (A), the political sphere (E) and civil society (O), and adaptive responses emerging from cabinet (J) and the administrative system (K), are the primary focus. The 'public management system' refers to the executive, i.e., cabinet (J) and the public sector (K), and 'governance' refers to the combination of all the entities in Figure 3.1. This chapter is concerned with the *dynamics within each of the economic, political and civil spheres and the interactions between them over time* (see also Cohen and Arato, 1994). These dynamics are dramatically escalating the challenges confronting public sectors in developing and implementing policies sought by the government of the day and are generating significant pressures to change certain practices back in the public management system (K and J). Pressures from citizens (G) acting individually and collectively (sometimes as direct clients of services) are also forcing themselves into processes determining public matters that affect them. Also important are the adaptive responses of public officials in the public management system to the changing forces in which they are constantly involved. The fourth focus is the framework of new public management ideas that are emerging in the international theory and practice in the western world. I will characterise these combined shifts in the history, context, theory and practice of public management as 'socio-political' movements. I use this abstract term to ensure it highlights the different assumptions it carries regarding the nature, purpose and conduct of public management, otherwise it will be tempting to introduce the methods and tools that come with it in superficial and eclectic ways.

Outside of New Zealand, these shifts are starting to be recognised by public management practitioners. One example is the Moran Report in the Australian Commonwealth (Advisory Group on Reform of Australian Public Administration, 2010). Another is the so-called New Synthesis project in Canada (e.g., Bourgon, 2009c). In the UK, think tanks such as the Work Foundation (e.g., Horner, Lekhi and Blaug, 2006) have been exploring new and interesting territory such as public value and deliberative democracy (although these notions will not be specifically discussed in this chapter; see Ryan, 2010). There has been limited and muted discussion of these ideas in central and line agencies in New Zealand (some signs of which are apparent in the recently announced 'Better Public Services' initiative),[4] and signs of practical initiative in some parts of some departments (as the illustrative cases later demonstrate) but little public or professional debate. The Future State project is, in part, an attempt to spark such discussion.

Emerging Ideas in Public Management

Several important ideas such as networking and governance, partnership and collaboration, participation and co-production are presently being discussed in the international public management literature. Some academics regard them as connected in some way (although not always obviously) and having deep implications for the future of public management. Some practitioners seem ready to adopt them but to treat them basically as 'tools', as new tricks that can be added on top of what is already done, ignoring their deeper assumptions and entailments, incorporating them within the dominant model as if nothing needs to change.[5] I argue that tokenistic adoption of these ideas is problematic.

4   See <http://www.dpmc.govt.nz/better_public_services/> (accessed 23 September 2011). It would be fair to say, however, that the matters addressed so far (at the time of writing) reflect corporate interests in managing the public sector rather than enabling innovation in managing so as to better achieve policy outcomes that increase public value. In this respect, the contrast with, say, the ideas surrounding the Moran Report (Advisory Group on Reform of Australian Public Administration, 2010) and the equivalent central agencies in the Australian Commonwealth, is telling. See, for example, <http://www.dpmc.gov.au/publications/aga_reform/aga_reform_blueprint/index.cfm>; and the recent work of the Management Advisory Committee <http://www.apsc.gov.au/mac/aboutmac.htm> (accessed 23 September 2011).

5   A good example of this relates to the notion of 'public value' where the BBC has adopted the notion and built it into its corporate vision (BBC, 2004), but without apparently realising

I align myself with those who believe these new ideas are connected and, in this chapter, suggest ways that those threads may be theorised.

It seems to me that the emerging ideas discussed below do cohere at a higher level of abstraction. To a greater or lesser extent, all of them address the nature of the *constituent relationships* (as opposed, say, to structures or hard systems) *within the public sector and within the government executive, and between the executive* (particularly the public sector) *and the providers and users of public services in civil society and the economy*. The emergence of these ideas is part of a fundamental but not yet unified rethinking about which type of relationship in which setting best realises the purposes of effective governing – how best to harness the capabilities and resources of the executive (K and J in Figure 3.1) in its interactions with the economy, parliament and other political activities, and civil society (A, E and O). The comparison, broadly, is between hierarchical, rule-governed relationships (bureaucratic relationships); market or quasi-market relationships based on impersonality, self-seeking individualism and calculative exchanges (economic relationships); and community-like relationships based on sociality, mutuality, reciprocity, trust and collectivism (community or network relationships) (Thompson, Frances, Levačić and Mitchell, 1991).[6]

At present, many argue that bureaucratic relationships belong to a time past (e.g., Hughes, 2003) although, in truth, they are still important in some areas of government activity. The market-oriented and public choice-derived reforms introduced in NPM remain appropriate in some cases but were applied universally in their implementation in countries such as New Zealand[7] and Britain, although less so in Australia, Canada and the United States. There are many arenas of government activity, however, which are fundamentally political and sociological and not economic. In these, an approach to public management built on community-like relationships is more appropriate – although what exactly this means and how it is to be realised is in the process of being worked out. Accordingly, I argue here that collectively these emerging ideas can be seen as representing a socio-political but contextually pragmatic critique of NPM. They point to a future that does not seek to replace market-based approaches to public management, since there are circumstances in which these can be

that public value presumes a fundamentally transformed relationship between user and provider, citizen and government – in ways close to those discussed below in relation to participation and co-production.

6 In classifying forms of co-ordination of social life, these authors use markets, hierarchies and networks. When speaking of relationships, I have chosen to characterise the third category as 'community-like', drawing a parallel with 'civil society' in the earlier part of my analysis.

7 There is argument at present over the level of intent. Some of those involved in the early design and development of the 1980s reforms argue that the model was intended to be more open, flexible and expansive than it has turned out. From this perspective, the implementation was too narrow, reductionist and transaction-based.

regarded as appropriate, but to balance them with community-styled approaches where economic or bureaucratic approaches are not appropriate. It also insists that the type of relationship that might work best in any setting – and hence the forms of organisation, practices, roles, methods and resources entailed by that assumption – is context-dependent and ultimately a matter of public value (Moore, 1995; see also Bennington and Moore, 2011; Kelly, Mulgan and Muers, 2002). In that sense I suggest these emerging community-oriented ideas do not represent an approaching 'post-NPM' era but are better understood as a 'non-NPM' or socio-political approach to public management that will increasingly predominate in some aspects of governing but in combination with market and bureaucratic approaches.

Before proceeding, an important caveat should be sounded. The ideas discussed in this chapter are presented more or less as typifications (what Weber in 1948 famously referred to as 'ideal-types') that accentuate their distinctiveness. They should not be taken as applicable to all organisations and practices all the time, particularly in their pristine form. This was a mistake made in the late 1980s and 1990s in relation to market-like approaches to governing. Singular, idealised frameworks applied universally should be treated with suspicion; there are too many necessary variations and context-dependencies in the public sphere for that to be wise. Instead, the ideas and trends discussed here are relevant to some parts of the public sector but less so to others. The twenty-first-century task is to decide which application – bureaucratic, market or community – is appropriate, and where it is not. Some government activities (e.g., where standardisation and routinisation are high and akin to a production environment; or where state authority needs to be asserted strongly) may be best run along traditional hierarchical and rule-based lines. Other purposes and activities may be well suited to a market-like form of public management. Fields of complex, long-term policy in relation to social welfare, education, health, the environment, sustainability and economic development, however, seem like prime candidates for community-like ways of working. This is where they may be most applicable.

It is within this overall framework that the following discussion tries to make sense of some important ideas emerging in contemporary public management.

Networks and Governance

Governing is no longer something done exclusively in and by government. It frequently occurs in and through wide-ranging networks that combine a broad spectrum of public, non-government and private actors who cannot simply be commanded or controlled by government. These networks become self-sustaining for the period that their particular issue is on the policy agenda and, when open and inclusive, harbour high levels of expertise regarding the nature of the issue, possible solutions and the conditions of implementation of any chosen option.

There is a large recent literature on the fact and significance of networks in contemporary governing (e.g., Denhardt and Denhardt, 2007; Howlett and Ramesh, 1995; Kickert, 1997; Kickert, Klijn and Koopenjan, 1997; Klijn and Koopenjan, 2000; Rhodes, 1997). Networks have long been recognised in the countries of western Europe (e.g., Netherlands; see Kickert, 1997, 2003) but are also becoming evident in Australasia – even more in Australia than New Zealand because of its federal system of government. In the full sense of the term, a 'network' is a form of enduring, goal-oriented organisation, a way of co-ordinating interactions between myriad actors with common interests (associations). Relationships between participants are purposive and even instrumental but also tend to be personal even where institutional. The network form of organisation stands in contrast to bureaucracies (positions, role-incumbents, hierarchy and rules) and markets (free individuals, self-directed preferences, calculation, value and exchange). Networks are also horizontal in orientation rather than vertical, relatively unbounded and porous to new members (e.g., Thompson, Frances, Levačić and Mitchell, 1991). Accordingly, networks can be understood as a characteristic form of organising multiple associations in a community-like approach to public management.

Networking as an organisational basis of governing increased dramatically in the last decades of the twentieth century and shows no signs of abating in the twenty-first (Kickert, Klijn and Koppenjan, 1997). In terms of Figure 3.1, the rise of networks is an historical effect of the push from civil society and the socio-economic environment into the politico-administrative system and, reciprocally, outreach by ministers and public officials into the civic and economic spheres. One result is the pluralisation of power that has occurred in developed democratic societies since the late nineteenth century (e.g., Held, 2006). As a result, governments have been increasingly forced to share their authority, and are less able to act autonomously or commandingly. They must find new ways of acting. As Rhodes (1997: 57) points out, the key challenge for government is 'to enable these networks and seek out new forms of cooperation'. Accordingly, governing in the future will be less about top-down leadership and control than enablement and facilitation from within. Networked governing also redefines parts of what it is to be a 'public servant' or 'official'. In articulating their vision, Denhardt and Denhardt (2007: 83–84), for example, envisage public officials not just as serving government but also acting as societal resources, as socio-political agents.[8] Their task will be to facilitate, broker and mediate emergent solutions to public problems from within the networks, by co-

---

8   This is not 'agent' in the subordinate sense defined in principal/agent theory but in the sense of situated, active agency (see Giddens, 1984). For a fuller account, see the discussion of constitutional issues later in this paper.

producing capability, resolving conflicts and building consensus – although how this agential conception of public service might play out in Westminster-based polities will be touched on later.

The ubiquity of networks today is partly responsible for a key shift in language over the last 10–15 years. Previously, the focus was government and public management. It now tends to be 'governance' (Kooiman, 2003) – so much so that one quizzical writer (Frederickson, 2007) has asked 'Whatever happened to public administration? Governance, governance everywhere.' Confusingly, the range of usages of the term is wide,[9] with some meanings made explicit and others implicit (Frederickson, 2007).

Literally, 'governance' refers to the 'act or manner of governing',[10] whereas the term 'government' refers to the static structures identified in the constitution or the abstract systems that comprise it. It seems to me that many authors focusing on governance do so based on an image of highly networked and complex processes of governing and with an interest in the dynamics of those processes. Governance could therefore be defined as a focus on the relationships, interactions and patterns therein of governing in contemporary societies; not of the structure and system in and of themselves but the patterns and dynamics emerging over time as governing is enacted through them. In less abstract terms, this means the ways in which officials, ministers, parliamentarians, users, providers, stakeholders and citizens routinely behave in particular contexts and over time (hence, what Kooiman, 1999, calls 'social-political' governance; see also Huxham, 2000; Kickert, 1997; Kooiman, 2003; Linquist and Wanna, 2010b; Rhodes, 1997; Salamon, 2002). In that respect, we can say it is an interactional view of governing that allows us to understand its history, trajectories and outcomes.

In that respect, therefore, 'governance' can be understood as a high-level (and still somewhat vague) abstraction referring to a mode of governing rather than a model of public management. It signals a switch in focus from structure to situated practice, analogous perhaps to recent reorientation in sociology from action or structure to their interplay (e.g., 'structuration', see Giddens, 1984) –

9 One not uncommon usage in Australasia outside of public management ('corporate governance') relates to the responsibilities and accountabilities of company boards and executives and how they control and direct an organisation, particularly in relation to legal and financial aspects of its operations. Among others, the World Bank speaks of 'public sector governance' understood in terms of the traditions and institutions by which public authority in a country is exercised. Various indicators of 'good governance' have been devised whereby countries can be compared at periodic intervals, namely, voice and accountability, political stability and absence of violence/terrorism, government effectiveness, regulatory quality, rule of law and control of corruption: <http://info.worldbank.org/governance/wgi/index.asp> (accessed 23 September 2011).

10 *Concise Oxford Dictionary*, 9th edition.

although that particular shift may be more interesting to public management theorists than practitioners.

Partnership and Collaboration

Governance may have a highly abstract referent; 'partnership' and 'collaboration' are more practical and empirical. They can be defined respectively as a type of relationship and a mode of interaction – terms that stand on their own but refer to behaviours that intersect in networked settings.

The notion of partnership has existed in public management theory and practice for several years, albeit with various meanings.[11] Germane to this is that discussion has emerged mostly in arenas of practice where the nature and effectiveness of the relationship between government and a third party in policy or service development or delivery is not adequately captured – or may be reduced or damaged – by defining it in market terms as did NPM. In that respect, replacing contracting out with partnership is simultaneously a critique of the market-based approach, an assertion of preferred meaning as enacted by the participants and a portent of the future. It should be understood as the dominant kind of relationship in a community approach to public management.

Contracting out and partnership are built on different assumptions (e.g., Powell, 1991). The former is associated with a market-oriented approach. A contracted relationship is founded on principal/agent assumptions, including the control of the agent by the principal. A partnership is a more organic, community-like relationship wherein power is shared and negotiated. Both (or all) parties bring something explicit and valuable to the relationship, especially knowledge and resources, such that it benefits both and within which they regard themselves as interdependent and mutually aligned. Unlike a principal–agent relationship, even if there is asymmetrical access to resources and hence the capacity to exercise power, no partner formally claims to be 'in charge'. Equalisation of power and resource sharing are fundamental. Trust too is a critical basis and one of the glues that maintain a partnership. So are sociality, mutuality and reciprocity.

---

11 A different use of the term 'partnership' has recently emerged as a way of delivering on large infrastructure projects without increasing the level of public debt incurred by government in achieving its goals (e.g., English and Skellern, 2005; Hodge and Greve, 2007). It refers to a 'public–private partnership' (PPP) between government and a private sector company, wherein the term is given a commercial and legal meaning, i.e., as an exchange rather than as reciprocity, and self-interest remains uppermost. Typically, as set out in the governing document, the partners share the cost of the project, with the private partner carrying significant risk, controlling the completed facility and drawing an income (some form of rent) for a specified period. At the end of this time, control returns to government. For the purposes of this discussion, this is not the notion of 'partnership' that is being considered.

Individuality and self-interest are subsumed. It is presumed that the terms of the relationship are that the goals are common, the differences will be collaboratively negotiated and the interactions will involve mutual adaptation. The relationship may continue for some time (rather than being time-limited as is usually the case with a contract) during which, it is believed, the richness and effectiveness of the relationship will increase. Informal interactions alongside the formal ones are assumed to be important. The character of any governing document – an agreement – will also be significantly different in its details compared with a conventional contract arising out of a competitive open tendering process and designed to control the contractor (see also Cribb, 2006; Pomeroy, 2007). In short, the differences between a market-based form of a relationship and one based on partnership could hardly be greater. Partnership should therefore be understood as a characteristic feature of a community-based approach to public management.

When working with others defined as partners, therefore, one way of interacting (perhaps even the defining way of interacting) is via 'collaboration'. One of the major realisations of the twenty-first century in public management is 'we cannot do it alone'. Joint working across organisational and sectoral boundaries has been one of the main responses and, again, we find an extensive literature on the topic, with terms such as 'co-ordination' and 'collaboration' figuring prominently (e.g., Agranoff, 2006; Armstrong and Lenihan, 1999; Huxham, 2000; Klijn and Koppenjan, 2000; Lindquist and Wanna, 2010b; Wanna and O'Flynn, 2008). At one level, within the politico-administrative system, knowledge has improved regarding the complex array of causal conditions underlying significant problems, particularly 'wicked' problems (Rittel and Webber, 1973) that require concerted action at the whole-of-government or sectoral level to create and implement holistic policy solutions. This obliged public sector organisations to start working together as a matter of normal practice. The need was even greater in jurisdictions that had separated and divided ministerial responsibilities and public sector organisations, and that have multiple strata of government. At another level, most of the complex issues confronting government extended out into the economy and civil society, so politicians and officials were obliged to reach out to actors in those spheres and bring them into the ambit of governing via the creation of policy and management networks. Various forms of joint working such as co-ordination and collaboration are now deemed essential and, indeed, are regarded as necessary conditions for effectiveness (e.g., Armstrong and Lenihan, 1999; Cooper, Bryer and Meek, 2006; Huxham, 2000). Working in these horizontal ways, of course, creates problems that are almost impossible to resolve within a public management system predicated on vertically aligned, single-organisation budgeting, management and performance. Something beyond conventional NPM and mere structural responses will be required to enable these developments in the future.

But there is something specific about 'collaboration' that merits closer inspection. Co-ordination and collaboration, for example, are often used as synonyms in public management discourse. When discussed in conjunction with governance, networking and partnership, however, collaboration means something more. As we discovered in an earlier research project (Eppel, Gill, Lips and Ryan, 2008), practitioners who take collaboration seriously differentiate it clearly. Collaboration is more than talking with each other (communication), agreeing to align activities (co-operation) or deliberately working together jointly (co-ordination). All four terms refer to modes of interaction, but the last three involve each party retaining its separateness and independence as a matter of course. 'Collaborating' parties cede their sovereignty, each subsuming their individuality within the collective goal of achieving the desired societal outcome. Self-interest is pushed to the background, and mutuality and collective interest are brought to the fore with little calculation of individual or organisational gain.[12] As in partnerships, all is shared: from power and authority, to funding and resources, to decision rights, responsibility and accountability. Within truly collaborative networks, in the same way that sharing replaces possession, trust replaces control, dialogue replaces monologue, and ongoing learning and adaptation replace planning and strategy (for a fuller discussion, see Eppel, Gill, Lips and Ryan, 2008). Collaboration therefore has a distinctive meaning and context. It is not difficult imagining communication, co-ordination and co-operation as important in effective market and bureaucratic relationships. Collaboration, however, seems likely only in community-like interactions. In that sense, I would argue that collaboration, like governance, networking and partnership, is part of a cluster of ideas pointing towards a socio-political approach to governing.

Another relevant point regarding collaboration, arising out of our earlier research, is worth noting. We concluded that one of the necessary conditions for effective collaboration is a thoroughgoing outcome orientation. Collaboration is not an end in itself, any more than is the shift towards governance, the advent of networks or engaging with others as partners. It emerges in interaction as participants in the network collectively learn their way towards solving the problem that has brought them together (Eppel, Gill, Lips and Ryan, 2008). In so far as the NPM approach is focused on outputs and exchange, and the bureaucratic approach on the integrity of processes, an orientation towards outcomes and the collaborative modes of interaction that can arise in pursuit of

12 The difference between co-ordination and collaboration is explicit in the calculative attitude struck by the central agency advice in New Zealand in relation to when and why to 'coordinate' (SSC, 2008a).

them points to distinctive features of a community-oriented approach to public management.

Teasing out some distinctive features of collaboration, partnership, networking and governance and drawing them together enables us to start sketching outlines of what government in the future – or certain parts of it anyway – might look like (see also OECD, 2000; 2001a). Clearly, it is different from the conception of bureaucratic or market-based governing. For example, hard-edged, self-contained organisations will give way to more porous ones that meld with intersecting networks. Budgets will need to be horizontal as often as they are vertical. Public service work processes and the competencies required would include engaging the public and political landscape, crossing boundaries frequently and with ease, and utilising and building trust-based relationships (Weber and Khademian, 2008; see also Denhardt and Denhardt, 2007: 83–84; Williams, 2002). Most of all, whole-of-government and sectoral approaches will predominate along with the contribution to be made to the collective goal by networking with civic and business groupings in articulating and realising those collective goals. The creation of partnerships will become standard practice. Government at all levels will behave not as a commanding, heroic or transactional leader but as a transformational, facilitative, collaborative one (Denis, Langley and Rouleau, 2007; Jackson and Parry, 2008).

Other writers are thinking along similar lines. Some, for example, explore the notion of 'collaborative governance' as an emerging approach to governing in the future (e.g., Linquist and Wanna, 2010b). Some have addressed different dimensions of what this might entail; for example, network governance (e.g., Denhardt and Denhardt, 2007; Kickert, Klijn and Koopenjan, 1997; Rhodes, 1997; Ryan, 2006); mechanisms, processes and new instruments of governance (e.g., Howlett and Ramesh, 1995; Jordan, Wurzel and Zito, 2005; Salamon, 2002); and the practices and capacities needed by public sector organisations and staff to be able to work within this new approach (e.g., Pollitt, 2003a; Weber and Khademian, 2008).

Participation and Co-production

In parliamentary democracies at the end of the twentieth century, with universal suffrage secure, rising levels of education and affluence meant that citizens were less willing to accept the unquestioned legitimacy and authority of experts and professionals in government. Increasing frustration with the democratic deficit (Horner and Hutton, 2011) – a lack of democratic accountability and control over the decision-making processes – led citizens more and more to demand direct participation in processes of governing – or, if alienated entirely and made powerless, to take up a position of cynicism and disdain and withdraw completely from involvement or interest. Bourgon (2009c: 203) puts it bluntly: 'People "want in". Closing our eyes to this reality may simply lead to further erosion of confidence in government and public sector institutions.' In terms of Figure 3.1, this refers to a powerful trend arising in civil society that has forced its way into the politico-administrative system, to which governmental and official actors have had to respond in kind. These dual determinations have occurred primarily in two parts of the system. Organised citizens and users in movements and associations have demanded access into policy advising and development processes. Individuals and groups have become more demanding in processes of policy implementation, delivery and review. It is worthwhile noting that sometimes these conflicts are major, involve many actors, involve deliberate changes in conscious behaviour on both sides and are newsworthy. At other times they may involve only small groups or individuals, occur behind the scenes and involve tacit behaviour. Even small moments can, over time, accumulate to the point where the impact is perceptible.

Governments in all western democracies have had little option other than to adapt by changing elements of professional practice. From the 1970s onwards, theory and practice in public management explored the idea of empowering citizens and consulting with affected parties about policy. Recently, the notion of 'participation' entered into discourse. Of course, participation has a long history in politics and political philosophy since it represents an important democratic ideal (e.g., Barber, 1984; Pateman, 1970). That same spirit has started flowing into public management. An active literature began to emerge in the 1980s and 1990s (e.g., Ranson and Stewart, 1994; see also Armstrong and Lenihan, 1999) to the point where even the OECD – a conservative organisation by any measure – published two books (2001b; 2009a) on the importance of citizen participation. In each of these works, participation is justified by the contribution it makes both to the overall quality of democracy and the effectiveness of management and policy.

By any measure, participation is a step beyond consultation, towards something surpassing established practice. Consultation is usually defined as seeking feedback on, say, a policy proposal that is already prepared and which those consulted can only modify, endorse or reject (Bishop and Davis, 2002; Stewart, 2009). Participation is a more engaged, intensive and open-ended relationship wherein the power to determine and decide is shared. Both clients and stakeholders contribute to and shape the policy and its outcome. It can occur in problem identification and policy development, as well as implementation and evaluation. Participation therefore assumes a deep, direct engagement between ministers, officials and citizens working on a common goal and built on mutual influence. Authority is diffused. 'Governor' and 'governed' lose their sharp distinction (Lenihan, 2009). Recent developments have accelerated the trend. Widespread computerisation, access to information via the internet and the increasing level of government information available electronically have enabled even higher levels of participation – although in new ways, not the 'town hall meeting' type of conception preserved by traditionalists. Freedom of information plus citizens' increased capacity to access, process and analyse information have challenged the traditional secrecy and the power of knowledge enjoyed by governments (OECD, 2003). Already, and even more in the future, whether they want it or not, officials and ministers are subject to much greater transparency, scrutiny and openness, with citizens participating to a greater degree than ever before. Bureaucracy would accord no play to consultation or participation. Market relationships between officials or providers and clients would allow consultation regarding the appearance, access to and experience of the good or service – but that is all. Participation presumes a community-like relationship between citizens, officials and the government of the day unlike anything that has gone before and that modifies the terms on which governing in contemporary societies is enacted.[13]

Co-production is one expression of these changes and is an idea that is presently very much to the fore (e.g., Alford, 2009; Bovaird, 2007; Boyle and Harris, 2009; Brandsen and Pestoff, 2006; Lindquist and Wanna, 2010b; Pestoff, 2006; Prentice, 2006; see also Brudney and England, 1983). Discussion usually starts from a critique of the notion of 'customer relationship' presumed by the marketisation of government services (e.g., Boyle and Harris, 2009; Boyle, Slay and Stephens, 2010; Ryan, 2004). NPM treats policy implementation as the top-down delivery of goods and services, where clients may have choice, but only from within a pre-determined range and form of provision. In contrast, co-production is defined as a participatory relationship between professional providers (whether government or non-government) and users (whether individuals, groups or communities). The full meaning of co-production is delivering public services in equal and reciprocal relationships between professionals, people using services, their families and their neighbours, in a partnership wherein clients are directly involved in the design and delivery of the form and content of the services required to meet their needs. Design and delivery are not things done to or for clients but are things done with them (Alford, 2009; Boyle and Harris, 2009).

In some respects, of the ideas considered here, participation and co-production

---

13 I have chosen not to discuss 'public value' in this chapter, mainly because of space constraints. Recent discussion of the notion (e.g., Bennington and Moore, 2011; Kelly, Mulgan and Muers, 2002) has highlighted the principle that 'public value is what the public value'. The implication is that citizens are deeply involved in policy and management, which itself has led to extensive discussion of 'deliberative democracy' (e.g., Held, 2006; Horner, Lekhi and Blaug, 2006), another notion with considerable possibilities for public management.

are those that speak most powerfully of the transformed understandings of governing they represent. These extend well beyond anything envisaged by new public management or public administration, as necessary responses to historical changes in train in the fundamental relationship between citizen and state, between a society and its form of government. They are socio-political understandings of public management, very different in their assumptions, constituents and application than their economic or politics-as-domination equivalents. In that respect, their connection to the progress of democracy is clear. They point to the need for a community-based approach to public management with obvious applicability in significant parts of the modern state. It seems to me, therefore, that the public sector of the future may be less inclined to stick with a single model of public management than to use an amalgam of several, each adopted and adapted according to the context and circumstances. In theory at least, in different places and spaces we may find any one of bureaucratic, market and community approaches and perhaps even a mixture of all three.

Emerging Practices in Public Management

New Zealand prides itself on the extent of devolution of operational authority to chief executives, but significant reforms or new sector-wide initiatives are almost always introduced top-down and driven by the central agencies. It is interesting therefore to note that official discourse, measured by the contents of central agency discussion and guidance documents and websites, contains very little on the socio-political approaches to public management canvassed above. 'Networks' and 'co-ordination' ('co-ordination' but not 'collaboration') are an exception but only slightly. However, in line agencies and especially at the point of implementation and delivery, public officials are confronted by the socio-political realities identified earlier and, despite any constraints they may experience coming from the existing system of public management, are adapting their practice to suit those circumstances and are teaching themselves new ways. As a result, there are pockets of innovation to be found in many places in the New Zealand state sector (Eppel, Gill, Lips and Ryan, 2008), some of which are consistent with the directions of change I am identifying here. Some of these initiatives are big, on-the-surface and proclaim their features (especially about partnership, collaboration and networks). Some are small, under the radar and are doing 'what needs to be done' with little fanfare. Four brief illustrations follow. I suggest that they are signs of the future. It may be that these signs are fragile and tenuous, that the bulk of public management practice continues to be based on bureaucratic and market principles and that these harbingers may not survive; on that point, only history will tell. It is essential therefore that they be recognised and applauded as leading the way.

It should be noted that the illustrations are focused on organisational intentions, what public managers say they are trying to do, without challenging the ostensive tidiness and confidence of presentation, or whether the beautiful words are matched by determination or achievement behind the scenes. I suggest that the mere fact of the language is sufficient marker of a new consciousness and a necessary condition for further development. In fact, there *are* issues for each organisation in enacting their intent. In some cases, practice has not particularly advanced from the old to the new, sometimes because of poor management or lack of ministerial support or aspects of the public management that actually get in the road. These and other issues are discussed in the final section of this chapter.

Cancer Control Networks

The Cancer Control Strategy is a good illustration of how networking, collaboration and partnership have entered into some parts of the New Zealand system. One part of the system is explicitly referred to as 'networks' (the Regional Cancer Networks themselves), but networking is the form of organisation that interconnects high-level and frontline activities underpinning the whole system.

In 2006 the Ministry of Health asked District Health Boards (DHBs) to collaborate in creating four regional cancer networks. The network strategy was a deliberate attempt to pull together the range, diversity and multiplicity of actors, including consumers, non-government organisations (NGOs), palliative care providers, Māori and primary care providers, and to have them collaborate at the regional and local levels to achieve the overall strategic goals of the Cancer Control Strategy and the Action Plan. To some degree, at least, the intent was to overcome the problems flowing out of fragmentation in the sector and competitive rather than collaborative ways of working (caused in part by the NPM reforms of the 1980s). The regional networks themselves draw on a wide range of providers, stakeholders and sometimes consumer groups. The explicit goals of these networks are to work across organisational boundaries and to devise collaborative ways to plan and deliver services relative to the needs of consumers and clients in their regions. The result is a structured framework of overlapping bodies with various kinds of advisory, policy, funding and delivery roles covering strategic direction-setting, policy development, national implementation and local implementation.

Collaboration is strong within and between the networks. As a recent evaluation pointed out (CCNZ, 2010), the networks reveal a growing sense of the collective 'we', leaving individual organisational agendas at the door. Still, however, organisational and budgetary silos and self-interest persist (members acting as organisational representatives rather than as contributors to a regional perspective), particularly in relation to strategic planning and budgeting; but that can be explained partly by the fact that too many organisations and individuals are struggling for access to too limited a range of resources. A spirit of partnership also flows throughout the Cancer Control Programme. To some degree the ultimate test of whether partnership has replaced principal–agent relationships is the nature of the financial relationship governing provision. In that respect, significant portions of the networks' activities are 'funded' rather than 'contracted', which implies a shift towards partnership. On the other hand, most relationships between DHBs and providers are in the form of 'contracts' for service (although possibly in a 'soft' form, closer to relational contracts).

Interestingly, in 2009, the Minister of Health set up a review of the health and disability system. This review concluded that clinical networks are one of the key avenues for improving models of care, particularly in relation to achieving desired outcomes. It notes:

> Clinical networks, which often also include managers and consumers, have been successful in some specialty areas in improving the coordination of care to deliver a more seamless experience for patients. For example, the regional cancer networks are important in bringing together all of the key people involved in caring for cancer patients in a way that can help address the problems created by fragmented care. More should be done to develop the influence of existing networks and develop new networks. (Ministerial Review Group, 2009: 15)

Further, the evaluation argues:

> The regional cancer networks are the first comprehensive regional network of this type to operate in New Zealand and are a new way of working, bringing together as they do a range of organisations and roles from funding and planning to providers across the DHB, primary care and NGO sectors with consumers to collaborate regionally. (CCNZ, 2010: 22)

Clearly, the Cancer Control Networks signal definite developments in relation to networks, collaboration and partnership. What is less clear is the extent to which participation and co-production are part of the networks – or the extent to which they were supposed to encourage a more participatory relationship between providers and users. It is apparent that focusing on the 'patient experience' is a priority. This suggests that even if a full-scale conception of co-production is not recognised, at the very least, the importance of 'client responsiveness' is. This is a step along the way.

Family and Community Services

If the emergence of participation and co-production by clients is unclear in relation to Regional Cancer Networks, it is strongly apparent in Family and Community Services and Whānau Ora. Family and Community Services (FACS) is the division within the Ministry of Social Development (MSD) that looks after service delivery, funding and contracting third-party providers. The language surrounding the activities of FACS is almost a paradigm case of the approaches to public management canvassed here.

FACS presents itself as an enabler of co-production (FACS, 2010). Families and communities are able to define and access the resources they need by, for example, improving family and community access to information and advice so they can easily get the help they need, and encouraging collaboration so families can get access to services in one place through one point of contact so that 'families and communities can find their own answers'. The important thing to note is that the active subject of those intentions is families and communities. FACS sets out to act as enabler and facilitator, working with clients to achieve what they want to achieve. This is not 'delivery to' but 'enabling access to what is sought', as promoted by writers on co-production. That said, the Community Response model of operations still under development at the time of writing intends giving clients 'a real say in how family and community services funding will be spent'. This 'information' will flow upwards to 14 Community Response Forums drawn from central and local government, and iwi and community providers, and will be synthesised in a community-funding plan for the region. This implies less a participation-in-planning model than institutional mediation of expressed need; that is, not apparently consistent with full-scale co-production. Assuming for a moment that this is a necessary device to ensure equitable distribution of resources and/or accountable processes of public money (and not just a residual desire by FACS to exercise control), it may hint at the trade-offs required to bring ideas such as co-production in service development and delivery to actual fruition.

The FACS language also speaks of partnership and collaboration: 'We can't do our work without our social sector partners or the many organisations active in New Zealand communities.' This, it claims, will be achieved by facilitating and working with its partners, leading, influencing and seeking out innovation, and supporting its partners to be self-organising and self-sustaining. There is also a heavy reliance on networks – or rather, 'networking' – since, unlike the Regional Cancer Networks, most are not formal, institutionalised networks. Networking is inherent: 'People working in social service organisations almost network in their sleep. It comes as a natural part of the make-up of people who like helping others.' Some of those networks run towards national, whole-of-government issues. For example, the Family Services National Advisory

Council (FSNAC) established in 2004 is a forum of senior representatives from government agencies and non-government organisations and people who provide iwi/Māori and Pacific people's perspectives. Other networks run to the frontline and are built around FACS's regional offices in major New Zealand cities, with membership comprising other central government agencies, local government, non-government agencies and community groups. Collaboration is designed to create and maintain service clusters for families in the specified region.

As a further sign of a partnership orientation, FACS is moving away from principal–agent relationships with providers, governed by legalistic contracts, to 'high-trust contracting'. The intention is to work with simple funding agreements focused on outcomes and to enable flexible, customised service delivery depending on the needs of the families and communities served. Partnership and collaboration are also evident in principles such as 'respecting and valuing each other and their expertise', 'acting with integrity and good faith', and 'having open, transparent, honest and timely conversations'.

Of course, it is one thing to use the language but another to enact the words. These may reflect the desire to act differently, but action still occurs within the framework of existing bureaucratic and market-based practice. If so, it can still be argued that the language signals the future but a key aspect of change, namely, unlearning the old practices and the assumptions, habits and routine that go with them as the first step in learning new ways, is still in process (6 et al., 2002).

It is worth noting that while this illustration has focused on the work of FACS, other parts of the MSD have also been moving in these directions. The Office for the Voluntary and Community Sector (now within the Department of Internal Affairs) has been working in this space for some years. Some Work and Income sites and case managers have also been pursuing these kinds of approaches for some time – an excellent example is the case of joined-up services in Papakura, discussed in Eppel, Gill, Lips and Ryan (2008). In other words, while the present Minister for the Community and Voluntary Sector has fronted a 'Government commitment to building strong community relationships' (New Zealand Cabinet, 2009), FACS is expressing a trend that has been emerging for some time and that predates the present minister.

Whānau Ora

Whānau Ora (family well-being) is an initiative with a political genesis that represents a special case of the socio-political determinants discussed earlier in this chapter. Driven by the Māori Party, it explicitly draws on tikanga (culture) and perhaps a desire for tino rangatiratanga (self-determination) guaranteed by the Treaty of Waitangi, but expressed in a certain way at a particular time in Aotearoa/New Zealand's political history. That said, many of the proposals underpinning Whānau Ora – an initiative still being developed at the time of writing – coincide closely with the ideas discussed above. In fact, even from the brief descriptions provided here, it is clear that Whānau Ora and FACS alone illustrate the extent to which these ideas are already making at least initial inroads into the theory and practice of public management in Aotearoa/New Zealand.

The goal of Whānau Ora is to improve the capacity of whānau (family) to be resilient and independent rather than dependent on government services. Expressed in public management terms, this will be achieved via co-production, participation, partnership, collaboration and networking. Most obvious is the emphasis placed on co-production and the participation of 'the client' (whānau) in defining the nature of their concerns and the mix of solutions and resources required to deal with them. Whānau Ora is distinctive in focusing on whānau: it seeks to empower families as a whole rather than separately addressing individual family members and their problems. It will also treat families holistically, thereby demanding cross-agency collaboration in delivery. Some whānau will want to develop their own ways of improving their lives and may want to collaborate with a hapū (kinship group), iwi (tribe) or non-government organisation. Other whānau will seek help from specialist Whānau Ora providers who will offer them wrap-around services tailored to their needs. Whānau will have a champion ('navigator') to work with them to identify their needs, develop a plan of action to address them, and broker access to a range of health and social services. The Whānau Ora worker or navigator's role will be to support whānau through this process and link them with government agencies or specialist services that can help them progress towards the solutions they have identified. Partnership, collaboration and networks in delivery are also central. Twenty-five providers have been selected to work directly with Whānau Ora, all collectives representing 158 providers across the country. It is worth noting also that, like FACS and 'high-trust contracting', Whānau Ora providers will have streamlined contracts that will be focused on results and will enable flexible delivery.

Central to achieving the goal of co-ordination and collaboration are Regional Leadership Groups (RLGs) comprising officials from the government agencies involved (including District Health Boards) and community members. These groups are also likely to play a role in ensuring a match of need and service provision throughout the networks via two-way flows of communication, resources and authority. As was noted in the FACS case, the test over time will be how direct and influential the flow from whānau through navigators to the RLGs will be. A full-blown approach to participatory planning and co-production would anticipate an open, deliberative and democratic process with open flows of information in both directions: expressions of need in one direction and political and institutional limits in the other. If system or technical mediation of demand occurs (as is likely) in non-transparent ways (in effect, interpreted only in terms of existing service-defined boxes and not co-designing or redesigning the boxes to fit the need), then this would be, at best, a half-way house. In that respect, as in many others, it will be interesting to see how Whānau Ora develops.

In fact, it may be interesting on many levels. Government's obligations to Māori following the Treaty of Waitangi have been debated for many years. The question is wider than just service design and delivery but it does include it (e.g., Ministerial Advisory Group on a Māori Perspective for the Department of Social Welfare, 1988; Waitangi Tribunal, 2011). As Durie argues, critical issues include the control and functioning of services delivered to Māori, whether as distinctive services (by Māori for Māori) or as members of a general New Zealand population. To contribute to Māori development, service design and delivery should involve a partnership (intended in the sense described earlier in this chapter) of Māori and Crown, if not fully controlled by Māori. Contractual relationships do not usually take this form. They may devolve some degree of function and authority to Māori providers but ultimately accountability and control lies with the state, not Māori. Contracts reinforce what Durie calls a 'service relationship' but not a 'Treaty relationship' (2004: 10). Whānau Ora, however, seems to go at least one step forward in this respect. If so, and developments continue proceeding down this path, a community-like approach to public management may make a small contribution to extending relationships between Māori and the Crown in the future, even though it may not have been a factor in Whānau Ora's creation.

Recognised Seasonal Employer

All of the illustrations presented so far suggest that the emerging ideas are most applicable in implementation and delivery. The final illustration suggests that they may be equally relevant in the creation and development of policy, particularly in situations of ambiguity, uncertainty and complexity. This case also demonstrates the large amount of learning (and unlearning) required to start working in new ways, and highlights the fact that these new ideas apply in both implementation and development (for details, see Hill, Capper, Wilson, Whatman and Wong, 2007; also Eppel, Gill, Lips and Ryan, 2008).

This programme enables an annual flow of seasonal labour for the viticulture and horticulture industries, including over 5000 returning workers (those who return, year after year) from the Pacific Islands. Previously, growers had difficulty attracting reliable and productive labour for the annual harvest. Moreover, the industry was full of regulatory issues and practices that were often contrary to policy and sometimes even illegal. Growers and distributors were concerned about the problems, as was government. From the outset it was realised that the problems were numerous and large and there was little agreement (and, in fact, there were fixed positions) among the various actors. The process to achieve agreement on policies that would resolve the issues would inevitably be long and laborious and needed to involve everyone. A simple, traditional top-down process would never work. It had to be a process of open-ended co-design. In other words, participation, co-production, partnership, collaboration and, eventually, the formation and use of networks to achieve policy goals and objectives were paramount.

The leading agency was the Department of Labour – or rather, a small number of public entrepreneurs from that and other organisations – which led an initial nerve-wracking and testing 16-month process of collective learning regarding the conditions applying in the industry. As solutions started emerging, some were piloted, trialled and evaluated, with the results being fed back into the collective discussion. The debate started with regulation and wound up completely rethinking the manner in which picking and packing would be conducted. Most of all, it redefined the sources, supply and employment of labour applicable in New Zealand. Extraordinarily, it did so in a manner that found common agreement. As options started to crystallise, other government and non-government parties, including Pacific governments, became involved, stretching the ambit significantly; for example, a change to immigration policy was required to enable the necessary transformation of labour practices inside the industry, and development goals for the contributing countries were later explicitly acknowledged. Participation and co-production were essential in the problem identification phase; and participation, collaboration and networks in the development phase. Without them there would not have been an effective policy for cabinet to sign off.

According to the Final Evaluation Report of the Recognised Seasonal Employer Policy 2007–2009 (DoL, 2010), these approaches to public management were fundamental to its success. They continued into the implementation stage and up to the present.[14]

Some Questions Arising

These four illustrations have been brief and descriptive but their significance is clear. The ideas being touted in the academic and analytical literature as emerging methods in public management such as networks, collaboration, partnership, participation and co-production – which I have defined as a

---

14 It is worth noting in passing that many aspects of the creation and functioning of the Recognised Seasonal Employer Policy, particularly in negotiating the complex relationships between industry, government and civil aspects of policy, were and are reflected in another case study that could have been used here, namely, the creation and allocation of fishing quotas in New Zealand – with the notable addition of the role of the Minister of Fisheries in fronting the ongoing processes.

community approach that contrasts with bureaucratic and market approaches – also show up, often explicitly and with enthusiasm, in some cases of emerging practice in Aotearoa/New Zealand. However, the fact that they show up in some pockets of practice but not in others – and that, where they do, the protagonists often suggest they act in those ways despite the system they work in and the fact that they often have to work under the radar – raises further questions. Some of these are discussed in the final section of this chapter. I do not pretend that what follows is comprehensive, any more than that my discussion of the key characteristics of a community-based approach to public management is complete. The questions asked below are only some of the obvious ones that come to mind when considering the overarching question underpinning the Future State project, namely, 'Where to from here and how?'

Where to From Here and How?

Do These Developments Require Formal Acknowledgement? Do They Replace Existing Ways? Do They Represent a Single Model for Universal Application?

It seems critical to legitimate a perspective on public management that highlights social and political aspects of managing in the public sphere, while also acknowledging the significance of the approach, means and methods discussed here. Compared with NPM and the bureaucratic era before that, they bring different assumptions to bear regarding the ends and means of public service and management within both the political system and society. Precisely because they embody different assumptions, these new forms of practice cannot simply be expected to emerge as discontinuous adaptations without legitimation and authorisation. Otherwise, individuals and organisations pursuing them are left dangling, wondering if they are doing the right thing and others will be wary of following suit. Promoting them is critical for the future state so that others can make sense of them (Alvesson and Sveningsson, 2008), first to unlearn the present and then to learn their way towards knowing when and how to employ them (Ranson and Stewart, 1994).

Both the political arm of the executive and the centre of the public service must legitimate and authorise the shift. Unfortunately, not many ministers in New Zealand appear interested in the nature and functioning of the public management system – other than in its relation to cost and fiscal considerations or whether public servants are being sufficiently 'responsive' to their wishes. They do not recognise the public management system as a whole (in Figure 3.1, K and J) as including 'us' and not just 'them' (public officials). Nor do many seem to grasp the institutional relationship between the system of government and the society that it is supposed to serve – they do in relation to the individualised and partisan electoral system (with which they are deeply concerned) but not the system as a whole. As a matter of practice and experience, some ministers do indeed grasp the need to get close to electors and the community in substantive ways, beyond the basic matter of maintaining their electoral stocks, but do not translate that knowledge into thinking about the implications for the design and functioning of the politico-administrative system. Some local government councillors and mayors are adept at relating to communities and, as local government plays a more significant role in the overall governance picture, may influence public management generally. Agencies and senior officials at the centre of the public sector also have a definite role to play. Exposition of these ideas and sector-wide leadership in encouraging the exploration and adoption of a community-based approach – where appropriate – will be important (in this respect the recent 'Better Public Services' initiative referred to earlier may prove important). It is also worth acknowledging that 'the centre' commissioned the research on which much of this book is based, so that too is a positive sign. The simple fact is, though, that ministers and senior public servants have a major role to play in authorising and encouraging energetic and committed exploration of new governance options and, if community approaches are to gain widespread attraction, government leaders must lead.[15]

In a jurisdiction that emphatically adopted a market-based, production-like approach to public management, however, it is essential a definite message is sent that this particular approach is not appropriate in some settings and contexts and that new and different ways have to be found. In multiple, small and *ad hoc* ways deep inside the public sector and in some ministerial offices, this is occurring, but what is badly needed is a much more public and inspirational display of leadership by both ministers and public sector leaders. The existing ways have acquired the status of normal, standard practice. Emerging practices have to swim against the tide of accepted ones. Since they have not been legitimated, this is more difficult than it needs to be. In this way, the present is getting in the road of the future and, as noted above, steps need to be taken to authorise these new approaches so the future can emerge (Ryan, 2011a; see also 6 et al., 2002; Douglas, 1986; Ranson and Stewart, 1994).

However, the story needing to be told is complicated. Overall, it is one of 'as well as', not 'instead of'. Despite the fact that public management in theory and practice tends to think in singular, universal models, it can be argued that multiple realities and mixed methods (ontological and methodological pluralism; Alvesson and Skoldberg, 2000; Blaikie, 1993) may be more appropriate to

---

15 An excellent recent illustration is the drive provided by Kevin Rudd, the Australian Prime Minister at the time, for the Moran Review (Advisory Group on Reform of Australian Public Administration, 2010).

governing in Aotearoa/New Zealand in the twenty-first century. In fact, the New Zealand model was once praised for its intellectual coherence (Schick, 1996), but enacted public management in 2011 in this country seems less and less like a singular, universal system (Lodge and Gill, 2011; see also Duncan and Chapman, 2010). It instead comprises an eclectic range of practices, some of which have arrived through disjointed and *ad hoc* incrementalism, even if the formal framework embedded in the governing legislation seems to assume a universal reality.

It is time to suggest that public management in different parts of the public sector might and should vary, and perhaps, vary widely across a jurisdiction – not in superficial ways but in ways that deliberately and demonstrably connect purposes, ends and means. The way to manage disaggregated, operational, routine, 'production-like' purposes in the public sector may necessitate one approach, but the management of holistic, complex, strategic fields of policy may require another. A socio-political approach may be most applicable in fields like health, education and other parts of the welfare state; economic and regional development; conservation and the environment; Māori and Pacific development; justice and corrections; and culture and the arts; but less applicable in fields like regulation and policing; customs; immigration, defence and intelligence; or the production, distribution and supply of goods and services such as electricity, water and telecommunications. Managers in those fields have been learning by doing in the face of uncertainty and complexity (see Eppel, Turner and Wolf, this volume), and their public management future clearly points in that direction. Conversely, bureaucratic and market-like approaches might serve best in parts of the governing system that depend on the assertion of the hierarchical authority of the state, or are routine and standardised and produce identifiable goods and services – although care needs to be exercised here. Public management systems tend to cram many matters of governance into the 'production' box, or in Kurtz and Snowden's (2003) terms, the category of the 'known' (Figure 3.2 below) and try to manage them all the same way. Unfortunately, doing so creates an appearance of progress in areas that are complex but simplifies and bounds problems in ways that ignore community knowledge and expertise, thereby risking little actual change and unintended (and unknown) effects (see also Eppel, Turner and Wolf, this volume).

In short, a socio-political perspective and community-based practices and methods may have wider applicability than at first seems obvious. The future appears likely to demand context-dependency and case-by-case consideration of what works best for society, and what best produces public value, as well as where, when and how. The result of such consideration would be a governmental system comprising many different forms and operating in many different ways.

Figure 3.2. Sense-making in a Complex World

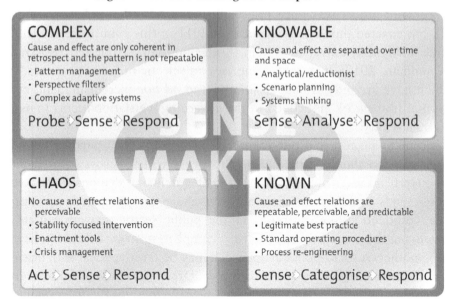

Source: Kurtz and Snowden (2003) pp. 462–83.

Do Past Approaches to Public Management Help or Hinder These Emerging Practices? If So, Do They Need to Be Revised?

Has the largely economics-based model of public management introduced in this country, like the bureaucratic model before it, left an institutional legacy embedded in everyday practice that enables or constrains these developments? In truth, the answer is unclear because systematic evidence is not available. That said, anecdotally, there does not seem to be much appreciation in the New Zealand public sector, especially in central agencies, of the manner in which underlying assumptions of a theory are embedded and institutionalised in the forms of practice derived from it, or the degree of influence they have in shaping the taken-for-granted, everyday realities carried around by organisational actors and the manner in which they conduct their work (Granovetter, 1985; Scott, 2008). A deep, careful and sociological look will therefore be needed to weigh up this question when it is confronted, as confronted it must be. Even if the eventual conclusion is that the framework can remain as it is, a major 'unlearning' exercise will need to be conducted.

However, practitioners constructing the types of emerging practices identified in the empirical illustration provided earlier often point to particular issues, seeing many (although not all) of them as constraints (Eppel, Gill, Lips and Ryan, 2008). One particular aspect stands out. The original designers hoped their model of public management would free up and enable public managers whilst making them accountable but it has not turned out that way. Elements of its design and certainly its implementation, particularly in recent years, have emphasised the control components of the model to the point where compliance now plays a very large role in everyday organisational practice and has stifled innovation in all but the most outstanding cases. Inadvertently, an iron cage has been recreated (Gill, 2011: Part Two). Another issue often mentioned is the effect of vertical, single-organisation accountability that gets in the road of efforts to collaborate (see Boston and Gill, this volume). The heavy reliance on principal/agent theory and the application of tightly defined contracts to govern delivery arrangements has proved problematic in many circumstances – as their supersession by FACS and Whānau Ora amply demonstrate. The effects of fragmentation and competition also fall into this category.

In preference to large portfolios, the public sector was broken up into smaller, fleet-of-foot, single-purpose organisations that were encouraged to compete among themselves and to use market mechanisms in contracting delivery agents – often themselves very small. Many government and non-government organisations now seem too modest to be sustainable and are fighting to retain a share of a limited and diminishing pool of funds. The struggle over resources has become even tougher, with fiscal austerity strategies brought on by New Zealand's unstable trading position and the global financial crisis, now exacerbated by the 2011 Christchurch earthquake. Another point worth making is that under NPM, the system required third-party providers to compete and community sector contractors learned to do so just like their private sector counterparts. Unfortunately, they still are. It is difficult to get organisations that have become habituated over many years to competing to reverse their practices and to start collaborating, even though their hearts and minds may favour different ways of working. Non-government providers also tend to have a relatively narrow band of competencies that contracting acts to limit. A more collaborative, community-like approach would enable connections between competencies and resources and shore up capability deficiencies between organisations.

New developments therefore demand collaboration, yet existing institutional arrangements make it more difficult than it needs to be. In this respect the Whānau Ora strategy of encouraging amalgamation between services has much to commend it. Equally, the heavy emphasis on tightly defined contracts to ensure accountability and control has led to many providers holding multiple small contracts with multiple funders, and a heavy compliance burden of reporting on process matters crowds out the time and space required to focus on outcomes and to innovate. In this respect, the FACS shift to 'high-trust contracting' is a welcome move, similarly for Whānau Ora, in so far as it opens the possibility of long-term collaboration, partnerships and network governance. This approach could and should be generalised.

Even if other aspects of the New Zealand approach do not prevent the development of new ways, they do not encourage or enable them. For example, the existing system of (often narrow) budgetary silos ('Votes') is said by some public entrepreneurs to hinder collaboration and horizontal management. Some of the 2004 amendments to the Public Finance Act were supposed to facilitate these kinds of developments (Treasury, 2005; see also Treasury Circular 2007/05, 2007), and Treasury officials have been known to argue that the possibilities are greater than have been taken up by departments. Some managers working at the local level have found they can 'find a way', but at a more macro level, where the sums are larger and accountability is more exposed, managers still say there are barriers. The apparent problem is compounded by the number of silos. It is also thought there are too many ministerial portfolios and discrete responsibilities and that the spread of each is too thin (Gill, 2008a). This means that agencies trying to work together may need to negotiate with multiple votes to enable collaboration. It may well be that ministerial portfolios and votes need to be aggregated around programmes of work directed towards outcomes. Provisions may also need to be created to enable horizontal expenditure that supports collaborative governance, perhaps subject to no more than ministerial approval.

As noted earlier, a focus on outcomes is a necessary condition for developing the socio-political practices discussed here. But outcomes in New Zealand's central government have had a chequered history. 'Managing for outcomes' was introduced in 2001 but, by the middle of the decade, went 'missing in action' as far as the central agencies were concerned (Gill, 2008b). Nonetheless, some agencies continued developing the idea, and organisations such as the Ministries of Social Development, Health, Education and Justice, and the Departments of Corrections, Conservation and Te Puni Kōkiri (see the case studies in Gill, 2011) now show definite signs of outcome-oriented internal cultures. It is not at all obvious, however, that recent initiatives from the centre such as the Performance Improvement Framework are as focused on outcomes as they should be, or that outcomes are embedded in the culture of the public sector to the extent they could and should be. Internal cultures in line agencies may provide sufficient foundations for further development – or they may not. Central leadership in this respect should be scaled up significantly.

In fact, trying to answer this question is difficult. The issues are complicated, some are operational and others go to the underlying system assumptions, and investigation needs to be much more detailed than can be done here. Moreover, practitioners are better placed to consider the issues than academic researchers. Accordingly, the matters noted above should be taken only as possibilities to explore. Without doubt, however, there seems to be a *prima facie* case that in some respects, at least, the existing model of public management in New

Zealand, embedded in legislation, guidance, circulars and the received wisdom of the workplace, needs to be significantly revised. Some parts may even need to be eliminated. Most of all, the end result should be one that deals effectively and adequately with economic and bureaucratic aspects of public management but does not constrain – and preferably enables – those aspects that need to run on community-like lines.

Do Current Organisational Cultures Constrain Innovations in These Directions?

Innovation in work organisation and practice can depend on the culture of an organisation and the manner in which managers manage. Some situations in the New Zealand public sector at present seem conducive. Many, however, do not.

It is often remarked that a 'culture of busyness' runs through many public service organisations in New Zealand, and it is certainly true that many middle and senior managers seem to work under conditions of high work intensity and constant disruption. In such settings there is little space or appetite for innovation. Operations, meeting targets, risk aversion and compliance are often the main focus, rather than strategy, policy outcomes, experimenting with new ways to achieve them, or creating an environment where the socio-political and hence community dimensions of governing can be given greater account in everyday practice. Management styles will tend towards command and control more than enablement, facilitation and transformation.

What explains this organisational state of affairs? Is it a simple case of bureaucratisation, wherein things are regularised, standardised, and made predictable, subject to hierarchy and governed by rules? That may be part of the mix but only a part; after all, the forces are both centripetal and centrifugal. Is it a failure of individual managers or chief executives to manage themselves and their context? That seems unlikely. If individual managers are replaced, the situation remains the same. Some of the explanation can be found in relationships with ministers. As Westminster officials, senior managers are obliged to be responsive to their minister; frequently, these days, that means multiple ministers. Senior managers therefore manage upwards. But the demands of ministers sway to political and not bureaucratic rhythms, driven by the hothouse of parliament, cabinet, caucus, funding negotiations, cabinet committee meetings, questions, the need to be briefed, policy options and performance reviews. These calls are constant and often urgent. The obligation to be 'responsive' shapes the workload of the ministers' officials and the cultures of the organisations they manage. This situation can be exacerbated if ministers demand 'obedience' rather than work in a Westminster-defined partnership. Whatever are the root causes of this 'busyness', organisational cultures generally seem to drive managers 'back to the rules' and are not conducive to building the capability required to 'serving beyond the predictable' that Bourgon (2009c) calls for.

Why discuss these matters? Emerging signs of the future such as those identified here need favourable organisational conditions to be realised and demand twenty-first century kinds of leadership and management (e.g., see Jackson and Parry, 2008: chapters 6 and 7; OECD, 2001c; also Bourgon, 2009c). That said, recent research (Eppel, Gill, Lips and Ryan, 2008) suggests that the source and site of innovations in the directions discussed here are to be found in the middle of organisations and policy communities, then extending outwards by diffusion, sometimes in spite of the constraints applying. Whānau Ora seems to be an exception. While apparently driven from the top, small-scale arrangements of its type have already been in existence and these are now being generalised. Encouragement or even passive toleration of experimentation is an important condition of progressive change, but if systemic conditions nurture organisational cultures and management styles that are obsessed with risk aversion and the control of contingency, not much of it will occur – as the public entrepreneurs with whom we spoke made very clear. If the trends identified in this chapter are to prosper, there needs to be a serious look at workloads, work intensity, workplace cultures and management styles, notwithstanding the (partisan) political and economic environment that continues to demand 'more from less'.

Do These Developments Raise Constitutional Issues?

If the cluster of ideas discussed here takes greater hold, then what is regarded as the normal, everyday work of some officials (middle- and senior-level officials particularly) will change significantly, in certain parts of the public sector, anyway. They will also bring the politics back into public management and, in effect, reconnect policy and administration. They will install the official as an active (although not independent) agent in relationships between citizen and state, and introduce an 'agential' conception of the role of the public servant. As such they raise issues that go to the core of the constituted relationship between ministers and officials in Westminster-based polities. The Westminster system and attendant conventions were constructed on the assumption of a bureaucratic model of public administration. In some respects, these issues were challenged by the economic (and managerial) model of public management. A community-like, socio-political model may challenge those conventions even more.

I am not alone in anticipating such challenges. For example, the Australian Public Service Commission (APSC, 2009: 1–2) has considered the implications of networking and collaboration for public service accountability and suggests:

Though accountability arrangements have evolved over the years, they still reflect the techniques and values of the industrial era in which they were developed. They are based on hierarchical modes of decision-making and sequential approaches to problem solving, and they require single points of accountability . . . The new modes of policy implementation are collaborative and can seem unstructured or messy. They require levels of risk taking, experimentation and engagement with communities that do not fit comfortably within current accountability and performance management arrangements.

Why might 'engagement with communities' create such issues? Williams (2002) discusses the differences between horizontal and vertical management in terms similar to those I used earlier in relation to networking, collaboration and partnership. Such engagement requires building and sustaining interpersonal relationships between diverse sets of stakeholders, fostering trust, managing power relationships and generating consensus. Public entrepreneurs engaged in this work say they engage in open discussion and mutual action from a position of shared power. Dialogue and reciprocity with partners are essential, as are flexibility, learning and restless adaptation, all acting anew on the new realities being constructed (Eppel, Gill, Lips and Ryan, 2008; see also Moore, 1995). *In toto*, this is political rather than technical work (although it may include technical work).

Seen from a Westminster perspective, bringing the political back into management and policy, as Stewart (2009; see also Rhodes and Wanna, 2009) notes, would be risky for officials. Conventional wisdom has them playing only a discrete role, acting on behalf of the minister and doing only what the minister would approve of – or has already approved of. In terms of the power to decide, the minister is in command. But if the description above is correct, some authority for initiating action would be ceded to officials and to participants because of the need for officials involved to negotiate and reciprocate in forging a mutual understanding and indeed to commit to it, in principle at least. Moreover, even if officials were acting with the knowledge and permission of the minister, the latter would need to accept that the journey might go to places other than those originally intended or hoped by the minister. The actual finishing place would be built on a consensus created by the participants, facilitated and forged in and through the work of officials acting on the basis of what they find before them – in other words, an outcome that has public value (Alford, 2008; Bennington and Moore, 2011). The minister would then be obliged to accept it. If it is not accepted, the minister would significantly undermine the official and the network, placing trust and legitimacy at risk.

Under such circumstances, minister–official relationships would need to be understood as that of interdependent partners, united in a common bond of achieving public value. Officials would be acting as the agent of the responsible government but in a manner wherein they exercise their 'agency' (Giddens, 1984). In this sense, agency refers to the capacity of individuals situated in a particular structure of relationships to act purposively within the setting in which they are situated and to enact their own motivated choices. The notion is similar to that articulated famously by Wamsley (1990) as 'agential' leadership. In terms of Westminster-derived practice, 'agential' action would not be equivalent to officials setting themselves up as 'platonic guardians' of the public interest or manipulating power for their own ends, as Rhodes and Wanna (2007) have misleadingly argued, but working at ways and means of getting public values expressed and brought to the policy process within a system of responsible government (Alford, 2008; Bennington and Moore, 2011).

How does this compare with the conventions associated with minister–official relationships in New Zealand? A common way of prescribing the relationship is to speak of something like 'unequal partners', with officials 'serving' the minister and the minister having the right to decide (see especially the *Cabinet Manual* 2008). They are united in the task of implementing the government's programme but bring different capabilities and authority to the task, recognising and accepting the legitimacy of the other ('with respect'; Prebble, 2010). There is an emphasis, however, on the power and rights of the minister and the obligations of the official to respond. Nonetheless, on the basis of 'free and frank advice', differences between ministers and officials are expected during policy development and debate is allowed, up to a point (Prebble, 2010). Policy analysis conducted by public servants occurs behind closed doors (although the 30-year rule in relation to cabinet no longer applies in New Zealand and the Official Information Act has significantly improved openness), and is expected to be technical and apolitical. Officials may consult with clients and stakeholders but only on behalf of their minister and according to the minister's agenda. Interaction with other parties and parliament is subject to the same constraint and only with express approval. Senior officials are at the minister's beck and call during cabinet deliberations and parliamentary debate. Implementation is treated as the operationalisation of the policy decision, and professional discretion in delivery is regarded as an issue of departmental control. Delivery does not engage with the client on matters of substance; need and provision are predefined and the client is made subject to the rules of eligibility, inclusion or regulation.

Read through an enabling lens, it is possible to imagine a minister or ministers working within a Westminster model appreciating agential action from officials, especially if those approaches seemed to be effective over the long term (as seemed to be the case, for example, with the 'Strengthening Education in Mangere and Otara' [SEMO] case study in Eppel, Gill, Lips and Ryan, 2008). It seems, however, that minister–official relationships are in general going in the opposite direction and that the historical understanding is under strain. For example, a forum of ex-ministers, senior public servants, commentators and academics in 2001–2 held in Wellington revealed a general disquiet with the state of affairs, but collectively was unable to agree on whether the core relationship has fundamentally changed or, if so, whether it should be described and prescribed anew. In the subsequent monograph, the discussion leader (James, 2002: 5) commented:

> This suggests we may be at a turning point, still able to stretch traditional concepts to explain and characterise the relationship but increasingly unconvincingly in some aspects of the relationship and perhaps in the not-too-distant future the relationship's totality. If the latter, it is now time to begin to reformulate the theory, norms and practices.

More recent research draws a similar picture. Lodge and Gill (2011: 155–6), for example, report that chief executives believe the shift from the widely hailed output production to collaborative outcome management is only limited. Further:

> While therefore some chief executives saw their main role as providing their minister with strategic 'free and frank' advice and being in a 'partner' role, others saw a change in their role toward an executive-type 'do as you are told' understanding: '[T]hey expect obedience'.

Moreover:

> It was, however, not just the presumed partner role that was under strain but also the (NPM-related) 'executive' understanding that politicians would grant their chief executives discretion to deliver outputs.

Anecdotally, it also seems that a significant proportion of officials at the second and third levels think of the relationship as one of simple hierarchy, that the minister is in charge, and they must do what the minister wants and do so immediately. There are also cases where ministers and governments are publicly critical and dismissive of the policy and management capabilities of their officials where the latter are unable by convention to respond. In these situations, risk-aversion, obeisance and a preoccupation with survival ('keeping your head down') should not be unexpected. All this suggests an unhealthy and unhelpful relationship between ministers and officials in a significant number of cases. Resolving it will need several lines of action. One will be ministers adopting a wider institutional understanding of the whole system of government in which they have chosen to work and the wider obligations they should meet (J, K and O in Figure 3.1, also E and A; for another detailed discussion of these and related matters, see Di Francesco and Eppel, this volume). Another is senior officials taking a stronger line in asserting their expertise, interdependence and agency.

In short, in a significant number of cases, there is a disconnection between where things are at and where things may go. The future for responsible government in New Zealand seems to suggest a 'partnership' between ministers and officials but one that is consistent with contemporary understandings of the term and in a context of collaborative governance, with officials acting in agential ways in serving the public and the government in a combined search for public value. This is different to a master/servant (superordinate/subordinate) or principal/agent model (for a discussion of 'shared accountabilities', see Boston and Gill, this volume). Whether this represents a constitutional change ('an Aotearoa/New Zealand system of governing'; Ryan, 2006), or whether it is only a matter of (re)interpreting the Westminster bargain in postmodern terms (which seems equally possible; e.g., Bogason, 2007) is at the moment unclear. Renegotiating the Westminster bargain may be one way forward. Starting afresh with a new type of bargain is another.

Conclusion: Creating the Future

Public management in New Zealand needs rethinking and revitalising. The model adopted from the late 1980s reformed many aspects of the earlier public administration model and improved the overall quality of governing in this country, certainly in relation to loosening up the administrative framework, budgetary and financial management, and increasing the level of managerial accountability of senior public servants. Time has moved on and the nature and extent of other challenges confronting the public management system have become apparent. Compounding the urgency, the fiscal concerns have recently returned after a decade of surpluses.

Some of those challenges were realised from the late 1990s and, for example, attempts to balance the focus on outputs with more attention to outcomes were part of ongoing developments. Whilst the centre did not implement this initiative effectively, managers in line agencies understood the lesson and continued developing their practice in outcome-oriented directions. As they did so, public managers in many places throughout the public sector in New Zealand, as much as comparable countries, also learned that, to be successful in the face of increasing complexity and uncertainty, new ways of conducting public management needed to be created. Their responses included methods such as networking, partnership and collaboration in order to work jointly with other actors in the economy and civil society who were essential to the success of policy. Equally, driven by a concern over the democratic deficit that contemporary western governments operating on conventional lines have been unable to overcome, citizens acting individually and collectively have been demanding access to policy and management processes in governing to an unprecedented degree. One response from public managers has been increasing acceptance of co-design and co-production as a necessary method of policy development and implementation.

Understood from historical, sociological and political perspectives, these developments – this movement towards governance as a mode of governing a society – remind us that there are many aspects of governing that cannot be expressed in economic or bureaucratic terms. They represent the impact of socio-political forces on the system of government that demand a response, a different kind of approach to public management that I have labelled a community approach. This is founded on different types of relationships between citizens, officials and ministers and the manner in which those interactions are conducted. It will be fundamental to developing new means and methods in public management for the decades ahead.

I argue, however, that these developments should not be promoted as a 'post-NPM' agenda, if that term is intended to mean that the NPM approach should be thrown in the dustbin of history to be replaced in its entirety by a community approach. In fact, even during the NPM heyday, practices derived from the bureaucratic era continued. This could be interpreted as a residue that lingered on. I suggest it tells us that some types of government functions are best conducted using a bureaucratic approach. Likewise, some government activities that are market-like should be organised and managed in market-like ways; that is, using the means and methods created as part of NPM. For the same reasons, those forms of government activity that are best conducted within a socio-political framework, particularly those wherein citizens and the state interact closely regarding complex policy issues that are uncertain in their definition and solution, community-like ways and means are more appropriate. The justifications for doing so relate both to the quality of democracy that is thereby realised and the effectiveness of policy and management when these methods are adopted. In other words, the future for public management is likely to entail a range of different approaches. Which is appropriate in a particular setting will depend on the social, political and economic context. Not all circumstances are best met by a single model. Accordingly, the form and content of the present legislation, guidance and embedded practice will need to be revised in certain ways to allow the emergence of the new, particularly if existing elements get in the road and would prevent them from reaching maturity.

This scenario suggests a complex future. The public management system in New Zealand will not be a closed system predicated on a single logic, but more like a complex adaptive system (e.g., Bovaird, 2008) constituted through ongoing interaction between the parts of the whole governing system (as in Figure 3.1). Which approach will be appropriate in which circumstances will need to be decided on substantive grounds that emerge from the whole economic, political and social context. In terms of another idea that is presently gaining traction but which has not been discussed in this chapter, public value in its multiple dimensions (Bennington and Moore, 2011) should be the determining criterion. It is also clear that for these developments to occur, attention will need to be paid to aspects of the politico-administrative system that go beyond public management understood in narrow technical terms. Fundamental to this is the constituted relationship between citizens, officials and ministers, with the behaviour of ministers and cabinet a critical part of the mix.

Achieving that future – or, rather, creating the future in whatever form it takes – will be testing for those who take on the task of leadership whether as ministers or as senior public officials. This analysis suggests that the model of change and reform employed in the past, a top-down approach driven from the centre, is only part of the story and perhaps a relatively small one. Learning and change should occur according to the principles of outcome-oriented collaborative governance identified in this analysis. Ministers, central agencies and Wellington-based head offices do have a role to play and it is an important one. Like the public managers behind FACS and Whānau Ora (or their apparent intent, anyway), however, they should function as system-wide facilitators, enablers and resources, available to all departments, ministries and agencies when thinking through what they need and when needing access to resources or removal of existing barriers. Capacity-building is critical, and investing in it is critical to the future. Of course, saying this assumes that all public sector organisations know how to be – and are willing to be – active agents in their own destiny. Partly because of the culture of control underpinning public management in New Zealand, some of those agencies are habitually reactive, doing only what they are obliged to do. They will need to be encouraged and supported as they move into the future. A full-scale programme of change management over time across the whole sector will be needed to trigger sector-wide changes to the structures, practices and cultures.

So 'the centre' will have an important role. But it should not be a centre that solely comprises central agencies, head offices and chief executive networks. The centre should take the form that keeps reappearing in the illustrations above and in other similar cases; namely, a horizontal network that combines and synergises the range of interests involved, drawn from spheres and levels inside and outside of government, and that learns its way forward, articulating the results of its deliberations and seeking participation of users. All of this, of course, must be driven by the understanding that, ultimately, the outcomes will be an effect of co-production with the citizens of New Zealand and the manner in which they choose to interact with government.

4

A Public Management Heresy?
Exploring the 'Managerial' Role of Ministers within Public Management Policy Design[1]

Michael Di Francesco and Elizabeth Eppel

'There is no worse heresy than that the office sanctifies the holder of it'

Lord Acton 1887

Introduction: The Sound of Silence?

One could be forgiven for thinking that public management is a wholly bureaucratic enterprise. Much of the change in public management policy during the past 25 years was designed principally to increase political control by modifying bureaucratic behaviour, most prominently in the case of New Zealand by framing the control problem in 'principal–agent' terms (Boston, Martin, Pallot and Walsh, 1996; cf Aucoin, 1990). However, the great bulk of scholarly examination of the design and performance of these policy changes is marked by the conspicuous absence of politicians, and in particular the role of ministers. In framing their explanation of the rise of new public management as a form of public service bargain, Hood and Lodge emphasise that the literature has largely overlooked how 'the managerial vision depends on a bargain or reciprocal exchange agreement *restricting* the behaviour of *both* elected politicians and public servants to make it work' (2006: 174, emphasis added). Others – 'controversially', by their own accounts – have raised the same issue in terms of comparative analysis of public management reform, noting that the 'incentives and penalties' facing politicians have 'been a "no-go" area for reformers' (Pollitt and Bouckaert, 2004: 156–8). On the role politicians play, the silence is deafening.

1   The authors would like to thank Jonathan Boston and Bill Ryan for very helpful comments on an earlier draft of this chapter. The chapter also benefited from formative discussions with Michael Barzelay. What follows, however, remains the responsibility of the authors.

What is perplexing, of course, is that the signals sent by ministers are *assumed* to matter within the operation of public management policies. As one of the principal architects of the New Zealand reforms has succinctly put it: 'Ministers have the ability to drive superior performance or to send distortions through the system that undermine the efficiency of a chief executive and a department' (Scott, 2001: 371). The defining characteristics of public management policies, particularly in New Zealand, are a range of now familiar organisational practices – such as management by performance control, structural separation between policy and delivery, and contracting – that depend on some level of ministerial interest in priority-setting and the value of management information; the very purpose of public management policy reform was to formalise a more modern concept of political and administrative control. Rather than detaching ministers from departmental work, these practices actually attach *greater* importance to the 'managerial' orientation of ministers' roles. Even after a quarter century of reform this seems not to have occurred, which has prompted calls for the next stage of policy change to include 'the requirements and conditions for politicians to conform more to the type of prescription that they require of others' (Bouckaert and Halligan, 2008: 205; see also OECD, 2005a: 72–74; Ryan, 2011a).

This chapter is a preface to this reform agenda, and an application to policy makers and researchers to countenance what we here term a public management 'heresy'. The heresy is to question the seemingly absent role of ministers within public management systems – the type of sanctification of office that Lord Acton cautions against – and to ask why efforts to improve public management continue to overlook the critical role of ministers in making management reforms work. In short, we argue that more must be done to align the behaviour of ministers with the systemic expectations they themselves have set.

The chapter proceeds in four steps. First, it frames key suppositions about recurring patterns in the way ministers engage with a defining aspect of public management policy, namely performance control. We call these patterns 'inherencies', and suggest that weak engagement is the product of asymmetries between formal role expectations and the levels of ministerial willingness and capability. The second section surveys conventional understandings of the role of ministers in Westminster systems and outlines a conceptual framework for investigating whether, and if so how, the managerial aspect of ministerial role description is reflected in selected performance control practices. We argue that to be effective these practices require ministers to be an integral part of (and not simply a figurehead for) departmental leadership and management. Next we examine declared ministerial role designation and practice in New Zealand and Australia respectively, as comparison jurisdictions. The following section (under the heading 'A Public Management Heresy?') catalogues the heresy by profiling the normative significance of a managerial role for ministers, surveying the asymmetries of willingness and capability that prevent ministers from taking these roles, and considering various means for enabling ministers to manage. We conclude by presaging the need for further, practice-oriented analysis of ministerial role definition in the context of public management policy design.

The Gap: Ministers and Public Management Policy

We suspect there exists a significant discrepancy between the design intentions of public management policy and the actual behaviour of politicians and, in particular, ministers of state. As already noted, the remarkable absence of scholarly attention in this area is one indicator, but to this we can add the reluctance (or is it simply disinterest?) on the part of current and former politicians to reflect on what are now considered quite orthodox approaches to organising government. To help orientate our exploration we need first to build scaffolding for our arguments and to explain what we mean by the gap between policy design and ministerial roles and behaviour, and why it is significant.

In a sense, the reform of public management systems seems quite self-evident. Prominent scholars of comparative government have described it as 'deliberate changes to the structures and processes of public sector organisations with the objective of getting them (in some sense) to perform better' (Pollitt and Bouckaert, 2004: 16). This tells us that any effort to understand the impact of reform should focus essentially on two things: the rules and practices that govern the way public organisations are expected to operate, and the purposes that are intended to be achieved by institutionalising those rules and practices. This has also been described as 'public management policy' to acknowledge that these types of rules and practices aim to *standardise* improvements to long-standing government-wide functions, such as planning, budgeting and employment (Barzelay and Gallego, 2006: 544–6). In this context, evaluating the impact of public management policies is really a type of constrained 'design science' exercise that compares the declared objectives of policy design with its operation in practice (Barzelay and Thompson, 2010). As noted elsewhere (Boston, 2000), a significant challenge in this type of systemic evaluation is disentangling issues of causality: are they principally design-related (flaws in the logic about the intended behaviour of actors) or primarily implementation-related (discrepancies realised in converting the design into organisational routine)?

Our specific interest is the way public management policies assign roles and responsibilities to both ministers and bureaucrats with a view to influencing the behaviour of *both* sets of actors. To illustrate, take that staple of modern management practice, performance control: public management policy design tends to assume a mechanistic link between the availability of performance information and its use by bureaucrats – whether direct or indirect – even though such utilisation remains one of the most under-researched areas of reform (Pollitt, 2006a). The even thinner literature on *ministerial* utilisation is confined largely either to councillor use at the local government level (principally in Western Europe: see Askim, 2009; Ter Bogt, 2004) or sporadic treatment in broader studies of managerial use of performance data in central government departments (for New Zealand, see Gill, 2011; and for the United Kingdom, refer to Polidano, 1998; Pollitt, 2006b). In general, there is highly equivocal evidence of political executive engagement with formal performance management regimes. Taking this practice area of performance control as a starting point, we can sketch some suppositions about the factors that may influence ministerial conformance with the declared objectives of public management policies.

We start from the proposition that there are certain characteristics intrinsic to majoritarian political systems where the accountability of executive government is based on Westminster principles. These features, a legacy of the long dominance of the two-party system, obviously structure the relationship between the executive and the legislature – responsible cabinet government is framed around the accountability of individual ministers to the legislature – and in so doing also give rise to powerful institutional rules and norms, especially the valency of political adversarialism and its framing of executive answerability.[2] We submit that these types of characteristics can be conceived as barriers that prevent systemic impairments being recognised and addressed – what we will call 'inherencies'. These inherencies can be of two types (Jasinski, 2001: 534–5): structural barriers (these might be political system rules, such as individual ministerial responsibility) or attitudinal barriers (the beliefs held by key actors that correspond with dominant political values, such as party adversarialism). These inherencies, we argue, are *neither openly acknowledged nor explicitly addressed in prevailing public management policy design* and potentially have significant impact on the way that declared policy objectives and design elements are institutionalised. Our key supposition, then, is that these inherencies manifest themselves in institutional reality as 'asymmetries' – or gaps – between declared policies and *both* the commitment imputed to key institutional actors and the observed behaviour of those actors.

As we have already suggested, an organisational practice that defines the more sophisticated designs of public management policy is what we call 'performance control of bureaucratic delivery' (Bouckaert and Halligan, 2008: 26–34, 134–51). This is an array of practices that use managerial

2 For a perceptive recent survey of the distinct cultures and norms governing parliamentarians and the political and bureaucratic executives in New Zealand, see Prebble (2010: 33–58).

concepts to formalise the specification and monitoring of performance standards as a means for exercising indirect – as opposed to direct hierarchic – control of bureaucratic (or non-government) delivery of services. Whether based on notions of agency (institutional incentives to align the interests of bureaucrat-as-agent with politician-as-principal) or management systems thinking (feedback mechanisms that permit controllers to identify and correct deviations from preset standards), such arrangements *assume* that the principals or controllers have some minimum level of commitment to the setting and monitoring of incentives or standards. As we have noted, the available evidence on politicians' utilisation of performance information suggests ministers do not actively engage with performance control. This gives rise to two key questions. First, does the *observed* behaviour of ministers reflect an asymmetry of commitment (ministers are unwilling to adhere to the declared objectives of performance control, i.e., they evade, ignore or feign observance), or an asymmetry of behaviour (ministers are incapable of adhering to the declared objectives of performance control, i.e., they have neither technical understanding nor skills)? Second, is such divergence generated principally by the types of inherencies described earlier, and if so, does this mean that the original design was flawed and therefore that ministers are likely to be highly resistant to further changes to public management policies? In other words, have public management policies been designed with sufficient understanding of the institutional context and political contest that shapes ministerial roles? The remainder of this chapter is about putting both policy makers and researchers in a better position to tackle these types of questions.

A Framework for Analysis: Mapping the Managerial Role of Ministers

So how might we go about examining the influence of public management policy change on the role of ministers? We think a useful starting point is to look at what has already been said about the institutional roles and responsibilities of ministers within Westminster-based political executives.[3] We can use this to do two things: first, identify the key roles usually attributed to ministers and, within these, assess the status of the managerial (or executive) function; and second, sketch out how specific organisational practices that are representative of public management policy change – in this case, performance control practices – might be reflected in these ministerial roles.

---

3   We confine this preliminary examination to ministers of state, acknowledging that in Westminster systems the role of ministers is increasingly framed by, and their agency exercised through, political staffers. For an overview of recent developments in Westminster (and other) systems, see Eichbaum and Shaw (2010).

Ministers – along with prime ministers and cabinets – form the apex of executive power in Westminster systems. There has long been a fascination with describing the constitutional position of ministers within cabinet – and New Zealand is no exception[4] – although surprisingly less analysis of the institutional roles and behaviours of ministers.[5] What exists tends to focus on the distinct career paths and socialisation of political and administrative elites; for example, the political skills required to succeed in parties and parliament, and the various factors – patronage, loyalty and so on – that inevitably influence selection as a minister (Aberbach, Putnam and Rockman, 1981; Peters and Pierre, 2001). The revival of ethnographic approaches to the study of elites – meaning the use of shadowing, diary analysis and non-participant observation to ascertain beliefs – is delivering increasingly detailed accounts of ministerial attitudes and behaviours, although somewhat divorced from analytical frameworks explaining institutional roles (Rhodes, 2005, 2007, 2011; Rhodes and Weller, 2001). Another perspective on the 'core executive' focuses on the key actors and institutions of central government and their relationship to one another (Dunleavy and Rhodes, 1990; Smith, 1999, 2000). A direct response to increasingly circuitous debates on the 'presidentialisation' of prime ministers in Westminster systems, this approach contends that power dependency is the defining characteristic of executive government. Its key insight is that the role and influence of prime ministers, cabinets, departmental ministers and bureaucrats are relational and contingent on how each actor deploys resources within changing institutionalised settings.

We focus on an important subset of core executive studies that is distinguished by the use of ethnographic research methods. These studies survey the relational power of ministers, combining detailed analysis of daily work schedules and ministers' own perceptions of their priorities and behaviour, to develop ministerial role classifications in central government in Australia (Tiernan and Weller, 2010; Weller and Grattan, 1981) and the United Kingdom (Heady 1974; Marsh, Richards and Smith, 2000).[6] Importantly for our purposes, these studies assess how role classifications have evolved over time by accounting for institutional change (such as the rise of ministerial staffs) and broader systemic

---

4   See, for example, Mulgan (2004: 73–98).
5   As we note below, an exception is McLeay (1995).
6   Unfortunately, these types of dedicated studies into ministerial roles and behaviours have not been systematically replicated in the New Zealand context. The most prominent exception is Elizabeth McLeay's study of cabinet and executive power in New Zealand which devotes a chapter to the role of ministers (1995: 108–25). McLeay uses interview data from two cohorts of ministers (1971–72 and 1991–92) to describe ministerial workload and gauge broad changes in ministerial role perceptions, although the analysis does not seek to apply role classifications as an organising framework to interpret and/or compare the New Zealand experience with other Westminster-type parliamentary systems.

change (especially the explosion in communications technology and the advent of a more contestable political marketplace).

The starting point, though, is what ministers actually do. Time and again these types of studies confirm that the job of a minister is hard: extraordinarily long hours, an unrelenting pace, the pressure of constant public scrutiny and the strain of having to juggle competing but equally important constituencies. To illustrate the range of task types, Table 4.1 gives a snapshot of the activities that an Australian federal minister undertakes in a typical parliamentary sitting week. What this table shows[7] is that ultimately ministers spend much of their time either in meetings or preparing for them, which means that like most top-level office-holders in large and complex corporate settings, they are – or should be – principally engaged in either digesting and communicating information or making and following up decisions.

Table 4.1 The Range of Ministerial Activities

	Activity Description	Hours spent per week
Department	Meetings with officials, briefing on and/or preparation for intergovernmental meetings, stakeholder meetings etc	6.4
Cabinet	Cabinet meetings, meetings with ministerial colleagues and MPs, delegations etc	8.5
Parliament	Caucus meetings, committees, tactics, question time	15.5
Private Office	Strategy and staff meetings, speech preparation, teleconferences etc.	4.0
Outside World	Media and press conferences, launches, functions etc	14.7

* Adapted from Tiernan and Weller (2010: 307-309). Hours averaged for a parliamentary sitting week. Excludes time spent on Cabinet preparation, reviewing and signing documents, and travel.

These task types are the means through which ministers perform four generic roles within Westminster executives: policy, political, executive and public relations (see Table 4.2). The policy role is about strategy-setting in government, although tellingly it usually distinguishes between 'policy setters' and 'policy takers'. The political role covers the arts of political judgement and persuasion that are so central to the effective advocacy of policy action. The executive role equates to the decisional and management aspects of organisational leadership that recognises the linkages between capability

---

7   And what is also emphasised by Tiernan and Weller (2010: 308).

and policy achievement. Finally, the public relations role emphasises the presentation and communication of policy, as well as the management of key stakeholder relations.

Table 4.2 Generic Ministerial Role Classifications

Role Classification	Description
1. Policy	Agenda setting, policy selection and authorisation
2. Political	Advocacy in Cabinet, party, parliament
3. Executive (or Managerial)	Departmental management and executive decisions
4. Public Relations	Relations with interest groups, media and public

* Adapted from Marsh, Richards and Smith (2000: 306).

Each role covers a slice of the occupational wagon wheel for ministers, although there is 'no single model of a minister' (Tiernan and Weller, 2010: 299–306). Instead, the weighting that ministers place on each of the functions will be dependent on circumstances, personal style, and the starting endowment of skills and experience. To capture this, analysts also refer to ministerial 'types' that describe the way ministers combine roles, for example, the policy selector (Heady, 1974) or policy driver (Tiernan and Weller, 2010) who effectively combines political and advocacy skills to shape their own reform agenda. The important point for the present discussion is the extent to which role types – and hence ministerial understanding of them – may have been reoriented by public management policy change. There are two key insights from the most recent studies.

First, there are significant differences between Westminster systems. Of most interest is that whilst the British studies distinguish an 'executive minister' role type, in Australia the expression of this role among ministers is so weak that it was not identified as a separate ministerial type. Having said this, it is also clear that the executive or managerial role of ministers is the least well understood. One explanation for this is the contradiction that operates at the core of Westminster conventions, in which the democratic ideal of a divide between politicians (policy) and bureaucrats (administration) coexists with the reality of policy interdependency. In this context, a management role for ministers is either frowned upon (for example, in the way that public service bargains exclude politicians from most personnel management decisions: see Hood and Lodge, 2006) or cast as exceptional, even eccentric behaviour (for instance, in the way that ministers such as Michael Heseltine in 1980s Britain or Simon Upton in 1990s New Zealand had strong interest in organisational management: see Riddell, Gruhn and Carolan, 2011: 23–25).

A second set of observations suggests that over the last 25 years systemic change (particularly media technologies and network governance) has had significant influence on ministers' roles, whereas institutional change (like public service contract employment) *appears* to have generated little discernable shift towards a more 'managerial' orientation. In the United Kingdom, the impact of media management on ministerial roles is almost overwhelming, and as a consequence the executive role is corralled with public relations as a strategy either to manage media image or effect agenda setting within 'obstructionist' departments (Marsh, Richards and Smith, 2000: 316–20). Similarly, the Australian survey of ministers' interactions with departments revealed that whilst the quality of policy advice and the quantity of agenda management had become increasingly important over time, the information needs of ministers (referred to derisively by one minister as 'CEO to the secretary's COO') displayed no greater managerial orientation (Tiernan and Weller, 2010: 311–14).

Of course, these studies were not designed to capture the specific impact of public management policy change on ministers' perception of their own roles. Nonetheless, they do confirm the existence of some interesting puzzles. If, as we propose, the performance control of bureaucratic delivery is a defining practice of public management, we would expect that over time it would have at least some expression in each of these role types: for example, the deployment of performance data in policy or programme advocacy, the use of performance information to frame answerability in accountability forums, and an increasing propensity for ministers to engage with target-setting and review in the management of organisational performance. Arguably, however, these performance control practices should be most prominent as part of the execution of a so-called 'managerial' role.

So how might these issues be examined? The approach we take here is to specify organisational practices that are representative of performance control within public management policies *and* designed to alter the declared (or formal) roles and responsibilities of both elected and appointed officials, including the way each is expected to interact with the other. In particular, we suggest that three representative practices are useful for exploring the managerial component of ministerial roles; each of them is designed to incorporate the use of performance information in organisational routines that are instrumental in the exercise of control, and each creates specific obligations on ministers to use performance information in support of the generic roles outlined in Table 4.2.

The first practice relates to the deregulation of public service employment and the use of fixed-term contracts to govern the appointment of top-level public servants. There are variations in the institutional rules – for example, independent regulator appointment in New Zealand versus internal appointment by prime ministers in Australia – but a common feature is the *use of performance agreements to manage the relationship between ministers and their chief executives.* This practice area covers a range of generic requirements for ministerial involvement in goal- or target-setting (agreements), the specification and amendment of performance standards and, whether directly or indirectly, the appraisal of performance. These requirements create declared obligations on ministers, and each is also intended to position performance control as part of a framework of cascading plans and agreements within government organisations.

The second practice covers the *incorporation and use of organisational performance information in the processes supporting decision-making by portfolio ministers.* The principal mechanism for this has been budget and financial management reform that conceives public sector activity as output, the standards for which can be specified and costed for the purpose of either funding or purchase by government. This type of policy change is exemplified through the accrual-based output budgeting systems implemented in New Zealand (Scott, 2001: 11–36, 169–96) and Australia (Wanna, Kelly and Forster, 2000: 260–8). Over time, these practices formalised accountabilities for outcomes achievement (ministers) and output delivery (public servants), and created specific responsibilities for ministers that required them (or their advisers) to comprehend managerial concepts of performance and associated accounting treatments, and to take an active interest in what was being funded and how performance plans were used to monitor accomplishment. This practice area covers a range of generic requirements such as ministers' participation in goal- and target-setting for the department; the reviewing of departmental performance; the use of performance analysis to support cabinet submissions; and the creation of structures within departmental organisations that facilitate ministerial engagement with performance planning, budgeting and reporting.

The third practice area covers the *procedures governing ministerial answerability for portfolio performance to other agents in the authorising environment, in particular the legislature.* In addition to overhauling financial management frameworks and the place of performance information within departmental decision-making, public management policy change was directed at altering the formal processes and content of budgeting and reporting accountabilities to the legislature; the intent was to shift the priorities and behaviour of public servants, parliamentarians and ministers away from traditional concerns with compliance and inputs. This practice area covers requirements for *ex ante* budget and performance plans and *ex post* portfolio reporting consistent with the accrual-based output budgeting formats; it creates a range of reporting instruments that are intended to *structure* ministerial answerability to legislative oversight forums.

In the two sections that follow we seek to describe, in a stylised way, the designated roles and responsibilities of ministers. We review the available evidence on ministerial engagement with these three representative practice areas at the national level of government in both New Zealand and Australia. Whilst the context for this chapter is better understanding of the potential for improving system design in New Zealand, we believe significant value can be drawn from a comparative analysis of institutions. New Zealand and Australia share administrative traditions but they also serve to contrast different approaches to public management policy, and the role of ministers within them (on which, see Boston and Halligan, 2009).

Ministerial Role Designation and Practice: New Zealand

Since 1912 New Zealand has had a Westminster-based system of government in which ministers are selected from the party or parties that command a majority in the parliament, and the public service is made up of professionals, recruited openly and appointed on merit. Increasingly, since the introduction of a mixed-member-proportional (MMP) electoral system in 1996, governments are formed through some combination of coalitions or confidence-and-supply agreements with other parties (Boston, Levine, McLeay and Roberts, 1996). The current pattern of relations between ministers and public service chief executives has been shaped by fundamental legislative changes made in the late 1980s (Boston, Martin, Pallet and Walsh, 1991; Scott, 2001). Whilst the architecture established by these reforms remains intact, periodic modification means that we can identify three phases of public management policy change: 'system establishment' under Labour (1984–90); 'technical–contractualist–managerial' development under National majority and minority governments (1990–99); and 'reform adjustment' under Labour-led administrations (1999–2008). The current National-led government has yet to stamp its mark on public management policy, although in the wake of the global financial crisis senior ministers have turned to tighter fiscal control and demanded chief executives focus on delivering smarter and less costly interventions that work (English, 2011a). If there is a third phase of evolution under way its form is still indistinguishable and therefore, as Boston and Eichbaum suggest, the key phases of policy evolution to date are two distinct ten-year periods that compare as qualitatively different 'systems' (Boston and Eichbaum, 2007).

Public Management Policy Change and Ministerial Role Designation

The first phase of 'system development' was famously initiated under the Lange- and Douglas-led Fourth Labour government. Three legislative 'pillars' – the State Sector Act 1988, the Public Finance Act 1989 and the State-Owned Enterprises Act 1986 – sit at the core of New Zealand's public management policy changes. These Acts reshaped the roles and responsibilities of ministers and government departments (Scott, 2001). While most policy advice and operational activities remained in government departments, some former functions were corporatised as separate trading organisations headed by a chief executive accountable to a minister through a board; in these cases the direct day-to-day responsibilities of ministers were confined largely to an 'ownership' interest (Mascarenhas, 1991; Scott, 2001). The legislative pillars also introduced a sharper distinction between the role of the minister and that of the chief executive, and since 1989 the remaining core government departments[8] have been headed by a chief executive with a fixed-term contract, rather than a 'permanent head'. The minister became responsible for providing strategic direction and making policy decisions; the chief executive was made more clearly accountable for the day-to-day operational decisions of the department; and, in particular, the management of staff became wholly a chief executive responsibility. Under these new arrangements, chief executives were given more latitude in the selection and use of resources to achieve cabinet-sanctioned goals (Boston, 1992; Scott, 2001).

The procedures for appointing chief executives and appraising their performance also changed in 1989. These arrangements have since been codified in the *Cabinet Manual* as administrative procedures (Cabinet Office, 2008). The portfolio minister is consulted when the chief executive position is to be appointed and then the advertising and selection of the preferred appointee is carried out by the State Services Commissioner. The position of chief executive is intended to be a politically neutral one appointed on merit for a fixed term of up to five years. Once appointed, a tripartite relationship exists: the State Services Commissioner is the legal employer and reviews chief executive performance against both the requirements of the position and priorities established by the minister, but ultimately the chief executive is responsible to the portfolio minister.

The second 'technical–contractual–managerialist' phase under the Bolger and Shipley National governments (1990–99) largely consolidated the core legislative changes, and codified them in cognate Acts, for example, the Fiscal Responsibility Act 1994 (Boston and Eichbaum, 2007). There was also an emphasis on procedures directed at departments and their chief executives, such as written performance agreements, output plans and performance pay for chief executives. For much of this period, the prime minister and ministers took the initiative at cabinet level to specify government's Strategic Result Areas (SRAs) as well as how departmental Key Result Areas (KRAs) should apply to groups

---

8   There were 32 departments subject to the State Sector Act 1988 at 1 July 2011. By comparison there were 34 in 1984 (see Boston et al., 1991: 237), although the number masks more significant changes made between 1984 and 2011 in the scope and arrangement of functions covered by government departments, Crown entities and state-owned enterprises.

of portfolios in support of budget prioritisation, departmental planning, and purchase and performance agreements (Boston and Pallott, 1997). Shipley even arranged her cabinet into ministerial teams with overlapping portfolios charged with working together under a lead minister (Scott, 2001).

This phase of policy change was, however, punctuated by key State Services Commission- and Treasury-commissioned system evaluations, the most prominent of which was *The Spirit of Reform* (Schick, 1996). This review praised the internal consistency and rigour of the output-based financial accountability reforms, but also noted the fragmentation resulting from dependence on bilateral contracts and their limitations in areas such as chief executive contracts. In effect, the Schick report articulated growing concerns about the impact of contractualist reforms on the coherence and ethos of the public service, and public management policy change in the third phase of 'reform adjustment' under the Clarke Labour-led government (1999–2008) was influenced by these evaluations. The new government moved away from the earlier contractual–managerial emphasis towards an approach based on public service values and standards of service to citizens. There was a corresponding shift in terminology from 'outputs' to 'outcomes' that might require the joint working of several departments, and this was reflected both in the replacement of departmental purchase agreements with 'output plans' and the installation of Statements of Intent to consolidate the chief executive performance agreements and departmental forecast reports prepared at the beginning of each financial year. Finally, the SRA/KRA process was replaced by the Capability, Accountability and Performance (CAP) process that sought to balance the short-term purchase interest of government with its longer-term 'ownership interest' in departmental capability (Boston and Eichbaum, 2007: 156).

We can note that transcending the shifts in policy change is an enduring presumption of a managerial role for responsible ministers; in the words of one of the principal designers: 'the whole system of government management relies on ministers carrying out their individual and collective cabinet roles with a considerable measure of competence' (Scott, 2001: 95). Such expectations, however, receive mixed treatment in one of the key declarations of ministerial roles, the *Cabinet Manual*. On the one hand, cabinet and cabinet committee procedures confine a minister's role to the setting of departmental 'policy direction and . . . priorities', whilst expecting them to be 'fully conversant with' and responsible for cabinet papers that, of course, are routinely prepared by public servants; and, on the other hand, broadening ministerial responsibility to embrace all spending decisions on 'outputs delivered by their departments' (Cabinet Office, 2008: 20–21, 67). It is not surprising then that some ministers – such as Simon Upton, a former State Services Minister – challenged the plausibility of the pivotal assumption of 'ministers expected to be energetic and well-informed purchasers, monitoring output delivery and bringing particular sanctions and pressures to bear as required'. It was, he said, 'a bold leap of faith to assume that ministers cheerfully fulfil all the requirements of the current [1999] public management system' (quoted in Boston and Eichbaum, 2007: 144–5). Next, we examine these discrepancies by assessing available evidence on ministerial engagement with the three representative practices of public management policy: chief executive performance agreements, organisational performance management and parliamentary scrutiny of the executive. In each of these areas the effective operation of the New Zealand system assumes an active role for ministers.

Chief Executive Performance Agreements

Delicately balanced and often unique to the individuals involved, the relationship between minister and chief executive is at 'the heart of government, linking political desire to action' (James, 2002: 1). Contemporary empirical studies that focus specifically on how performance management process has been used to structure these key interactions in New Zealand are scarce; what research evidence exists has often been gathered incidentally from broader investigations of departmental accountability and organisation change management.

Formal processes requiring the responsible minister to set and review chief executive performance began in the 1990s with year-long written agreements, which systemic evaluations found were not well integrated with other accountability instruments (such as the output and financial reporting responsibilities of the chief executive) (Boston, 1992; Schick, 1996). In the only dedicated review of the process, Whitcombe (1990) found that ministers and chief executives alike saw the written performance agreement and review process as overly bureaucratic and insensitive to the specific and changing priorities of the minister. Chief executives thought that the minister had too little input into the process: '[t]he key person is the minister . . . brought in by a round-about process' (Whitcombe, 1990: 122). And the nine experienced ministers interviewed by Whitcombe were split in the value they saw in the process. One saw it as 'an excellent discipline' and 'had spent a day working out what he thought should be in the performance agreement, his goals and a timetable and thought that it had helped him to think through all aspects of the department's operations'. However, this proved to be the exception as, overall, ministers showed little enthusiasm for a signed agreement and placed little emphasis on the formal review process.

By the mid-1990s, as Boston and Pallot (1997) observe, the cascading system of government-wide SRAs and more specific KRAs flowed into departmental planning and accountability documents and executive performance agreements, and lent a coherence that had previously been lacking; the system also enjoyed broad support among ministers, chief executives and the central agencies. However, as we have noted, SRAs/KRAs lapsed with the change of government at the end of the 1990s, replaced by a greater emphasis on the balance between short- and long-term priorities. Today, departments develop a Statement of Intent to operationalise government's policy objectives, which is signed by the responsible minister. The Statement of Intent process was entirely consistent with system design assumptions of an active strategic governance and management role for ministers. Again, in the words of Scott (2001: 95), the policy changes envisaged ministers:

> using the system to drive the government organisations under their control to change priorities and to achieve continuous improvement. They do this by close involvement in the strategic planning of the department, in the detailed attention to the contents of the chief executive's performance agreement and the budgeting behind it, in careful and balanced formal reviews of performance, and in periodic informal discussions with the chief executive and other senior staff about performance.

However, based on his experience as a chief executive in the 1990s, Scott concluded that 'not all ministers have these capabilities'. Nor, it appears, the inclination: in his participant roundtable investigation of the relationship between ministers and chief executives, James (2002) found that formal performance-based management – in conjunction with the impact of other systemic changes, in particular open government information – had reinforced the conventional distinction between policy and management.[9] While ministers have 'correctly refused to take responsibility for activities reserved to the chief executive', they 'often extend this refusal to management generally and pushed chief executives and other public servants forward to defend programmes and errors to Parliament and the news media' (James, 2002: 72). A development in the current Key government, which is neither consistently nor broadly enough applied to suggest a (re)awakened recognition of the role of ministers, is the Prime Minister's use of letters to ministers setting out government priorities for a portfolio (e.g., the justice sector), which are in turn iterated in letters of expectations with chief executives.[10]

---

9   This traditional distinction between ministerial leadership and departmental administration was also reflected in the ministerial role perceptions reported by McLeay in her earlier study of Cabinet ministers (1995: 120–2).

10 Personal communication in interviews with senior public servants. While this approach has been followed in the justice portfolio – covering the Ministers of Justice, Police, Corrections, Courts and Social Development – it has not been applied in the equally challenging Environment group of portfolios.

Organisational Performance Management

Departmental performance is subject to scrutiny from many quarters – ministers, the State Services Commission, the Office of the Controller and Auditor-General, and parliament. Much of what we know about ministers' participation in organisational performance management has been gathered in the context of studies of department performance. In his study of performance accountability within the New Zealand reforms, Norman observed a 'collective sigh by senior public servants about the unwillingness of politicians to engage with the rational planning that the public management model prescribes'; according to one chief executive, 'we need to prioritise, but this is exactly what politicians most dislike doing' (Norman, 2003: 112–13). This need not have been the case. Provision was made in the system design for ministers to use 'purchase advisers' to align output purchasing decisions to government priorities and to ensure that ministers were not simply signing off on the output decisions of their departments. Despite each minister being allocated a budget to purchase such advice, there was no systematic use of this provision, although in part this was because of concerns about how the employment status of purchase advisers contravened the statutory separation of political and public service appointments (Eichbaum and Shaw, 2009).

As the focus on organisational performance evolved in the 1990s, informal means to balance the formal system's emphasis on annual outputs were sought out, and some chief executives initiated 'advisory boards' with external membership to assist them in the steering and governance of their departments. These arrangements arose in the general absence of more active interest by ministers in the full range of departmental responsibilities, and contained within them the potential for conflict with the ministerial role. In one case at least, a minister in the 1999–2002 Labour government objected to the private sector membership of his department's advisory board and insisted that the chief executive terminate the board because he and his associate ministers had 'adopted a firm hands-on approach to our oversight' (Scott, 2001: 118).

Other studies have emphasised the inter-dependency between ministerial expectations and the ability of a chief executive to bring about shifts in departmental performance. Wyn (2007) found that a clear statement of a minister's expectations for, and trust and confidence in, a chief executive was critical to the latter's success in, for example, managing organisational change. These expressions of confidence can become strained in circumstances of ongoing public attention on departmental failures. An overall positive trend in measured performance improvement under these circumstances might be discounted because of media focus on a few events. While ministerial expressions of dissatisfaction act as a strong motivator that a chief executive can use to encourage change, the negative effect on morale works against this.

Other performance management and accountability case studies have also revealed something of the approach ministers adopt in providing guidance on strategic direction and feedback on performance (Dormer, 2010; Gill, 2011; Norman, 2003). A consistent finding is the informal, non-explicit means by which ministers tend to convey their wishes to public servants, summed up in one minister's interview comment that 'no one in their right minds thinks that we use [the formal accountability documents] to manage performance' (Dormer, 2010: 15). In particular, Norman (2003: 147) noted how uneasily such an imposed conception of organisational rationality sat with some ministers:

> Trust matters more than anything else in the relationship between the chief executives of policy ministries and ministers. Documentation doesn't help build such trust and can get in the way . . . the real substance of accountability to the minister does not come through formal processes and documents, but through weekly meeting and informal exchanges. The formal system is only relevant where there are problems.

Even so, central agencies and the political executives they serve remain committed to the component elements of public management policies established in the late 1980s. In 2010 the State Services Commission developed a new approach – the Performance Improvement Framework – for the formal review of departmental and chief executive performance (SSC, 2010a). The current Key National-led government has articulated a 'new responsibility model' as part of the state sector response to the fiscal pressures imposed by the global financial crisis of 2008–9. This model, as the Minister of Finance explained (English, 2011a: 57), 'requires ministers and chief executives to clarify exactly what results they want', and will apply:

> the basic tools of ministerial and chief executive accountability, and thus spend a good deal of time ensuring that discussion between the Prime Minister and his ministers exactly reflects these expectations over the next two or three years . . . as ministers, we must keep demonstrating political support for change and reinforcing the mandate that chief executives can use tools and make changes without fear of political consequences.[11]

Parliamentary Scrutiny of Performance

Parliament is also an important agent of the authorising environment in which ministers and chief executives operate, particularly through the pressure its select committees apply in the scrutiny of output specifications and performance (and, more commonly in recent years, independent special

---

11 The last part of this quotation, which seeks to reassure chief executives of a 'safe space' in which to experiment with policy and delivery tools, may be more a case of wishful thinking.

inquiries or major inquiries into aspects of performance) (Prebble, 2010: 173–82). A department's Statement of Intent is subject to scrutiny by the relevant select committee as part of the Estimates Review process that accompanies annual parliamentary approval of the government's budget, a check intended by the system designers to provide parliamentary scrutiny of ministerial priorities. In this, select committees are assisted by the Office of the Auditor General, which provides analysis of outputs, expenditure and performance based on their audits of departments. Because the Statement of Intent is aligned to government priorities, the responsible minister might also choose – or be asked – to appear before the select committee, although the reality is that all too often it is public servants who are subject to scrutiny in a forum where the political contest takes the lead, and detailed interest in taxation and spending is not the norm (Prebble, 2010: 170–2). At the end of the financial year, the chief executive is responsible for providing an annual report to parliament on what has been achieved against the Statement of Intent. The Audit Office reviews these reports and the Auditor General periodically selects specific areas for greater scrutiny and reports these reviews to parliament. Departmental annual reports are also scrutinised by a select committee, and the chief executive may be held to account for matters covered by the report through both the select committee and media scrutiny. Informed by briefings supplied by the Audit Office, select committee questioning can be quite robust, often skirting around the political, making this a challenging forum for politically neutral chief executives.

In the design of the formal system, the minister is held accountable for policy decisions by parliament and the public through the media and the election cycle. In his insider's survey of the institutional sparring between parliament and the executive, Prebble (2010: 170) credits select committees with wringing detailed information out of departments during their financial reviews, but also sees them 'far from reflecting a wish to debate the big picture', often immersing themselves in minutiae and trivia for political point-scoring. He is also critical of parliamentary debate about spending priorities, which rarely focuses on the larger strategic position and fiscal trajectory. Others agree that there is little evidence of parliamentary use of even high-level output- or outcome-based performance information to scrutinise the executive (Hitchener and Gill, 2011a: 92). The original system design intended select committees to play an active role in reviewing departmental performance. On the one hand, MPs can ask questions of ministers (and do, some 20,000 in 2009 alone) and may use the Official Information Act 1982 to get hold of policy details; on the other hand, at least one of the principal reform architects has lamented the reluctance of select committees to 'own' the review domain, noting that this may be a product of MPs' lack of exposure to questions of performance in large and complex organisations (Scott, 2001: 180).[12] The last word should probably go to a former Auditor General who pinpointed 'the absence [of] any explicit requirement for ministers to report their performance . . . against stated goals or outcomes' (Boston, Martin, Pallot and Walsh, 1996: 302). This is without doubt a performance accountability hole in need of filling, since the defence of government performance in the select committee forum is left largely to chief executives while the scrutiny of parliament focuses mostly on selected issues of political import.

In conclusion, assumptions about the respective roles, relationships and expectations of ministers and chief executives stem from the State Sector Act 1988 and the Public Finance Act 1989 as well as the conventions more recently codified in the *Cabinet Manual*. The scarcity of empirical studies on ministerial engagement in the last quarter century indicates there is a gap in our understanding of how these roles are enacted in practice and how they enable or hinder public sector performance. Whilst quite clearly practice has evolved over this period, role expectations for ministers are expressed rather than documented, and what slender evidence there is indicates that most ministers have little appetite for providing strategic leadership and 'managerial' oversight of their portfolios through sustained practice of this aspect of the role.

Ministerial Role Designation and Practice: Australia

At the national level in Australia,[13] the Westminster tradition has been interpreted and institutionalised within the core executive in distinct ways. Chief among these are the continuing vitality of the cabinet system for collective decision-making combined with comparatively high levels of ministerial discretion – even in the face of augmented power structures around the prime minister – as well as the endurance of the Westminster 'myth' as a rhetorical device for maintaining a rough equilibrium in the professional relationship between politicians and public servants (Rhodes, Wanna and Weller, 2009: 155–86). Within these traditions, political executives have been 'assertive' in pursuing performance-based managerial reform as a means of increasing control (Halligan, 2010a: 134–5) and, as in New Zealand, public management policy change in Australia is characterised by distinct episodes of reform. In this section we examine the record to extract a current reading on ministerial roles, and sift through the available – often proxy – evidence to assess ministerial practice.

12 In particular, Scott cites one former minister who considered that 'MPs haven't the time or inclination in many cases to really get inside the accountability documents that give committees unparalleled insights into both ministerial and corporate governance.'

13 We acknowledge that the evolution of ministerial roles could also be investigated at the sub-national (state and territory) government level. We confine our discussion to the Australian (federal) government principally to align cross-country comparison at the *national* level.

Public Management Policy Change and Ministerial Role Designation

In the modern era of administrative reform in Australia there are principally three episodes of public management policy change: 'managerialism' under the Hawke and Keating Labor governments (1983–96); 'marketisation' under the Howard Liberal–National Coalition government (1996–2007); and what has recently been christened 'integrated governance' under the Rudd and Gillard Labor governments (2007 onwards) (Halligan, 2010b).

The 'managerialist' agenda under the Hawke–Keating Labor government was in essence a continuation of the reformist inclinations of the truncated Whitlam Labor administration (1972–75), in particular, its clash with bureaucratic inertia and the presaging of 'accountable management' as a means for enhancing ministerial control. Under Hawke, and with diminishing intensity Keating, public management policy change was characterised by two streams of management improvement. The first of these comprised structural reforms to impose greater rationality on the functional design of government organisations (for example, the 1987 'Bastille Day' machinery of government changes) and to transform the nature of delegated authority from inputs and process compliance to outputs and results achievement ('making the managers manage' through beacon initiatives such as the financial management improvement program, program management and budgeting and the introduction of program performance statement reporting to parliament) (Holmes and Shand, 1995; Task Force on Management Improvement, 1992). The second stream covered initial reforms to dilute permanency in public sector staffing conditions. These included legislative changes introducing fixed-term appointments for departmental (rather than 'permanent') secretaries who were to manage 'under the minister', and the creation of a mobile elite of senior executive service managers. Later, under Keating, the performance appraisal of public service executives was expanded and aligned with corporate planning.

Returning to government after 13 years, and initially highly suspicious of public service loyalty, the Coalition under John Howard presided over the second 'marketisation' reform episode (Bouckaert and Halligan, 2008: 230–55; Halligan, 2000). Three streams dominated. Like its predecessor, the first of these was structural reorganisations, although this time framed around decentralisation and contestability in service delivery, including expansive use of contracting and the creation of artificial markets (most prominently in the delivery of welfare services). The second stream both consolidated earlier financial management reforms and assembled a 'product and costing format' to enable contestability. The Financial Management and Accountability Act 1997 clarified the financial and governance accountabilities of departmental heads, and the accrual-based Outcomes and Outputs Framework, introduced in 1999, integrated delegated financial and programme management authority with detailed cost and performance information requirements. Outcomes and outputs became the basis for *ex ante* and *ex post* accountability reporting to parliament. The third stream was the seismic shift in public service staffing towards individual contracts and the primacy of workplace bargaining. The transition was marked by the Public Service Act 1999, which confirmed deregulated general employment categories and sealed the prime ministerial 'hire and fire' arrangements for the appointment of departmental secretaries.

The third episode of 'integrated governance' reforms under the Rudd and Gillard Labor governments is still playing itself out. This period is marked by a reversal of the employment deregulation agenda – although noticeably not for top-level public servants – and a judgement that market-inspired decentralisation was in fact leading to administrative fragmentation. Under Rudd, public management policy change events included rationalising national systems of intergovernmental service delivery – especially through the Council of Australian Governments process – and addressing fragmentation in national administration through more 'active management of the APS as a consolidated entity' (APSC, 2010: xviii). The change agenda was set in place prior to Rudd's fall by the Moran Review, which sought to reconnect policy analysis and service delivery and to reinvigorate a collective responsibility for institutional coherence (by, for example, establishing a new Secretaries Board to reinstitute an *esprit de corps* among the bureaucratic elite) (Advisory Group on the Reform of Australian Government Administration, 2010; Lindquist, 2010).[14]

We can discern that a common thread to these three policy change episodes is the augmentation of ministerial direction and the maturation of organisational routines for converting this into control via performance management. But what do the changes mean for the declared role of ministers? Two sets of institutional rules help to mark out formal ministerial role descriptions within the changed public management policy environment.

The first of these are key statutory provisions. The basic law – Section 64 of the Australian Constitution – provides that ministers are appointed 'to administer' departments of state; this formulation of words is somewhat unusual in the Westminster world in that it codifies ministerial responsibilities that are *broader* than the conventional ascription of 'policy'. Supplementary provisions in the

---

14 Although consistent with the broad argument made in this chapter, at least one commentator has criticised the Moran Review's focus on bureaucratic leadership as 'marginalising' the role of ministers by playing down their 'partnership' with public servants and reinforcing 'a dominant and misleading model of public management': see Mulgan (2010: 293–6).

Public Service Act 1999 formalise conventions of responsible government and the superordinate status of ministers: the public service is accountable 'within the framework of Ministerial responsibility to the Government, the Parliament and the Australian public' (s10); departmental secretaries are appointed to manage their departments 'under the Agency Minister' (s57(1)) and must assist their minister to fulfil 'accountability obligations to the Parliament to provide factual information, as required by the Parliament, in relation to the operation and administration of the Department' (s57(2)).

The second set of institutional rules is composed of guidelines for the operation of the cabinet system. Whilst their application is always subject to prime ministerial style, they do reinforce the practical requirements for collective cabinet responsibility and in effect declare key expectations about the role of individual ministers in 'managing' their portfolios. The most recent update of the *Cabinet Manual* (DPMC, 2009), for example, places a premium on ministerial compliance with cabinet submission rules; locates responsibility for cabinet submissions with ministers (even where, as is routine, the detail was prepared by officials); and expects that ministers are responsible for implementing and following up cabinet decisions affecting their portfolio. In recent times we can also note that these administrative aspects of the cabinet system have been reinforced by the way some prime ministers have sought to systematise 'performance management' of ministers. A good example is the role of 'charter letters' issued by Prime Minister Howard (although discontinued by his successors) in conjunction with administrative arrangements orders to clarify portfolio priorities, set out ministerial performance expectations and institute formal annual reporting requirements. According to one departmental secretary, this process played some role in signalling the importance of ministerial engagement with departmental strategic planning and agreement-setting processes (Podger, 2009: 22–23, 65–66).[15]

There is then – in declared public management policy in Australia – both a long-standing requirement for ministerial 'administration' of portfolios and an enhanced expectation about the way in which ministers might fulfil this role type, particularly through the organisational routines defined by performance management. We now examine each of the three performance control practice areas – using largely proxy evidence – to establish whether the so-called 'managerial' role has weak or strong expression.

---

15 There are, however, conflicting accounts about the provenance of 'charter letters'. The inference from Podger's description of the process is that the letters were a prime ministerial initiative that became bureaucratised, while a recent history of the Department of the Prime Minister and Cabinet suggests that the issue of charter letters was an 'old practice' – since at least 1987 – that was resuscitated by bureaucratic initiative in the mid-2000s (see Weller, Scott and Stevens, 2011: 143–4).

Chief Executive Performance Agreements

Now that ministers – more accurately, prime ministers – in Australia have clear power to appoint and determine the performance standards of departmental secretaries, how do they make use of the process? As we have already noted, there are important differences between top-level appointments in Australia and New Zealand: the former is bipartite (the prime minister appoints and oversees the performance appraisal process) and the latter is tripartite (in all but name, the independent State Services Commissioner both appoints and appraises). The performance review process in Australia, whilst legislated, is unquestionably more opaque than in New Zealand, and the role of ministers in setting and assessing performance is attenuated through the dominant role of the prime minister. The evidence of ministerial attitudes and engagement with this key instrument of performance control is both scant and contradictory.

We can note that scrutiny of the performance appraisal process is framed by the perceived influence of fixed-term appointments on the independence of the senior public service, and in particular the pliable criteria for performance assessment. The broader debate about politicisation is largely beyond the scope of this chapter.[16] We remark only that available academic analysis suggests either that 'cowering' behaviour seems mainly to be a characteristic subjectively identified by secretaries in other secretaries (Weller, 2001), or that the locus of politicisation may be better traced by the way performance control practices embed expectations about 'responsiveness' at lower levels in the organisational chain (MacDermott, 2008).

Not surprisingly, the primary source of evidence on ministerial use of performance appraisal processes is public servants. The circumstances for some of them, such as Paul Barratt who was in 1999 the first and last secretary to challenge dismissal, suggest that performance appraisal is nothing more than a thin veneer for the exercise of ministerial whim. Others, especially serving practitioners, have provided assurances that ministers – and especially the prime minister – take the responsibility of performance-rating secretaries 'very seriously' and that the process permits ministers to use all available evidence to send 'a clear message' to non-performers (Briggs, 2007: 501–3; Shergold, 2007: 368–70). However, such industriousness is contested. Andrew Podger, a former Public Service Commissioner under Howard, unveils the inner workings of an ersatz agreement-setting process: for him the use of the term 'contract' is misapplied ('there is no negotiation involved or tailored provisions') (2007: 136). And whilst he agreed that Prime Minister Howard approached the process earnestly, ministers' involvement in annual performance review meetings was

---

16 On which see Mulgan (2008b) for a masterful survey and interpretation of the recent literature in Australia.

seen as 'a chore' potentially subject to capricious application of political and managerial criteria (Podger, 2007: 142–3). In sum, and apart from reinforcing the dual and conflicting nature of secretary accountabilities – responsible in law to the minister but appointed by the prime minister – the available evidence suggests highly variable and contingent commitment by ministers to the *procedures* of this type of performance control.

Organisational Performance Management

The use of organisational performance information to support decision-making and management by portfolio ministers is surely emblematic of public management policy change. As we have noted, it covers a range of practices, from ministers' participation in setting goals and targets for the department, to the use of performance analysis to support cabinet deliberation. Again, these types of unseen ministerial behaviours tend to remain beyond the reach of external observers, and so we rely largely on verification by other means.

A good starting point is the Australian Public Service Commission publication *Supporting Ministers* (now superseded), which sets out guidelines for using formal planning and performance management procedures to mark out the 'roles and responsibilities' of ministers and agencies (APSC, 2006). As we have already noted, these included the strategic direction provided by John Howard's charter letters, and their linkages with performance-assessment processes for the agency head, as well as the invitation by departments of ministers (and more commonly their staff) to attend corporate planning processes to 'set out expectations' and agree performance indicators for budget performance reporting to parliament. Such procedures were also extolled as good departmental practice by the Public Service Commissioner at the time, Andrew Podger (2009: 35, 65–66):

> Strategic planning, directly involving ministers, can help build the necessary relationship. Strategic plans focus on 'why' and 'how', complementing policy platforms, charter letters and portfolio budget statements that determine 'what' achievements are expected and the resources involved. They can be regarded as high-level agreements between the minister and the department and should be formally endorsed by the minister.

Proxy indicators suggest that ministers were neither engaged nor supported in the way this exposition suggests. Earlier, we noted that the Outcomes and Outputs Framework, implemented by the then Department of Finance and Administration in 1999, was intended to provide the architecture for systemic performance control. Chief among its objectives were aligning departmental outputs with outcomes specified by the government, and establishing a management and accountability system based on key indicators of performance. The framework dominated management improvement and accountability reporting activity during the 2000s, but was also subject to external censure (ANAO, 2007; SSCFPA, 2007). The underlying criticism was that the outcomes and outputs architecture was adornment, around which public officials worked. Whilst outcomes – the desired impact of policies – were required to be specified by ministers (and endorsed by the Finance Minister), there was evidence to suggest that this was highly variable. Just as tellingly, information on outputs and outcomes was seldom incorporated within agency management reporting, indicating little or no alignment between internal management reports and external Portfolio Budget Statement reporting (ANAO, 2007: 24, 26–27). As one audited agency summarised: 'the framework had not replaced existing interest in reports based on organisational structure, programmes and cash based reporting. Instead [the framework had] introduced additional layers of reporting . . . [and] outputs are generally not useful as a tool for monitoring . . . performance' (ANAO, 2007: 74). This is revealing, since, as we will see in the next section, parliamentary oversight processes ascribe more importance to Portfolio Budget Statements precisely because they are tabled as 'ministerial documents'; yet ministerial ownership, and the signals sent within departments about the framework, both appear to be very weak.

One final gauge of ministerial commitment to performance control by way of organisational performance management is from the vantage point of cabinet and its experimentation with a Cabinet Implementation Unit (CIU) (Wanna, 2006). An artefact of an administration transitioning from reform activism to delivery management, the CIU was designed by the prime minister's key advisers to mimic the type of consolidated performance reporting produced for company boards. When established by the Department of the Prime Minister and Cabinet in late 2003, the role of the CIU was both prospective (to strengthen strategic implementation analysis and planning, particularly in the cabinet submission process) and retrospective (to monitor and report on implementation progress and problem-solve systemic obstacles) (Wanna, 2006: 357–62). Most prominently, the CIU generated quarterly 'tracking' reports for both the prime minister and full cabinet using a 'traffic light' warning system to report against implementation milestones. Reflecting experience reported elsewhere in this chapter, whilst the prime minister took an active interest, most ministers gave the process limited attention (and then usually only their own department's rating). As a 'corporate board' exercise, the initiative was heavily qualified, and 'other than the PM there [was] not much sense of a governing board mentality or behaviour at cabinet' (Wanna, 2006: 367). In fact, if anything, the CIU provides additional evidence of the remarkable commitment of Prime Minister John Howard – or his closest political advisers

– to the form of performance management, as well as correspondingly weak transferral of this to his ministry.

Parliamentary Scrutiny of Performance

The final practice area covers public management policy change to alter the formal processes and content of budgeting and reporting accountabilities to the legislature. In summary form, these comprise requirements for *ex ante* budget and performance plans and *ex post* portfolio reporting consistent with the accrual-based outcomes and output budgeting format. The intention was to *reframe the terms* of ministerial – and bureaucratic – answerability to legislative oversight forums: 'the hope of reformers was that changing the formal content of accountability . . . would encourage a corresponding shift in the priorities of parliamentarians and the public' (Mulgan, 2008a: 248). Inevitably, this type of change also sought to recalibrate prevailing doctrines of individual ministerial responsibility to parliament; whilst these conventions no longer operate as 'strict liability' for ministers, the new format for performance accountability did seek to reorientate the way ministers *explained* actions carried out under their authority (although not necessarily alter the way political adversarialism as an 'inherency' gravitates towards error and blame). This is not the place to join the debate on ministerial responsibility (although plainly this is of direct relevance to any proposal to renovate the managerial role of ministers). For the moment we focus on available evidence of ministerial engagement with the new forms of accountability reporting, as gauged by the proxy measure of parliamentary utilisation.

Two recent contributions suggest that, whilst performance has seeped into the dialogue of parliamentary oversight, there is only circumspect evidence of its deployment by political executives (Mulgan, 2008a; Thomas, 2009). Parliamentary scrutiny of the executive in Australia and New Zealand is most obviously distinguished by the former's upper house – the Senate – and the strength of the shared norms of transparency and responsibility that underpin its largely self-developed role as a chamber of review (on which, see Uhr, 1998: 141–8). As we have already encountered, the key documents for parliamentary scrutiny are both prospective (the budget estimates and accompanying Portfolio Budget Statements) and retrospective (departmental annual reports). The defining characteristics of these documents, however, tend to determine 'the attention they receive' in Senate questioning of ministers and public servants; as a formal budget paper the Portfolio Budget Statement is a ministerial document and hence more likely to be tested (Thomas, 2009: 392). The question that both Thomas and Mulgan explore is the extent to which the accountability priorities of politicians have, in fact, shifted over time. Using direct references in Senate

Estimates committee transcripts as a crude measure, both researchers arrive at similar conclusions: there has been some diffusion of the language of outputs and outcomes, including a general trend of questioning away from inputs (costs and personnel), but this has not been matched by explicit committee utilisation of the performance-reporting documents to frame discussion of concepts and data (Mulgan, 2008a: 458–60, 466–7; Thomas, 2009: 394–5). Having said this, parliamentarians have also clearly signalled that reporting by outcomes and outputs on an accrual accounting basis did not provide usable information; their strong preference – which has since been acted on – was for budgeting and reporting at the more familiar 'programme' level.[17] What the research does indicate – although more by exclusion – is that there is little evidence of ministers having been either required to respond to scrutiny driven by performance reporting or actively deploying the reporting format to structure answerability around performance narratives.

A Public Management Heresy: Enabling Ministers to Manage?

It is now time for us to take stock and to examine in more detail the heresy that may accompany claims to a managerial role for ministers. First, a recap. This chapter is exploratory in nature. At the beginning we suggested that a defining element of public management policies was organisational practices that institutionalised performance control of bureaucratic delivery. Whilst these practices assign formal managerial-type roles and responsibilities to ministers and appointed officials, practical and conceptual analysis of public management policy tended to concentrate on the latter. We further proposed that a number of inherencies operating within Westminster-type parliamentary systems may act as a brake on ministers' management behaviour, *vis-à-vis* their other roles, and that these may exhibit as asymmetries of commitment (unwillingness to commit to a managerial role) or behaviour (absence of understanding or skills to apply a managerial role).

Evidence of these types of asymmetries was sought in the experience of ministerial engagement with selected performance control practices in New Zealand and Australia. The case studies revealed a number of important themes; not surprisingly, and likely reflecting the strong statutory basis for its policy change, the extent of ministerial estrangement appears to have greater intensity in the New Zealand case.

First, the case studies confirmed that there has been limited investigation of the role of political executives in public management policy in New Zealand and

17 See JCPAA (2002) and SSCFPA (2007). The initiative to simplify parliamentary budget reporting was labelled 'Operation Sunlight' and is discussed in Hawke and Wanna (2010: 69, 73–74).

Australia, which is surprising because both jurisdictions were reform pioneers and are classified as mature 'performance management' regimes (Bouckaert and Halligan, 2008: 134–5). Second, the focus of policy change in both jurisdictions has been on the bureau side of the bargain. Reform was something done to correct the self-interested (or disinterested) behaviour of bureaucrats; in both jurisdictions can be found expressed – if only partially documented – expectations for ministerial 'engagement' that pay cursory attention to whether and how the behaviour of political executives can actually be modified. In New Zealand, for instance, there is no doubt the State Services Commission fully discharges its statutory role to monitor closely chief executive and departmental performance, but ministers and parliament appear to have too few incentives to pay more than passing attention (preferring, as we would expect, to focus on those aspects of performance reporting with political implications).

A third theme characterising policy in New Zealand, and to a lesser extent Australia, is the way a sharper distinction between the strategy-setting role of ministers and the freedom of top public servants to determine means was framed by a reciprocal creative tension, even though the systemic assumptions about ministers executing this management role have been more honoured in the breach. While a very few have recognised the potential benefits of – and diligently attended to – this part of their role, most seem not to bother when sanctions or other incentives are not operating. Finally, it appears that in the place of most ministers' personal rejection of the managerial aspect of their role is a plethora of *ad hoc* arrangements. Some of these, such as purchase advisers in New Zealand and hastily conceived 'board of directors' experiments in both countries, while addressing a perceived need, have potential for conflict with the legislated roles of ministers and chief executives. Unfortunately for the effectiveness of public management policies, this suggests that ministers may indeed be hemmed in by the political contest 'inherency' discussed at the outset of the chapter, and relatively indifferent to any role expectations for ongoing improvement in the performance of their departments.

The Public Management Heresy: Naming the Problem

Earlier we surveyed ministerial role classifications and noted that the managerial function was under-conceptualised. By this we meant that the departmental management role for ministers within Westminster-type parliamentary systems is either expressly excluded (in the pure application of the traditional 'policy–administration' divide, ministers determine policy and its implementation is managed by professional public servants), or strongly contested (the inter-dependency between politicians and public servants may approach, in the words of Parker, 1993: 143–7, a 'policy partnership' but the executive role classification is a necessary evil or 'chore' of residual status). These perspectives are reflected in the most recent arguments over the impact of public management change and the re-assertion of the 'proper' constitutional role of ministers and officials, for example, to dismiss public value activism as the 'repackaging of bureaucratic self-interest' (Rhodes and Wanna, 2009: 180) or to expose performance control routines as insulation devices designed to transfer or shift ministerial responsibility (what some analysts would call agency tactics for 'blame avoidance') (Hood, 2011: 69–79).[18] What tends to be overlooked in these types of analyses is that there are – and have always been – competing interpretations of the relationship between ministers and bureaucrats within Anglo-American political traditions, and these oscillate in their emphasis between 'neutral competence' (constitutional technician) and 'political responsiveness' (executive instrument) (see, for example, du Gay, 2002). These debates are unlikely ever to be resolved, and our view is that the unchallenged focus on the bureaucratic side of the equation constrains what might be possible within public management policy design.

Tentative as they are, we believe our case study observations show why public management policy designers should take the 'managerial' role of ministers more seriously. To begin, we happen to agree with the premises of most public management policy: ministers matter in the way they affirm what should (and ultimately does) get done in government, and their level of engagement with the formal management systems that transmit these signals can be a critical factor for organisational functionality (or dysfunctionality). Just as importantly, we consider that the role of ministers tends to be overlooked in both policy design and analysis because the responsibilities of ministerial office are taken as 'received' rather than being shaped by, and aligned with, community or even professional expectations. Another way of conceiving this is that the delegations of trust to ministers take the form of 'terms and conditions established more by the trust-claimer than the trust granter' (Uhr, 2008: 39). Finally, and relatedly, taking seriously a managerial role for ministers may inoculate against the risks that flow from a reified separation of policy and management, in particular, decision-making by ministerial elites 'cut off from the practical knowledge and policy insight that arises from operational activities' (Scott, 2001: 97).

The 'heresy' of which we speak then can be put quite simply: despite declining levels of public trust in government (SSC, 2000), again paraphrasing Lord Acton, the role of ministers is 'sanctified' within Westminster systems and, because of this, public management policy design is often reluctant to infringe on the norms and prerogatives that define those office-holders. The heresy, in short, is to contend that the role of ministers in public management policy design should

18 See also Hood and Lodge (2006: 172, 181–6). Similar arguments about the nature of 'indirect governing relationships' within public management reform can be found in Flinders and Buller (2006).

be both more explicitly addressed *and* prescribed. The question, of course, is how? Defining a managerial role for ministers should not be about rule-making for its own sake, such as codifying management proficiency (or even worse, instituting this as a type of prequalification process for ministerial office). Nor is it about slavishly holding the working conditions of politicians to the same rigours of managerial and contract prescriptions (a good example of how quickly this can slide into absurdity is performance pay for parliamentarians: see Davis and Gardiner, 1995). Rather, we propose exploring options for encouraging the 'professionalism' – rather than the 'professionalisation' – of ministers; by this we mean improving the competency of ministers in line with community expectations about how they should discharge the obligations of their office. That performance control is now an orthodoxy of much public management policy, and one enthusiastically endorsed by political executives, is one reason why ministers *should* develop a greater willingness and capacity to take an organisational leadership role; one that actively inserts ministers into the way managerial process and information flows structure what Askim calls the 'decisional stages' of agenda-setting, decision-making and post-decisional monitoring (2009: 458–63).

Based on our case studies and a distillation of the broader literature surveyed under the heading, 'A Framework for Analysis', we develop a preliminary taxonomy of how ministers seem to approach such a managerial role using two sets of 'asymmetries' framed around managerial knowledge and skills, and commitment to the managerial role (see Table 4.3, opposite). It is a heuristic device; we readily concede that ministerial roles are subject to and constrained by a host of factors including prime ministerial power, variations in policy issue saliency, the strength or complexity of mobilised opposition, a punishing work schedule, and of course highly variable starting endowments of skills, experience and motivations. Nor is the device exhaustive; the taxonomy identifies three possible combinations of asymmetries, and suggests how these may manifest in practice and how they might be addressed through policy change to increase ministerial receptivity to and capability for a managerial role.

To illustrate the taxonomy it is useful to look at two extreme combinations: the exceptional (low-likelihood) case of a minister being committed to a managerial role but possessing neither knowledge nor skills (the bottom left cell), and the more commonplace (high-likelihood) case of a minister rejecting or evading the managerial role and having neither knowledge nor skills (the bottom right cell). In the first example, the validity of a managerial role is accepted but willingness is not matched with capacity; the suggested remedy is institutionalised support for developing and applying relevant skills (such as strategic management, corporate governance and so on). In the second example, repudiation of the managerial role is reinforced by the way other authorising agents (such as the prime minister, parliament or the media) may look past accountabilities in this area as well as the strong incentives that a minister may have simply to off-load this task-type to others (such as political staffers or departments themselves); the proposed remedies combine skills development and the deployment of more invasive 'choice architecture' (Thaler and Sunstein, 2008) to validate the managerial role for ministers and channel their behaviour along these lines. As Table 4.3 also shows, other variants of the asymmetries can be envisaged and each would be addressed with different combinations of soft skills development and harder procedural motivators.

Table 4.3 The Managerial Role of Ministers: A Taxonomy of Asymmetries

		A/SYMMETRIES OF COMMITMENT (WILLINGNESS)		
		Minister accepts and is committed to a managerial role	Minister feigns commitment to a managerial role	Minister evades or rejects a managerial role
A/SYMMETRIES OF BEHAVIOUR (CAPABILITY)	Minister understands managerial role and has skills	(a) Low. (b) Very few ministers are both committed and able	(a) Low-Medium. (b) Ministerial interests – e.g. promotion – best served by 'optics' (c) Validate role, improve incentives to conform	(a) Medium. (b) No clear accountability incentives to accept role. (c) Validate role, improve incentives to conform
	Minister has neither under-standing of managerial role nor skills	(a) Low (b) Few ministers are likely to combine commitment with no experience (c) Institutionalised support for developing and applying skills	(a) Medium (b) Focus on other ministerial roles – e.g. political – or delegate role to others (c) Institutionalised support for developing and applying skills, stronger incentives to conform	(a) High (b) Accountability incentives confirm minister's attitudes, delegate role to others (c) Validate role, improve incentives to conform, institutionalised support for applying skills

* Each cell sets out: (a) current likelihood of occurrence (b) description of situation and (c) possible options for remedy.

Enabling Ministers to Manage: Scoping Options

So how might the managerial role of ministers be re-engineered within current public management policy design?[19] We expand on some of the remedies identified in Table 4.3 to outline a range of options to enable ministers to manage, that is, to promote greater conformance with the systemic expectations established (the example of which we have been examining is performance control). We draw on developments and thinking from across the Westminster world to sketch out four possible remedies.

The first is *promoting professionalism* in the managerial (or executive) role of ministers. As already noted, 'professionalism' – the combination of qualities connected with trained and/or skilled people – should be distinguished from 'professionalisation', which is often associated negatively with careerism and the rise of a professional political class (see generally Borchert and Zeiss, 2003).[20] The setting of competency standards and the acquisition of the necessary skills can be approached in a number of ways. An obvious means is quite simply through better preparation for office: the use of structured induction and the expansion of formalised 'professional training' of ministers to embrace not only legal and ethical obligations but also expectations about roles that formal guidelines prescribe for the planning and management cycle, such as contained in some cabinet manuals (Pollitt and Bouckaert, 2004: 157; Riddell, Gruhn and Carolan, 2011: 43–50). The training and guidelines could focus on information exchange and performance conversation expected at each stage in the cycle, tailored for the prior experience of ministers. Another, not unrelated, option is to work directly through legislatures to step up the pressure on ministers – as a select group of parliamentarians – to fulfil their offices with regard to standards set by their peers.[21] The greater potential (if not actuality) of minority governments in both New Zealand and Australia makes this viable. An interesting example is the current strengthening of Australian Parliament Codes

---

19 At the outset we referred to the exploratory nature of this chapter as being a type of 'constrained design science' exercise. One self-imposed constraint has been to work within *current* public management policies to identify opportunities for modification. Even though the chapter identifies and questions political system inherencies, by and large, better definition of the 'managerial' role of ministers seeks modifications designed to improve current arrangements. One obvious alternative is to consider significantly more fundamental reform to public management policy settings, something we only touch upon in the fourth of our 'remedies'.

20 The modern conception of professionalism in politics was formulated by Max Weber in terms of 'vocation', distinguishing those who live *for* rather than *off* politics (see Weber, 2004).

21 The argument for enhanced professionalism for politicians, through greater 'self-regulation' of their various accountability relationships with the legislature, is made in the Australian context by Uhr (2005a, 2005b).

of Conduct – as well as the proposed Parliamentary Integrity Commissioner contained in the 2010 parliamentary agreement between the Australian Labor Party and the Greens – specifically to extend chamber oversight to ministerial activities and accountabilities.

A final set of options for this remedy rests with the levers available to prime ministers and comprises options that are particularly challenging because they must confront the political constraints on defining 'ministerial effectiveness'. They include the extension of existing ministerial codes of conduct to embrace redesignated core role descriptions and accountabilities (Australian Government, 2010; see also Uhr, 2005a); more formalised use of performance management by prime ministers to set performance expectations for ministers, encourage skills acquisition through senior and junior minister 'mentoring' arrangements, and actively review ministerial performance (possibly with an eye to including such performance in the allocation of portfolios); and, finally, recognition that considering new conventions for minimum ministerial terms (say three years) may be one way of framing the implicit performance assessment – and stemming the not insignificant costs – associated with 'ministerial churn' (Cleary and Reeves, 2009).[22] That said, we do acknowledge that such a menu of remedies rubs against the deep grain of attitudinal inherencies. Could ministers really accept a job description accompanied by on-the-job training? Perhaps more fundamentally, who would be best placed to conduct such training: past or present ministerial peers, learned academics, respected businesspeople or – perish the thought – senior public servants?

The second remedy – *injecting external experience* – is actually a dual-purpose response to claims of both 'amateurism' (that ministers either can or should not be experts) and 'professionalisation' (the narrowing of career paths for politicians). Westminster conventions – and in Australia, the Constitution (s64) – require ministers to be drawn from members of parliament; the introduction of external experience has usually been a task for party pre-selection or, more directly, appointment to ministers' private offices. However, recent British experimentation with the appointment of cabinet-level and junior ministers from outside parliament – the GOAT ('government of all the talents') appointments – provides one template for introducing 'non-parliamentary expertise' with the specific objective of targeting 'experience in big management tasks' to key portfolios (Young and Hazell, 2011: 15–17; see also Riddell, Gruhn and Carolan, 2011). Certainly, such outside appointments are less difficult in Britain – executive prerogative on the appointment of peerages permits easier passage into the upper house – but there is also comparable experience

---

22 For an empirical 'principal–agent' analysis of the relationship between prime ministerial assessment of ministerial performance and ministerial resignations (or 'turnover'), see Berlinski, Dewan and Dowding (2010).

in Australian state governments of appointing, in the context of whole-of-government strategic planning frameworks, prominent external figures to cabinet committees as a way of bolstering technical expertise in both policy and governance (Government of South Australia, 2007: 43; NSW Government, 2006: 142).

A third remedy is *enforcing governance and managerial responsibilities*. This is really a variant of the second remedy in that it tends to rely on the use of independent expertise to guide ministers in their broader governance obligations. A recent development, particularly within the core executive, is the codification of departmental governance structures that replicate private sector corporate governance guidelines. Again, Britain provides us with an emerging model through the Cameron Coalition government's new requirements for the establishment of departmental boards *chaired by Secretaries of State* (cabinet ministers) and comprising significant membership of external (independent) appointments (Cabinet Office, 2010; HM Treasury and Cabinet Office, 2011). These boards are sentinel developments for three reasons. First, as mentioned, these boards mimic the duties and obligations of corporate 'boards of directors': they are expected to determine 'policy' and 'give advice and support on operational implications'. Second, whilst departmental boards have been operating at least since the mid-2000s (HM Treasury, 2005), the new protocols explicitly reduce civil service membership *and* create a new position of lead non-executive director who will serve as a 'mentor and advisor to the Secretary of State' in their role as chair (HM Treasury and Cabinet Office, 2011: 6–7; McClorey, Quinlan and Gruhn, 2011: 2). Third, to quote McClorey, Quinlan and Gruhn again (2011: 4), perhaps most significantly the arrangements place new demands and obligations on Secretaries of State to:

> influence further the running of their departments and introduce business-like practices. Much of the Boards' work will focus on the monitoring of performance, risk and other technical issues, all of which will demand a deep understanding of organisational change and financial management. In this context, the role of Chairman will be fundamental in driving the content, tone and style of debate at Board meetings.

Whilst the shift to departmental boards has been criticised for creating authority nodes that potentially compete with (rather than enhance and clarify) ministerial responsibility (Wilks, 2007: 457), there is little doubt that the expectations for ministers to engage with organisational management and performance is being taken to a new level. Thus conceived, departmental boards are an instructive example of how the 'architecture of choice' approach could be used to shift role perceptions.

The fourth and final option is exponentially more ambitious: it aims to tackle aspects of political system inherencies – chiefly adversarialism and answerability as a 'culture of blame' – by *establishing external consensus-based accountability structures*. To date the political contest in which ministers compete holds stronger incentives for shaping the behaviour of ministers than the legislated roles and responsibilities they themselves have enacted. This option aims to augment public management policies through targeted cultural change in the wider authorising environment: the focus is on changing behaviours currently driven by perceptions of the political contest by ministers and chief executives (and, by extension, parliament, the media and the general public). Some analysts have described this option as 'breaking the blame game by moving to a more community-based and consensual multi-party approach to improving performance, and as part of that, to make shared arrangements for policy making' (Gill and Hitchener, 2011a: 498; Gill and Hitchener, 2011b). Modification of the authorising environment in this way involves relocating political responsibility for assessing performance to deliberative structures that may be more effective in promoting policy improvement. One model is multi-party accords that set societal goals and performance benchmarks and delegate reporting and monitoring to statutory independent bodies; examples flourish at the sub-national level of government, including the long-lived Oregon Shines strategic performance framework in the United States (Young, 2005) and, closer to home, the Tasmania Together state planning process in Australia (Crowley, 2009), both of which institutionalised whole-of-government performance management with independent administration through 'progress boards'. Whilst highly dependent on political compromise for their establishment, once achieved, changes in these types of institutional settings can, at the very least, signal strong preferences for a more constructive performance dialogue and matching expectations for engagement by politicians.

Conclusion

This chapter has been an exploration of uncharted areas in the design and performance of public management policies in New Zealand and Australia. This had both conceptual and practical objectives. On the first, we have argued that orthodox analysis and design of public management policy is deficient in two key ways: first, policy change directed at bureaucratic structures and behaviours ignores the critical role that ministers must play in making management reforms work; and second, such policy change is commonly designed in ignorance of key inherencies in Westminster-type parliamentary systems that inhibit the necessary behavioural change in politicians. The exploration has been framed by the lens of ministerial role classification in Westminster systems, and has examined the under-conceptualised managerial role that we consider requires ministers to be an integral part of (and not simply a figurehead for) departmental leadership and management.

To meet our practical objectives we contend that defining aspects of public management policy – in particular, performance control practices – are dependent on the managerial role orientation for ministers becoming much more prominent. Using a survey of available – and by necessity proxy – evidence on political executive engagement with performance control practices in New Zealand and Australia, we have suggested that this role of ministers is a 'missing link' in the design of governance structures. In effect, we speak a public management heresy by profiling the normative significance of a managerial role for political executives within Westminster-based government systems like New Zealand, and suggest a number of means for enabling ministers to manage. These include using training and standards-setting to promote professionalism among ministers, exploring ministerial appointments from outside parliament to inject external experience, using governance structures as 'choice architecture' to impose leadership and managerial responsibilities on ministers, and, finally, chipping away at the key inherency of adversarialism by experimenting with consensus-based accountability structures to shift ministerial accountabilities for performance. Each of these options is designed to change the way ministers see their own role, and to promote greater self-awareness in the way ministers send signals to other actors operating within the public management systems they themselves have installed.

Our firm view is that this chapter is only a beginning; it has explored a number of terrains that from any perspective remain disturbingly under-researched and under-conceptualised. These range from dedicated, participant-centred investigation of the role of ministers – and especially the 'executive' role of ministers that was expected under current public management policies to become much more pronounced – to the investigation of the extent to which both parliamentarians and ministers (including their agents, such as ministerial advisers) approach and utilise managerial information as part of these every-day roles. Our understanding is that very few of these critical issues have been investigated in New Zealand (and have been subject to only marginally more scrutiny elsewhere). We concede that these questions will be hard to conceptualise, and the subjects of inquiry even more difficult to pin down for sustained investigation. But they lie at the heart of any consideration of practical ways of enhancing systems of public management and, just perhaps, the real heresy would be continuing to overlook them.

5

Affordability and Sustainability: Tweaking is Not Enough[1]

Bill Ryan

One of the major issues ahead identified by the Future State project was that of fiscal affordability and sustainability (Gill, Pride, Gilbert and Norman, 2010: 34–35, 37). Drawing on the Treasury's 2009 medium-term fiscal outlook, the Future State Stage 1 report noted expectations that the next 40 years will bring a severe fiscal squeeze. Projections in the 2010 fiscal outlook are similar (Treasury, 2011a). When the earlier document was being written, the implications of what has since become known as the global financial crisis of 2007–9 were only just becoming apparent. Since then international growth has continued to be sluggish and public debt has become a major problem in some western European countries such as Greece and Portugal. Major programmes of cutback have been introduced in Britain, and the United States is struggling with the cost of bailouts and the legacy of debt-funded military interventions elsewhere in the world. In New Zealand, the disastrous Christchurch earthquakes of 2010 and 2011 had yet to occur, many costs of which government has to meet directly and indirectly including through the Earthquake Commission, placing even more pressure on New Zealand's short-to-medium-term fiscal position. These matters are dealt with in the 2010 version of the Treasury fiscal outlook.

According to the Future State report, while fiscal constraint will need to be maintained in years ahead, the New Zealand structural deficit will likely be modest by international standards. This is because New Zealand has a strong Crown balance sheet and low levels of public indebtedness relative to comparable countries. Demand and supply factors, however, will maintain pressure. On the demand side, demographic changes due to an ageing population will put upwards pressure on superannuation and healthcare costs. The complexity of aged care is also likely to mean a need for other types of services. Supply issues include the relative cost of government services that rely on skilled labour, for which wage rates tend to rise at a rate faster than those for unskilled labour (Gill, Pride, Gilbert and Norman, 2010: 37).

---

1   My thanks to Derek Gill and Chris Eichbaum for comments on earlier drafts.

In these global circumstances, the need for fiscal consolidation is recognised both in New Zealand and internationally. According to the Organisation of Economic Cooperation and Development (OECD, 2011: 33–34), most member countries are committed to rebalancing public income and expenditure and reducing public debt relative to GDP and will do so for the foreseeable future (OECD, 2011: 88–89). This will include reducing expenditure in those parts of the public sector that are seen to be wasteful or inefficient. There is public concern in many countries about unemployment or wage effects of reducing the public sector, and citizens continue to demand increased services delivered according to increasingly higher standards. These issues take us back to fundamental questions about the purpose of government in society. As the OECD (2011: 33–34, emphasis added) notes:

> Achieving fiscal consolidation has triggered a public discussion on *what should be the appropriate role of government in society and the economy* . . . Consequently, sound, sustainable public finances will result from an agreement between governments, citizens and businesses about what level of services the government should provide (and to whom) and how the public will pay for them.

In an equally portentous remark, the Future State report cast doubt on whether conventional ways of addressing major issues will be up to the task. Gill, Pride, Gilbert and Norman (2010: 37) declare:

> Responding to this challenge by 'doing more with less' will not be sufficient. The public policy challenge is to develop the step changes in policy design and delivery that address the drivers so the trajectories of spending are reduced.

They illustrate their argument by referring to the 'race to the bottom' in law and order policy. This is a tough-on-crime approach that stresses punishment. Crime rates in New Zealand have been stable or dropping, yet incarceration rates have been rising and are now high on an international scale, with attendant costs in running the justice and corrections systems. The report authors argue that, rather than focusing on apprehension and punishment in relation to the relatively small numbers of people involved in crime, the focus should be breaking the cycles of dysfunction that cause the problems in the first place. This they refer to as 'changing trajectories': putting aside what has been done in the past and following a different, innovative path, something at which New Zealand has previously shown itself to be adept (Gill, Pride, Gilbert and Norman, 2010: 37).

Two points from this discussion are central to the rest of this chapter. The first is that 'doing more with less' will not be sufficient and that step change is required ('tweaking is not enough'). The second is that a collective debate is needed to reconsider the democratically agreed role of government in relation to society and the economy and hence the level and purposes of government expenditure, so that the nature of the step change required can be decided.

Government's Approach to Affordability and Sustainability[2]

Three recent speeches – by the Finance Minister to the Australia and New Zealand School of Government (English, 2010) and to the Institute of Public Administration New Zealand (English, 2011b), and the Statement to Parliament delivered by the Prime Minister in February (Key, 2011) – draw an explicit link between government expenditure and New Zealand's economic performance in weathering the global economic difficulties and the one-off effects of the Christchurch earthquakes. Government expenditure is said to be too high and, given present trends, unsustainable. Government will also have to deal with the approaching demographic bulge, which is expected to cause health and aged-care expenditure to rise dramatically. Strategies for making savings are being put in place, including controlling the level of public sector spending relative to GDP and net debt ('providing better and smarter public services'). Government's immediate concern is to return to budgetary surplus by the middle of this decade. According to the Finance Minister, 'Public spending restraint is no temporary aberration. It is effectively permanent' (English, 2011b).

What has been proposed? Do the initiatives in relation to public sector performance promise significant savings? The following discussion comes from a public management perspective, not economics. It does not consider debates within the economics discipline regarding the optimal level of government expenditure relative to national production, or the rights and wrongs of reducing (or increasing) government spending in difficult economic times. Some schools of economic thought argue it should be minimised. Others argue the opposite (e.g., compare Kibblewhite, 2011, with NZCTU, 2010; see Buchanan and Musgrave, 1999; also Hall, 2010; Hood, Emmerson and Dixon, 2009). This chapter focuses instead on what might be said about affordability and sustainability from a public management perspective (including organisational and management theory) that is sensitive to socio-political considerations. Later it looks at one set of ideas being offered by some economists working inside public management that illustrates what going beyond 'tweaking' to a 'step change' might look like – what sort of possibilities might need to be considered.

Government has the view that the present circumstances provide a classic 'burning platform' (Pollitt, 2011) to which it is responding. It wants to 'rebalance' the economy and get the budget back into surplus by reducing government debt (acknowledged by government to be lower than that of many OECD countries

2 Parts of this and the following section first appeared in Ryan (2011b) published in *Policy Quarterly*.

but, like many, trending upwards since 2008; e.g., OECD, 2011: 65).[3] The early public justification was built on familiar political rhetoric: 'The previous government's decision to massively ramp up spending in the 2000s left behind a large, structural deficit, and a bloated public sector that by 2008 was crowding out the competitive sectors of the economy' (English, 2011b). Government's solution will be 'building better outcomes from public services by being clear about New Zealanders' priorities, by minimizing waste, scaling up what works, getting rid of what doesn't, and generally focusing our investment on changes that bring results' (Key, 2011: 12). According to the Minister of Finance (English, 2011b), these will come in three areas: clear priorities, achieving high-quality services and reducing waste.

Government acknowledges its obligation to maintain the core functions of government but intends reducing government expenditure relative to the size of the New Zealand economy. Its general (if cryptic) position is that 'This is not a time we can afford to indulge in a whole lot of "nice-to-haves". . . [that] come at the expense of necessities and at the expense of fairness to people with more need' (English, 2011b).

Government's present priorities are vulnerable children, welfare reform, education, housing, health and accident compensation, justice, law and order, and public safety. Within that, allocation decisions 'belong to the Government itself, consistent with its political mandate and accountability to the New Zealand public. So the Government will continue to make decisions about what to stop increasing, scale back, or stop doing altogether' (English, 2011b).

The language here is also familiar to those involved in public sector reform over the last 20–30 years. Government says it wants a modern, responsive public service that provides good value for money. In relation to service delivery, it expects to see the same level of innovation and responsiveness it believes is found in the market economy. Public service agencies are said to be risk averse. In order to feel the keen edge of competition, contestability will be increased. More services will be provided by non-government organisations, iwi and private sector providers.

Government plans to halt the recent increase in the number of policy positions in Wellington[4] (characterised as 'bureaucracy' and therefore, by implication, wasteful), and to put more resources into frontline delivery, reducing the complexity confronting clients of services and making delivery seamless. This

3 For a fuller picture of trends of all OECD countries from 1996–2009, see <http://stats.oecd.org/Index.aspx?DataSetCode=NAAG_2010> (accessed 26 September 2011).

4 In fact, the subsequent Review of Expenditure on Policy Advice (2010: 12) found that most of this increase had occurred in the Ministry of Foreign Affairs and Trade (MFAT). If MFAT's policy advice expenditure is removed from the total estimated cost of policy advice, nominal growth was approximately 16 per cent (-0.6 per cent real).

applies particularly to transactional services delivered to New Zealanders in their homes and businesses. Servicelink, an integrated delivery initiative being developed by Inland Revenue, the Department of Internal Affairs and the Ministry of Social Development, is held up as an example.

As reported in the 2011 Fiscal Strategy Report, the 2011 Budget projected savings of $5.2 billion over five years, directing $4 billion of these savings to new initiatives, mostly frontline services in health and education. Some savings will come from reducing public sector operational costs although most will come from adjustments to the policy framework, plus changes to KiwiSaver, Working for Families and student loans, the costs of which have recently escalated. The Treasury forecasts a return to fiscal surplus in 2014/15 with increasing surpluses in following years. Core Crown net debt is projected to peak at less than 30 per cent of GDP and to decline steadily beyond 2015 to be no higher than 20 per cent by the early 2020s (see Figure 5.1). Treasury believes that this will be achieved despite absorbing the cost of the Canterbury earthquakes (Treasury, 2011a).

Figure 5.1. Core Crown Net Debt

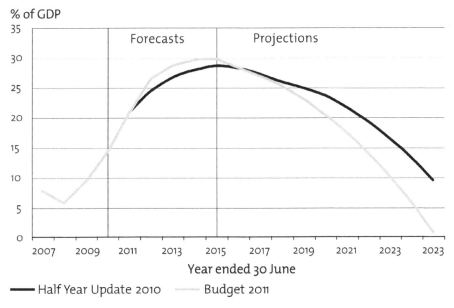

Source: Treasury (2011a: 50).

Several initiatives to rationalise public sector operational (not policy) costs are already well established or getting underway. In early 2009, government imposed a cap on staff numbers in core government administration (Wellington) and gave priority to frontline service delivery staff. In August 2010, it also set up the Review of Expenditure on Policy Advice 'to provide advice on the cost and quality of policy advice, as well as the alignment between policy expenditure and the Government's priorities'.[5] Attention is being focused on the high number of central government departments and ministries compared with other jurisdictions (for details, see English and Ryall, 2011). Mergers have already commenced although, so far, these have been relatively minor. The more general concern is that there are 'too many departments and ministries', although government is stressing that structural change is only part of the answer. Work has already begun on rationalising back-office functions, common services and processes (Better Administrative and Support Services, BASS). Here, the 'aggressive' harnessing of technology and collaboration in provision of common and corporate services (e.g., between Treasury, the Department of the Prime Minister and Cabinet, and the State Services Commission) is expected to contribute significant savings. Overall, according to the Minister of Finance, 'This direction is likely to lead to fewer government agencies over time, to stronger governance across agencies where it is needed and for agencies to be more frequently based around common services and processes' (English, 2011b).

One mechanism for achieving saving is tight new operating allowances at a maximum of $1.1 billion a year, reducing annually to 2014/15 (Treasury, 2011a: 43). Government has set the overall goal but is asking chief executives to make the 'key savings decisions'. The same applies to the so-called efficiency dividend. This is an annual claw-back but is differentiated according to agency size. Organisations with total output expenses over $200 million are being subject to a 6 per cent efficiency dividend with 3 per cent applying to those under that line. This device is intended to drive on-going efficiency and productivity improvements and to generate savings consistent with the four-year budget plan (Treasury, 2011b).

Another mechanism is the Performance Improvement Framework (PIF). Described as 'a joint central agency initiative to help senior leaders drive performance improvement across the State Services',[6] PIF was introduced in September 2010 as an evaluation of practices, systems and processes in each organisation. It is intended to work as much through self-reflection as through external, expert-led assessment. In relation to PIF and the efficiency measures, government has praised chief executives for the work done so far. It continues to emphasise it is 'open to ideas and propositions from the public sector' and that it 'wants to work with public servants' (English, 2011b).

5   See <http://www.treasury.govt.nz/statesector/policyexpenditurereview> (accessed 26 September 2011).
6   See <http://www.ssc.govt.nz/pif> (accessed 26 September 2011).

Savings, Efficiencies and Cutbacks as the Path to Affordability

Economy, efficiency and cutback are familiar strategies for keeping government affordable, with renewed attempts in recent years spurred by every new perturbation. The idea that austerity might be permanent is relatively new. If so, are these time-honoured tactics adequate to the task? In truth, academic research on their effects and effectiveness is limited (Pandey, 2010; Pollitt, 2010, 2011). More than 30 years ago, Levine opened up questions about cutback management and organisational decline. His interest lay in the 'great questions of political economy and the more earthly problems of managing public organizations' (Levine, in Pandey, 2010). Throughout the 1980s academics developed an interest in the field but then it waned. Recently, tightening economic conditions have re-ignited interest (Pandey, 2010), but the best that can be done by public management academics, as Pandey (2010: 564) suggests, is to ask 'somewhat inconvenient questions that get swept under the rug to accommodate seemingly more pressing issues'.

Recent experience has emphasised that savings are 'ferociously difficult' to achieve (Pollitt, 2010: 9). Even under the strong anti-government and privatisation agenda of Britain's Thatcher government, aggregate spending was maintained. A recent comparison, undertaken by Hood, Emmerson and Dixon (2009) of cuts in Britain in the 1920s (led by the 'Geddes Axe' committee) and the 1970s–80s, confirms the difficulty in modern times of achieving the same level of reductions that were gained in earlier years. The work undertaken by the Future State team looking at the changing role of the New Zealand state during the past 20 years (i.e., reductions in government activity following public sector reform) came to a similar view. Gill, Pride, Gilbert and Norman (2010: 64) examined various dimensions of government in its roles as consumer, employer, producer, investor, borrower, spender and taxer, and concluded that:

> Overall – despite rhetoric about the New Zealand revolution – the size and role of the state has been remarkably stable in New Zealand. The one notable exception to this statement was the state reducing its role as a producer of market goods and services (through privatisation).

Trade-offs are an inevitable part of expenditure reductions. Conventional economics wisdom says that reductions are needed in circumstances like those of the present and the savings need to be considerable. But most government spending is on transfers and social programmes, with a relatively small proportion spent on public service operations. The greatest potential for savings therefore lies in cutting programmes, but this can be electorally unpopular. Reducing operational expenditure is more electorally acceptable but the potential pool is small relative to total public expenditure and the level of savings required. Moreover, there are practical limits to what can be cut out of the public sector since a certain level of operations and capability must be maintained in order to ensure that government even functions – to say nothing of what might be needed in the future as a result of the demographic bulge. There is, in effect, a 'bottom line' for effectiveness.

So what approaches are available to governments? Pollitt has created a framework focused on broad strategies for managing 'during financial austerity', as shown in Table 5.1. What can be said about these strategies? Table 5.1 provides a summary of what is known. The following discussion elaborates on these points and adds others.

Table 5.1. Three Savings Strategies

Approach	Advantages	Disadvantages
'Cheese-slicing'	Sounds egalitarian ('everyone must meet his share'). Ministers avoid directly choosing which programmes will be most hurt. Detailed decisions delegated to programme specialists who probably know what they are doing (and can be blamed if their decisions turn out to be unpopular or hurtful).	Programme specialists may make politically unpopular choices. And/or they may make self-interested choices which hurt effectiveness whilst protecting service providers (themselves). May also incentivise budget holders to pad their budgets so that there will be 'fat' to be cut next time round.
Efficiency gains	Sounds less threatening/more technical ('doing more with less'). So it may be claimed that savings can be made without too much pain.	Usually requires considerable innovation – organisational and technological changes which may not work, or may not work for some time. Probably will not yield enough by itself to correct the present fiscal imbalances.
Centralised priority-setting	Looks more strategic and leaves politicians directly in control. Enables the government to protect the most effective programmes (if they have reliable data on effectiveness)	Ministers become visibly and directly responsible for painful choices. And, unless they consult carefully they may make choices with consequences they do not fully foresee, but they are unlikely to understand the internal complexities of the services which are being cut.

Source: Pollitt (2010: 13).

Across-the-board cuts, referred to by Pollitt as 'cheese-slicing', have a long history. The attraction of this approach is that it can achieve small but significant reductions in expenditure in a relatively short period of time. It also sounds comparatively fair in that all are expected to share equally in the burden. From a political perspective, a government can appear to be taking strong action in the face of crisis and avoid taking responsibility for cuts to particular programmes by leaving detailed cuts to public managers. From a democratic perspective, however, this is problematic. Public managers making those decisions are not themselves directly accountable and may make managerial decisions that serve organisational or system interests rather than those of clients. Further, across-the-board cuts do not differentiate between well-managed, lean organisational units and poorly managed ones with 'fat'. This means that efficient and effective programmes are treated the same as inefficient and/or ineffective ones that can absorb the reductions (the same can apply to efficiency dividends). In fact, cheese-slicing creates incentives for managers to 'pad' their organisations and programmes so that the next time that approach is applied they have reserves that can be cut (Pollitt, 2010).

Centralised priority-setting is the opposite of across-the-board cuts. Programmes known to be effective are retained and prioritised, whereas those that are not are either dropped or scaled back. From both political and democratic perspectives, this approach has benefits. It appears to the electorate and the public service as more strategic (although not perhaps to providers and clients whose programmes are stopped). It leaves ministers in control and accountable and enables government to retain those programmes it favours or believes can be justified. The downside from the ministers' perspective is that it makes them transparently responsible for choices that may be unpopular with significant parts of the electorate. It may not have been feasible to consult widely in their preparation and so the cuts will be a shock to those affected. There may also be unanticipated consequences, in terms of impacts both on other programmes and on overall client outcomes (Pollitt, 2010).

The biggest difficulties with this approach, however, may be technical. Central to making it work is evaluation of the range of programmes under consideration that is both good and extensive. According to the OECD (2009b), not many governments have such information. In New Zealand, with so little evaluation conducted (Ryan, 2011a), the situation is even worse. Equally, prioritisation tools such as matrices and filters are relatively under-developed (Pollitt, 2010). Otherwise, governments use political criteria such as electoral popularity on which to base their decisions. Technical analysts may recoil from this approach but, because government will eventually be held accountable by citizens for their decisions in public debate and elections, it is legitimate. In terms of public value and societal well-being, however, there is no guarantee that the results will be effective or equitable.

Strategies for Improving Economy and Efficiency

'Efficiency gains' sound less controversial but, in fact, are more difficult. Many in the general population have a view that bureaucracy and the public service are inherently inefficient and wasteful such that partisan accusations are all too easy to make – destructively so since a well-run bureaucracy is an excellent instrument for achieving certain types of routine and regulatory public functions. Moreover, when ministers demand new levels of efficiency, particularly when economic times are difficult, the professional pride of public managers in producing maximum value from the resources put at their disposal also comes to the fore and they take on the challenge. Actually, they have little option since protest would be seen as self-interest or unresponsiveness. From the ministerial angle, demanding efficiency gains, as noted in Table 5.1, sounds less threatening to citizens than, say, across-the-board cuts, and carries a note of careful technical consideration that will likely win votes. However, deeper analysis that draws on managerial and organisational research suggests the potential for such cuts to bring about clear and positive benefits is more problematic now than it might once have seemed. 'If–but' considerations abound.

Economy and efficiency (including productivity) drives are obvious responses to fiscal difficulties. From any perspective, inefficiency and waste should be eliminated and the freed-up resources saved or put to more productive use. As Pollitt (2010) notes, however, such crusades have been a constant fact of life in public sectors for the last 30 years and more. It is probable that most if not all of the 'low-hanging fruit' has been picked. That there might still be considerable quantities of redundancy and waste lying around as suitable candidates for cutting-out seems implausible. The more searching out has already been undertaken, the more the law of diminishing returns seems likely to apply. The potential now for significant savings achievable via efficiency drives, relative to the aggregate costs of running a government, is likely to be marginal.[7] Affordability, therefore, is unlikely to be addressed significantly as a result.

A similar point can be made in relation to demands for increased productivity. Service work is notoriously resistant to productivity improvements (see, for example, OECD, 2005b), but staff ceilings, staff reductions and work intensification have all been tried in New Zealand as elsewhere (e.g., UK Audit Office, 2006). Again, with so much already achieved over recent years, it is unlikely there are many undiscovered pockets. High workloads and long hours exacerbated by short-staffing due to staff ceilings are everyday realities for

---

7   As may prove to be the case with BASS.

many in the public sector (e.g., for women, see Donnelly, Proctor-Thomson and Plimmer, in press). This suggests that work rates are already high and that further intensification would be destructive, leading to increased sick and stress leave, burn-out and staff departures (Battaglio and Condrey, 2009; Pandey, 2010) – indeed, continued expectations of staff reductions and capping are already creating these negative effects. Industrial strife may also follow, particularly if managers and staff perceive that ministers have reneged on the bargain that structures relationships between ministers and officials (Kelman, 2006; Pandey, 2010). Moreover, in New Zealand policy organisations, a significant amount of everyday work for policy staff involves servicing the daily needs of cabinet and ministers in their executive and parliamentary roles (Review of Expenditure on Policy Advice, 2010). Ministers are unlikely to want dramatic cutbacks here.

The credibility of still expecting significant savings from efficiency drives is therefore doubtful. They can also be damaging, testing the popularity of the government and system legitimacy in several ways. If they lead to service reductions (e.g., reducing hours of service, distribution networks or the numbers of local outlets), the tolerance of citizens and the legitimacy of the government can be tested – quite apart from equity issues raised by impacts on those least able to afford continued access or to resist (see also Pandey, 2010). Sound evidence and plausible reasoning are needed for service reductions and other cutbacks to be accepted by the electorate. If communicated openly and effectively, citizens and officials may accept the adjustments for the period of time they are required, but they will not if the reasoning appears implausible or unjustifiable, particularly if they offend a general sense of egalitarianism. Equally, reductions and cutbacks driven by ideology, populism or language games – rhetorical references to 'bloat', 'waste' and 'bureaucracy' are little more than 'boo-hurrah' words (see Ayer, 1936, on 'emotivism' in language) – may resonate with some elites and voters. They will be resented, however, by service users and public officials, especially where inefficiencies have previously been eliminated. Dutiful service to the government of the day by officials may continue, but with declining productivity due to work intensification and without much commitment to performance improvement, thereby countering other savings strategies. It is an unwise government that ignores or undermines organisational and staff health and safety in the present and their capability in the future, and one-off savings drives now may bring about short-term economic gain but also long-term substantive damage. Economy and efficiency (including productivity) are eternal organisational values but should be applied as normal ways of working and driven from within, as part of professional public management, not occasional bush-beating expeditions driven from without.

Mergers: Consolidation or Collaborative Governance?

A particular issue arises in New Zealand regarding the number of public organisations that appear to be comparatively large – or, to be more precise, to be made up of a large number of small organisations and a handful of large ones. *Prima facie*, savings might be possible if the number was to be reduced. If cost reductions are the question, mergers might also be part of the answer. However, this is a difficult issue fraught with risks. High human, financial, capability and industrial costs can follow mergers such that wise governments are inclined to avoid them (OECD, 2005b; see also Gill and Norman, this volume) – as the present government seems to recognise (English, 2011).

The simple fact is that New Zealand appears to be in a bind. 'The New Zealand model of public management' in the 1980s and 1990s broke up the existing large, multi-faceted government bureaucracies to create a larger number of smaller, single-purpose organisations. As a result, this country has significantly more separate and specialised organisations in the public sector than most comparable countries – as the present government has noted with alarm (English, 2010). It would seem to be commonsensical that high levels of separate silos mean separate and distinct corporate and common service units, information systems, senior managers and chief executives, more than would otherwise be required (or available) to run a public sector the size of New Zealand's. That said, the Future State report noted that the counterfactual is unclear. Some polities such as those in Scandinavian countries with significant numbers of separate public organisations and relatively high levels of annual public expenditure relative to GDP also demonstrate strong economic growth (Gill, Pride, Gilbert and Norman, 2010: 30). The sheer number, therefore, may be less important than the relationship between vision, strategy, structure and function according to which a society is governed – which should be the principle applied to such considerations in New Zealand.

Nonetheless, organisational and strategic barriers created by the present level of fragmentation and separation, and hence the costs involved in negotiating them, have been acknowledged in New Zealand for over a decade (Ministerial Advisory Group, 2001; see also Schick, 1996). The time, money and resources required to achieve strategic, cross-government solutions (and the costs to clients traversing them in accessing services) are likely to be higher than in relatively non-fragmented systems. Government has accepted arguments along these lines and, as a result, in March 2010 and 2011, announced some mergers and, in August 2011, further disestablishments and transfers of functions.[8] Other decisions of

8 For an overview, see the press release by the Minister for State Services, Tony Ryall on 11 August 2011, <http://www.beehive.govt.nz/release/reduction-state-agencies-confirmed> (accessed 26 September 2011). It is interesting to note that these decisions will result in total estimated savings of $92 million in the four years from 2012/13 (after the transitions are

this type may follow.

However, the 'but' remains. As Norman and Gill (this volume) point out, there has been too much reliance on restructuring in New Zealand sometimes as a substitute for resolving fundamental issues that go more to matters of practice, behaviour and values. Further, there is no guarantee that mergers in and of themselves will produce major savings in the short term anyway; in fact, savings may be only limited and the break-even point well into the future. As is well known, the direct costs associated with mergers can be significant, to say nothing of indirect and consequential costs, downtime, loss of morale and reduced productivity over the time that organisations are being combined. Further, if restructuring is thought of as a means of achieving more efficient whole-of-government solutions, lack of co-operation and collaboration in the public sector is just as evident *within* some organisations (between, say, branches or units) as it is *between* organisations; mergers might therefore internalise the problems of fragmentation without necessarily solving them. Anyway, assuming that organisations represent necessary and/or desired government functions (there should, after all, be a necessary connection between the elements of a government's vision and the structure of the public sector – the latter should follow the former), these still have to be conducted regardless of the particular configuration of the machinery of government. If core activities still need to be funded, then the only current costs that might be saved are those arising out of dealing with fragmentation when attempting to integrate and create whole-of-government solutions. These may be significant, but not of the order that government might need to keep government affordable according to the Treasury outlook.

Mergers, however, could be an old-fashioned solution. It is likely that public sectors in the future will be more like complex adaptive systems based on web-like structures and processes (networks), rather than (at best) centre-line systems built on cybernetic principles as at present (Bovaird, 2008). If so, mergers might be less essential in preparing for the future than creating integrative, collaborative mechanisms that combine not just levels of government and multiple public sector organisations under collective, whole-of-government goals, but also the multitude of community and private sector organisations involved in policy development and implementation. In other words, the future is likely to be the world of 'governance' being discussed by some leading-edge public management writers (e.g., Kooiman, 2003; Rhodes, 1997; for more on this see Ryan, this volume). These ideas, however, are still only 'ideas'. Notwithstanding their emergence from practice, their constituent theories, concepts, models and tools

---

complete). Ongoing savings thereafter are estimated to be $22 million per annum. These are not trivial savings but are quite small compared with the magnitude of the government's savings programme.

are still underdeveloped. Considerable work is required well into the future to bring them to fruition. They do not stand, therefore, as answers to immediate fiscal concerns.

Moreover, New Zealand would face particular challenges in moving in these directions. The legislative and conventional underpinnings of our public management system are founded on divided ministerial responsibilities, on single and vertical organisations, and on competition. The foundational changes required to move to a collaborative governance future would be very considerable indeed and, in the short-to-medium term, would require more, not less, government expenditure. This is not an argument for not taking on this idea but for recognising the nature and extent of the challenges involved should it be taken up.

Innovation: Is Tweaking Enough?

As noted in Table 5.1, another catch cry for reforming governments is 'innovation', based on the tacit assumption that it leads to greater efficiency and effectiveness (e.g., UK Audit Office, 2006). Not much is known about how innovation occurs in the public sector[9] (Hartley, 2005; Pollitt, 2011). It demands a willingness to take risks. A degree of organisational slack also helps. So does an atmosphere of trust, an appetite for experimentation and a culture of learning. Conversely, budgetary constraints, greater work pressures and staff lay-offs squeeze out reserves, discourage risk-taking, lessen trust and reduce the tolerance for failure (for overviews, see Pandey, 2010; and Pollitt, 2010). They can force organisations backwards into mechanistic structures and cultures. Cuts can also reduce the capacity of organisations to provide effective and publicly valuable service delivery, something that motivates many public servants (Pandey, 2010). Pollitt (2011) notes that recent expenditure reductions imposed on UK local authorities led to safeguarding of core services and wiped out innovations and recent initiatives. Efficiency and innovation are both part of public management but, in difficult times, achieving one can counteract the other.

That said, outcome-oriented public officials – those focused most of all on achieving good outcomes for clients – sometimes continue to innovate, despite the system they work in and even when resources are constrained. Examples of this behaviour were clearly apparent in research conducted recently in New Zealand (Eppel, Gill, Lips and Ryan, 2008). Innovation is risky and most of these public entrepreneurs and their fellow travellers felt obliged to work under the radar in

---

9   Some work was done in the central agencies following the Review of the Centre but does not seem to be available on the public record or on central agency websites.

the initial stages. More to the point, generalising or scaling up the conditions of success they stumbled upon or created would most likely be expensive in the setting-up and development stages. It would be courageous guardian angels (senior managers) who would approve and authorise such arrangements while cost structures are under pressure. In short, genuine innovation does occur, but is not motivated by or likely to lead to significant savings – in the short term, anyway.

In fact, innovations in service development and delivery are being touted elsewhere as potential affordability measures, not via toughening of quasi-market methods or reassertion of top-down controls upon which NPM was based ('one more shove'), or cheese-slicing, prioritising or efficiency drives, but something very different. Signs of these new ways are apparent in Britain in talk of localism, mutualism and social enterprise underpinning the Conservative government's 'Big Society' agenda. They also appear in notions such as 'radical efficiency' (e.g., Gillison, Horne and Baeck, 2010; see also Hartley, 2005, for a wider view) being developed by some think tanks in that country (and publishing their work through the National Endowment for Science, Technology and the Arts, NESTA). These types of ideas surfaced first in 'third-way' approaches to governing (Giddens, 1994) adopted by the Blair Labour government but that are now being extended – perhaps paradoxically – by the new Conservative government (on 'red Tories' and their search for progressive policies, see Blond, 2010). 'Third-way' thinking tried to find a middle way between socialist and *laissez-faire* approaches, integrating economy and state, in contrast to seeing them as opposed. Creations such as radical efficiency, if adopted, might achieve two purposes at one stroke. The total call on public resources (public expenditure and public debt relative to GDP) could be reduced by relying more on civic resources (social and human capital) to achieve mandated policy goals: in short, this would mean more community-based governance. Equally, social capital would be strengthened and the new governing arrangements legitimated by a citizenry participating in the creation and maintenance of those arrangements.

In this respect, radical efficiency is worth examining in closer detail, if only as an example of its key principle; if austerity is now permanent, savings can no longer be achieved by tweaking the existing system – as both Giddens and Blond and the authors of the Future State project pointed out. More fundamental change is required. I explore it not to suggest it provides 'the answer' to affordability questions, but because it illustrates a kind of forward-looking, innovative thinking that might be worth canvassing in New Zealand. In doing so, I note too that radical efficiency is consistent with other ideas about public management in the future that are discussed elsewhere in this volume, so its prescriptions may have some degree of prescience.

Radical Innovation Where Tweaking is Not Enough

The value of radical efficiency (e.g., Gillison, Horne and Baeck, 2010; see also Bunt, Harris and Westlake, 2010) lies mostly in its acceptance of the need for fiscal constraint now and in the future and its determination to rethink the terms of the debate. It also makes clever use of the work of the economist Schumpeter (1943). One well-known aspect of that author's work deals with periods of transformation in private markets following a period of crisis brought about by 'creative destruction' of the old. New forms emerge through and because of destruction of the past, initially in small ways by local entrepreneurs but growing to reshape the industry or economic sector in which they are involved.

The radical efficiency authors have extracted key principles from a range of case studies drawn from around the world which, they say, demonstrate the power and foresight of local innovation in the face of system constraints. Practice, not theory, is their source. Gillison, Horne and Baeck (2010: 2) conclude:

> In the short term, radical efficiency can help to tackle the unprecedented financial pressures in public services – evidence from our case studies suggest savings of between 20 per cent and 60 per cent are possible, alongside better outcomes. If the UK can realise the potential for radical efficiency that we have seen in cities and states around the world then this would amount to both huge savings for government and better outcomes for citizens.

Governing in the future will not be solely the Fordist-styled production-, outputs- and performance-focused approach to public management now dominant in Britain (like New Zealand), or based around standardised services delivered nationally and managed by central government, whether provided directly or contracted out ('standardised welfare state for mass [passive] consumption'; Gillison, Horne and Baeck, 2010: 2–10). This model, say the radical efficiency authors, is at its limits. It can no longer be tweaked sufficiently to meet the economic challenges of the future. What is needed, they argue, is a paradigm shift[10] in the way in which ministers, officials and citizens think anew about public problems, solutions, insights, customers, suppliers and resources. Radical efficiency is about generating new ways of conceptualising 'services' that achieve genuine gains in their value and efficiency: in essence, seeing them as production and not consumption. Localism (in the sense of localised variations created within an overarching national, strategic framework) and a different relationship between central

---

10 I argue in chapter 3 of this volume that the future will involve not a substitution of one paradigm by another but by context-dependent choices between bureaucratic, market and community approaches to public management.

government, local government, civic associations and social capital must be the base on which a new approach is built.

So how are these savings to be achieved? Their answer is emphatic but not straight-forward, parts of which challenge conventional economic thinking. 'For some', say Bunt, Harris and Westlake (2010: 38):

> the simple answer is to open up many more state-delivered public services to much greater private competition – to create private-dominated markets in public services. But a Schumpeterian-inspired analysis of innovation in public services actually points to a more fundamental issue than types of providers, namely the design of the 'market' in public services. Schumpeterian-style progress is unlikely to occur unless providers are in effect able to change the rules of provision and the 'market' is designed in such a way that it encourages and rewards the replacement of less effective approaches by new and better approaches.

Previous attempts to cut costs have focused largely on achieving marginal efficiency gains within existing service delivery models, thereby reinforcing incumbent approaches rather than stimulating radical ideas for service redesign. These have included streamlining administration, resource sharing, cutting services, reducing or stopping expenditure on some categories of clients (e.g., low priority or wealthy clients), or delaying or cancelling planned expenditure (e.g., asset or infrastructure renewal or expansion). None of these, however, will any longer produce the level of government expenditure reduction needed to meet the immediate or long-term fiscal challenges, including increasing demands for services (e.g., with the predicted demographic bubble, services for the aged). What is needed is long-term transformation (Bunt, Harris and Westlake, 2010: 6–12).

First, government – central government in particular – has to develop new ways of repurposing and redirecting resources so that allocations and commissions enable rather than inhibit the new to emerge (Bunt, Harris and Westlake, 2010: 36). It has to 'let go' and instead of managing top-down, learn how to set agreed, overall national outcomes then create conditions wherein local leaders who are 'committed, passionate and open-minded who may come from anywhere', including those in and connected with local government and civil society, can innovate in ways that are appropriate for the local setting (Bunt, Harris and Westlake, 2010: 22–29). The 'Total Place' pilots in Britain are identified as a good example (see also, HM Treasury, 2010; for a Total Place pilot built on radical efficiency, see NHS Croydon and Croydon Council, 2010). Instead of wringing minor efficiencies out of existing systems that are 'legitimised by history rather than need' (Gillison, Horne and Baeck, 2010: 11), central government must let local public entrepreneurs or providers, or even clients themselves, acting as their own providers, rethink the problem as did, for example, the officials and civic leaders in Croydon. The idea is to start with the policy goals specified for clients ('quality of life') – noting that clients may be communities, groups or individuals – and then to work backwards to what is needed, rather than starting with the dead weight of what already exists and considering how to modify it (Bunt, Harris and Westlake, 2010: 30–37).

'Radical efficiency' also presumes 'co-production' with clients (see also Alford, 2009; Boyle and Harris, 2009). If, in solving the problem, clients individually and collectively are reconceptualised as 'producers' rather than 'consumers', and also as active agents, and their communities, neighbourhoods and families are treated as partners (Boyle and Harris, 2009), then the design and funding of means to achieve public policy outcomes look very different ('work with the grain and the spirit of families, friends and neighbours'; Bunt, Harris and Westlake, 2010: 38–44). Defining clients in these terms is close to the sociological notion of 'agency' (conceptualising individuals in relation to structures; e.g., Giddens, 1984) and the idea of 'strength-based' approaches to social development[11] (e.g., Saleebey, 2008) – and can also be associated with early intervention and prevention. According to radical efficiency advocates, combining these principles will lead to more effective, more appropriate and ultimately cheaper ways of solving complex problems than are possible in the present.

It is worth noting in passing that the radical efficiency authors demand a high level of rigour and enquiry in understanding human needs, developing new kinds of strategies to deal with them and evaluating the efforts to date (learning and evaluation). In that way, ongoing formative approaches to knowledge (rather than formalistic *ex ante* analysis or *post hoc* evaluation) enable understanding and management of ongoing risks and not simply their avoidance (Bunt, Harris and Westlake, 2010: 45–54; see also Eppel, Turner and Wolf, this volume).

'Savings' therefore, in one sense, refer to expenditure reductions made possible by eliminating old programmes and services in favour of redefined, more targeted ones that draw resources from a wider range of sources, thereby reducing the relative share that needs to be contributed by government. More effective services that achieve their goals first time or prevent the problem arising in the first place would obviate the need for remedial or alternative services and the costs associated with them. This is a reasonably conventional understanding of 'savings' and how they might be achieved. A more complex appreciation comes from reconceptualising our thinking about total public value, where it comes from and how it is constituted (Moore, 1995; see also Kelly, Mulgan and Muers, 2002). If clients are defined as partners and the resources they bring to the relationship as more than money, then, immediately, the array of economic, political, technological, social, cultural and human forms of capital to which

---

11 For an example, see the Māori potential framework used by Te Puni Kōkiri.

they have access and of which they are a part, become available as resources for use (and reuse) in the policy process. They then become 'inputs' into the process. 'Supply' and the 'market' are constituted in different terms and would operate according to different dynamics. Moreover, the end result, the outcome, may well be achievement of the particular policy goal sought by government but may also include definite increases in the stocks of human and social capital maintained by clients and which accumulate across the society as a whole (to say nothing of the public value derived from legitimising the new forms of governance; see Bennington and Moore, 2011). The strength, resilience and well-being of communities would increase. Were these to be achieved, then the 'calculation' of value inputted and derived would be radically different from the criteria that presently define understandings of the 'costs' of governing and its relationship to the economy. It would be a much broader conception of what constitutes 'economic' activity and would sit alongside the social and political values that citizens would ascribe to government, its actions and its effects, the totality of which would enter into the public value created by government and hence the 'efficiency' (and, ultimately, the 'affordability and sustainability') of government.

Clearly, the conception of 'resources' and 'efficiency' employed here is wider than just finances and goes beyond mainstream fiscal thinking. In fact, say Bunt, Harris and Westlake (2010: 10), 'money sits outside this model'. 'Resources' are also understood in social, human and public terms and not just monetary or even organisational terms. In this sense, the radical efficiency agenda points away from market-failure economics (including public choice theory) that contribute to contemporary public management in Britain and Australasia (e.g., Buchanan and Tollison, 1981; for an overview, see Dollery, 2009) to something positive. It also assumes a shift from a 'tax-and-spend' conception of government to one of 'social investment' (e.g., Giddens, 1994; also Aiginger, 2004, 2005; Jessop, 2003; Lister, 2004; Newman and McKee, 2005). This would change significantly the terms in which total public value is defined, budgeted, funded, commissioned, accounted and evaluated (on measuring economic performance and social progress more broadly, see Stiglitz, Sen and Fitoussi, 2008). It would not seek to replace conventional economic calculations of welfare but to expand them and insist that the total picture of inputs, outputs and outcomes includes social and political values. We have already noted connections to 'third-way' approaches to public management; Smyth (2007) suggests that thinking along these lines being conducted by some economists in Britain and Europe is tantamount to working out an 'economics of the third way'.

How credible is radical efficiency? It points in promising directions and represents the kind of innovative thinking needed for the future but, as presented, caution seems warranted. These particular documents are produced for advocacy purposes, seeking to inspire strategic thinking rather than convincing via detailed technical analysis. These purposes may be valid but there must be substance behind the rhetoric. The case studies are selective and interpreted optimistically. The claim of dramatic savings is redolent of many reform advocates of recent years. United State Vice-President Al Gore's National Performance Review (Gore and Peters, 1993), for example, promised 'a government that works better and costs less' but did not apparently do so (cf. also Osborne and Gaebler, 1992). Advocates of contracting-out of 20 years ago also promised significant reductions, but in most cases the gains have not been realised (Hodge, 1998). The current passion for public–private partnerships may be destined to produce the same outcome (Hodge and Greve, 2007). On the other hand, as the OECD seems to propose (noted above), serious rethinking is required about the relationship between government, markets and society, and this social investment approach is doing just that[12] – moreover, strengths-based approaches combined with early intervention and prevention are already well established in many fields of social policy.

Radical efficiency is not yet a coherent body of work, but it may become so. My point in discussing the idea is not to promote 'radical efficiency' or 'social investment' as necessary solutions to affordability and sustainability in the future – although I note again that they align with other emerging ideas in public management (e.g., co-production, participation and collaboration). If nothing else, much more thinking needs to be done, particularly by progressive economists themselves. Such ideas, however, confirm the need for and possibility of innovation in grappling with the future in public finance as much as anything else, and that the future state may have to transcend the particular market-failure schools of economics that have dominated thinking about government and markets in New Zealand and Australia in recent years. As we have seen, alternatives are already gaining traction in Europe. The Council of Australian Governments is also taking an interest, as evidenced in its 'new national reform agenda' aimed at social investment in human capital development as a twenty-first-century growth strategy (e.g., COAG National Reform Initiative Working Group, 2006; see also Smyth, 2007). Small signs of a possible shift may be occurring in New Zealand with the recent announcement that Treasury will start using 'standard of living' indicators in policy advice (Treasury, 2011c).

One point should be emphasised. The level of public investment needed to ensure that approaches such as radical efficiency actually work across a society

---

12 It is also worth noting that the 'Total Place' pilots in Britain feature in the radical efficiency publications, and HM Treasury regarded them as sufficiently worthy to produce an extensive and cautiously positive report on their progress (HM Treasury, 2010).

would be substantial. The work cited here shows that small experiments along these lines are abounding in countries such as the United States, Britain, Australia (and New Zealand, even though the radical efficiency authors drew no case studies from this country); but scaling up and generalising these ways of working to the system level, mobilising capability and building capacity in civil society would necessitate a heavy level of public spending and public sector commitment. Social investment and other strategies designed to redefine governance are not about government handing the task over to someone else and walking away. They require seeding, support, facilitation and enablement (see also Young Foundation, 2010). Government remains the embodiment of the collective will and the repository of public resources for equitable redistribution; its obligation would be to facilitate the strategic development of future-oriented capability both inside and outside of government. The short-term call on public funds may be significant to achieve the long-term goal of a more affordable and sustainable government sector.

Whether this has been accounted for by the radical efficiency writers in their claims of savings is not clear. Without social investment, these ideas would be no more than rationalisations for a minimalist state agenda ('neoliberalism with a human face'; Jessop, 2006), the same accusation levelled by the left at the whole third-way movement (and, in Britain at present, by some civil society organisations affected by government cutbacks whilst promoting the 'Big Society'). Were such an approach introduced in New Zealand *without* the commitment to social investment – in other words, cutbacks to social protection without the redirection of resources to the local and community levels – the results could be socially disastrous for populations that are already struggling. On the other hand, a transformation of the goals of government and the means of governing along the lines envisaged here – with a clear commitment to public resourcing of the transformation – could contain the seeds for sustainable and affordable government in Aotearoa/New Zealand for decades to come.

Conclusion

As the Future State report pointed out, countries like New Zealand face a pincer movement into the future of difficult economic conditions, increasing and shifting demands for government services, and the simultaneous need to keep taxation low and remain competitive in global markets. The ongoing affordability and sustainability of government is a profound concern but the best ways forward are far from clear.

What arises out of this analysis is that mainstream instruments such as marketisation, cutback, prioritisation and efficiency drives designed to reduce government expenditure relative to national production have provided equivocal results. The numbers in New Zealand remain within a relatively narrow band. We could say therefore that they have not worked. We could equally say that the situation has remained relatively stable. It is also clear that, managerially and organisationally, they show no particular promise of producing the kinds of reductions called for by conventional economic thinking in relation to affordability and sustainability. As the radical efficiency writers suggest, the times may demand transformational thinking – or in future state terms, a step change. Alternative approaches such as social investment theories of governing may or may not be part of the future, but the type of thinking they represent points clearly to the need to break out of unreflective repetition of the past.

Ultimately, of course, when considering affordability and sustainability, despite all the lower level and technical arguments, a truism remains. What are deemed to be appropriate and sustainable levels of government expenditure depend on the ideas and values underpinning particular theories of society, markets and government. There is no universally applicable position. The range of positions occupied by various countries showing significant growth reinforces the point (OECD, 2011: 67). And the appropriate economic approach and policy settings for any particular society at any particular time will be a matter of the particular public consensus prevailing at that time. However much some economists might like it to be so, it is not a question to be decided on the numbers. It is a political decision.

At present, in New Zealand, the balance between each of those factors is decided by relatively closed technically expert groups and the government of the day that, together, largely adhere to a particular branch of economics. Some hold that line in doctrinaire ways, others are more eclectic, and others again take a pragmatic position with their concerns defined by international capital markets and rating agencies. There is some public debate around the relationship between government, economy and society and the preferred level of government expenditure but, by and large, there is not much collective discussion of the extent of the problem now and in the future, the choices available and their implications, or the conception of the 'good society' that New Zealanders want. Public economics is a complex arena of knowledge that should not be reduced to slogans, but New Zealand's civic institutions for making the ideas accessible, for debating the concerns of the various interests involved, for enabling deliberation and choice and guiding the government of the day towards an acceptable set of policies – and, hence, the step change needed for the future – are relatively weak compared with countries like Australia, Britain and some member states of the European Union. Governments and public managers today and tomorrow in this country will need to respond to the economic issues as they see them, but the greatest challenge confronting the future state is how to engender the kinds of societal deliberation of key questions. They include how New Zealanders want government to act, what balance we seek between economic growth and social well-being, the levels of taxation we are able to bear, and to whom resources are redistributed and to what degree: overall, what we take to be the level of affordability and sustainability we want to achieve for government in the future and how to maintain that position.

6

Complex Policy Implementation: The Role of Experimentation and Learning

Elizabeth Eppel, David Turner and Amanda Wolf[1]

Introduction

It is hard to imagine a sports team winning consistently without a coach. Coaches make innumerable decisions in the unique contexts of games that steer and co-ordinate the team's actions given the rules, the players' skills and lessons learned previously. In the real time of a match, coaches' prior assumptions are put to the test in light of their judgements of what seems possible to attempt on the day. New and updated understandings arise from the interactions with the opposing team, leading to adaptations on the spot. Although analogies can be pushed too far, policy implementers function surprisingly like coaches. They specialise in translating policy aims into action according to given rules, expectations and circumstances, and they often exercise a significant degree of discretion. Like coaching, the job of implementation is not limited to the simple operational matters of putting a plan into action; coaches and implementers engage with other aspects of the 'game', such as attracting resources and sifting through alternative strategies to find a winning one. Implementation thinking begins when new policy ideas are proposed and extends through the evaluation of policy outcomes. Nevertheless, compared to the intensity of attention to coaches' contributions to game results, implementation – putting policy ideas into practice – is rarely accorded star billing in the policy game, except when matters go spectacularly wrong. Indeed, most implementation research takes its cue from failures. The picture painted by the coaching analogy, emphasising coaches' contributions to success, is hard to detect explicitly in public management commentary and guidance.

As early as 1997, Hill wondered if implementation was 'yesterday's issue', a backwater unlikely to reward serious consideration. Barrett, too, in her 2004 reflective essay, urged renewed attention to implementation studies, including

---

1   We wish to thank the public sector managers who met with us to share confidentially their experiences and insights about complex implementation, and to acknowledge their contributions to the findings presented in this chapter.

the integration of implementation into the entire policy process. By the 1990s theorists had begun to escape earlier argument traps, for example, about whether to approach implementation from the top down or from the bottom up. However, the advent of new public management practices attenuated any gains for implementation practice (Barrett, 2004). In New Zealand, as elsewhere, implementation fell out of fashion when new public management came into fashion.

Some features built into the new public management system conspire against concentrating on implementation. Dichotomising policy and delivery, or outputs and outcomes, or provision and consumption of services diverts integrative instincts. In such an environment, policy governance interests centre mainly on ensuring good front-end, 'evidence-based' policy advice, on generic operational matters such as financial accountability and on the back-end results from good operations. Such a perspective renders implementation out of focus, hidden in a black box where 'good' policy decisions convert somehow into a range of self-evident activities. Yet, effective implementation management requires better insight at the specific level analogous to that exercised by coaches with accumulated knowledge of their teams and game.

A change in perspective is underway, bringing implementation – and hence its management – into focus. Encouragingly, the new perspective offers genuine advances in support of the ultimate aim of better citizen outcomes, not nostalgia for the past and its particular myths. In one clear statement, the chief executive of one of New Zealand's largest departments identified departments' need to think about what they do in an outside–in, developmental evaluation paradigm, from the citizen back to the processes, systems and structures designed by the department to implement policies (Hughes, 2011). Another chief executive, considering environmental policy challenges, said 'our focus needs to move beyond providing more evidence about why [any particular] policy tools are desirable, to one that looks at the *context* in which they are deployed' (Reynolds, 2011: 4, emphasis in original). Both chief executives urge managers to approach the implementation of policy as a series of thoughtful decisions *conditioned by what is outside*. They point to a fairly radical shift, entirely deserving to be labelled a 'new perspective'. Good policy ideas and well-managed resources and processes require intimate and continuing connection with outside ideas and resources in their context. In New Zealand, good examples of such outward-focused practices can be found. Managers show that they understand tacitly the basis of what we will refer to as 'complex implementation' and that they can respond appropriately in that environment.

While recognising that each implementation exercise varies in its complexity, managers need to know what factors make a difference and how to transfer better what they know across policy domains. Accordingly, it is time to articulate the elements of strategies to augment the conventional, design–implement–evaluate cycle with ones more attuned to complexity and context. These elements flow from understanding what is meant by complexity in the policy process, combined with a pervasive and practical capability for experimentation and learning. This capability derives from pragmatism, and is essential for working with complexity. In short, an open, context-sensitive and complexity-aware orientation is proposed in place of the old 'policy process', which has been neatly conceived as a series of stages, masterminded and controlled by agencies.

Aims and Overview

This chapter offers public managers a theoretical platform to support an 'outside–in' perspective, illustrates it with practice examples, and identifies desirable support capacities and capabilities at various levels of the public management system. It contributes to understanding how public sector agencies operate effectively in conditions where there are 'wicked' problems and multiple perspectives on problem causes and solutions. We shift attention deliberately from front-end efforts to link policy design and consequent outcomes logically to alternative ways of thinking about and 'doing' policy. Managers we talked to described practices more consistent with an outside–in perspective, and considered the conventional policy sequence unrealistic and unhelpful. The conventional model was accepted by only one manager in one of New Zealand's classically 'operational' departments. Findings highlight the need for a consistent strategic view of end goals, some means for testing changes, and the capacity to identify and assess progress in order to refine and redirect effort. Support for these practices involves ensuring appropriate permission to experiment; early and sustained activity conducted outside the responsible agencies; and open, flexible access to multiple sources of expertise. Implementing agencies and the policy management system need to take every opportunity to incorporate learning fully into their understanding of the agency's role, capability requirements and future focus.

This introductory section concludes with an elaboration of the concept of complex implementation, which captures the way even relatively simple policy ideas become complex when the ideas move from simply stated policy objectives into tangible actions by, and affecting, many actors. In the rest of this chapter, we set out some themes appropriate for describing and understanding complex implementation, drawing on public policy, public management and complexity literatures. We then present our experimentation-and-learning model, followed by a justification grounded in the pragmatic tradition. The chapter then sets out findings from New Zealand practice, based on a range of case studies and discussions with policy managers. This section is followed by specific suggestions for Parliament and select committees, cabinet, chief executives and senior departmental leadership, leadership collectives and the central control agencies to support experimentation and learning in complex policy implementation.

Complex Implementation

Policy objectives can often be simply stated, even if the underlying problems are complex. Two examples are 'sustainable water use' and 'less family violence'. Typical interventions to meet policy ends can also be stated in crisp, plain language, even when people disagree on specific details. An intervention may set volume and discharge standards to maintain or improve water cleanliness, or broadcast messages to stimulate awareness and community action to prevent family violence. When accompanied by compelling logic, these interventions seem obvious on paper. As is well known, however, once put into action, few interventions achieve policy objectives fully as intended. The causes of so-called implementation failures include flawed policy, flawed operational activity and unanticipated conditions. Key assumptions may have been overlooked in the logic argument, leading to a decision to implement a policy that is poorly suited to its objectives. Activities necessary to implement the policy may have been underfunded or foisted onto an inadequately prepared target, reducing the likelihood that even a good policy will deliver on its objectives. Unexpected external conditions may have intervened when a policy was rolled out, derailing even a well-designed and well-operationalised policy from its path.

This picture of the complexity of policy implementation calls into question the adequacy of much advice to improve policy implementation. For example, May (2003) claims that 'a central issue for implementation scholars is the extent to which noteworthy distortions can be anticipated and addressed as part of the design of a given policy' (p. 223), thereby mitigating flawed policy as a cause of implementation failure. Good policy work, it is claimed, also looks ahead to the implementation phase, assessing risks for failure, embedding contingent responses in the design, and so on, to mitigate failures due to flawed operational activity and, to some extent, to reduce the sphere of the unexpected. Without question, many potential failures can be avoided through these practices. However, when considering the full influence of conditions in the world, their variety and interaction, as well as the nature and diversity of human behaviour, it is clear that there will always be a potential for things to go awry.

Treating policy implementation as complex requires that public managers understand a fourth class of the causes of implementation failure – in addition to flawed policy, flawed activity and unanticipated conditions – namely, a failure to be alert to the inevitability of the complexity of policy implementation that arises from multiple, iterative human actions. Some conceptualisations of the policy process create problematic assumptions for a complexity-aware practitioner. Complex implementation calls for practices that eschew a linear model of the policy process, in which implementation follows phases of problem definition (supported by evidence from previous policy activities) and intervention design, comparison, selection and decision (Bardach, 2005; Dunn, 2008). This model assumes sequential processes, culminating in a whole with a discrete end point. Whole policy processes imply boundaries between them and external environments. Indeed, many theories refer to environments from which causal factors arise (Hill and Hupe, 2009; Kingdon, 1995; Sabatier and Weible, 2007). They treat such external environments as fixed, affecting but unaffected by changes in public policy processes (Howlett and Ramesh, 2003; Sabatier, 2007). Public policy actors, too, are taken to affect, but be unaffected by, the policy process.

In place of a linear model we propose an iterative experimental–learning process, in which actual policy activities evolve in response to new information from the implementation field. From a very early stage, the processes involve actors outside the government agencies responsible for the policy. Policy design and implementation are co-produced along with policy outcomes, with evaluative learning marshalling that process. Those involved exercise a capacity to sense anomaly and ask questions, and to revise and update activities accordingly. Government sets broad objectives (as always), but then authorises policy implementers to apply government tools and resources toward their iterative solution, *in the absence of a comprehensive, predetermined plan.* In this different conception, organisational and individual practices promote more effective policy implementation, facilitating learning by experimentation. In the best cases, organisations will also capture knowledge about complex implementation and maintain it institutionally to understand better the current and future environment.

Complexity Themes

What may be described as complex is subject to a large and varied literature, as is the matter of responding to complexity. In this section, we canvass the literature in order to derive and present some themes appropriate to our aims. The public management literature includes several explanations for causal mechanisms operating in policy processes understood as complex, nonlinear and social interactions between actors. Among the explanations are that the bounded rationality of actors limits how exhaustive and comprehensive policy processes can be (Lindblom, 1979; March and Olsen, 1984); that interdependent actions of street-level bureaucrats during the implementation process lead to nonlinear transfer from policy design to implementation (Lipsky, 1980; Pressman and

Wildavsky, 1973); that serendipitous combinations of problems and solutions arise during 'windows of opportunity' (Kingdon, 1995); that disproportionate information attention and processing lead to punctuated equilibria (Jones and Baumgartner, 2005); and that formation of advocacy coalitions (Sabatier and Jenkins-Smith, 1993) or horizontal relations between networks of actors (Kickert, Klijn and Koppenjan, 1997) explain processes.

Some scholars have drawn on selected complexity concepts to elucidate understanding of aspects of policy processes such as 'complex adaptive system' and 'co-evolution' applied to decision-making (Gerrits, 2010; M.L. Rhodes and Murray, 2007); 'adaptive systems' and 'self-organisation' applied to implementation (Butler and Allen, 2008); and 'self-organisation' and 'emergence' in the management of administrative networks (Meek, De Ladurantey and Newell, 2007). Teisman and colleagues have proposed a complexity-informed approach to understanding and managing complex governance processes (Teisman, van Buuren and Gerrits, 2009), while Sanderson (2009) and Morçöl (2010) have examined complexity theory applied to designing and managing policy processes.

These understandings and explanations of the complex in public management in light of the wider complexity literature – particularly that dealing with complexity in organisations and social systems that have some commonalities with policy processes – suggest a set of interconnected themes comprising a holistic complexity lens. The lens (which is argued more fully in Eppel, 2010) assists managers to make sense of interactions between individual and organisational actors in public policy processes. This sense-making is, we propose, a starting point and touchstone throughout the implementation process; it directs managers' gaze (hence the 'lens' motif), but does not constrain it.

Features of a Complexity-informed View of Policy Processes

The System Whole

The iterative interaction of human actors constitutes a complex system whole (Byrne, 1998; Cilliers, 1998). A complex system cannot be understood as the sum of its parts, or reduced to its parts to assist understanding (Bohm and Hiley, 1993; Kauffman, 1993; Waldrop, 1992). A system whole is made up of individual human actors and social groups of human actors, which may be formal (e.g., organisations) or informal. These human actors organise themselves at various levels, interact with each other, and comprise wholes that change and are changed by other systems they interact with (Allen, Strathern and Baldwin, 2006; Byrne, 1998; Cilliers, 1998; Midgley, 2000).

Nested, Interacting and Interdependent Systems

Complex systems nest within larger and larger complex systems (Kauffman, 1995). Organisations are human complex systems. Units within them are part of a complex system whole (Mitleton-Kelly, 2003; Richardson, 2008). With components in common, nested systems show 'self-similarity' because the characteristics identified at one level of the system (e.g., the individual) are also present at successive levels (e.g., the organisation). Understanding these interdependent systems needs a holistic view (Byrne, 1998).

Multiple Interactive Systems Create Feedback Mechanisms

Reflexive influence patterns, which arise from the ongoing interaction between actors in the system, can result in feedback loops. Negative feedback reverses or compensates for changes elsewhere, resulting in macro-stability. Internal features of organisations – such as structures, hierarchies, rules, controls, cultures, defensive routines and power relations – are held in place by feedback loops locking an organisation into a particular stable pattern (Morgan, 2006). Positive feedback loops amplify changes by reinforcing the direction of change, and can cause sudden, unpredictable and destabilising effects.

Adaptation and Co-evolution Within and Between Systems

Over time, reflexive interactions between actors lead to adaptation between groups of actors (systems) (Kauffman, 1995) and organisations (Boisot and Child, 1999; Stacey, 2003). From a complexity perspective, the 'external' environment is an interacting system (Gerrits, Marks and van Buuren, 2009; Midgley, 2000) and, therefore, changes in the environment may not only stimulate system change, but the environment will also undergo change in response. As a result, there is co-evolution and adaptation of one group of actors (a system) and their environment (Gerrits, 2010).

Change Through Self-organisation and Emergence

Consciousness, learning and language arise from interactions between actors in social systems (Blackmore, 2005; Watzlawick, 1984). Human actors reflect internally on their experiences and recognise patterns that help them make sense of their environment (Weick, 1995, 2001). Humans respond to the complexity of their environment by either side-stepping complexity through the simplification and codification of responses or by holding multiple and sometimes conflicting representations of environmental variety, and therefore retaining a repertoire of responses. Pattern recognition can also lead to unpredictable effects when a novel stimulus is set against previous learning (Weick, 1995). Thus, every change produces the stimulus for further change in each actor by self-reference to the individual actor's internal sense-making. This self-organisation by multiple actors can lead to the emergence of new relations and patterns of actors. Overall change in socio-economic systems occurs as a result of changes that affect the micro-diversity resulting from feedback loops, adaptation and emergence (Allen, Strathern and Baldwin, 2006; MacIntosh and MacLean, 1999). Emergence of new levels of order occurs through self-organisation of system parts in reinforced patterns around 'attractors' (Richardson, 2008).

Open Systems and Socially Constructed Boundaries

Groups of humans making up a social system are open to their environment (Cilliers, 1998; Kauffman, 1993, 1995). The boundaries of these systems are not constant or fixed but are social constructs – artificial or socially imposed reference points – which define the limits of knowledge considered pertinent to the system and to the human agent who generates that knowledge (Gerrits et al., 2009; Midgley, 2000). Organisations are open to a flow of energy, actors, information and ideas. While individuals can plan their own actions, they cannot plan the actions of others or the interplay of plans and actions, and organisations can be seen as processes for joint action.

Stability, but Not Equilibrium

Despite sometimes stable macro-appearances, complex systems are in fact 'far-from-equilibrium' (Byrne, 1998; Cilliers, 1998; Eve, Horsfall and Lee, 1997; Kauffman, 1993, 1995; Richardson, 2008). Such systems can suddenly and unpredictably undergo trajectory changes (Prigogine, 1987). Far-from-equilibrium systems often exhibit tensions or paradoxes, as changes in the feedback loops destabilise the system (Stacey, 2003), often disproportionately to the stimulus (Kauffman, 1995; Prigogine and Stengers, 1984). At these change points, new patterns can self-organise and emerge from the seemingly chaotic without external intervention. Social systems are both chaotic and stable depending on when one observes them (Eve et al., 1997).

The History of the System Influences its Starting Point for Change

The history of earlier changes, starting points and feedback loops can create 'path dependencies' (Prigogine and Stengers, 1984). Stabilising path dependencies arise when negative feedback loops undo externally imposed change or limit what happens next. Stable systems are more likely when there is a single, strong attractor influencing feedback loops. Less stable systems are characterised by multiple, weak attractors (influencers of feedback loops). Furthermore, the size, precise timing and nature of change in a complex system cannot be predicted in advance because of the sensitivity of the system to its initial starting position and contingency of the interactions between the system parts.

A Holistic, Complexity-informed Lens for Public Policy and Management

The complexity lens shows characteristics that might be found at work in policy processes viewed as wholes. This way of seeing could support practitioners in 'wicked' problem situations where messy, unordered and chaotic systems of public policy and management are only partially understood through the application of traditional lenses (Australian Public Service Commission, 2007). Thus, they can recognise that it is impossible to control the evolution of complex systems in conventional ways. The lens alerts managers to appreciate that the interactions between actors are not predictable in advance and can produce novel changes (surprises). Because of the ongoing nonlinear interactions of actors, there are likely to be a number of different interpretations of what is occurring and what might happen next (Dennard, Richardson and Morçöl, 2008; Klijn and Koppenjan, 2004; Teisman et al., 2009).

Managers cannot reduce the system whole to its parts to assist their understanding, since many individuals, institutions and processes interact interdependently. Using a complexity-informed lens, however, they can not only focus on the dynamics of policy processes, but can also recognise the direction, contents, speed and intensity of changes in a system. For instance, interactions between policy participants, institutions and processes might consist of negative feedback loops, which undo changes, and positive feedback loops, which amplify changes by reinforcing their direction, creating change in a system whole. Feedback loops can result in stability around an attractor (e.g., a new policy document, institution, information), or in destabilising and chaotic disturbance leading a system suddenly and unpredictably to re-organise itself around a new attractor (e.g., an unintended effect of policy change). The size of a response (e.g., budget cuts) is not necessarily proportional to the initial stimulus. The self-organisation that occurs during adaptation and co-evolution of far-from-equilibrium social systems that are also complex can result in emergence of new phenomena. A complex social system is sensitive to its history, which affects the starting point for any change.

Complex social systems, such as policy sectors or government agencies, are open, which can lead to changes in their composition and the exchange of information, resources and ideas with their environments. What policy designers and implementers might regard as 'environment' and 'internal' are actually the product of iterative social interactions and negotiations. Moreover, the social construction of system boundaries in policy processes means that managers must understand the goal conflicts that impede more effective exploration of policy problems and the identification of workable solutions. It follows that understanding of policy problems and solutions will lack coherence if boundaries as identified and maintained by different policy participants are ignored, with consequent difficulties for managing policy processes.

Understanding and explaining public policy processes as complex nonlinear social interactions between multiple actors requires sense-making across at least three nested interacting complex systems: the real world system, such as communities where family violence occurs; the policy and public management system; and the policy processes system, i.e., the policy designers, implementers and those the policy intends to affect. Sense-making describes practical approaches to working in complex circumstances and processes used to examine reality from multiple perspectives (Weick, 1995, 2001). Compatible techniques include uncovering different perspectives in narratives (Allison, 1971), drawing on phenomenological frameworks (Kurtz and Snowden, 2003), frame reflection (Schön and Rein, 1994) and boundary critique (Midgley, 2000).

Institutional theory points towards the distinctive, interacting roles assumed by individuals, organisations and constitutional/legislative systems (Hill and Hupe, 2006; Ostrom, 2007). The complexity lens allows managers to focus on the interdependent roles and nonlinearity in systems over time. Interdependent interactions occur as responses to changes made in another organisation. Actors might self-organise to form new organisations or levels of organisation. Activities across one level of organisation, such as changes in rule-setting, spontaneously generate behaviours at another level of organisation, such as decision-making by public officials.

The complexity themes applied to policy processes indicate the need to involve affected people in policy design and implementation. Policy networks conceived as parts of open, interacting policy systems reveal interactions that might shape policy processes and their game-like dynamics. In place of one best solution, desirable changes of trajectory in the system can be sought through internally consistent accommodations between actors. Monitoring change to check consistency with the desired direction and real-time evaluation will help avert the consequences of unintended, and sometimes unwelcome, changes that inevitably arise as complex systems adapt and co-evolve with emergent phenomena.

Policy designers and implementers require approaches to help identify participants, boundaries, system attractors and feedback loops in ways that are consistent with the change being considered. Awareness of complexity concepts and the tools designed to work with them could assist public policy managers to describe and understand the systems in which they want to intervene and the processes they might use to do so. Policy processes so understood would take into account the dynamism and emergence within all of the systems involved. Thus, there would be a resistance to simplification that masks complex dynamics and attention to details, monitoring for points of change and difference from what is expected, while maintaining a focus on the trajectory of the whole compared to the outcome wanted.

To summarise, the complexity lens focuses on the boundaries that might exist in the perceptions of varying actors, which helps in understanding how these boundaries are constructed and the ways in which they might facilitate or impede intended changes. By forcing managers to identify existing attractors and feedback loops, the lens assists in identifying the dynamics already present in the system where policy change is wanted. Policy intentions will interact with the extant system dynamics created by previous policy changes and their interaction with the system. The lens reveals that a system might seem stable and temporarily resistant to change, and then might suddenly and unpredictably change. Managers can be alert to the inevitability, but not precise predictability, of self-organisation among the parts of the system and the emergence of entirely new phenomena, some of which will be beneficial to the desired change and some unwanted. Thus, the means to achieve a particular intended policy change trajectory cannot be specified in any precise way and will require close monitoring of system changes for early signs of unintended effects.

Modelling Complex Implementation

It is widely appreciated that policy formulation should take account of a full range of implementation variables: who is expected to do what, when, with whom, with which resources and so on, and with what sorts of likely behavioural responses to those activities. Hill and Hupe (2009) canvas a range of definitions of implementation, concluding with a preference for defining implementation as what happens between policy expectation and (perceived) results. Moreover, policy and action are a continuum in the implementation process: paraphrasing Anderson (1999, quoted in Hill and Hupe, 2009), policy is being made as it is implemented and implemented as it is made. Good policy design 'looks ahead' to implementation and evaluation, thus collapsing analytical distinctions (Hill and Hupe, 2009; McConnell, 2010).

Complexity, as summarised in the previous section, highlights the lack of conventional means of control through 'looking ahead'. Sanderson (2009: 705–6) claims:

> change, instability and disequilibrium are the norm . . . the path of change can be highly sensitive to initial conditions . . . traditional cause-effect assumptions cease to be valid; elements of systems are mutually dependent . . . in effect the behaviour of a complex system emerges as the holistic sum of the dynamic interaction between its component parts over time.

Policy actors are themselves implicated in this behaviour, as the policy process system interacts with other systems, including the real world addressed by policy (Eppel, Lips and Wolf, 2011). Complexity implies limits of policy analysis and management to change social phenomena. Yet, the imperative remains to try for a better world.

Managers understand that there is often no one-way door from the agency to the world through which a formulated policy is 'carried out'. As policy activities play out, policy management iterates according to what is learned from evaluation and other feedback and what changes ensue from political directives. In complex implementation, managers thus face several salient conditions:

- A policy seeks to change or influence the behaviour of many independent actors (organisations, community groups and/or individuals) over whom there are no direct means of control. There is a range of activities, involving various agents, which could influence the overall policy outcome.
- The knowledge required to bring about the desired change is highly distributed in the communities, organisations and individuals where change is to take place and is unknowable at the point when policy decisions are being made. That is, there is no central node where knowledge considered necessary for well-controlled decisions can be mustered, made sense of and managed.
- Of necessity, policy actors simplify aspects of the situation; matters that are consequently overlooked may become relevant and known only over time and through action.
- Objectives may be clear only at the highest and most abstract level. Lower-level perceptions of the nature of the problem, appropriate elements of solutions and mandates may be contested.

One set of responses to the challenges of complex implementation seeks to retain the traditional, tried-and-true approaches, but to work harder within them. Scott and Baehler (2010) describe these as 'rational comprehensive', centred on the notions of a policy cycle and analytically distinct steps or stages in that cycle. Typical stages are: identifying problems and gathering information/ evidence; developing, comparing and choosing options; and implementing, monitoring and evaluating. In working from problem to recommendation, rational–comprehensive analysts identify and theoretically classify problems and match them to suitable theory-based solutions (Bardach, 2005; Weimer and Vining, 1999). Rational approaches are associated with 'evidence-based policy making', in which the central task of policy analysis is the application of rational-scientific methods to examining problems and gaining knowledge of causal linkages between policy interventions and their outcomes (Banks, 2009). In complex problem areas, proponents of evidence-based policy urge 'more powerful tools' and the use of 'more sophisticated specialist knowledge to enhance . . . capacity to design and implement successful policies' (National Audit Office, 2001, quoted in Sanderson, 2009: 701). Banks (2009) recommends in the Australian context a set of 'ingredients' for better policy, encompassing re-doubled efforts, better analytic capability, better data sets, adequate time and so on.

The second set of responses to complexity is characterised by the rejection of some part of the expected or traditional responses, and their replacement with new elements of practice. Scott and Baehler's (2010) 'network participatory' approach provides part of the picture, conceiving of policy actors and their networks in a horizontal weave. This approach can be detected in increased emphasis on 'joined-up government'. A requirement is a 'dense web of connections between policy and management functions to ensure that government's activities are effective, efficient, and aligned with society's fundamental values' (Scott and Baehler, 2010: 16). Networks are held to offer insights into complexity in the form of the multiple perspectives and experiences available. But there remains an underlying presumption of a single point of control and decision. This 'single point' refers to a discrete policy that can be named and the organisational ownership of the policy (even if the ownership is shared).

To aid better articulation of public management practitioners' repertoire of practices, and to push against their boundaries, we contrast the conventional approach to policy-making with a new model, based on the conditions summarised above.

Figure 6.1 assumes that policy design and implementation follow a linear, staged process, most of which occurs within the responsible government agency. Existing knowledge is marshalled and options are identified and compared, taking account of implementation requirements. A policy or programme is implemented outside of the originating agency, and is evaluated later. The evidence from evaluation may lead to further policy changes being developed internally and implemented externally. The focus is on getting the policy 'right' through the successive iterations.

The model remains effective in some situations, but often complex, uncertain and changing conditions make it difficult to anticipate sufficiently what must be done to implement policy. Policy managers regularly lack the fundamentals that the rational–comprehensive approach assumes they can rely on, such as an adequate information base; clear role assignments; and predictable influence patterns, timeframes and milestones. Complex implementation calls for a repertoire of practices that augments the extant practices of within-agency analysis and management, consistent with the model shown in Figure 6.2.

Figure 6.1. Agency-centred Model of Policy Design and Implementation

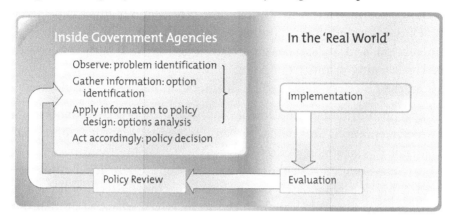

Figure 6.2. Experimentation and Learning Model of Policy Design and Implementation

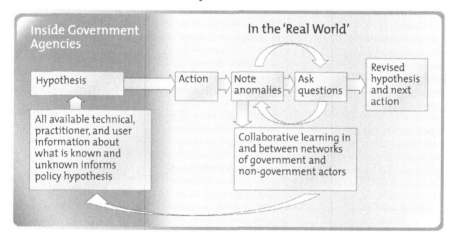

Figure 6.2 shows that more of the policy process occurs outside the government agency. The understanding of the problem formed through the traditional means of policy analysis is treated only as a tentative hypothesis that requires testing in the real world, outside the government agency. Testing takes the form of actions with collaborators such as individuals, community groups and NGOs. These actions result in feedback that contributes to a review of the original policy hypothesis. As a result of the repeated iteration of this process, the policy design will be modified to retain those actions that produce changes towards the desired outcome, and to abandon actions that do not produce demonstrably good results. Thus, the policy design is a work in progress, constantly adapted to take into account ongoing change occurring outside in the community. Different individuals with different experiences bring

different perspectives to a situation. Over time, the perspectives shift through interaction. They interfere with or reinforce others in a manner expected from a complexity-informed understanding of feedback loops. In this model, policy implementation and policy design occur together and both are constantly updated as learning results from doing.

In sum, the practices suggested by the model in Figure 6.2 would be:

- Experimental: Policy implementation would be practised explicitly as experimentation, and public servants would be accorded appropriate latitude to learn from action.
- Learning-oriented: On-the-go learning would arise from repeatedly searching for what does not fit the expected pattern, followed by actions that take into account new perspectives arising from plausible explanations about what is occurring.
- Accountable: Policy implementers would be accountable for their experimentation and learning and for successive iterations of policy design. However, they would not be accountable for outcomes as conventionally understood, since outcomes would be understood as a function of interactions between policy objectives, context and the full range of actors involved in implementation.
- Collegial: Policy implementers would be able to learn from the work of others, to build up gradually an evidence base focused on complex policy implementation.

Experimentation and Learning: The Pragmatic Tradition

Focusing on complex implementation directs fresh attention to learning. Because learning is clearly an element of policy practices generally, some distinctions are needed. As shown in Figure 6.2, the emphasis is on 'learning as you go', the locus of which is out in the world (in the problem–solution 'situation', or in the 'game'). But there is no single, target objective end to the learning process since objectives differ. The learning involves more than the accumulation and reflection on bits of knowledge because people get tied up in their learning and, hence, learning cannot be abstracted away from learner. Therefore, attention to the person who is learning matters as much as does the impetus for learning. This concept of learning derives from pragmatism. In this tradition, beliefs, not evidence, provide grounds for acting. People compare their beliefs with observed challenges to those beliefs. The pre-eminent disposition is the ability to see inconsistencies and to be surprised. The detection of the unexpected in the course of focused observation requires thinking that challenges existing understanding. Surprise, and the genuine doubt it entails, sparks new questions and new ways of seeing that may lead to a refined hypothesis. Observed effects of actions targeting desired ends are used to update both what is desired and how those ends might be best pursued (Bromley, 2008).

The pragmatism of Peirce, Dewey and James is enjoying a resurgence of interest in the context of complexity, as several developments in the literature illustrate. This literature emphasises experiment and learning, often in a 'design' framework. According to one review, 'designerly practice involves envisioning and trying out solutions, it requires science, but also intuition, emotion and aesthetic judgement' (Baerenholdt, Büscher, Scheuer and Simonsen, 2010: 5). Four 'pragmatic' illustrations are profiled below, showing aspects of design practice and experimentation for policy contexts. Regardless of whether pragmatism is explicitly invoked, the illustrations convey the nature of what is required and enabled when an outside-in, context-aware perspective is adopted.

First, consider Pawson's 'basic agenda for research synthesis' (2006: 25):

> The nature of causality in social programmes is such that any synthesis of evidence on whether they work will need to investigate how they work. . . . The central quest is to understand the conditions of programme efficacy and this will involve synthesis in investigating for whom, in what circumstances, and in what respects a family of programmes works.

'Family' likeness refers to the shared intervention theory in mentoring programmes or 'naming and shaming' interventions, to take two of Pawson's examples. Each policy instance can shed light on how the intervention works in general, as well as what is needed in specific contexts. Realist synthesis is thus an iterative process. Researchers respond to new data and new ideas, follow 'surprising' leads and think on their feet (Pawson, 2006: 102). The end point is a better understanding of the complexity of a policy mechanism and how it behaves in different contexts, in order that users are better able to apply their learning in new contexts. Realist synthesis – ostensibly an approach to develop even more robust evidence in complex situations – clearly shifts the burden of success to learners and their practices of learning.

A second example considers 'design experiments'. The experimenter iteratively implements and assesses interventions by 're-specifying' and 're-calibrating' them until a successful outcome is reached. In a policy setting, a design experiment resembles a frequently changed pilot programme. Unlike a classic experiment, in which a specific 'treatment' effect is isolated in order to draw conclusions, the design experiment is an 'action research' method that seeks to perfect the treatment through a stream of adjustments to it (Stoker and John, 2009). The experimenter should not 'dive in'. Rather, it is necessary to think ahead, have clear questions and be equipped with hypotheses to test (Stoker and John, 2009). Design experiments, which result in custom-made interventions, address the common critique that experimental results from a study in one context may not be replicable in another.

Design thinking in policy suits the core nature of the activity. As May notes, 'policy design is the process of inventing, developing and fine-tuning a course of action' (2003: 224) in order to address a policy problem. The Danish MindLab, sponsored by three ministries, studies and applies design thinking in a range of cases. MindLab's director claims that design thinking is 'the discipline of melding the sensibility and methods of the designer with what is technologically feasible to meet people's real world needs' as well as 'an attitude, or a way of reasoning' (Bason, 2011: 2). Tax departments in Australia and New Zealand are among leaders in design thinking for policy.

A third example originated 40 years ago, when clinical epidemiologists distinguished 'explanatory' and 'pragmatic' trials (Maclure, 2009; Roland and Torgerson, 1998). Pragmatic trials share features of realist syntheses, seeking 'to answer the question, "Does this intervention work under usual conditions?", whereas explanatory trials are focused on the question, "Can this intervention work under ideal conditions?"' (Thorpe et al., 2009: 464). Pragmatic trials meet policy makers' needs for information for decision-making (Maclure, 2009). They may involve 'compromises for expedience', which may be arrived at through a process of *ongoing* negotiation between the policy maker and the researcher (Maclure, 2009: 1001, emphasis added). These trials may not contribute markedly to biological (or 'mechanistic') knowledge (as would an 'explanatory' trial). Instead, they provide a 'real-world test in a real-world population' (Maclure, 2009: 1003). Nevertheless, the real value in the trials is that they test a number of 'individual interventions', either because of the variation within one trial, or by combining learning from several related trials:

> Often there is uncertainty about what, in fact, is 'optimal' and the best way to find out is by designing 'pragmatic' trials that include a range of factors that may (or may not) increase the likelihood of good outcomes (or reduce the likelihood of adverse effects) and undertaking subgroup analyses when appropriate. (Oxman et al., 2009a: 486)

The context in which the trials operate is, as in realist syntheses, centrally important. The circumstances are held to include the relevant factors that act on, or modify, the effectiveness of the intervention (Oxman et al., 2009b).

The fourth illustration is methodological. Within a burgeoning literature on mixed methods in research and evaluation, pragmatism is fairly ubiquitous (Biesta, 2010; Feilzer, 2010; Greene and Hall, 2010). Feilzer establishes that 'the approach most commonly associated with mixed methods research . . . is pragmatism, which . . . focuses on the problem to be researched and the consequences of the research' (Feilzer, 2010: 7). Mixed methods approaches, to the extent they integrate methods and epistemological stances within a single study, are neither purely positivist nor purely constructivist. Feilzer summarises, 'pragmatism as a research paradigm supports the use of a mix of different research methods as well as modes of analysis and a continuous cycle of abductive reasoning while being guided primarily by the researcher's desire to produce socially useful knowledge' (Feilzer, 2010: 6). Abductive reasoning results in hypotheses; it supplies 'new ideas' that can then be pursued in an inductive–deductive process. Abductive reasoning, introduced by Peirce, is characteristic of pragmatic logic (Stewart, 1997). In an abductive syllogism, some event comes as a surprise. Some assumptions or circumstances would make the event unsurprising. Since the event is observed, the assumptions are deemed a plausible explanation.

Feilzer favours the pragmatic paradigm because it 'sidesteps the contentious issues of truth and reality, accepts, philosophically, that there are singular and multiple realities that are open to empirical inquiry and orients itself toward solving practical problems in the "real world"' (Feilzer, 2010: 8). She favours a 'realist' epistemology, noting that 'any knowledge "produced" through research is relative and not absolute, that even if there are causal relationships they are "transitory and hard to identify"'(Feilzer, 2010, quoting Tashakkori and Teddlie, 2009). The examples of the design experiment and pragmatic trials capture the same notion, and also make explicit the importance of testing ideas and using experiments to *find better questions to ask* (and so to implement a more effective intervention) in the situation at hand.

The pragmatic tradition underpinning these practices is a philosophical framework that (among its tenets) views knowledge as both constructed and a function of organism–environment transactions, believes truth comes from experience, and is problem-solving and action-focused (Greene and Hall, 2010). Pragmatists 'live and act together' in a world 'for which [they] have a shared responsibility' (Biesta and Burbules, 2003: 108). Pragmatists see the 'world as a place where things happen or they don't . . . where progress is achieved by way of experimentation, trial and error. . . . pragmatism is a mind-set and a world view' (Harrison, 2009: 5).

In pragmatism, knowing is about doing, not having. 'When faced with new and unfamiliar choices, the process of learning precedes choice: we are forced to work out our beliefs about the situation as we contend with the situation' (Bromley, 2008: 5). Bromley argues that in a policy context, we must be able to offer reasons for beliefs about the outcomes of available options. Further, since the future is changing as we seek to go there, we reason to defeat this indeterminacy. This is not some specialist capability – it is an acknowledgement of how people in practice respond with reasoning, not calculation (Bromley, 2008: 4).

Pragmatism suggests that all knowledge is fallible and that 'individuals rearrange their perceptions/experiences to form new ideas' (Snider, 2000: 129). Knowledge is always open to additional interpretation. Its focus is on inquiry, its qualities, and what the inquirer knows or does not know, not on knowledge as object. Inquiry, especially in Dewey's formulation, rejects 'a sharp dichotomy between theoretical judgements and practical judgements' (Hookway, 2008, s1, para 1). We must, according to Stewart, 'be willing to test the consequences of our beliefs or explanations, particularly when doubt arises . . . [and] using human judgment rather than merely mechanical calculations, test [our] explanations *and* assumptions against those problems that [our] explanations and assumptions are supposed to solve' (Stewart, 1997: 21, emphasis in original).

Peirce's 'method of methods' for acquiring and developing knowledge was 'synonymous with the experimental method of the sciences' and indeed of learning in everyday life (Stewart, 1997: 1). The process of questioning as we go implies integration between thinking, planning, trialling and objectives-setting, in which 'thoughts about possible outcomes in the future are created once we find ourselves in the context of action: what should I do? We work out what we think we want as we work out what we think we might be able to have (to get)' (Bromley, 2008: 4).

Inquiry is cumulative, as is learning throughout life. Peirce wrote that 'reasoning should not form a chain which is no stronger than its weakest link, but a cable whose fibres may be ever so slender, provided they are sufficiently numerous and intimately connected' (quoted in Hookway, 2008). Mixed methods research develops cables of this sort when done well. Haack reinforces this point, claiming that 'scientific evidence [is] a tightly interlocking mesh of reasons well-anchored in experience' (2003: 3). In this alternative picture, 'evidence' is embedded in an extensive web, and is not universally 'true'.

Charles Beard, observing public administration in the early twentieth century but foreshadowing current evidence-based policy thinking, favoured 'apolitical efficiency' (Snider, 2000: 123), was concerned with 'tangible consequences and with what works' (Snider, 2000: 134), and was adamant that administration be stripped of any possible arbitrariness. As a consequence, administrators were required to adopt impersonal knowledge practices, and engaged social scientists as 'technical servants to social administration . . . providing sheer methods and facts' (DeHue, 2001: 288). 'Social scientists rapidly adapted to the new demands and began to focus on knowledge that was instrumental rather than reflexive, standardised rather than discretionary' (DeHue, 2001: 288–9).

The resurgence of interest in pragmatism is explicit in Sanderson's call (2009: 209) for 'intelligent policy making':

> in which we accommodate the complexity surrounding the application of intelligence in policy making, treat our policies as hypotheses to be tested

in practice, to be piloted where feasible and appropriate and to be subject to rigorous evaluation, and in which we learn from these processes and apply the intelligence thus gained to future policy thinking and decisions.

Importantly, Sanderson does not require that we reject the analysis behind the urge to use evidence for policy; evidence is limited, but its instrumental rationality offers many attractions in the face of complex problems. The aim is to find ways to make 'stronger use' of evidence, but without mere redoubled efforts. For Sanderson, the basis for the new option is provided by recognising the importance of experiment: in the case of complex systems, experimentation may be a required aspect of government intervention.

The policy literature offers a particularly rich seam of thought on policy as experiment, notably Campbell's 'experimenting society', which has had great influence in policy evaluation and the evidence-based policy movement (Dunn, 1998). According to DeHue, 'Campbell argued also that policy making *always* is social experimentation and pictured the social scientist as "methodological servant of the experimenting society"' (2001: 284, emphasis added). If a policy was inefficient, or harmed people, it would be replaced by a new experiment, and society would gradually discover better policies. This history explains the preference that continues today for randomised controlled trials. Knowledge became confined to what was already known or assumed, not to what it would 'be reasonable to believe about the outcomes of available actions' (Bromley, 2008: 4).

In the policy context, a pragmatist looks at a policy intervention in its whole-world context with an emphasis on outcomes. Such a perspective is fairly recent. In New Zealand, it is reflected in the outcomes orientation to policy (instead of a problem orientation) and in a systemic or strategic orientation (instead of a piecemeal, 'programmatic' orientation). Pragmatism also provides a justification for the learning-as-we-go model presented in Figure 6.2, which in turn reflects the themes summarised by our complexity lens.

However, there are always limits. For example, there are limits to pilot testing and evaluation, especially in a small, diverse country such as New Zealand. Pragmatism suggests that more effort ought to be shifted to 'learning as we go'. In addition, it is necessary to think more precisely about who is the 'we' who is applying intelligence and learning. Complex implementation suggests the 'we' is increasingly not only the people inside the bureaucracy. Different individuals with different experiences bring different perspectives to a situation. Over time, the perspectives shift through interaction. They interfere with or reinforce others in a manner expected from complexity theory's treatment of feedback loops. But the tendency is for a narrowing of reasonable working hypotheses (Bromley, 2008: 5). According to Bourgon and Milley, 'to address complex problems, governments must improve their ability to tap into the collective intelligence of society' (2010b: 40). Interaction in complex systems leads to actions that have the qualities of experiment, of trial and error. In the policy context, policies are considered as 'hypotheses', not programmes to be rolled out. The uncertainty inherent in the system calls for 'gentle policy action' (Sanderson, 2009, quoting Elliott and Kiel, 1997: 65). Note that the *gentle* action, not the qualities of the actions such as their adaptability (so often recommended in complex situations), is the aim.

Characteristics of Complex Implementation in Practice

Scott and Baehler (2010) underline the strengths of the rational–comprehensive and network approaches. Nevertheless, while there is adequate acknowledgment that policy implementation work needs to be more context-aware and process-focused, the idea that a 'best' course of action can be identified and selected centrally and then implemented in the world is retained. The clarion call is just to work *harder*, in ever more clever ways to project policy effects into the future, to draw on a better range of evidence, to partner more effectively with others both inside and outside government – and so on – in order to arrive at a more informed decision about whether to introduce a new or revised policy, the shape of that policy and to plan for its implementation. There are strong incentives for practitioners to invest in this extra effort, given present accountability and responsibility arrangements, and the need for agencies to feel comfortable with their level of control in planning policy continuations or revisions.

Practice belies this notion: there are numerous examples in which the pragmatic experimentation and learning model predominates, and effective 'control' is decentralised and democratised. A range of cases and discussions with policy managers undertaken in 2011 was drawn on to document the experimentation and learning pragmatic model in action. Interviewees came from diverse sectors: education, taxation, international trade, security and border control, community development and justice. These discussions took place in light of findings from New Zealand case studies. One case examined the Land and Water Forum (Bisley, 2010; Eppel, 2011a; Land and Water Forum, 2010). The Forum, pursuing a collaborative governance approach that was relatively unknown and untested in New Zealand, created a policy framework for water use, where policy progress had previously been stalled. The approach allowed multiple perspectives to be taken into account and competing values and priorities to be balanced. A second highly relevant case looked at family violence prevention (Eppel, 2011b; McLaren and Stone, 2010). The Family Violence Prevention Campaign was considered as an exemplar of action learning about a policy situation. In this case, family violence prevention activities were constructed by leveraging community knowledge and resources.

A relatively simple idea, 'It's not OK', was used to build a shared understanding of the problem in communities and to motivate local action.

We analysed the case studies with the aid of the features of the complexity lens set out above. A long list of observations resulted, which were used to develop an interview schedule. Interviewed policy managers were also invited to consider the models presented in Figures 6.1 and 6.2, before narrating an example of complex implementation they selected. The remainder of this section summarises and illustrates some findings from the New Zealand case studies and interviews, presented as a set of themes, with short illustrative quotations drawn from interviews conducted in April and May 2011 with policy managers in Wellington.

Wicked Problems

Complex implementation is often associated with 'wicked' problems. These are problems, such as family violence, where there are multiple perspectives on problem causes and solutions; where there are no clear, unambiguous and lasting solutions; and where systemic responses are required (Australian Public Service Commission, 2007). When government policy systems try to tackle such problems, no matter how thorough their analysis, there is likely to be as much unknown as known, and other actors, outside of government agencies, hold some of the information and expertise required for understanding the problem and its solution. There may be less need for brand new interventions, but more need for flexible, adaptable, tailored uses of what is already available. Even relatively simple problems, such as raising the GST rate, can be complex in their implementation because of the multitude of actors involved in the implementation and their different priorities.

> Government agencies can't do it by themselves – they have to be in the outside world, everyone with a stake has to be taken seriously and the agency has to take all their stakeholders with them.

Work with Small Steps

A strong egalitarianism in New Zealand favours some implementation approaches, which can be most clearly appreciated in their absence, as when a triage approach is occasioned by emergencies. In emergencies, actions cannot be thoroughly planned and cross-checked against the criterion of equal treatment, and the environment exerts significant influence on what happens, for whom and with inevitable 'errors'. Even in the absence of a crisis, progress toward policy objectives may occur unevenly and in small bursts. In the Family Violence Prevention Campaign, a senior manager noted the importance of being 'tight on the goal and purpose, but loose on the means' so that community-led change could make an active contribution to the outcome.

Clear Vision and High-level Goals

A statement of vision, and the articulation of high-level goals, is an important first step in any complex implementation. Sometimes goals will not be agreed at the outset, and part of the implementation process must include reaching a shared agreement across all the relevant actors about what the goals should be. This, in turn, involves understanding the expectations created by the political and public mandate outside of the government agency, and understanding what might be involved in achieving the vision for different actors.

> Information is not knowledge. There is a need to understand the complexity of how others view the same information.

> Getting and keeping a mandate to work towards an outcome – this can come directly from government or more indirectly from 'out there' and people and businesses that see a problem that needs fixing.

Networks of Actors

In complex implementation, there are networks of interdependent actors both inside and outside of government agencies, not all of whom will initially understand the vision or outcome. Some of these might have aligned interests and support the outcome, and others might not. Ignoring the latter could imperil the implementation.

> You have to get everyone at the table and they have to hear each other because that is part of the process of socialising the issue and building understanding that might lead to agreement on what needs to be done.

Learning as You Go

A strategy for coping with complex implementation is to treat it as an experiment – a learning exercise – where each step in the implementation is an opportunity to gather more information, reassess assumptions and modify the implementation plan accordingly.

> [Peter] Senge had the right idea – you set a milestone you can see or that feels tangible enough to be achievable, and then when you get there you stop and assess things again before setting the next milestone. You can't map it all out at the beginning because there is so much that you don't know.

> I think it is the acceptance of the experiment – and not having to have everything planned and developed. If we had spent our time on intervention logic and stuck to that, we wouldn't have been able to be as nimble.

Sense-making and Reflection

Complex implementation requires ongoing sense-making (Weick, 1979) and deep reflection to unearth discrepancies between actual and intended or espoused practice by each of the actors.

> People do not always say what they mean/do; or mean/do what they say.

> I noticed [in the department] that when we got negative feedback, people went 'oh we should control that! – shut it down!' We resisted that. We listened to it. We didn't shut it down. And we didn't get completely rattled by it either. You can't control that sort of thing. You have to work with it.

Similarly, paradoxical ideas may be present in the field, and it can be better to work with paradoxes than to resolve them artificially.

> [One stakeholder] argued for a more restrictive rule, but the underlying rationale turned on their interest in maintaining the maximum amount of flexibility.

Knowledge Gaps and Untested Ideas

Even when there is a research and evidence base to draw on, there will be knowledge gaps, especially about local-level dynamics and how individuals, communities and organisations might respond to the policies being implemented. Therefore government agencies need to be more aware of what they do not know.

Implementation actions might be seen as exploratory exercises to test tentative theories and ideas, and to 'find out'. Even when a policy decision and its implementation appear simple – for example, 'raise the GST rate from x to y at time t' – implementation is complex because the ideas the government agency might have about *how* this should be done are untested by the actions and constraints on the actions of people the policy affects. Policy implementation can be prototyped and tested in the real world. 'Policy design' translates policy decisions into a working plan that will operate as intended in the real world, as opposed to a theoretical model with unknown real-world performance.

> We spend a lot of time prototyping what the implementation might look like and then testing that against the real world.

> Our approach to implementation has changed completely. Where once upon a time, the implementation thinking did not really begin until the policy development was well down the track, we now begin to design the implementation, hand-in-hand with the policy development, right from the outset.

Anticipation of Surprises

Complex implementation results in unexpected interactions and results. Therefore, as well as a willingness to learn from what is occurring, attention to variance is also needed to spot the emergence of phenomena and patterns of behaviour that were not intended. Surprises should be anticipated and some of these will support and accelerate the intended trajectory of change.

> There are ways that we do things that create a whole that is greater than the sum of the parts. We are doing the opposite of what a conventional public servant might do. . . . We had to believe that a point comes where you no longer have to drive everything. The ownership gets wider and the distributed network has taken over and [is] driving it. . . . So many projects never get to that stage because public servants are afraid of stakeholders. They are risk averse.

Where the patterns of behaviour that emerge undermine the intended direction of change, they need to be disrupted early before their effect comes to dominate the overall direction of change.

> You need to be collecting data about what happens during implementation and making it available in the policy community so that you are already thinking about the next [round of] review as you implement the changes.

> A promise to monitor the effects of what you do takes away the high stakes of change because if it looks like turning to custard you can do something about it before it is too late.

Distributed Information, Decision-making and Accountability Networks

The information needed for implementation design and monitoring of implementation is highly distributed among actors, many of whom are outside government agencies. As independent decision makers, these actors will act according to their own interpretation of what is occurring and what they think is going to happen next. In this context, accountability for what happens is problematic. Government agencies need to be clearer about what they do and do not know and also for what they are accountable. In complex implementation, this might take the form of evidence of change in the intended direction, rather than performance of specific actions.

> We teach problem definition and solution generation before you have even talked to people. And then we pick a solution, plan the design and then you implement it. That is just fine when you know what you are working with and there is high agreement about the problem and the solution. But where you have a high level of uncertainty about what works and how to grapple with it . . . then the same old–same old will not work. We had to learn to chart a course and keep the navigation going and not lose sight of the goal.

Supporting Factors

Discussions with policy practitioners about their experiences in complex implementation resulted in identifying a range of factors that support an experimental approach to policy implementation. Among the lessons of experience were the following:

- An experimenting approach to implementation requires both a mandate for a strategic goal and the permission to pursue that goal flexibly, learning from and adapting to new challenges.
- Detailed plans and objectives have to be allowed to emerge through practice.
- Planning for implementation needs to start early, alongside policy development.
- Multiple types and sources of expertise are required.

Complex implementation requires some skills and capabilities. Policy practitioners need relationship skills to interact with the diverse individuals, organisations and communities that might hold some of the information and resources needed to achieve the policy goal. They need to be able to deal with ambiguity and changing situations without losing sight of that goal. They also need to be sufficiently flexible and nimble in their thinking and actions to take advantage of the serendipity that will arise during implementation.

An experimenting, learning approach to complex policy implementation requires the support of evaluative findings. To provide a basis for learning and further policy development in complex and fluid implementation situations, evaluation approaches need to be flexible and attuned to the needs of key decision makers. Some recently developed evaluation approaches meet those needs. Developmental evaluation, as described by Patton (2011), provides one example of an evaluative approach that fits well with complex implementation. Developmental evaluation brings information to bear in support of a process of innovation and change. It suggests ongoing dialogue with different stakeholders. In developmental evaluation, participants may ask not only what implementation activities are in place and why, but also to what extent the initial policy plan remains appropriate and what new elements may have been added or may be needed. Developmental evaluators keep tabs on issues that have emerged, unanticipated consequences that have been observed, new learning about the implementation process and important factors for future policy development.

Patton's views on evaluation emphasise questioning, and thus align with a pragmatic mindset. 'Questioning is the ultimate method' (Patton, 2011: 288). The activity of questioning starts *in situ* and becomes a means of intervention, of 'questioning as we go' (2011: 289), affecting not only the evaluation report but also the very policy that is reported on. Thus, Patton privileges the role of the evaluation professional as part of the policy/implementation team. The evaluator is a learning facilitator, a conduit bringing evaluative thinking practices to those in need of it, a 'friendly critic' or a 'burr in the saddle' (2011: 25).

Support from the 'centre' is also required. There are at least five relevant levels, each of which can offer support in different and complementary ways:

(1) the chief executive and senior leadership of individual government agencies;
(2) collectives of chief executives or deputy chief executives who adopt a leadership/championship role with respect to a particular outcome;
(3) the central agencies of State Services Commission, the Treasury and the Department of Prime Minister and Cabinet, which develop and monitor policies and guidelines affecting all government agencies;
(4) the ministerial executive of government that makes up the cabinet; and
(5) Parliament and its machinery, such as select committees.

Table 6.1 shows roles for each of these levels to support experimentation and learning in policy implementation.

Conclusion

This chapter began by drawing attention to the often-overlooked activity domain between policy development and results achievement, namely that of implementation. It sought to revitalise managers' attention to implementation in a manner consistent with complexity scholarship. It set out a model to guide managers engaged in complex implementation, and grounded a justification for the model in the pragmatic tradition. While reporting detailed empirical studies is outside the chapter's scope, we drew on several New Zealand case studies and augmented them with illustrations of aspects of complex implementation from a series of interviews with policy managers. We detected a range of ideas for ways in which managers could be supported that are implicit in these studies and interviews, and these are summarised in Table 6.1. Our overall conclusions follow.

Table 6.1. Supporting Actions from the Centre

Support required	Support action	Action level*
Clear accountabilities	Hold people accountable for setting and pursuing strategic goals, effectively developing initial policy, and learning from changed or emerging circumstances.	1,2,3,4,5
Adaptable, experience-based framing of 'success'	Ensure flexibility in policy implementation to achieve more lasting community-driven results, mindful of the need for mutual adaptation between all the actors, inside and outside of government.	1,2,3,4,5
Risk accepted by oversight bodies	Task steering groups to allow 'fast fails',through which learning and adaptation occur, and to therefore moderate extreme risk aversion in their control and accountability functions.	1,2,3,4
'Tight' focus on purpose and outcome but 'loose' focus on means	Align roles and expectations: Ministers, CEs and senior management: clear messages about the changes they want. Policy designers: provide flexibility in the means by which objectives can be achieved. Policy implementers: invest in understanding the actors and how they might actively support change, not simply comply.	2,3,4,5
'Champions' groups and direct involvement in change	Encourage CEs and deputy CEs to be directly involved in a complex implementation, to broaden and embed new capability through their personal investment in achieving an outcome, and to convey to policy practitioners operating in complex implementation that they have champions who understand the nature of the processes being created.	1,2,3
Organisational learning culture	Regularise ways to learn from implementation experience, enabling organisations to more fully understand the multiple perspectives its client groups and to apply this knowledge in future strategic thinking and planning. Establish effective organisational memory – a capacity for retaining lessons of experience.	1,2,4

Support required	Support action	Action level*
Room for experiment	Explicitly permit complex policy implementation and allow time and room to engage with actors who need to be part of the change. Allow for communities to self-organise around policy attractors and for desirable behaviour to emerge. Permit other actors to lead actions in support of the policy objective. Acknowledge implementation as an adaptive 'new beginning', not an end.	1,2,4
Privilege questions	Pursue the questions that are important, knowing that answers are not assured at particular times, but that the pursuit will help make progress towards the policy objective. Information on what is not known may be as valuable as information on what is known.	1,2
Transdisciplinary skills	Consider the diversity of skills needed for policy development and implementation design, and build more transdisciplinary teams comprising individuals with skills and knowledge based outside government.	1, 3
Communication capability	Develop relationship and communication skills for work in inter-organisational settings, which have diverse values, cultures, and policy-relevant skills.	1,3

*See text for definitions of action levels

Complex and 'wicked' problems require new ways of doing policy implementation. New ways of doing implementation entail:

- collapsing the conventional distinction between policy design and implementation;
- augmenting the conventional model, in which policy is designed in-house along with a substantial implementation plan that is subsequently rolled out and managed, with a model in which policy/implementation is produced outside under the pervasive influence of the complexity, uncertainty and ambiguity of the problem;
- embracing an ongoing learning orientation, which complements existing problem and outcome orientations, with the locus of learning out in the world (in the problem–solution–outcome context);
- redefining the objectives of policy evaluation by accepting that much of the knowledge that is necessary for the success of the policy emerges as part of policy/implementation practices and must be gained and applied on the fly; and

- developing a deliberate organisational learning perspective to evaluate and learn from practitioners' experiences about a sector, its processes and how outcomes are achieved during complex implementations.

In short, successfully implementing policy for many policy problems is complex. It involves a whole system and multiple, open mechanisms that lead to emergent processes and outcomes, in a web of relationships and influences, almost all of which are not able to be controlled by the implementing agency. Aspects of implementation as a complex process may also apply to problems that are not themselves considered to be complex.

Although policy analysts and advisers have little difficulty generating lists of things that might be done – some advisory service here, a social marketing campaign there or a community partnership somewhere else – their existing theories and evidence about how and why policy 'works' serve as mere starting points, and the real work of design and implementation co-evolves in continuous contact with the changing nature and knowledge of the problem and the outcomes that are produced. This recognition requires a reframing of the role of the policy evaluator as a person who applies skills in presenting knowledge in context to implementing and implemented-upon actors, getting alongside them and bringing them along. For implementers, a key implication is the need for experiment-conducive management systems and rules of accountability.

In complex policy situations, characterised by large stakes and uncertainty, as well as in the everyday policy decisions that can have profound implications for individuals' well-being, a strong case can be made for learning as we go. A renewed pragmatic practice brings experience into the many efforts to create the futures we want. Making use of evidence seamlessly requires applying continuously a habit of mind that asks not 'what are the facts?' but 'what is the next question?'

While the nature of complex problems and policy implementation means that there will never be a fully transparent and shared body of knowledge about what works to effect desired outcomes (nor stable ideas of what outcomes are possible), the public sector as a whole can seek to overcome four challenges:

(1) that the initial efforts might not be as good as they could be because collaborative learning is limited;
(2) that the nature of the lessons to be gained from experience might be misunderstood as context-specific substance rather than transferable process elements;
(3) that the transferable lessons of experience might be unavailable to wider policy communities; and
(4) that those who follow have to (re)discover the lessons of experience for themselves.

Addressing these challenges requires policy designers/implementers to learn as they go and to allocate sufficient time to that learning, both as a share of time devoted to all policy tasks and as a new temporal rhythm in general. Successful complex implementation requires a dogged focus on the future common good and a commitment to work gradually and to talk our way there.

7

Working Across Organisational Boundaries: The Challenges for Accountability

Jonathan Boston and Derek Gill

Introduction

Accountability is critically important in many spheres of human endeavour; the management of the public sector is no exception. Without accountability, the risks of poor performance and the misuse of public resources are greatly increased. And without accountability, parliament cannot exercise proper control over the political executive and government agencies. Robust accountability is thus a prerequisite for democratic government and, more generally, for good governance.

But often the goal of strong accountability is complicated – if not thwarted – by the fact that it is *shared*. It may be shared between two or more people and/or between different organisations; it may also be shared across different tiers of government (i.e., national and sub-national) and between both public and private entities. Shared accountability of this nature is, in fact, remarkably common. This is strikingly so at all levels of government. Under a system of cabinet government, for instance, there is collective decision-making, and many responsibilities are shared. Likewise, the policy outcomes desired by governments – whether economic, security, social or environmental – typically require the collaboration of multiple agencies, sometimes involving both governmental and non-governmental bodies. Such collaboration may include formal partnerships or more informal arrangements. Either way, a degree of joint accountability for the results is entailed. As a result, public officials often face multiple accountabilities – upwards, laterally, outwards and even downwards.

Yet, where accountability is shared, many problems can arise. The lines of accountability may be unclear. The opportunities for blame-shifting are increased. Sanctions for poor performance may be difficult to apply. Similarly, where performance is praiseworthy, it may be unclear who most deserves the credit. Within the public sector, these problems can make some individuals and agencies reluctant to participate fully or enthusiastically in joint working arrangements. Inter-agency collaboration and co-operation may thus be undermined. Given that joint working is often vital for achieving desired outcomes, addressing the issues raised by shared accountability is critically important.

To compound problems, New Zealand's public management reforms of the mid-to-late 1980s (and largely unchanged since then) have almost certainly exacerbated the challenges of working across two or more agencies, not least because of the reform's strong emphasis on vertical, straight-line accountability. This includes a focus on departmental chief executives being accountable to their portfolio minister(s), and explicit, hierarchical reporting lines (and related accountabilities) within departments. The emphasis on *vertical* accountability mirrored the 'best practice' business unit structures of the late twentieth century, with a matching of authority and resources to ensure 'no excuses' accountability for delivering outputs against pre-defined policy outcomes. Further, despite the increased emphasis on 'outcomes' since the late 1990s (as reflected, for instance, in the planning process for *Statements of Intent*), there has been no change in the underlying reporting lines embodied in the reforms of the 1980s (see Gill, 2011: 37–140). At the same time, inter-organisational arrangements involving *horizontal* accountability are increasingly being formalised, with shared accountability for the achievement of specified outcomes. For instance, departmental chief executives are working more intensively in mandated clusters or sector groupings, such as the natural resources sector, the justice sector, the social sector and so forth. Box 1 discusses the implications for the external accountability documents of the social sector. These examples pose questions about how joint working can best be encouraged, or at least facilitated, in an accountability framework that is fundamentally hierarchical in nature.

The Future State project (discussed in chapter 1 of this volume) has examined how new ways of working within New Zealand's public sector might be encouraged. Of particular concern has been the question of how to improve the quality of public services and the cost-effective delivery of desired outcomes through better joined-up government, including improved inter-agency collaboration and co-operation. This is critical because many policy issues will require increasingly cross-organisational and inter-connected responses. Cross-jurisdictional work, no doubt assisted by technological innovations, is also likely to intensify. Horizontal relationships will thus be of vital importance. Formal hierarchies obviously supply the benefits of clarity and stability, but 'clan' and 'network' solutions are often more likely to provide the flexibility to respond to complex and fast-changing issues. How can the tensions created by the competing requirements of clarity and flexibility be reconciled?

With such questions in mind, this chapter explores the nature and implications of shared accountability in the state sector, with particular reference to New Zealand. We begin by considering some key concepts and their interrelationships.

This includes the nature of accountability, the distinction between vertical and horizontal accountability, the relationship between accountability and responsibility, and some of the sources of confusion surrounding the concepts of accountability, responsibility and blame. Next, we outline the key features of New Zealand's model of public management, highlighting its emphasis on formal, vertical, straight-line accountabilities (and their related unbroken chains of command). In so doing, however, we draw attention to the limitations of vertical accountability models within a Westminster-type parliamentary democracy, and the extent to which, in practice, there are significant departures from such models.

Following this, the chapter explores the reasons for, nature of and problems associated with joint working in the state sector. This includes an analysis of the drivers for joint working, the wider policy context, the intensity and scope of joint working, the design of governance arrangements and the options for accountability. Finally, we explore the policy levers available to accommodate new modes of inter-agency working. This leads to a consideration of the vital role that central agencies need to play in facilitating innovative practices within the public sector.

Note that the focus here is on *joined-up government* (i.e., joint working by government agencies) rather than *joined-up governance* (i.e., jointly deciding policy or service delivery matters with civil society). Joined-up or collaborative governance involves engaging with and empowering citizens/clients/businesses in the process of decision-making on policy development and/or service delivery. Of course, joint working often involves a degree of collaborative governance, but it need not. For instance, the classic functions of the state include providing internal and external security through the protection of borders from foreigners and the detection and incarceration of domestic criminals. To be effective, these functions typically require joint working (involving two or more government agencies). However, they do not need collaborative governance; indeed, that may impede effectiveness. Thus, while collaborative governance is important, it is beyond the scope of this chapter.

Key Concepts

Let us first explore the nature and implications of accountability and responsibility (and related concepts) in a governmental context. A major goal of policy makers within the democratic world in recent decades has been to enhance political and bureaucratic accountability. Under the influence of new public management (NPM) and related managerialist philosophies (see Hood, 1990), a number of common approaches have been adopted. These include better quality information on what governments do and how they do it, better specification of expected performance (both in relation to individuals and organisations), and improved reporting, monitoring and performance assessment. Additionally, many governments have sought to improve public access to 'official' information, enhance parliamentary scrutiny of governmental agencies and create new institutions, such as the Ombudsman, to scrutinise the conduct of those exercising public power.

Few countries have been more earnest in their quest for greater governmental accountability than New Zealand. As Schick (1996: 87) has argued:

> Taking accountability seriously is a genuine triumph of New Zealand public management. Other countries give lip service to holding managers accountable; New Zealand has robust mechanisms in place to enforce accountability.

This is not to suggest that the public management reforms of the late 1980s have resolved all the accountability issues within New Zealand's governmental institutions. To be sure, much has been achieved. Government agencies are now more accountable, not just in managerial and financial terms but also politically; and the nature of the responsibilities of ministers and officials has been clarified and, where possible, more carefully delineated. Yet, as discussed later in this chapter, certain problems remain. Critics of the reforms, for example, claim that the doctrine of individual ministerial responsibility has been weakened and that the emphasis on 'accountability' has gone hand in hand with a diminished sense, or understanding, of 'responsibility'. Such concerns were galvanised by the Cave Creek tragedy in April 1995 when 14 young people lost their lives as the result of a collapse of a viewing platform on conservation land (see Gregory, 1996; Noble, 1995).

The Nature of Accountability

What, then, does 'accountability' actually mean, and how does it relate to the separate notions of 'responsibility', 'answerability' and 'blame'? There is an extensive literature on such matters (see Gregory, 2003b; Mulgan, 2003). In brief, accountability is about a person rendering an account, or answering, to someone else for his or her actions or conduct. As Jones and Stewart (2009: 59) put it: 'Accountability implies an obligation to explain to someone else, who has authority to assess the account and allocate praise or blame for what was done or not done.'

More specifically, accountability can be thought of in terms of a triadic relationship: 'X' is accountable to 'Y' for 'Z'. For the accountability relationship to operate effectively it is necessary to know who 'X' is, who 'Y' is and the nature of 'Z' for which 'X' is to be held to account. If any of these elements is missing or unclear, the accountability relationship will be weakened, if not undermined altogether. Hence, as Stanyer (1974: 14) points out, 'Accountability always embodies a precise logical structure.' Gray and Jenkins (1985: 138) have advanced the same idea more elegantly:

> To be accountable is to be liable to present an account of, and answer for, the execution of responsibilities to those entrusting those responsibilities. Thus accountability is intrinsically linked to stewardship. Stewardship involves two manifest parties: a steward or accountor, that is, the party to whom the stewardship or responsibility is given and who is obliged to present an account of its execution, and the principal or accountee, that is, the party entrusting the responsibility to the steward and to whom the account is presented. There is however a third party in this relationship: the codes on the basis of which the relationship is struck and by which it is maintained and adjudicated.

Drawing on agency theory, Anderson and Dovey (2003: 5) suggest (in a thoughtful analysis of accountability and how the concept operates within the New Zealand model of public management) that accountability involves:

> a relationship based on the provision of information about performance from those who have it to those who have a right to know it, either because they have the power to reward or sanction, or because they have a 'right to know'. As a formal device, it includes both agent responsibilities (to inform) and principal responsibilities (to provide incentives – to reward and sanction). Its primary purpose is to close the performance management loop.

They go on to outline six important questions to ask in relation to any accountability arrangement:

1. Who will be held to account?
2. Who will hold them to account?
3. How and when will they be held to account?
4. For what will they formally be held to account?
5. To what standard?
6. With what effect (reward or sanction)?

There are, of course, many different kinds of accountability, each of which emphasises different values: legal (the rule of law), political (responsiveness), professional (expertise), managerial (effectiveness), financial (probity), and so on. In any given context, therefore, it is important to consider which particular form (or forms) of accountability is operative and to what extent it is effective and sufficient (see Stone, 1995). As Mulgan observes, there are many dimensions of accountability (*who, to whom, for what and how*), stages (*information, discussion and rectification*), and levels (*individual and collective*). To quote, 'Many different typologies have been advanced . . . but no one typology has emerged as standard or generally accepted' (Mulgan, 2003: 30).

For public servants in a parliamentary democracy like New Zealand, multiple forms of accountability apply (such as political, bureaucratic, legal, financial), together with accountabilities to multiple principals. For instance, departments are accountable to their portfolio minister (or ministers) and to the prime minister and cabinet; they are also accountable to parliament (typically via select committees), to the courts (for compliance with the law), and to the Controller and Auditor-General (and, at times, other Officers of Parliament). Equally, line departments are held to account by the central agencies, and the State Services Commissioner undertakes performance reviews of departmental chief executives. These multiple relationships are shown in Figure 7.1 in which the thick lined double arrow represents a broad and strong accountability and the narrow double arrow represents a more limited accountability. In fulfilling their public duties, therefore, public servants face multiple masters and a veritable plethora of reporting requirements and accountability mechanisms. Some are process-oriented and focused largely on compliance; some are behaviourally focused and concerned with integrity and probity; while yet others are output and outcome focused, and are thus primarily concerned with performance.

As Bovens (2007: 196) observes:

> Over the past decades, this Weberian, or in Britain Diceyan, monolithic system of hierarchical political and organisational accountability relations has been under serious pressure and is slowly giving way to a more diversified and pluralistic set of accountability relationships.

These pressures include strengthened notions of individual accountability (as exemplified by the Nuremburg trials), and the growth of the audit culture strengthening outwards horizontal accountability.

At the same time, it is important, as Jones and Stewart (2009: 59) argue, not to stretch the notion of accountability inappropriately 'to encompass certain relationships that fall short of genuine accountability'. For instance, in Figure 7.1 departments and other public agencies in parliamentary democracies are not generally *directly accountable* to citizens, voters, customers, clients, users and stakeholders. They are nonetheless *answerable* to them, at least in the sense of being *responsive* to their needs and interests, including, where appropriate, listening to their concerns, explaining government decisions, undertaking dialogue and providing information. In the absence of the ability to impose direct rewards and sanctions, no formal accountability relationship exists.

Vertical and Horizontal Accountability

Another important distinction of relevance to this analysis is that between vertical (or hierarchical) accountability and horizontal, lateral or mutual accountability (see Considine, 2002; O'Donnell, 1998). Vertical accountability refers to any relationship involving 'unequals' (i.e., in relation to power or authority) where an 'inferior' person (or agent) is directly accountable to a 'superior' person (or principal) for the performance of a particular task. Principal–agent relationships of this kind are extremely common. They occur within all organisational hierarchies (e.g., public organisations, private firms, NGOs), but also within the political system more generally. Under a Westminster-type system, public organisations are answerable to ministers, ministers in turn are answerable to parliament and MPs in turn must answer to voters.

Figure 7.1. Multiple Principals

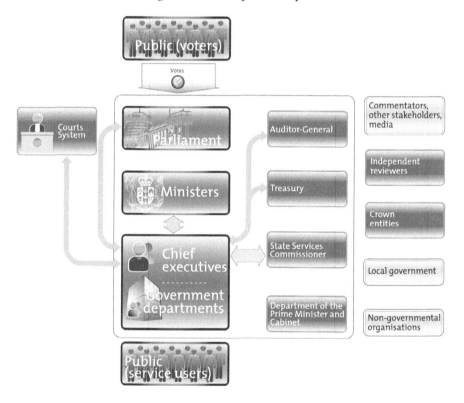

Unlike vertical accountability, the notion of horizontal accountability refers to situations where the people involved are more-or-less *equal* in authority or standing, and where a person (or persons) holds another person (or persons) accountable for their actions or behaviour. Such situations arise in various dimensions of life, such as marriage (or marriage-like relationships), partnerships, relationships between nation states, relationships involving professional peers, and so forth. That said, for horizontal accountability to operate effectively, there must be a sense in which the two parties are not on an absolutely equal footing with respect to the matters for which one is accountable to the other. Put differently, the accounting party must, at least in the relevant sphere of competence or activity, be in a position to exercise the power to impose sanctions and rewards – often through recourse to external sources of authority. Situations involving horizontal accountability thus entail an asymmetrical relationship of some kind, even if the parties in question are not in a typical principal–agent relationship.

Horizontal accountability can arise in at least two different ways. In the first instance, it occurs when one organisation is accountable to another of a similar status (e.g., a department to the courts system, as shown in Figure 7.1). This can be distinguished from the horizontal accountability that arises where two or more public agencies work together to deliver a particular result. As is discussed later in more detail, accountability for joint working essentially boils down to two main possibilities: sole or joint. Joint working can either be governed by a lead organisation that assumes sole accountability for the activity and its results, or governance and accountability can be jointly shared by the participants. A mix of the two may also be possible in some circumstances.

To complicate matters further, distinguishing between vertical and horizontal accountability is not always clear-cut. Consider contractual relationships: in theory the parties are equally free not to enter the contract; in practice, however, there may be a dominant seller or buyer. In such circumstances, one party can often largely determine the terms of the contract. Similarly, it might be argued that contracts between governments and non-governmental organisations are inherently unequal. After all, governments can typically exercise considerably more power (whether legal, moral or political) than parties in the private or voluntary sectors. Is it reasonable, therefore, to regard civil society actors as being equal to governmental actors? Scholars differ in their views on such matters. Irrespective of the answer, it is important to note that individuals (and organisations) can be jointly accountable for something (e.g., an activity or outcome), regardless of whether they are equal in power. Thus, both equal and unequal parties may be jointly accountable to a superior party. Sharing accountability, therefore, does not entail an equality of power or status, but such inequalities are an important tension that must be managed if shared working is to be effective.

Responsibility

Whereas 'accountability' has primarily to do with rendering an account, 'responsibility' is a much broader and richer concept (see Martin, 1996: 2). In particular, it embraces the idea that the consequences of a person's action or inaction matter and individuals have certain obligations or duties – moral, if not legal. Thus, as Gregory (1995a: 19) has put it:

> much more so than accountability, responsibility will usually place a burden of choice on a person; it may sometimes give rise to agonising moral dilemmas; it always demands a capacity for reflective judgement. A person, official or whomever, may give an account of the choices made, but responsibility requires one to contemplate reasons for those choices and to live with the consequences that flow from them. In this sense, therefore, accountability is a necessary but by no means sufficient component of responsibility.

There are several other important distinctions between accountability and responsibility. First, accountability is typically externally imposed; hence, it usually involves other parties. By contrast, responsibility can be (and often is) internally imposed; it involves a *felt* obligation or duty – generally, but not always, to others. Second, and related to this, whereas accountability implies that a person is answerable to someone else for something, a person can be responsible *for* something without necessarily being responsible *to* anyone for it (Mulgan, 1991). For instance, in a hierarchical organisation – like a government department, police or army – each person has certain functions or duties, and is responsible to a superior for satisfactorily performing them. But, and this is of crucial importance, whereas accountability implies answerability to another person (or persons), the same is not true with respect to responsibility. Hence, the point at which the buck stops, the place of ultimate authority, may be a point of genuine (and possibly great) responsibility without the person (or persons) who exercise this responsibility being responsible to any other person (or persons).

Thus, as Mulgan (1991: 4) observes, in the case of a limited liability company, the chief executive is directly responsible to the board and the board, in turn, to the shareholders. But the shareholders, although they bear ultimate responsibility for the fate of the board and the company, are not responsible to anyone. Likewise, in a parliamentary democracy some claim that the final political authority lies in parliament, others that it rests with the people. If it is the people, then, it can be said that the people are collectively responsible – in a broad sense – for the government of the country, but they are not responsible to anyone else.

Bear in mind, too, that the terms 'responsible' or 'responsibility' can have a number of different meanings, depending on the context. To illustrate, a cabinet minister can be seen as having the *authority* (or responsibility) to govern, a *duty* (or responsibility) to govern, a duty to govern *prudently* (responsibly) and a duty to govern *on behalf of others* (responsibly). A minister is also *liable* or *culpable* (responsible) for his or her decisions. In such a situation, the minister will also be accountable (e.g., to the prime minister, parliament and his/her electorate). It is important in any particular context, therefore, to be clear about the nature of the 'responsibility' to which one is referring.

Sources of Confusion

The problem of determining who is responsible (or accountable) for what and deciding what should be done when things go wrong is frequently the subject of confusion. This is no less the case in government than in other spheres of human endeavour. In fact, there are some particular features of government – including size, institutional complexity, multiple and overlapping jurisdictions, and the nature of the tasks being undertaken – that make it all the harder to determine where responsibility lies and to call individuals to account. Aside from the issues of shared accountability (that are addressed later), there are at least five important sources of confusion surrounding accountability in the governmental arena:

- a failure by the principal (e.g., a minister) to specify what is required of his or her agent (e.g., a departmental chief executive);
- a failure to understand the nature of the responsibilities attached to particular roles;
- a failure to distinguish responsibility and blame;
- a failure to recognise the difficulty in many situations of locating (or allocating) blame and applying sanctions; and
- a failure to recognise that in the event of evidence of maladministration the absence of a resignation does not imply that people have failed to exercise their responsibilities or that no one has been held to account.

The first of these reasons – the problem of performance specification – is well documented and readily understood. This does not always mean that there is a simple solution. It is often difficult, if not impossible, to specify precisely what is required and how performance will be assessed. Such problems are an inherent aspect of the difficulties affecting certain public sector organisations. Indeed, many activities are located within the public sector precisely because they involve serious problems of contract specification, monitoring and enforcement (e.g., policing, defence, the conduct of diplomacy).

Second, individuals have a number of different kinds of responsibilities. Many of these are associated with the particular *role* or *roles* that are being performed (e.g., the role of parent, employer, representative) (see Mulgan, 1994: 142). Those who lead organisations – whether they are a departmental chief executive, school principal, newspaper editor or a managing director – have very broad and demanding *role responsibilities*. In effect, they are responsible for everything that goes on within their organisation. This includes a duty of care for their employees, as well as for those affected by their organisation's operations (e.g., students, clients, customers or members of the public).

Third, there is often a failure to distinguish between responsibility, on the one hand, and blame or culpability on the other (see Holmes, 2010). Some people appear to think that if 'X' is responsible, then 'X' is automatically to *blame*, personally, directly and morally, if something goes wrong. Hence, if a minister is politically responsible for the administration of his or her department, it is assumed that the minister is personally to blame, and thus morally culpable, whenever mistakes are made by departmental officials. But such a view confuses the notions of responsibility and blame. One can be responsible for something without necessarily being to blame. This was the position of Bob Semple (the Minister of Works) in defending his position in response to the Turakina–Fordell tunnel disaster of 1944. His position was essentially, 'I am responsible but not to blame.' Of course, if a minister has personally contributed to a mistake being made (whether through acts of commission or omission) or directed officials to do something that was plainly wrong, then he or she is both responsible and to blame.

Fourth, when things go awry there can be significant difficulties identifying who is to blame, determining the appropriate sanctions and then applying these sanctions. The recent regulatory failure surrounding leaky buildings provides a good example of the complexities involved. Leaky buildings were not due to a simple cause like technology failure. Rather, they were the outcome of a complex interaction of several factors, among them new technologies, new regulatory standards, installation practices (the use of sealants), lack of awareness of the 10 cm clearances, new products (untreated timber) and a lack of owner maintenance (Mumford, 2011).

More generally, difficulties in allocating blame can arise because the evidence may be unclear or insufficient; and/or because of the large number of people implicated (with varying levels of responsibility), legal difficulties surrounding the application of particular sanctions, and the strong pressures to avoid actions that will cause political embarrassment. Alternatively, there may be political pressures for 'heads to roll' even though such action is unjustified. Within a Westminster-type constitutional framework, there are particular difficulties associated with the allocation of responsibilities within the cabinet (e.g., is the problem in question a matter for collective responsibility or individual ministerial responsibility or both?); and also between ministers and government agencies (e.g., if a departmental blunder has occurred partly, it seems, as a result of underfunding, how should the respective political and managerial responsibilities be assigned and what sanctions should be applied and to whom?).

Finally, there is a widespread view, certainly in New Zealand, that in the event of evidence of maladministration, someone – and preferably a minister – ought to resign. Only a resignation is seen as providing evidence that responsibility has been taken and that the associated guilt has been expiated. While such a view is understandable, it fails to recognise the range of sanctions that applies in the public realm (including the loss of reputation, a loss of votes by the government at a subsequent election or even just the embarrassment that can be generated by public discussion in the media) and that resignation, as the ultimate sanction, is appropriate in only a limited range of circumstances. Arguably, ministers should not be expected to resign over matters for which they are vicariously but not directly responsible, unless the issues in question are very serious (see McLeay, 1996). Against this, a resignation would be proper when a minister has deliberately lied to parliament or sought to secure improper personal advantages from the exercise of his or her ministerial authority. In practice, ministerial resignations, both in New Zealand and other parliamentary democracies, are relatively rare when the matter involves only vicarious responsibility. But in the event of a major policy failure, it is not uncommon for the relevant portfolio minister to offer his or her resignation, perhaps as the 'honourable' thing to do; prime ministers are then at liberty to accept or reject such resignations depending on the gravity of the situation and whether the minister in question is expendable.

Vertical Accountability and New Zealand's Model of Public Management

Having considered the nature and implications of accountability and responsibility, let us now turn to explore the dynamics of accountability – including its strengths and weaknesses – under the New Zealand model for public sector management. The New Zealand reforms of the late 1980s and early 1990s have been extensively studied, resulting in both enthusiastic reviews and critical commentaries. As Boston, Martin, Pallot and Walsh (1996: 382) observe, since the mid-1980s, 'virtually every aspect of public management in New Zealand has been redesigned, reorganised, or reconfigured in some way'. Unlike the public management reforms in some other jurisdictions, the quest for greater accountability was a fundamental driver of the New Zealand reforms. To quote Schick (1996: 9), 'Accountability has not been an afterthought in New Zealand, as it has in other countries that have implemented reform. Instead it has been robustly designed as an integral feature of the reformed public service.' A key premise on which the reforms relied was that, with effective accountability systems in place, robust performance information would generate better performance.

We will not traverse the theoretical, philosophical or political origins of these reforms as these matters have been well documented elsewhere (e.g., Boston, Martin, Pallot and Walsh, 1996). Instead, we explore the emphasis of the reforms on accountability – and in particular, their focus on *vertical* accountability. While the reforms introduced a number of innovative and path-breaking changes, there was also considerable continuity. In particular, New Zealand had enjoyed a long tradition of a non-partisan public service and a lack of ministerial involvement in staffing matters, and these features were retained. Indeed, some would argue that they were strengthened by the reforms.

Of the essential elements of the previous administrative system that were embraced in the new regime, three deserve particular mention:

- the role of the State Services Commissioner in appointing and overseeing the performance of departmental chief executives;
- the importance of ministers not interfering with the day-to-day operations of their departments; and
- the requirement for departmental chief executives to demonstrate consistently and constantly their 'serial loyalty' to ministers and the government of the day (Hood and Lodge, 2006).

While in theory the new accountability regime placed a powerful emphasis on vertical or hierarchical accountability (i.e., from voters to parliament, to ministers, to departmental chief executives, to senior managers, and so on down the chain of command), in practice the regime is much more subtle and complex; the simple, elegant, vertical cascade of accountability is thus more apparent than real. Five complications or qualifications deserve comment.

The first complication concerns the role of the State Services Commissioner in appointing and reviewing the performance of chief executives. Interestingly, given the importance of accountability to the formal system, the State Sector Act 1988 does not provide a clear answer to the question of to whom a departmental chief executive is accountable. Under the Act, the State Services Commissioner is the employer of all public service departmental chief executives on behalf of the Crown. The Act established a complex triangular relationship between departmental chief executives, ministers and the State Services Commissioner. In short, departmental chief executives have a dual accountability – to the Commissioner in respect of their standard of probity and integrity and to their responsible minister in relation to organisational performance (see Figure 7.2). The Commissioner's primary focus within this triangular relationship has been to enable the relationships to operate as effectively as possible. More specifically, the Commissioner has been concerned to establish minimum standards of probity, integrity and conduct for chief executives and their staff, and to review chief executive performance on behalf of the responsible minister. In his Annual Report for the year ended 30 June 2001, the Commissioner at the time, Michael Wintringham, commented on the triangular employment relationship, as follows:

> although the chief executive is *employed by* the State Services Commissioner, he or she *works for* their Responsible Minister. I can think of no other employment relationship where the terms *employed by* and *works for* are not synonymous. (SSC, 2001: 5, emphasis in original)

The State Sector Act 1988 is explicit about the general duties and powers of chief executives, and implies a prohibition on ministers' involvement in departmental staffing matters. Parliament's Standing Orders also set out some aspects of ministers' roles and responsibilities in relation to parliament. On operational matters, convention as codified in the *Cabinet Manual* imposes greater restrictions on ministers than those set out in legislation. The *Cabinet Manual* (2008: para 3.5) states that:

> Ministers decide both the direction and the priorities for their departments. They should not be involved in their departments' day-to-day operations. In general terms, Ministers are responsible for determining and promoting policy, defending policy decisions, and answering in the House [of Representatives] on both policy and operational matters.

Figure 7.2. Triangular Accountability Relationships

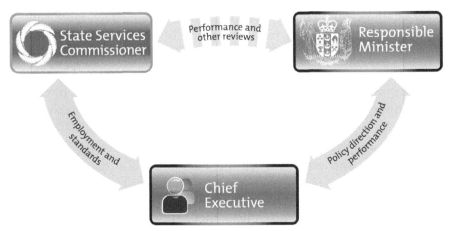

Hence, a departmental chief executive in New Zealand is responsible (in accordance with s32 of the State Sector Act and other relevant legislative provisions) for ensuring that the department operates efficiently and effectively, that the responsible minister is provided with policy advice, and that the staff of the organisation carry out their duties to obey the law, implement government policies, and follow departmental rules and guidelines. If something goes wrong within the department, the chief executive is answerable to his or her minister and is responsible for putting the matter right and ensuring that the same mistake doesn't happen again. If chief executives fail to fulfil such responsibilities, they face the prospect of being dismissed, or at least not being reappointed when their employment agreements expire. The Commissioner plays a central role both in reviewing what went wrong and in managing the performance of the chief executive in question.

The second complication to the simple regime of vertical accountability is continued fuzziness in the respective roles and responsibilities of ministers and chief executives that inevitably creates accountability issues, including the risk of accountability deficits. In a parliamentary democracy like New Zealand, ministers are *politically* responsible (to parliament and the public) for what their departments do, while chief executives are *managerially* responsible for the operations of their departments. Necessarily, these respective responsibilities overlap; they cannot be precisely delineated, as if chief executives' responsibilities begin only where those of ministers end (or vice versa). As Schick (1996: 42) has rightly put it:

> Fuzziness is inherent in an arrangement that assigns political risk to the Minister and managerial discretion to the chief executive .. . . as long as both the Minister and the chief executive have their hands on the rudder, one or both may be called to account, even when one has limited control over the other's actions.

Such shared and overlapping responsibilities are inevitably the source of some confusion and tension. Some people appear to assume that if person 'X' is responsible for 'A', then person 'Y' cannot also be responsible for 'A'. Hence, if a departmental chief executive is responsible for the management of a department, then a minister cannot also be responsible. The implication, in other words, is that there can be no shared or joint responsibility for departmental administration. But such a view is erroneous. There are many areas of life where responsibilities are shared between two or more people – boards of companies and the rearing of children are obvious examples.

It is sometimes argued that under the new model of public sector management, ministers are responsible for choosing *outcomes* and selecting *outputs* to achieve these outcomes, while chief executives are responsible for producing the outputs purchased by ministers in accordance with the relevant purchase agreement. Ministers, according to this view, are no longer in any sense responsible for the management of their departments; these responsibilities now rest solely with chief executives (see SSC, 1997: 5). Such a construction is, of course, a restatement of the old policy/administration divide. According to this view, ministers are only responsible for policy matters; they are not responsible for matters of administration. These are the rightful domain of departmental heads.

But again, such a view fails to understand the broad nature of a minister's role responsibilities as the *political* head of a department within a parliamentary democracy. This role carries with it the political responsibility for everything the department does, or fails to do, in carrying out the policies of the government and administering the laws of the country. As such, ministers are answerable to parliament and the public for the activities of their departments, whether or not they have knowledge of these activities. Hence, if a department is clearly operating inefficiently, the relevant portfolio minister must explain to parliament what is going on, why it is going on and what will be done about it. And the minister must, as part of his or her role responsibility, ensure that something is actually done to put things right. In short, ministers have *explanatory* and *amendatory* responsibilities.

The third complication to the simple vertical cascade is the lack (in most cases) of a simple one-to-one relationship between ministers and their departments in New Zealand. Unlike comparable jurisdictions, including Australia and the United Kingdom, where departments serve only one lead minister, the situation in New Zealand is relatively complicated. Leaving aside associate and junior ministers, three distinct arrangements can be observed for lead or senior ministers. The most common arrangement in New Zealand is where one department serves multiple lead ministers across a range of portfolios (e.g., the Ministry of Social Development in mid-2011 had three cabinet ministers with five different portfolios between them). The second most common arrangement is where a department has only one minister (e.g., the Solicitor General works solely to the Attorney General). The least common arrangement is where one portfolio is serviced by two or more departments (e.g., in the past the Minister for Biosecurity was served by two departments). Almost all large departments in New Zealand have multiple portfolio ministers, one of whom – the 'responsible' minister – has overall oversight of the performance of the department. Leaving aside the difficulties of achieving co-ordination in the face of so many political masters, the fact that many departments serve more than one minister raises issues of multiple accountabilities.

A fourth complication has arisen since the introduction of proportional representation in the mid-1990s, namely the establishment of coalition governments with ministers drawn from two or more parties. This means that chief executives and their departments not only serve multiple masters but also masters from different parties. This does not present particular difficulties when the coalition is cohesive and the relationships among the ministers are cordial. But this is not always the case, particularly as the coalition comes under strain. Various dilemmas can arise. For example, what should a chief executive do if a portfolio minister from a minority party asks him/her to do 'x' but not tell the central agencies or ministers from the major party? Is the chief executive primarily accountable to his/her minister or to the government as a whole? Arguably, the answer is that the chief executive is primarily accountable, in such circumstances, to the cabinet. As such, he or she should inform the head of the Department of the Prime Minister and Cabinet about what the minister has asked and their request for secrecy.

Box 1: Horizontal sector leadership meets vertical accountability

Cabinet, as part of a range of initiatives aimed at transforming state sector performance, formally mandated in 2010 that the Ministry of Social Development (MSD) assume a sector leadership role in the social sector, spanning health, education and justice for delivering 'outcomes focused social services' <http://ssc.govt.nz/sites/all/files/cabpaper-lifting-performance-and-service-delivery_0.pdf>. This mandate raised accountability questions as the chief executive (CE) of the MSD was to be accountable for ensuring that barriers were identified and removed and the mandate had the potential to cut across other CEs' accountabilities. In turn, this posed questions about how the various responsibilities should be reflected in the formal accountability documents.

In New Zealand's public management system, the *Output Plan* and the *Statement of Intent* are largely framed in terms of vertical responsibilities. The expenses involved in cross-sector leadership are insignificant compared with the overall Vote for Social Development, so the risk was that the leadership role would receive no explicit recognition in the formal system.

After tensions of the cross-sector leadership role were reviewed in 2010 with the Treasury and the State Services Commission, formal accountability emphasising 'capability' and 'activity' was adopted. The initial focus was to learn from pilot projects intended to improve outcomes for young people, as these could be expected to stretch current legal, contracting and financial systems.

Accountability for such cross-sector work would be reporting on progress against such work, with relevant activities agreed with ministers and resources shared across agencies, but with the MSD taking the lead to ensure progress (see MSD, *Statement of Intent*, 2011: 10–12). In a sense, this is a Procrustean bed, a forced fit to an existing standard, using a work-around to combine a horizontal role within a vertical accountability framework. There was no formal recognition of the followership responsibilities of the other agencies in their respective accountability documents.

A fifth complication is the increased pervasiveness and formalisation of joint working (both across government departments and agencies, and between the public and private sectors) and the challenges this raises for accountability. Inter-organisational working arrangements are increasingly being formalised, with greater shared accountability as departmental chief executives work in mandated clusters or sector groupings. The spread of joint-working arrangements is explored further below. Box 1 discusses a particular example of the social sector forum including the Ministries of Health, Education and Social Development. It suggests that the cross-cutting role of lead agencies is not readily accommodated within the formal external accountability documents as these emphasise vertical accountabilities. Likewise, the 'followership' responsibilities of the contributing partner agencies are not recognised at all in their respective accountability documents.

In summary, while New Zealand's model of public management emphasises – and relies heavily upon – formal, vertical, straight-line accountabilities, in practice there are limitations to such models within Westminster-type parliamentary democracies. In New Zealand these include the triangular relationship between ministers, departmental chief executives and the State Services Commissioner; the continued fuzziness in the respective roles of ministers and chief executives; the lack of a one-to-one relationship between ministers and departments; the complexity of working under proportional representation; and the rise of formalised, inter-organisational working arrangements. In practice, these represent significant departures from simple, vertical, straight-line accountabilities.

Joined-up Government: The Whys and Wherefores

We turn now to our primary concern, namely, the reasons for, nature of and problems confronting joined-up government, and particularly the issues that joint working pose for the design of accountability arrangements. We proceed here as follows. First, we consider why joined-up government is often needed and why it is likely to become more important over the coming decades. Second, we discuss the different kinds of problems that confront policy makers and especially the fact that these vary with respect to their stability and knowability. This has important implications for how joint working should be managed and governed. Third, we explore the various design options for working together and their implications for governance structures, accountability arrangements and the sharing of responsibilities. In so doing, we highlight three interrelated factors that are crucial to successful joint working: first, the policy choices with respect to both the intensity and scope of joint working need to reflect the nature of the problem being addressed; second, the governance arrangements need to be constructed and operated so as to encourage a shared sense of responsibility for the tasks being undertaken; and third, the formal accountability arrangements need to be clear-cut and congruent with the governance structures.

Why Joined-up Government is Needed

Generally speaking, the default way of working for state servants in New Zealand is within their organisations, with vertical reporting arrangements. This is confirmed by the survey conducted as part of the Managing for Performance project (under the auspices of the Institute of Policy Studies) which indicated that joint working is the exception rather than the rule. To illustrate, managers were asked how much time they and their staff spend on various activities including managing joint projects or relationships with other organisations. Overall, 24 per cent of managers reported that a lot or nearly all of their time is spent working jointly, but the amount varied depending on the nature of the activity (Gill, 2011: 384). This figure was significantly less than the percentage reported for direct services, directly enforcing regulations, reporting and internal services, but slightly higher than for policy advice and managing contracts with providers.

Typically, in New Zealand joint service delivery augments the default way of delivering services hierarchically via single organisations. It provides the opportunity for greater adaptability and flexibility to respond to changing circumstances. In such contexts, a joint group or network has the advantages of being able to access the capabilities and resources of their respective home organisations while retaining the agility of a small start-up organisation. At the same time, however, joint groups are vulnerable to internal group dynamics and disruptions from changes in the external environment.

Currently, while joint working is not the dominant mode of operating within the New Zealand government (see Box 1), it seems destined to become increasingly important. The need for cross-agency working arises in the modern state because of the way large bureaucracies are structured into multiple organisations and because a multitude of arms-length and third-party providers deliver publicly funded services. These arrangements generate a multiplicity of inter-organisational boundaries, and these boundaries, in turn, have numerous consequences: they create behavioural incentives, they establish rights and responsibilities, they generate barriers to the flow of ideas and information, and they foster inter-organisational competition. Boundary problems of this nature are inevitable regardless of how the government organises itself and contracts for services. Moreover, relationships between citizens/business and the state are complex and multiple, with a preponderance of many-to-many, rather than tidy one-to-one, relationships. To illustrate, consider the different state agencies with which citizens must interact when they face a major life event – such as if they move towns, if they go from education to work, if they shift from welfare to retirement or if they experience a major change in health status.

Moreover, the literature suggests that there is an increasing need for joint working across the state sector, not least because of several major drivers. These include:

- *Growing interdependencies*: for instance, there is a drive for improved alignment in response to trends (that long predate NPM) for more publicly funded services to be delivered by third-parties.
- *Rapid technological change*: for instance, new technologies are enabling real-time collaboration (authentication) and open systems are allowing greater integration opportunities (e.g., the Ministry of Agriculture and Fisheries and the New Zealand Customs Service have a common IT system at the border). The effect of many new technologies has been to change the transaction costs of joining up relative to operating as a hierarchy or silo.
- *Increased expectations of citizens and business for integrated services*: citizens expect governments to provide the same sort of integrated on-line services (such as drivers licensing) as occur in the private sector.
- *Increased complexity in the issues that governments are required to address*: this involves a move from the machine-age problems (e.g., paying benefits on time) to the 'wicked' problems (Rittel and Webber, 1973) of post-industrial societies (e.g., family violence and dysfunctional families). Addressing 'wicked' problems is likely to require the involvement of a number of players, with a growing realisation that 'we can't do it on our own'.
- *Increased reach of the domain of government*: the state has continued to expand from its classical origins, where the focus was largely limited to internal and external security, to the modern state with the emphasis on the four well-beings (i.e., social, cultural, economic and environmental).

Presently in New Zealand, there are three other immediate imperatives for increased inter-organisational collaboration: the fiscal driver to do more with less; the need to respond to unexpected events such as natural disasters, not least the major earthquakes in and around Christchurch; and the need to develop coherent responses to the big, longer-term policy challenges, such as enhancing labour productivity, coping with an ageing population and decarbonising the economy. For such reasons, the issues surrounding the design, governance and effectiveness of joint working are likely to become even more important over the coming decades.

The Policy Context and Joint Working

The design of joint working arrangements depends on a range of factors. One of these is the level of complexity of the policy problems and the extent to which the choice and mix of activities required can be reliably known in advance. Figure 7.3 shows how policy issues can be delineated according to the stability and knowability of the cause-and-effect relationship of the problem being addressed. On the right-hand side of Figure 7.3 are known and knowable issues. The former are often called 'tame problems' (see Rittel and Webber, 1973), in the sense that cause and effect are knowable in advance and are stable and predictable. The solutions are knowable, but may not have been implemented because of difficulties of bridging the boundaries between organisations. The latter – knowable – issues are 'expert problems' that can be centrally driven, using expert systems for service delivery based on output and outcome measures. For issues on the right-hand side of Figure 7.3, the conditions are such that effective working across boundaries can be guided by evidence-based policy or good practice derived from intervention logic, output and outcomes measurement, and the use of either relational or classical contracts to acquire services. For these sorts of problems, having a sole expert decision maker who is responsible for decisions can be expected to yield better results than relying on collective decision-making.

Figure 7.3. Complexity and Policy Problems

COMPLEX	KNOWABLE
Cause and effect are only coherent in retrospect and the pattern is not repeatable	Cause and effect are separated over time and space
• Pattern management • Perspective filters • Complex adaptive systems	• Analytical/reductionist • Scenario planning • Systems thinking
Probe Sense Respond	Sense Analyse Respond
CHAOS	KNOWN
No cause and effect relations are perceivable	Cause and effect relations are repeatable, perceivable, and predictable
• Stability focused intervention • Enactment tools • Crisis management	• Legitimate best practice • Standard operating procedures • Process re-engineering
Act Sense Respond	Sense Categorise Respond

Source: Gill, Pride, Gilbert and Norman (2010: 26), based on Kurtz and Snowden (2003).

On the left-hand side of Figure 7.3, by contrast, relationships between cause and effect are not knowable in advance; nor are such relationships necessarily stable or predictable. This is the world of complexity and chaos. *Complex* issues, where cause and effect are evident only in retrospect, are 'wicked' problems and are more likely to require a decentralised approach using tacit knowledge and partnerships. *Chaotic* issues, where even in hindsight cause and effect are difficult or impossible to determine, are 'intractable problems'; to the extent that they can be addressed they require a decentralised approach based on tacit knowledge. The 'wisdom of crowds' (Surowiecki, 2004) is a simple idea with significant implications. It suggests that groups of people are better than sole decision makers or small elites at solving problems and reaching wise judgements. In complex situations the 'wisdom of the crowds' through collective decision-making is likely to reduce sole-person risk. Sole-person risk particularly arises when a single decision maker faces complex issues.

Accordingly, when designing the institutional arrangements for joint working, it is important to consider the stability and knowability of the cause-and-effect relationship of the problem being addressed. For instance, in the world on the left-hand side of Figure 7.3, there is no stable intervention logic and there are no robust performance measures, and the outputs required cannot be reliably known in advance. In this zone, joint working will often be essential, but will need to be goal-orientated, emergent and spontaneous (as discussed in chapter 6 on policy implementation). As properties are emergent, the activities undertaken will need to morph – possible very quickly – as events change. Ideally in such situations, any joint working arrangements should be flexible, with the timeframes for accountability reflecting the fact that making progress on complex and chaotic issues can take many years. Unfortunately, this does not mesh well with the typical timeframes of public sector accountability systems, which are usually annual (or even shorter).

How to Work Together: The Design Options

Having considered the drivers for joint working and the different policy contexts within which such arrangements may arise, let us now explore some of the options for working together. From an institutional design perspective, two issues are of immediate relevance, namely, the intensity and scope of joint working. Generally speaking, as the intensity and/or the scope of joint working increases, so too will the formality and complexity of the required governance arrangements. As will be evident, the issues of intensity and scope are connected.

The Intensity of Joint Working

The intensity of joint working can vary across a spectrum as depicted in Figure 7.4. At one end of the spectrum, there is co-existence, which is not really joint working in any meaningful sense. At the other end of the spectrum, there is full collaboration, where there is shared commitment to common goals and shared responsibility for actions and outcomes. A good example in New Zealand is the integrated delivery of social services by central government agencies to two whānau in Papakura (Eppel et al., 2008). Between these extremes are communication (shared information), such as the Justice Sector Information Strategy; co-operation (shared resources), as exemplified by the National Maritime Coordination Centre; and co-ordination (shared work), such as authentication.

Thus, a key design issue is not simply *whether* to work together but, if so, with what intensity. Interestingly, both academics and practitioners suggest that the presumption should be in favour of choosing the least intensive form of joint working compatible with realising the desired goals. For instance, the guidance provided by the State Services Commission in 2004 was, in effect, 'don't work together unless you have to'. The clear implication is that low intensity should be preferred over high intensity, and that joint working should be selective. Deep, systematic engagement should be reserved for priority issues where collaborative working is more or less essential. Likewise, Pollitt (2003b) argues for a selective approach, contending that joint working should only be used where the potential benefits outweigh the risks and costs, and where the issues are significant and specific.

Figure 7.4 also highlights the different implications for responsibility depending upon the intensity of joint working. At one extreme, *communication* involves a limited negative duty of no surprises; while at the other extreme, *collaboration* involves a positive duty to deploy resources at your disposal to ensure collective success, if possible. In the latter case, responsibilities are typically shared rather than clearly separated and there is reliance on others over whom there is no direct control and little ability to impose sanctions or provide rewards. By contrast, the implications for the formal accountability system are more limited: in all the cases (other than *collaboration*) the resources are likely to remain under the control of the individual agencies that undertake defined tasks. Higher intensity joint working under collaboration raises more complicated accountability issues because of the difficulties in separating contributions, as discussed below.

Figure 7.4. Intensity of Shared Work and the Implications for Responsibility

Continuum of Inter-Governmental Integration				
Relationship Description				
Coexistence	Communication	Cooperation	Co-ordination	Collaboration
Relationship Formality				
Informal	→			Formal
Accountability Relationship				
N/A	No surprises	Not get in the way and help where possible	Actively align activities	Actively ensure goal achievement
Relationship Characteristics				
Self Reliance	Shared Information	Shared Resources	Shared Work	Shared Responsibility
No formal communication	Informal meetings e.g. web exchanges	Formal e.g. face to face meetings	Sharing on a regular formal basis	Formal partnership
Policies & services developed in isolation	Irregular exchange of practices	Regular exchange of staff, info practices	Regular exchanges & specific undertakings	Shared policies and/or practices
Autonomy emphasised	Autonomy retained	Autonomy attenuated	Autonomy further attenuated	Autonomy further attenuated still
May have common concerns	Getting together on common interests	Getting together on common projects	Working together on shared projects	Working together to common goals

The Scope of Joint Working

Related to the level of intensity of joint working is the question of scope. At least seven dimensions of scope can be identified:

- *Duration*: temporary (e.g., taskforces), intermittent (*ad hoc* groups) and permanent (standing committee);
- *Focus*: mainly policy development, mainly service delivery, or both policy and service delivery;
- *Societal reach*: central, regional or local government; NGOs; for-profits; and independent observers and experts;
- *Vertical reach*: to chief executive or ministerial oversight;
- *Horizontal reach*: membership that is open versus closed, narrow versus wide, the role (if any) of the central agencies, etc.;
- *Breadth*: limited focus on specific transactions versus wider focus on shared outcomes; and
- *Orientation and purpose*: simple commitment to alignment of activities and outputs versus commitment to more complex common outcomes.

The mathematics of network size provides the intuition for problems of intensity and scope. For each extension in horizontal reach, which adds a node to the network, the number of links between member organisations grows exponentially. Shared governance of networks relies heavily on trust and this is harder to sustain when there is a larger number of actors. Provan and Kenis (2008: 241) argue that a shared governance network is more likely to be effective where the number of network participants is low and the goal consensus is high. By contrast, they suggest that 'lead organisation network governance will be most effective when trust is narrowly shared . . . there are a relatively moderate number of network participants, when . . . goal consensus is moderately low' and the required network-level competencies are moderate.

Governance Arrangements: Hard and Soft Factors

Once the intensity and scope of joint working have been determined, the next challenges are to ensure that the appropriate governance arrangements are selected and that these serve to encourage the required level of shared responsibility for the task in hand. There are two main types of design choices for governance arrangements: the first cover the 'hard' or 'objective' factors (e.g., are they the right group?) relating to the systems, structures and institutions involved; the second cover the 'soft' or 'subjective' factors (are they governed right?) relating to people and relationships.

More specifically, the 'hard' factors include choices on a number of dimensions, such as:

- *Structure*: Is a structure established and if so is it an *ad hoc* inter-departmental committee (IDC), a standing IDC or a task force?
- *Decision rights*: Does the group have decision-making powers or only an advisory role?
- *Participants*: Is membership of the group open or closed, narrow or wide, limited to experts or much broader? What is the required level of skills and competencies?
- *Formal mandate and commissioning*: Is a formal top-down signoff (e.g., from ministers, chief executives or senior management) required, or is the group that emerges (and morphs) driven from the bottom up by the participants?
- *Formality of rules*: What are the terms of reference, goals and roles and how formal are they?
- *Processes*: How are contracts, project plans and formal agendas used?
- *Leadership*: Are leadership responsibilities shared or is there a lead agency? If the latter, is it the largest dominant agency or another party?

- *Support structures:* Is there a formal dedicated secretariat or a revolving secretariat? What are the systems for setting agendas and knowledge management?
- *Staff:* Are there explicit staffing positions established and are they filled by secondments, temporary or permanent appointments?
- *Resources:* Is there an explicit budget and how substantial are the available resources?
- *Mode of control:* Are the modes of control predominantly person-centred, formal bureaucratic, output-based, cultural-/clan-based or reputation-based?
- *Priorities:* How are the inevitable tensions between the vertical organisational priorities and the horizontal pressures arising from the joint work to be resolved?
- *Performance information:* What information will be available on activities, outputs and outcomes?

The key 'hard' choices in the design of institutional arrangements are between what have been called *externally governed* and *participant governed* arrangements (see Provan and Kenis, 2008: 235). An example of the former is the body overseeing the allocation of domain names – ICANN or Internet Corporation for Assigned Names and Numbers. Participant-governed arrangements can be separated into *shared-participant governed networks*, where leadership responsibilities are shared, and *lead-organisation governed networks*. In the latter case, one of the parties involved will be selected to provide overall leadership (or at least serve as an honest broker). Often, this will be the largest agency, but it need not be.

Other 'hard' factors can also be important, but this will depend on the context. Leadership and followership, for instance, are typically critical components of successful joint working (Bryson, Crosby and Stone, 2006). Interestingly, however, a formal top-down mandate from the cabinet, although a useful supporting condition, is neither a necessary nor sufficient condition for joint working to be effective.

In practice, in New Zealand a number of models to address the governance and leadership of joint working networks can be observed. These include: shared joint leadership, as in the case of 'Strengthening Families' where there was no fixed secretariat or designated leader; lead organisation leadership, which in the case of the Social Sector Forum has been formally mandated by the cabinet; and minor agency leadership, as in the case of the National Maritime Coordination Centre where Customs was selected to provide honest-broker leadership of the network (see Eppel et al., 2008).

In addition to these 'hard' systems concerned with administrative capabilities, there are also 'soft' or subjective factors to do with creating social capability, positive group dynamics and behaviours, and a sense of shared responsibility. The literature on corporate governance suggests that getting the 'hard' factors right is neither necessary nor sufficient for achieving high quality governance. In other words, getting the structure right is only part of the story. To quote Edwards and Clough (2005: 26): 'Hard factors take us some way but simply adopting them is not enough – we need to focus on . . . interrelationships and behaviours and the policies and procedures that support effective behaviours.' In a similar vein, in inter-agency working the 'soft' factors are crucial for building trust and performance within the group as well as for outside legitimacy. These 'soft' factors include:

- the initial conditions: whether there are relationships, processes or structures already in place;
- the distinctive phases of the group dynamics – starting, getting together, working together, sustaining – and how the group's resources need to be augmented by learning and organisational support;
- dealing with the diversity of institutional logics and perspectives and building alignment in world view or a shared conception of the problem;
- framing and reframing the issues to build a shared purpose, shared problem, shared vision and shared sense-making;
- power: are differences in relative power managed?
- leadership: personal leadership (understanding self and others), team leadership (building the group), visionary leadership (creating and communicating shared vision), ethical leadership (adjudicating disputes and sanction conduct), and entrepreneurship;
- followership: the role of personalities in influencing group behaviours and norms;
- path dependence: getting early runs on the board that lay the foundations for the longer haul;
- managing conflict;
- dealing with emergences and emergent issues; and
- how key roles – such as guardian angels, public entrepreneurs and fellow travellers – are enacted (see Eppel et al., 2008).

These 'soft' factors are often the most difficult to address in the context of joint working. Without the skills in the team, a shared narrative based on a common view of the problem and the purpose of the exercise, inter-agency working will be trapped in low-level co-existence and communication with limited shared responsibility. Building the required level of shared responsibility requires aligning both the 'hard' and 'soft' factors. In many situations, this is neither easy nor straightforward.

Joint Working and Accountability

As noted earlier in the chapter, any analysis of accountability raises at least six questions:

1. Who will be held to account?
2. Who will hold them to account?
3. How and when will they be held to account?
4. For what will they formally be held to account?
5. What is the required performance standard?
6. And what are the available rewards or sanctions?

In the context of joint working – especially at the collaboration end of the spectrum (see Figure 7.4) – who should be held to account and for what? Realistically, there are only three options, at least in terms of the formal accountability system: accountability can be concentrated in one actor (i.e., one person or organisation), or it can be diffused or shared across a number of actors, or there can be a mix of concentrated and diffused accountability. Each approach has strengths and weaknesses (see Mulgan, 2003).

In the first situation, one actor serves as the single point or focus of accountability. This person or organisation is thus responsible for the whole operation, including both procedural and substantive matters. The relevant actor is therefore answerable if things go wrong; there can be no question, in other words, as to where the buck stops. For such an accountability regime to work effectively, the relevant actor must be able to exercise an appropriate level of control over what is done and how. Otherwise, there will be a mismatch between responsibility and control. Likewise, such an approach implies that the activities of the various participating entities are reported in an integrated manner (even if some separate reporting also occurs).

Under the second approach, accountability is diffused, with each contributing organisation being answerable for, and reporting on, its own contribution and performance. Hence, unless integrated reporting is explicitly mandated, reporting will be fragmented with no single entity accountable for reporting on a holistic basis. Where one participant takes the lead role, reporting will typically be integrated but answerability for actions remains dispersed. Shared accountability under joint working can obviously generate a number of problems with rectification because of the lack of clarity about who exactly is responsible when things go awry. In such situations, the parties may engage in buck-passing and blame-shifting. As Jones and Stewart (2009: 63) highlight, there is a risk that 'Shared accountability becomes, in practice, joint irresponsibility, where no one is accountable.' Other problems may arise if there are different principals to whom the various agents are accountable and if these principals have differing expectations about performance, contrasting subordinate goals, or different information and reporting requirements. Other things being equal, such problems are likely to grow exponentially as the number of organisations (and related principals) increases.

A third possible approach is to mix concentrated and diffused accountability. That is to say, there is shared accountability for some of the required tasks or outputs, but in other cases accountability is focused on one actor (or, alternatively, several actors may be separately responsible for a series of different tasks). There do not appear to be any current examples of this model in New Zealand. Nevertheless, there is the potential to develop this approach, for example, by using the levers set out in Table 7.1, as will be discussed shortly. In all likelihood, this approach will have the advantages and disadvantages of the other two options.

In determining whether formal accountability should be concentrated or diffused, several criteria are relevant. The first is separability, namely, the ease with which tasks or outputs can be broken into discrete parts. In short, can the performance of individual discrete activities be adequately specified and measured separately? The second is interdependence – that is, the extent to which the results depend on the actions of others over which one has little or no control. Where activities are clearly separable, measurable and not interdependent, specific responsibilities can be allocated to the various parties and the relevant party can be held to account for meeting the required performance. In this situation it is clear who is accountable when mistakes are made and who is responsible for rectification. Other things being equal, where the tasks or outputs are not readily separable and/or they are highly interdependent, there is a stronger case for shared accountability. Yet, as noted, this is likely to result in fuzzy accountability for remediation. However, this may be the price that must be paid to secure the gains from a joint commitment to shared action in a context where separability is low and/or interdependence is high. In short, each solution poses problems, and it will not always be obvious which approach is likely to yield the best overall outcomes.

To illustrate, consider the vexed case of the defence forces acquiring and managing new military capabilities. There are six somewhat overlapping but distinct phases in the life of each specific capability:

1. the strategic policy decisions;
2. development of capability specifications;
3. acquisition;
4. introduction into service;
5. operation and maintenance in service; and
6. decommissioning and disposal.

In New Zealand, the provisions of the Defence Act 1990 currently mean that the Secretary of Defence is primarily accountable for the strategic policy and acquisition phases, while the Chief of Defence Force is primarily accountable for the other four phases. But the reality is more complicated because information and expertise must often be shared and because the 'hold-up problem' can arise. As was evident in the late 1980s and early 1990s, the Secretary of Defence is unable to deliver on his or her accountabilities without the active co-operation of the Chief of Defence Force. To achieve good outcomes, therefore, they must work together effectively.

Finally, there is the issue of *to whom* those involved in joint working are accountable. There are various possibilities here, depending on the context. Figures 7.5 and 7.6 outline different cases of shared accountability where two or more organisations are jointly responsible for undertaking a common set of activities or delivering an agreed outcome. In Figure 7.5, there are two organisations involved, but they serve a common principal. Accordingly, accountability relationships are relatively straightforward – although issues may still arise in allocating praise or blame if there is a poor understanding of how the two organisations are supposed to work together and if the various tasks are non-separable and highly interdependent. By contrast, in Figure 7.6, there are four agents responsible for a particular activity or outcome, but they serve two separate (and potentially competing) principals. Additionally, agent 'B' reports to two separate sub-principals. Such situations will inevitably raise greater co-ordination and accountability issues.

Implications for Practice

As will be evident from the preceding discussion, the issues surrounding joint working and accountability in a governmental context are complex – and potentially quite confusing. This may be frustrating, but it reflects the nature of the world. As our analysis highlights, the challenges for policy makers and state sector managers are likely to be all the greater where the problems being addressed are 'wicked', where the tasks that need to be undertaken are non-separable and difficult to measure, where there is a high degree of organisational interdependence, where there are multiple (and potentially competing) principals, and where the formal accountability regime (and hence the primary external incentive structure) is hierarchical and thus poorly aligned with the requirements of shared accountability. But even where the policy problems are relatively 'tame' and the various tasks are separable and measurable, joint working still generates difficulties. It is not surprising, therefore, that joint working arrangements are typically hard to organise and manage, and that accountability for performance is often weak and muted. Given this situation, how might progress be made?

Figure 7.5. A Simple Example of Shared Accountability

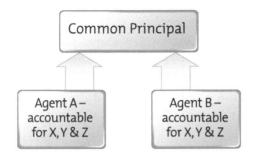

Figure 7.6. A More Complex Example of Shared Accountability

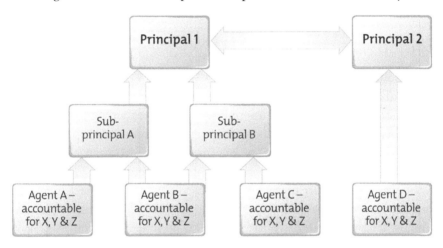

One approach is to consider the various kinds of public management levers that are (or potentially could be) available to policy makers and how these might be deployed to enhance accountability in the context of joint working. Table 7.1 outlines some of the possible levers that could be deployed in New Zealand. They are structured under five headings – leadership, learning, resources, policy and frontline practice; and grouped into two categories – minor modifications to current policy settings and more significant changes. Plainly, each of these possible modifications will have both strengths and weaknesses. Obviously, too, the relevance and merits of any particular lever will depend upon the context and vary case by case.

Among other things, Table 7.1 highlights the fact that the central agencies – the Department of Prime Minister and Cabinet, the State Services Commission and the Treasury – have a key leadership role to play as advisers to the government on public management in grappling with ambiguity and supporting new ways of working. These roles include:

- leadership and legitimisation – creating the environment that facilitates these different ways of working;
- building a network of networkers and joining up the joining uppers;
- promoting learning opportunities about working jointly, including emphasising the skills and capacities required for working jointly; and
- developing tool kits for identifying ways of working matched to the context and the problem that build the requisite sense of shared responsibility and commitment.

Like all good leaders, there is an art in knowing when to help and when to get out of the way. At the same time, central agencies cannot do this independently. They need the support of the line agencies and the staff who work in them. Co-operative working is thus essential.

Conclusion

By international standards, New Zealand has long enjoyed a high degree of governmental accountability. This applies to all levels of government (i.e., national and sub-national), and equally to the political and bureaucratic arms of the state. Prior to the major constitutional and public management reforms of the late 1980s and early 1990s, political legitimacy stemmed largely from an electoral system that typically gave a single party a majority in parliament and hence the right to govern. In this world, bureaucratic accountability was organised hierarchically and was primarily concerned with probity and rule-following to achieve the policy goals set by ministers. With the public management reforms, however, bureaucratic accountability was refined and extended, with much more emphasis being placed on organisational performance. This led to greater transparency and openness, clearer expectations, improved reporting and monitoring, better information, and enhanced parliamentary (and extra-parliamentary) scrutiny of governmental agencies. We readily acknowledge, of course, that the new arrangements are far from perfect. Indeed, as explained in this chapter, various complications and tensions remain, not least over the respective responsibilities of ministers and officials (or between politics and administration). In part, this is because in the realm of democratic government certain responsibilities cannot be neatly divided up and parcelled out to separate 'players'. But the reforms undoubtedly brought some significant improvements to the overall framework of governmental accountability; this is to be welcomed and celebrated.

Looking ahead, given the nature and complexity of the issues facing humanity – whether locally, nationally or internationally – both joined-up government and collaborative governance are likely to be increasingly important. The resultant sharing of power and responsibility is bound to pose new challenges for political and bureaucratic accountability. The focus of this chapter has been on the accountability issues raised by joined-up government (i.e., where power and responsibility are shared among the governors) rather than collaborative governance (i.e., where power and responsibility are shared between the governors and the governed). This is not to suggest that the latter is unimportant, but it requires separate consideration.

Table 7.1. Policy Levers to Improve Accountability for Joint Working

Focus	Minimal modification	More significant modifications
Leadership		
Ministers	Fewer ministerial portfolios PM priority letters emphasize cross-agency priorities Letters of expectation between ministers and CEs Crown entities emphasize sector priorities Formal cabinet mandate for cross-agency work	Formalized Strategic Management System
Central agencies	CE performance expectations include joint work CE remuneration partly tied to contribution to joint work Additional requirements for cross-cutting work in: • Statements of Intent, Output Plans, Statements of Service Performance • Annual reports Sector Performance Improvement Framework reviews Network of networks learning fora Appointing joint-work champions	Lead sector CE involved in appointment process for other sector CEs Lead sector CE undertakes, jointly with the State Services Commission, performance reviews of sector CEs
Individual Agency Leadership	Staff Selection – jobs are defined to include joint work and collaborative skills are sought Staff Development – coaching and training in joint working Staff reward – implicit and extrinsic motivators support joint working	
Learning	Joint evaluation strategies Learning fora Pilots and trials	
Resources	Multi-output class and multi-year appropriations	Multi-agency appropriations (using a lead agency)
Policy	New requirements for particular policy initiatives along the lines of Regulatory Impact Statements	Amend Cabinet Manual and CAB 101
Frontline practice	Lead contractor for third-party contracts Job descriptions include joint-work competencies Practice manuals include joint-work practices	Common risk screening tools

As highlighted in Figure 7.4, joined-up government can take a number of forms – from communication at one end of the spectrum to collaboration at the other end. In determining which form should be adopted – and hence what the most appropriate governance and accountability arrangements might be – the following matters need to be considered:

- the policy context, and especially the complexity of the problem being addressed (e.g., to what extent can the choice and mix of activities required be reliably known in advance?);
- the desired intensity of joint working (e.g., is it communication, co-ordination, co-operation or collaboration?);
- the desired scope of joint working (e.g., how many organisations are involved and how much goal alignment exists?);
- the options with respect to various 'hard' factors (e.g., whether externally governed or participant-governed arrangements are preferred and, if the latter, whether shared-participant or lead-organisation arrangements are preferred);
- the options with respect to various 'soft' factors (e.g., the preferred style of leadership, conflict management and issue framing); and
- the separability and interdependence of the tasks to be undertaken or the outputs to be delivered (e.g., whether the performance of individual discrete activities can be adequately specified and measured separately).

We do not wish to pretend that answering these questions will always be easy. Indeed, in many cases there is likely to be much uncertainty as to the best way forward, with conflicting views over whether the preferable form of joint working should be more towards one end of the spectrum or the other. However, whatever the precise choices, a number of points need to be underscored.

First, while formal accountability arrangements matter – not least because of the incentives they generate – they are not the only thing that matters. In the context of joint working – especially, but not only, at the collaboration end of the spectrum – it is vital for all the participants to share a sense of 'ownership' for what is being done and a felt duty or obligation to contribute. A strong sense of shared responsibility is thus essential, whatever the formal accountability regime. This objective will be more difficult to achieve, however, if the 'soft' and 'hard' governance arrangements are not properly aligned.

Second, concerning the respective merits of concentrated versus diffuse accountability, our analysis suggests that, in the context of joint working, concentrated accountability is likely to work best when the required tasks are clearly separable (and measurable), interdependence is low and sole-person risk is minimal. This implies that the policy problems are relatively 'tame' in nature. Conversely, shared or diffuse accountability appears to be preferable when the tasks are difficult to separate, interdependence is high and collective wisdom is likely to reduce sole-person risk.

Third, given the increasing importance of joined-up government, there is a need for some creative thinking about how the policy levers available within the public sector can be more effectively deployed (and/or modified) to encourage new and successful forms of joint working. As we have argued, this needs central agency leadership. It also requires a willingness to place more emphasis on horizontal accountability mechanisms.

Finally, while hierarchies and vertical accountabilities are bound to remain central features of any public management system within a parliamentary democracy, state servants need to be mindful of the increasing expectations for them to deliver 'results' and to do so a in context of ongoing fiscal restraint and mounting 'wicked' problems . This will require innovative practices, a new openness to collaborative arrangements and a broad conception of accountability. On this theme we leave the last word to Considine (2002: 22):

> In the new world of enterprising government, the public official is expected both to honor his or her official mandate and to move freely outside the hierarchical constraints of government in search of collaborative and quasimarket relationships with contractors, competitors and coproducers. This multidimensional agency power suggests that accountability cannot be defined primarily either as the following of rules or as honest communication with one's superiors. Rather, it now involves what might be thought of as the appropriate exercise of a navigational competence: that is, the proper use of authority to range freely across a multirelationship terrain in search of the most advantageous path to success.

8

'E-Government is dead – Long live networked governance': Fixing System Errors in the New Zealand Public Management System

Miriam Lips

Introduction

Government's use of Twitter as a critical communication platform to exchange information with the people of Christchurch immediately after the February earthquake; starting up your own business within five minutes through the Companies Office website; crossing international borders without the customs and immigration checks performed by a Customs officer but by self-service using an e-passport combined with face-recognition technology: these are real-life examples of the profound impact information and communication technologies (ICTs) are having on the New Zealand public management system and its external relationships. It is undeniable and even inescapable perhaps that ICTs will be a critical infrastructure for the future state. However, the complexities related to this topic area of what is often called 'e-government' are vast and should not be underestimated. Indeed, persistent traumas around the failure of large e-government initiatives in the past, such as INCIS, still resonate with many public officials. As a result, some see the introduction, management and use of ICTs in the public sector as 'dangerous enthusiasms' (Gauld and Goldfinch, 2006) that should be treated with caution.

Consequently, in order to get a better grip on the system requirements and conditions needed for the shaping of the ICT-enabled future state, it is of vital importance that we try to unpack these complexities. This is what I will do in this chapter. First of all I explain that a significant part of these complexities is caused by narrow perspectives on e-government and misleading expectations of the transformational potential of technology in public sector reform processes. Such assumptions and opinions often lead to recommendations of future models and solutions that are not aligned with the managerial, governmental and democratic realities faced by public sector leaders. Another set of complexities has to do with the dominant focus on the technical tools in e-government initiatives, causing situations in which e-government users, the wider social context and the institutional environment in which ICTs are being used are easily forgotten. I therefore argue that, in order to get a deeper understanding of the changes happening across the public sector (including its external relationships), and of the transformational outcomes and implications of these changes, we need more empirical research into the actual use of ICTs. Finally, I stress that we need to explore opportunities offered by moving away from a government-centric approach towards public service development and delivery, while at the same time shifting towards new ICT-enabled citizen-centric service models, such as Networked Governance. I conclude this chapter by summarising a few system errors which, in my view, need to be fixed in the current public management system in order to make any progress with the design of an effective and efficient ICT-enabled future state.

'We are governed by technology' . . . Yeah Right!

The arrival of new technologies has always captured the lively imagination of reformists. We know that earlier technological revolutions, such as the book press, electricity, the automobile or the telephone, have profoundly and systematically changed our society. We often look back at these transformative events as seismic shocks with a strongly upward-progressing outcome. In so doing we usually fail to see the 'muddling through' processes that actually accompanied the initial utilisations of these technologies, the learning curves that have occurred from the moment that the technologies were introduced. For example, the telephone was introduced not with the intention of allowing people to speak to other people long distance but to enable them to listen to opera. Another example is the automobile: it was initially used as a replacement for horse-led carriages on farms, and was never conceptualised as a vehicle for driving long distances between cities. Both examples demonstrate that newly available technologies are sometimes used for purposes that were never part of their original design, as people have used them and seen their potential – often almost serendipously.

Consequently, technology-related transformation should not be considered as a predictable, easy, quick or straightforward process. And yet, throughout the history of e-government visions, strategies and initiatives taken by governments around the world, we can observe strong ambitions and even higher expectations for e-government outcomes, due to the acknowledged transformative power of ICTs and in particular the internet. For example, in 1993, when the term 'electronic government' was first introduced in the Clinton–Gore administration's National Performance Review document, 'Reengineering Through Information Technology', there was a clear and explicit expectation that the internet would create the government of the future. In New Zealand, the 2006 e-government strategy goals demonstrated a strong belief in the transformational changes in the public sector and its external relationships as a result of ICTs:

- by 2007, ICTs will be integral to the delivery of government information, services and processes;
- by 2010, the operation of government will be transformed as government agencies and their partners use technology to provide user-centred information and services and to achieve joint outcomes; and
- by 2020, people's engagement with government will have been transformed, as increasing and innovative use is made of the opportunities offered by network technologies (see <http://www.e.govt. nz/guidance-and-resources/previous-e-government-strategy-2006>).

The 2007 and 2010 examples demonstrate a common perspective on the relationship between technology and society. This perspective is called in scholarly terms 'technological determinism' (MacKenzie and Wajcman, 1985): the idea that the intrinsic capabilities of technologies drive societal developments. According to this perspective, technologies have effects on society that are inherent, autonomous and independent, rather than caused, conditioned or shaped in any way by society. Technological determinists therefore perceive technology as a governing force in society, and e-government as a driver of transformational change in the public sector or, as Henman puts it, 'it is undeniable, we are governed by technology today' (2010: 3).

In opposition to this technological deterministic perspective, scholars have come up with an alternative perspective of the social shaping or, in its most extreme form, social determinism, of technology (Homburg, 2008; MacKenzie and Wajcman, 1985; Orlikowski and Barley, 2001). According to this perspective, technologies are not exogenous to or independent of societal factors, but shape, and are shaped by, the social and institutional environment in which they are used. Consequently, although technology and institutional context, more specifically 'e' and 'government', are often treated as separate domains, they need to be seen as interacting with each other (Homburg, 2008). Therefore, the transformational potential embedded in ICTs cannot be considered as a given. Rather, the outcome of e-government is dependent on the actual use of the technical functionalities and capabilities of ICTs in a particular institutional context with certain rules, norms and values.

In recent times, we can observe a shift in the underlying perspective of many e-government strategies around the world: moving away from a technological deterministic perspective, there is an explicit acknowledgement in many countries that technology is not *driving* change, but is an *enabler* of change. Increasingly, this explicit acknowledgement goes together with an implicit understanding that the institutional context, in which ICTs are used, is critical to the outcome of an e-government initiative: an emerging awareness that e-government is very much a public management issue, rather than a technology issue. Consequently, e-government should no longer be owned by an IT department, but by public management leadership.

In the New Zealand public sector, we can observe this shift in perspective, for instance, in the replacement of the 2006 e-Government Strategy by the 2010 Directions and Priorities for Government ICT Strategy. In this Cabinet Paper, pointing out how central government will more collectively lead the use, development and purchasing of government ICT over the next three years, the Ministerial Committee on Government ICT has proposed a strategic framework with five Directions and fifteen Priorities, which fit within a governance structure that goes right to the very top levels of government (see <http://www.ict.govt.nz/directions-and-priorities?OpenDocument>). For instance, according to this medium-term strategy, ministers and agency chief executives will make strategic decisions together about government ICT investment priorities and funding; funding models will be developed that incentivise collaboration across government; a Government Common ICT Capability Roadmap will provide a combined 'line of sight' across a portfolio of services, projects and new initiatives; and agencies will be able to make products and services available to one another as part of their core business. It is to be expected that by implementing these Directions and Priorities, public sector leaders will become increasingly aware of the critical importance of treating e-government as a complex public management issue, rather than a predictable, straightforward technological transformation project.

New Public Management or Digital-era Governance?

For a long time, technology and public management, or 'e' and 'government', have been treated as separate domains in government agencies. A similar tendency can be observed in academe, with some good exceptions to the rule (e.g., Bellamy and Taylor, 1998; Borins et al., 2007; Fountain, 2001; Snellen and Van de Donk, 1998). Typically, many scholars have considered the 'e' to be a technological or information systems (IS) topic and 'government' on the other hand to be owned by scholars in public administration and management. Commonly, E-government (usually with a capital 'E') was considered as a typical IS topic, without much difference in treatment between E-government and E-commerce, as both topics use the same technological platform. In the same vein, many public administration and management scholars did not perceive e-government to be of any relevance to them (Meijer, 2007). This strong disciplinary separation also led to a situation in which those public administration scholars with an interest in e-government were usually more or less exclusively focused on the public administration aspects and impacts of e-government, without opening the 'black box' of the ICTs involved (Lenk, 2007).

The absence of an interdisciplinary or at least multidisciplinary treatment of e-government in the mainstream of scholarship in both IS and public administration has led to neglect and ignorance around the 'government' aspects among IS scholars and around the 'e' aspects among scholars in public administration and management. It may not be surprising therefore that those public administration scholars with an interest in e-government and its impact on the public sector may demonstrate a naive belief in the transformational potential of ICTs and the governing capabilities of these technologies (Taylor and Lips, 2008). For example, some argue that the new public management (NPM) model is dead and is replaced by a so-called 'Digital-Era Governance' (DEG) model (Dunleavy et al., 2006a and 2006b). Due to newly available pervasive information-handling opportunities, this public management reform model is seen as a response to emerging public sector problems resulting from NPM reforms. The DEG model can be characterised under the following three themes (Dunleavy et al., 2006b; Lips et al., 2009: 841):

- *Reintegration*: ICTs will put back together many of the functions and expertise clusters that NPM separated into single-function organisational units. Examples are the use of digital identity management systems to facilitate joined-up government or to re-strengthen central processes in order to reduce duplication across government.
- *Needs-based holism*: ICTs will simplify and change the entire relationship between agencies and their clients, moving away from the NPM focus on business process management and towards a citizen- or needs-based foundation for organisation. Examples are ICT-enabled public service reorganisations around a single client group or ask-once processes supported by reusing already-collected citizen information.
- *Digitisation changes*: electronic channels become the central feature of administrative and business processes. Examples are new forms of automated processes where no human intervention is needed in an administrative operation, such as electronic monitoring of customers (e.g., patients) or increasing transparency, and offering citizens to track and self-monitor the processing of their service applications.

The foreshadowed Digital-Era Governance model raises the fundamental question of who or what is actually governing here. According to the authors, their public management reform model is not technologically deterministic (Dunleavy et al., 2006b: 225): but what then is it? If it is not technological determinism, it needs to be a form of social shaping or even social determinism: that is, not technology as the single driving force, but the mutual shaping of technology and the social and institutional contexts that determine the public management reform outcome. This situation points at the critical importance of, for instance, leadership, political support, available funding, accountability structures and enabling legislative frameworks, which would need to be aligned with the technical application in order to achieve the DEG themes of reintegration, needs-based holism and digitalisation. So if DEG is indeed the future model of public management, the question then becomes how this public management reform model could be 'institutionally enabled' rather than technology driven? And that leads to another important question: is NPM dead in New Zealand?

As demonstrated by the earlier mentioned Directions and Priorities for Government ICT Strategy, NPM, or, better perhaps, the current public management model in New Zealand is very much alive and trying to enable a more efficient and effective use of ICTs across the New Zealand public sector. It is a good example of how the social shaping perspective can be observed in the practice of public management: how the introduction and use of ICTs are being shaped by, and are shaping, the institutional and social context in which the New Zealand public sector operates. Consequently, we are not facing a situation in which one public management model is being replaced by another, an *'either–or'* situation where the NPM model is being replaced by DEG, but an *'and–and'* situation in which we are dealing with a gradually evolving public management model in which the introduction and use of ICTs is increasingly institutionally enabled and embedded. This acknowledgement of the critical importance of institutional enablement for an effective introduction and uptake of ICTs not only points to the type of system requirements and conditions needed for the New Zealand public management system in order to move away from existing paper-based and towards digital-era based forms of government and governing; it also suggests that the unique institutional and social constellation of the New Zealand public management system requires e-government solutions that fit these particular contexts, rather than solutions that are directly 'cut and pasted' from overseas jurisdictions.

Surveillance State versus Service State . . . or the Fair State After All?

If technologies are not driving but enabling change, and do so in interaction with the institutional and social environment, the question then becomes *how* ICTs are shaping the institutional and social context in which the New Zealand public sector operates. If we allow ourselves to open the black box of ICTs, we can observe that, by their very nature, ICTs are generating, facilitating and acting upon information flows. Castells (1996) and others (see for instance Freeman, 2007, for an overview) refer to this phenomenon as the ICT paradigm. They identify this new socio-technical paradigm through five major characteristics. Firstly, the most important characteristic is that ICTs *act on information*. Because information is an integral part of human activity, it is expected that the effects of ICTs will be *pervasive*. Another characteristic of this ICT paradigm is that ICTs facilitate and accelerate a *networking* logic into social forms of organisation. This is closely related to a fourth characteristic of ICTs offering *flexibility* and the ability to reconfigure organisations, institutions and relationships. And lastly, due to processes of digitisation, there is a growing convergence of technologies into highly *integrated* information systems.

These technological affordances can both create new information relationships within the public sector and between government and citizens, and enable changes to existing information relationships. For example, the following changes to informational relationships are generally observed as a result of introducing ICT-enabled identity management systems in e-government service relationships with citizens (Camp, 2003; Lips et al., 2009: 837; Marx, 2004):

- Information can flow freely and in ways that are difficult to trace, also compared to information in face-to-face or paper-based transactions within the confines of a physical locale and relatively closed networks.
- Information can be copied and stored at almost no expense.
- There is an increased merging of previously compartmentalised identity information on the citizen.
- Transactions become information dependent, and transactional histories become more detailed and easily available to many.
- Trust depends on transactional history reports rather than on personal recognition.
- An increased blurring of lines between public and private places makes citizen identity information more publicly available.

Whether such informational changes present themselves in the end depends on the *actual use* of the ICT-enabled information in a particular institutional and social context. Taylor (1998) refers in this respect to the 'x-raying' vision of applying an ICT paradigm or 'informatisation' perspective to the study of public administration and management: by doing empirical research centred on the use of ICT-enabled information flows in the public sector and its external relationships, we are able to develop a much deeper understanding of the changes happening to and within the public sector, and their transformational effects, compared to other approaches to the study of public administration and management. O'Neill (2009: 61) further unpacks the nature and scope of

ICT-enabled transformational change in the public sector by making a useful distinction between instrumental transformation or 'doing things differently', and systemic transformation or 'doing different things'. Whereas 'doing things differently' means a radical change in the existing administration, information management and service delivery practices of government agencies that may also have a consequential impact on organisational structures and/or management practices, 'doing different things' means a radical change in existing governance arrangements of public management including constitutional responsibilities and accountabilities, fiscal management, legislation, regulation and decision-making rights over public resources.

As an example, based on the same informational trends mentioned above, scholars and practitioners point to fundamental changes that may happen to informational relationships between government and the citizen as a result of the introduction and use of new ICT-enabled forms of citizen identity management in public service environments (Lips et al., 2009). Interestingly, however, although both clusters point to the privacy implications of these new digital forms of citizen identity management, there seem to be almost opposite perspectives on the directions and outcomes of these fundamental changes, with little supporting empirical evidence for either of these two perspectives (Taylor et al., 2009). Some hold the view that the introduction of these new information systems will enable the transformation of public service provision to citizens (Varney, 2006), offering governments the opportunity to break down 'vertical' silos and deliver integrated, more effective services that meet the holistic needs of the citizen (Dunleavy et al., 2006b). This so-called 'service state' perspective on ICT-enabled public sector reform anticipates increased trust and empowerment of the citizen in her relationship with the state (Lips et al., 2009). Others, however, point out that the introduction and use of these ICT-enabled systems will facilitate increased surveillance of the citizen, leading to substantial information imbalances in citizen–government relationships (London School of Economics, 2005; Lyon, 2001; Murakami-Wood et al., 2006). This 'surveillance state' perspective on ICT-enabled public sector reform anticipates erosion of trust and a substantial impact on democratic citizen rights (Lips et al., 2009).

Empirical research into the actual use of new ICT-enabled forms of citizen identity management by government agencies in a variety of e-government service environments in the UK shows that no particular perspective is dominant: characteristics of both perspectives were visible in these UK case studies, simultaneously and in parallel. Moreover, all observed citizen identity information practices were within the legal restrictions of UK data protection legislation and not violating a UK citizen's privacy or other democratic rights (Lips et al., 2009). Consequently, depending on the actual use of ICT-enabled information in a particular institutional and social context, the same informational options can lead to outcomes that can be classified either under a surveillance state perspective or a service state perspective.

These research findings also suggest that there may be discrepancies between agencies' information management intentions and their actual use of that information. Similarly, e-government service users' perceptions about agencies' use of citizen identity information may differ from agencies' actual practice. For example, recent research[*] into the attitudes of New Zealanders to the sharing of personal information in the course of online public service provision (Lips et al., 2010) shows that research participants had little knowledge about the use of their personal information by government agencies. Participants provided their information to public sector agencies in order to get a service, but they usually did not understand how their information would be processed or used, why they needed to fill in multiple forms with the same information, how and to what length their information would be stored or kept, and who would have access to their information – issues that might in fact support the adoption of a surveillance state perspective among research participants. A particular area of concern to a number of them was the accuracy of personal information stored and processed by government agencies, especially information used for categorising clients and determining eligibility for services.

However, with exceptions among individuals highly dependent on social services – including Pasifika, Māori and self-employed individuals – the large majority of the research participants saw the New Zealand government as a benign and trusted institution that operates in support of the existing social contract between the citizen and the state: that is, an institution that plays privacy by the rules, using citizen identity information proportionally and for the intended purposes in order to offer service 'rewards' to citizens behaving in accordance with the rules and to 'punish' citizens breaking those rules. According to this so-called 'fair state' perspective, participants saw clear collective and often also individual benefits of sharing citizen identity information with and across government agencies, including improved public service effectiveness and better value for money for the taxpayer. One of the participants explained: "I don't see any downside as long as you play the game. If you have nothing to hide, I don't really see it as an issue."

The Shift Towards Networked Governance

ICTs are not only shaping and being shaped by the institutional context, such as privacy legislation, but also by the social context in which they are used. In the case of many e-government initiatives, the social context includes government agencies or other public sector institutions, as well as the (external)

---

[*]   This research was commissioned by the Inland Revenue Department.

users of e-government services. Compared to other countries in the world, a very high proportion of the New Zealand population uses the internet. From a 2009 representative survey about internet use in New Zealand (Smith et al., 2010), we know that 83 per cent of the population are active internet users; and of the 17 per cent who do not currently use the internet, about one-third are ex-users, but two-thirds have never used it. Four-fifths of the internet users check their email at least daily, half the users are members of social networking sites like Facebook and over a half of users use internet banking at least weekly (Smith et al., 2010: i). One of the most popular websites in New Zealand is Trade Me, the New Zealand version of eBay. In August 2011, Trade Me had more than 2.8 million active members, with an average number of 695,193 visitors each day (Nielsen Online, <http://www.trademe.co.nz/About-Trade-Me/Site-Stats>). Compare this with approximately 60 per cent of the population who use the internet for getting government information, and around 30 per cent who access secure public services and pay taxes and fines online (Smith et al., 2010).

It may not be a surprise therefore that some public officials wonder why the New Zealand government cannot be similar to successful online business models in the private sector, such as the Air New Zealand model where customers can make bookings and organise their check-in online without the mediation of a frontline staff member. However, if members of the general public are asked about their channel choice preference in their relationships with government, a question we asked recently in the earlier mentioned study (Lips et al., 2010), the answers actually show a move away from a standardised, dis-intermediated Air New Zealand model. Participants indicated that they are individuals with unique, complex circumstances: they do not necessarily tick all the boxes presented to them on the standardised online form in their service interaction with a government agency. As a result, they prefer to discuss their unique circumstances with a human being, so that they are confident about getting the right service. The same study also shows that, instead of choosing between particular channels, such as face-to-face and online, many participants think and act 'multi-channel': they first download the online forms so that they know what will be asked of them, and then they go into a government agency to get the right service more quickly and from a staff member they trust.

The more fundamental question that emerges from these research findings is: why *should* the New Zealand government be similar to successful online business models in the private sector, such as the Air New Zealand model? Is there something unique perhaps about government, which requires the design of new ICT-enabled *citizen*-centric service models, instead of copying business models that are narrowly focused on particular groups of *customers*?

Interestingly, based on anecdotal evidence, we also know that the people who are influencing the institutional arrangements of the New Zealand public management system often do not actively use or understand (new) ICTs. Nowadays, many senior public officials consider these technologies to be costly and risky, and believe that they will lose control in one way or another if they allow these technologies to be used in their business environment and external relationships. This may explain why government agencies are only scratching the surface of the enabling opportunities offered by ICTs in their relationships with citizens, particularly if we compare that with developments in society (e.g., the electronic use of Facebook, Trade Me, internet banking and Air New Zealand).

New Zealand is not the only country that is looking into ways to improve the uptake of e-government services. In a recently published OECD-study 'Rethinking e-Government Services: User-Centred Approaches' (OECDc, 2009), the dilemma between the promises of e-government initiatives and the lagging user take-up in the large majority of OECD countries is further explored. One explanation for the low uptake of e-government services across OECD countries, especially when compared with the quality and quantity of e-government services available, has been the common 'build-and-they-will-come' attitude among e-government service providers: users, and in particular their unique needs and expectations, were often forgotten in the design of 'government-centric' e-government services focused on increased efficiency and effectiveness. Furthermore, for many years, the dominant focus on technology has overshadowed the need for institutional changes in the public sector, such as structural, legal, organisational and cultural changes, which are finally being acknowledged as prerequisites for designing integrated, 'citizen-centred' e-government services (OECD, 2009c).

With increasing pressures from society to become more efficient and effective, particularly also as a result of the global financial crisis, governments around the world are moving away from a dominant focus on the 'e' of e-government and are putting more and more emphasis on the 'government' aspects of e-government, i.e. the institutional and social context in which e-government is being developed and used, and on the outcomes for e-government users (OECD, 2009c). In shifting towards an ICT-enabled citizen-centric approach to public service development and delivery, the following design questions will be of major importance to governments (OECD, 2009c: 13–14):

- How can governments enable and support a participatory and inclusive approach to public service development and delivery in order to ensure that citizen needs and expectations are met?
- How can governments use ICTs to empower citizens to create their own services that meet their individual needs?

- How can the public sector itself transform into a coherent whole, meeting users on their terms and not under the terms set by governments' administrative organisations, traditions and cultures?
- How can the current division of responsibilities and the organisational structures within the public sector be rethought to accommodate a whole-of-public-sector approach to service development and delivery?

In New Zealand, we can observe several practical examples of this new ICT-enabled citizen-centric service model of 'networked governance'. For instance, immediately after the Christchurch earthquake in February 2011, social media were used by both citizens and government agencies to find victims, keep people in the disaster-zone up-to-date, and arrange for primary needs, such as water, electricity and toilet facilities. Another good example is the Student Army, an initiative where thousands of students mobilised themselves via Facebook to help clean up the effects of liquefaction after the September and February Christchurch earthquakes (an initiative financially sponsored by the Ministry of Social Development following the February earthquake).

Another example of ICT-enabled citizen-centric service delivery is the NZ Transport Agency's Feet First programme (see <http://www.feetfirst.govt.nz/>). The Feet First programme encourages primary school children to walk to school safely with a caregiver, friend or organised walking group at least once a week during school terms. The benefits of children getting to school using 'active transport' are significant, and include improved levels of fitness and health, less money spent on petrol, reduced energy use and fewer vehicle emissions, learning safe transport habits for the future, less congestion at the school gate, and more social interaction for children and their families. The programme is actively supported by a website where children and schools can share their stories and pictures about how fun walking to school can be and find out what other children and schools are doing. They can also participate in a picture book competition and find curriculum materials on road and rail safety around schools. In 2009, 426 New Zealand schools participated in the programme.

Fixing System Errors in the New Zealand Public Management System

In a recently published UK Institute for Government research report entitled 'System Error: Fixing the flaws in Government IT' (Institute for Government, 2010), Ian Watmore, a top UK public servant with extensive experience in the private sector, was quoted saying: "IT in government is as difficult as it gets" (Institute for Government, 2010: 9). E-government offers many challenges but, it seems, few solutions that satisfy everyone, manifested for instance by many high-profile and costly failures in the past. One of the authors of the report explains that this is rarely the fault of the underpinning technology: policy complexity and complexity management (Eppel, 2010); project delays; budget problems; commercial and supplier problems; inadequate change management processes; high cost of change; complex cost-benefit analyses of large, multi-year e-government projects; incompatible systems; conflicts with existing legislation; and low user-uptake, are all examples of complex public management issues related to the implementation and use of ICTs in the public sector and its external relationships. The authors observe that, despite costing billions of dollars per year (approximately £16 billion per year in the UK), e-government seems to be locked in a vicious cycle of struggling to get the basics right and falling further behind the fast-paced technological environment with which citizens interact daily (Institute for Government, 2010: 9). However, they explain that "most attempts to solve the problems with government IT have treated the symptoms rather than resolved the underlying system-wide problems. This has simply led to doing the wrong things 'better'" (Institute for Government, 2010: 9).

These lessons and insights from the UK suggest that we should be more focused on fixing the 'system errors' in our current public management system if we would like to make effective use of ICTs in the future state and its external relationships, such as through networked governance arrangements. I would therefore suggest fixing or at least addressing the following system errors and perspectives in the New Zealand context:

- moving away from a technology perspective on e-government and acknowledging the critical importance of treating it as a complex public management issue, with a consequence that the introduction, management and use of ICTs in the public sector and its external relationships need to be discussed at the strategic level of all-of-government and government agencies, not just among chief information officers or within ICT departments;
- an appreciation that we are not facing an 'either–or' situation in which one public management model is being replaced by another, but an 'and–and' situation of a gradually evolving public management model in which the introduction and use of ICTs is increasingly institutionally enabled and embedded;
- the lack of cross-government learning about successes and failures around introducing and using new technologies in the New Zealand public sector and its external relationships;
- an acknowledgement that ICTs are generating, facilitating and acting upon information flows across the public sector and its external

relationships, with potentially pervasive effects, while appreciating that changes and effects will depend on the actual use of the ICT-enabled information in a particular institutional and social context;

- understanding that successful online business models in the private sector or e-government solutions from overseas jurisdictions may not work in the unique institutional and social constellation of the New Zealand public sector;
- enabling institutional approaches to participatory and inclusive public service design and delivery; and
- shifting from government-centric service models towards new ICT-enabled citizen-centric approaches to public service provision.

In my view, if we could fix these system errors and address these issues, the New Zealand government could very well become a world leader in digital-era, 'new' new public management.

9

Restructuring: An Over-used Lever for Change in New Zealand's State Sector?

Richard Norman and Derek Gill

'If all you have is a hammer, everything looks like a nail', management theorist Abraham Maslow observed in 1966.[1]

Is restructuring the hammer of organisational change in New Zealand's state sector? A State Services Commission (SSC) survey of state sector employees in 2010 identified that 65 per cent of the 4600 staff sampled had been involved in a merger or restructure during the previous two years, a sharp contrast with a similar survey of the federal government of the United States, which found that only 18 per cent were affected. These statistics raise questions that form the basis of this chapter: why, how and to what effect are state sector organisations restructured in New Zealand?

Our research started with a review of empirical data on restructuring and of perspectives from the literature on restructuring in the public and private sectors. We then explored these perspectives in three separate focus groups in May 2011, with chief executives, human resource managers, and Public Service Association (PSA) delegates and organisers. Not surprisingly, chief executives (CEs) who initiate restructuring have a considerably more optimistic view about its role and impact than those who are affected by it. Annex One is a reflection piece written by one of the most experienced New Zealand public service chief executives, Christopher Blake, Chief Executive of the Department of Labour (and Chief Executive of the New Zealand Symphony Orchestra from 2012), which provides a balance to the more sceptical argument presented in this chapter.

We conclude that restructuring has indeed become the 'hammer' of organisational change in New Zealand, a result of the 'freedom to manage' formula adopted in the late 1980s to break up a unified and 'career-for-life' bureaucracy that was seen to respond too slowly to the economic crises of the 1980s. Restructuring has become almost an addiction, reinforced by short, fixed-term contracts for chief executives and a belief among those chief executives that their employer, the State Services Commission, expects them to be seen to be 'taking charge'. Restructuring is a symbol of and sometimes a substitute

1 Maslow (1966: 15).

for action. It treats organisations as though they are mechanical objects with interchangeable parts rather than as living systems of people who have choices about the extent to which they will commit to their work. Organisational change receives considerably less scrutiny than funding proposals for major capital works. We advocate that restructuring should be subject to such scrutiny and chief executives need to act more like stewards of their organisations and less like owners.

Restructuring: Data Sources and Interpretation

There are two sources of data available from the SSC on restructuring in the state sector.[2] The integrity and conduct survey (conducted in 2007 and 2010) collects information on the number of *employees* affected by restructuring. In addition, an inventory of Machinery of Government changes mandated by cabinet records the number of *organisations* potentially affected by externally sanctioned restructuring.

The integrity and conduct surveys undertaken by the SSC include a question: '[Has your] Organisation been involved in a merger or restructure in the last two years?' In 2010, of the 4641 staff surveyed, 65 per cent replied 'yes', 27 per cent 'no' and 8 per cent 'don't know'. This was a significant increase from 2007 when the answers were 55 per cent, 33 per cent and 12 per cent respectively. This distribution is remarkably consistent across all types of organisations in the public sector and is not restricted to the departments and ministries that comprise the public service proper. Sixty-five per cent of staff in public service departments, 66 per cent in Crown agents, 66 per cent in DHBs and 64 per cent in other Crown entities replied 'yes'. The response to the identical question in the US (Ethics Resource Centre, 2007: 50) for 2005 was 18 per cent. While the American statistics can be seen as an extreme because federal restructuring requires approval of Congress, the contrast is striking. Restructuring may be as prevalent in Australia as New Zealand, judging by experiences of students for the Masters of Public Administration delivered by the Australia and New Zealand School of Government (ANZSOG). One of us (Norman) works with these classes of 130 students annually, and has found that consistently more than 80 per cent have been personally affected by restructuring during the previous three years.

The SSC's inventory records changes that needed a cabinet mandate for legislation, i.e., changes in names, legal form or establishment/disestablishment. It does not include chief executive or internally initiated changes that do not require legislative change. No direct estimates are available for the frequency of chief executive-initiated restructuring, although Gill (2008a: 29) reports a

2   We are grateful to Frank Peek in the SSC for comments on the data sources and analysis.

practitioner's estimate that 50 per cent of CEs restructured their departments in the first year in the role.

We analysed the SSC inventory of data, assigning each machinery of government change to one of four types:

- change in legal name only;
- change in legal form;
- undertaking a new function or losing an existing function; or
- merger or break-up of an existing organisation.

Any double counting of organisational types was netted out.

The two sets of data on employees and number of organisations can, with some caveats, be compared. The SSC Integrity Survey asked respondents about the previous two years. For public service departments, only 10 per cent (on an organisation-weighted basis)[3] or 2.4 per cent (on an employee-weighted basis) were subject to a cabinet-mandated change over a three-year period 2008–10, whereas (on an employee-weighted basis) 66 per cent of public servants reported being involved in a merger or restructuring during the two years before 2010. These results suggest that restructuring in New Zealand is mainly internally initiated rather that cabinet mandated. In fact, internally generated restructures in New Zealand exceed the *total number* reported in the US federal government service. In comparison with the United Kingdom, where prime ministerial concerns about portfolio allocations are a primary driver (White and Dunleavy, 2010), restructuring in New Zealand is predominantly chief executive driven.

In the New Zealand system, the departmental CE is more akin to the combined chief executive officer and chair of the board of a United States private corporation. New Zealand chief executives have broader authority to act than in perhaps any other jurisdiction, or what Schick (1996: 46) describes as 'virtual carte blanche to run their departments':

> New Zealand chief executives must do certain things that career managers in the Public Service generally have not been accustomed to doing. They must weed out weak managers, shed redundant workers, re-examine or sever long-standing relationships with suppliers, actively recruit from outside the Public Service, negotiate the wages of senior managers, revamp operations, abandon low-priority activities, manage their assets, commit in advance to output and cost levels, take responsibility for the volume and quality of services, negotiate employment, purchase and performance agreements, respond to numerous inquiries from Parliamentary committees and central agencies, represent the department to the

---

3 Organisational weighting gives the same weight to each agency regardless of size, whereas employee weighting is based on the number of people not the number of organisations. The SSC survey data are employee weighted.

media and public, be responsive to the Minister, and more. They must drive the department to be more efficient, productive, and responsive. They must act as if their own job is on the line and their own money is being spent.

This gives them very considerable powers to shape the organisation as they wish.

Perspectives from the Literature on Restructuring Practices

Governments restructure for internal and external reasons (OECD, 2005a). Internal causes include the quest for management improvement by, for example, splitting or merging agencies or aligning or separating policy-making and implementation. External reasons for change include the emergence of a new policy priority, often in response to a crisis. A commonly cited international example is the creation of the United States Department of Homeland Security after the 2001 attacks on the World Trade Centre in New York, while the recent example in New Zealand is the creation of the Canterbury Earthquake Recovery Authority. Budget deficits have been a major driver of restructuring in New Zealand since 2008, as savings have been sought by merging agencies and back office functions.

The previous section discussed how, in contrast to the UK, restructuring in New Zealand is initiated predominantly by chief executives. A key motivation in Britain for restructuring is political pressures within cabinet to align portfolios around new priorities or to reward politicians with a larger department. In New Zealand, there is not the same requirement for one-to-one relationship between departments and the lead minister. As Boston and Gill discuss in chapter 7 of this volume, three distinct arrangements can be observed for lead portfolio ministers in New Zealand. The most common is *one department, many ministers*. Less common is an arrangement of *one minister, one department* or *many departments, one minister*.

A major driver for restructuring in New Zealand during the 1980s and 1990s was the theory drawn from new institutional economics which advocated that organisations should have 'simple and clear purposes', particularly the separation of policy, delivery and regulation in order to align incentives for officials and reduce 'opportunistic' behaviour (OECD, 2005a). Looking at a range of countries, Dunleavy et al. (2006a: 470) describe new public management (NPM) as a recipe of 'disaggregation, incentivisation and competition'. While the overall number of public organisations and the official doctrines applied by the State Services Commission have been remarkably stable for the last decade (Gill 2008a; Lodge and Gill 2011), a shift in thinking is evident in the last three years. Now the structural focus is to 'shift the burden of proof towards amalgamation' (DPMC, 2011a: 1). Whereas much restructuring of the 1980s and 1990s was to disaggregate larger organisations, the trend since 2008 has been to bring them back together, as seen with the merging of the Foundation and Ministry for Science and Research and the merging of the Ministry of Fisheries with Agriculture and Forestry.

This shift in emphasis raises the question of the contribution of structure to organisational performance. One influential approach is the 'McKinsey Seven S' model shown in Figure 9.1, which was popularised by *In Search of Excellence* by Peters and Waterman (1982). According to the McKinsey model, improved performance comes when all the seven 'Ss' are lined up. Peters and Waterman distinguish between the 'hard' or visible elements of organisational life such as structures, strategy and systems, compared with the 'soft' people-based elements of skills, staff, style and shared values. The authors note that, contrarily, the 'hard' issues, with their emphasis on documents, measurement and the easily visible, are actually 'soft' or easy to deal with. The 'soft' dimensions of organisational life, focused on the distinctive contributions of shared values and people, are 'hard' or difficult.

Figure 9.1. The McKinsey 7S Model

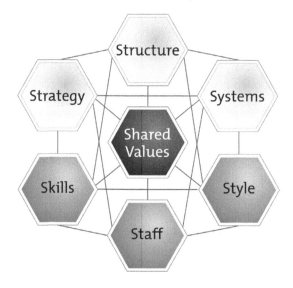

Source: McKinsey 7S model: see
<http://www.mindtools.com/pages/article/newSTR_91.htm>
(accessed 1 October 2011).

A different conceptualisation of the role of structure is provided by Bolman and Deal (1997), who characterise 'structure' as a metaphor that prompts thinking about organisation as factories or machines. Perhaps it is not surprising that restructuring is a favoured tool for public sector agencies when the term 'the machinery of government' is still widely used to describe the form and functions of government. Applying the machinery metaphor has an effect described by Morgan (2006: 13): 'If we talk about organisations as if they were machines, we tend to expect them to operate as machines: in a routinized, efficient, reliable, and predictable way.' Morgan explores alternative metaphors for organisations, including the brain, and organisations as cultures, organisms or political systems. Similarly, Bolman and Deal (1997) liken organisations to families (the human resource approach), jungles (politics rule), or to a carnival, temple or theatre (symbolism is important).

The 'How' and 'Effect' of Restructuring

Processes for the 'how' of restructuring have been well established in the New Zealand state sector since the first moves in 1986–87 to break up large, long-established departments to create state-owned enterprises, focused service delivery entities and policy ministries. More than private sector employers, public agencies are constrained in how they proceed with restructuring, and legislative provisions for 'good employer' practices create greater consistency and focus on fairness that in the more diverse practices of the private sector. To some extent these processes result in an overstating of the use of restructuring in public organisations, which must follow formal processes where smaller, private sector organisations can be more informal.

Restructuring affects staff when it removes security of employment and puts staff into a competition for positions in the restructured organisation. Such competition inevitably tests the loyalty of staff, whose focus shifts to individual economic survival rather than service to the organisation or wider public. Cascio (2002) distinguishes between numbers-driven change and 'responsible restructuring'. 'Downsizers' constantly ask themselves, 'What is the minimum number of employees we need to run this company? What is the irreducible core number of employees the business requires?' A second and smaller group of 'responsible restructurers' see employees as assets to be developed. They ask themselves, 'How can we change the way we do business, so that we can use the people we currently have more effectively?' Further:

> The downsizers saw employees as commodities, like microchips or light bulbs, interchangeable, substitutable, and disposable, if necessary. In contrast, responsible restructurers see employees as sources of innovation and renewal. (Cascio 2002: xii)

The responsible restructurer has a much greater likelihood of retaining organisational citizenship behaviours, such as:

- altruism (e.g., helping out when a co-worker is not feeling well);
- conscientiousness (e.g., staying late to finish a project);

- civic virtue (e.g., volunteering for a community programme to represent the firm);
- sportsmanship;
- courtesy (e.g., being understanding and empathetic, even when provoked).

Another contentious issue in restructuring is the pace of change. Is it better to move as quickly as possible to reduce uncertainty? Or should a measured process of consultation be followed? An example of the first approach was the change process led by Sir Roger Douglas during the 1980s, in which he advised: 'implement reform by quantum leaps. Moving step by step lets vested interests mobilise. Big packages neutralise them. Speed is essential. It is impossible to move too fast. Once you start the momentum, never let it stop' (Roger Douglas, in a speech to the Australian Education Council Conference, Adelaide, 6 December 1990, reported in the *Evening Post*, 24 October 1991). One consequence of this speed of reform was that New Zealand voters opted for proportional representation politics in part to put brakes on first-past-the-post majority rule. For organisational restructures, the speed of change remains a key issue, as can be seen in the varied responses of the focus groups.

New Zealand research about effects of restructuring is rare. The one significant study, based on change in the 1980s, reviewed the effect of restructuring of state-owned enterprises (Duncan and Bollard, 1992). A case study of the creation of the Ministry of Social Development in 2001–2 (SSC, 2003) examines the change processes used for that merger. Recent analysis of four restructures in government departments in Britain (White and Dunleavy, 2010) provides useful insights. These researchers identified problems such as lack of time for planning, lack of funding, overloaded staff and little central support. These restructures had largely been driven by cabinet changes, often initiated by the prime minister to reallocate political portfolios. Different pay rates in merging organisations created a major challenge. The result could be substantial costs in terms of finance or morale in either upgrading those on lower rates or suppressing pay increases for the better paid. White and Dunleavy conclude that the results from restructuring are disappointing as the costs are higher and the benefits take longer than expected to be realised. They pose the question: can we afford productivity dips and to wait for at least two years before realising the concrete benefits of reorganisation?

Disappointing returns on restructurings are not limited to the public sector. One widely cited study of private sector mergers concludes that fewer than 25 per cent of all mergers achieve their stated strategic objectives (Marks and Mirvis, 2001). Research into private sector organisations benefits from an ability to compare bottom-line profitability pre- and post-merger, whereas public sector mergers are particularly difficult to research. 'Public value' (Moore, 1995), a proposed counterpart of bottom-line private value, is inherently difficult to measure and political in its definition.

Figure 9.2. Productivity Dip in Most Mergers and Acquisitions

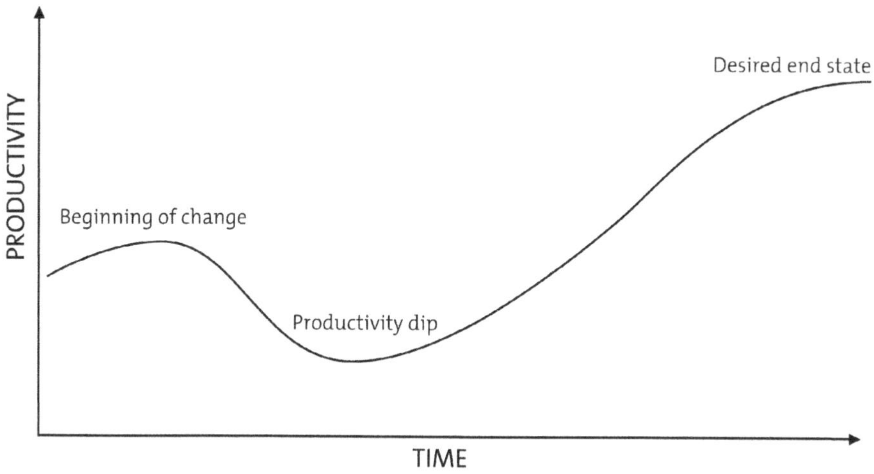

Source: White and Dunleavy (2010: 79, figure 34).

The initial research thus reveals an intriguing puzzle. On the one hand, analysis of the data shows extensive, repeated restructures in the New Zealand state sector, the majority of which were internally initiated rather than externally imposed. On the other hand, the available evidence suggests that the cost of restructuring was significant, with benefits taking around two years to be realised. In a number of recent cases, outgoing chief executives led restructuring immediately prior to stepping down, only to have the new incoming CE trigger a further set of changes in their first year in the role. Are the costs of restructuring recognised by practitioners? And why do they restructure? We therefore sought practitioners' views on why and how restructuring has been conducted in the New Zealand state sector.

Practitioners' Perspectives on Restructuring Within the New Zealand State Sector

We explored the topic of restructuring with three groups that could be expected to have very different perspectives on the topic: chief executives, human resource managers, and union delegates and organisers. These groups were given the opportunity to contribute anonymously through decision support software that enabled individuals to brainstorm and vote on ideas.[4] The workshops focused on four questions:

4   The software used was WIQ from Ynsyte, at <http://www.gowiq.com/ynsyte/home.php>.

1. Why is restructuring used as an organisational change tool and is it used too frequently?
2. How well in your experience is restructuring carried out within New Zealand public sector organisations?
3. What are the results from restructurings?
4. How could restructuring processes be improved?

Notable insights from these sessions included the pressure perceived by chief executives to restructure in order to demonstrate that change is happening, and the scepticism of human resource management specialists compared with chief executives.

Why Restructure?

The chief executive group was small in numbers (five), but it had longer to discuss restructuring than the other two focus groups. Firstly, the group challenged the survey figures quoted earlier about the extent of restructuring, suggesting these overstated the case by including 'technical' restructures. Reasons for restructuring noted by this group included changing formal mandates, political pressure, budget reductions and the need to align an organisation to new expectations. The intention of a restructure internally was to change and improve the mix of capabilities and if necessary to shore up deficiencies. For a CE coming in new, there may be a need to 'reboot' an organisation and 'decouple' it from a non-performing past. Structure needed to be aligned with vision, strategy and desired performance. Restructuring was a way a new chief executive could clarify expectations for a department seen as poor in capability by politicians.

PSA delegates agreed with the reasons that prompted change but thought restructuring seemed to be the 'only improvement tool' that government knew how to use. Human resource managers thought that restructuring has become almost a 'preferred and first-choice method for tackling individual performance problems', a way of avoiding potentially long-drawn-out performance processes.

According to the CE focus group, newly appointed chief executives frequently decide that existing second-tier management is not able to deliver on expectations for change. If an outsider has been appointed as CE, it is probably because an external jolt has created a different environment from that which the existing management team has been prepared for. One CE referenced Charles Darwin and observed that 'adaptability is the key to survival – rather than strength or intellect'. Restructuring was put forward as an important part of the process of shaping organisations to be fit for purpose. Often that needed different people on a management team, people comfortable with 'uncertainty and driving down costs'.

As one CE put it, 'context is everything'. The current budget environment that requires savings and the funding of redundancies out of baseline revenues creates restrictions that state sector managers have not had to face for some time. 'That pushes you to get it absolutely right. You do try to hold on to the talent you have and avoid losing the mobile people.' A fundamental difference, however, between public and private sectors is the need to work within a single-year appropriation, compared with the private sector flexibility of posting a significant loss in a year marked by restructuring. The five-year appointment term of public service CEs increases the imperative to restructure at the beginning of the term. A typical cycle involves restructuring the second tier in the first and second years, using the third and fourth years to anchor change, and hoping to see the benefits come through by year five when the focus of the CE would be on reappointment or a different and perhaps larger role.

Human resources managers, whose roles involve them in implementing restructures, were considerably more sceptical about reasons for restructuring and the results. This group agreed that restructures 'happen too frequently, sometimes to satisfy political ego'. It was the 'easiest lever to pull and often not the most effective', in contrast to less tangible cultural change based on continuous reflection about organisational performance. Restructuring often creates action but not forward motion and is a way to 'be seen to be doing something'. For union organisers and delegates, restructuring was about 'reducing staff', 'reducing budget', 'cost cutting, not innovation'. This focus group had the resigned acceptance of a reactive role, responding to management initiatives.

Is Restructuring a Substitute for Effective Performance Management?

In terms of the McKinsey 7S model, structure was seen by chief executives as a key lever to align organisations with strategy. An alternative view was that restructuring is used as a substitute for a systematic effective performance management. The HR focus group certainly thought the latter was the case, voting that restructuring was 'frequently used to tackle long-standing performance issues' without the legal risks of performance management processes. Such restructuring masks 'fundamental flaws in the organisational culture' and is 'a dishonest alternative to managing poor performance'. The group thought restructuring had become 'a default position for performance managing leadership teams', and was used instead of 'hard conversations' about the real issues. The PSA group experienced restructuring as 'a CE wanting to impose her/his priorities on the organisation' and for 'new CEOs to stamp their look or branding on their new fiefdom'. It was a 'great tool for management where they can get rid of perceived dead wood and trouble makers'.

Not unexpectedly, chief executives had different and positive views about their roles as change makers. One CE commented:

> Leaving non-performers in displaced positions can undermine efforts to lift performance – they can compete for leadership, and you can look as though you've avoided the tough calls.

Elaborating on the performance challenges they had experienced, CEs reflected on finding that 'long term performance issues at the second tier' had not been tackled. One CE thought it would be possible to get a team to work effectively and took four months to find it could not.

Through a combination of verbal and on-line discussion, the CE group exchanged views about the pressures on leadership. The comment 'none of us are appointed to the job as baby sitters' set the tone for a discussion about realities of the CE role, which included the value of 'building affiliation and allegiances through appointing (one's) own team'. 'You can't drive change as one person. You don't have a magic stick – if you're going to change you to start with a team that you believe can help you drive that change.' From the outside was an 'unexpressed expectation' of central agencies that a CE is 'perceived not to be decisive is you don't change the top team'. One chief executive reflected on the experience of being seen as 'too slow' by central agencies, a reaction that abated after a restructure.

CEs are conscious of the pressure of fixed contracts, usually five-year terms, which mean that 'change needs to occur early in your tenure, to ensure you reap the expected rewards'. 'Five years is a relatively short time to ensure change is completed and embedded – so you need to do it quickly.'

How to Go About Restructuring?

Structural change can be initiated in order to change the shared values and organisational culture, or change can start with culture first and then move to structure. CEs suggested culture change is easier to achieve if a hard-edged approach is first taken to introduce 'a new leadership in the organisation to drive it'. As one CE put it, 'if you want cultural change, you need to be hardnosed. It takes too long to teach old dogs new tricks, if you can do it at all!' One CE reflected on the importance of avoiding giving a 'false expectation that this will be the last change' – creating a need to 'unfreeze, change, and refreeze' quickly. CEs saw attempts to move on culture change first as less certain, while human resource managers preferred this approach.

CEs agreed that for larger restructurings, 'a powerful and compelling case for change' is best made through a set of principles. 'Principles that are sound and communicated well generate better buy-in and healthier culture.' Structural change has to be reinforced by cultural change, a focus on important values. Restructuring is just the start of the process needed to deliver change, and is more likely to succeed if staff are involved in the design, taking longer with consultation, but then implementing swiftly.

The HR focus group was particularly concerned about consultation and communications, agreeing that 'managers don't always communicate enough and changes can drag on', that there can be 'issues around communication if there is a perceived agenda', and that 'too often consultation is a sham process that has little effect on what the CE wanted to begin with'. The group thought that change was 'usually well managed in terms of the risks of personal grievance cases, but not well managed in terms of bringing people along'.

The PSA focus group believed that to be effective, a restructure should involve 'staff input into the dialogue and process', rather than simply following a 'pre-conceived idea': 'Sometimes it is done effectively and staff have buy-in – usually when there is early engagement of staff, unions and management working together.'

One of the perennial issues in organisational change is the choice between rapid 'big bang' change and gradual, organic change. For CEs, bottom-up consultation can work well if the goal is to achieve small adjustments that can enable business as usual. However, if the organisation needs rebuilding and repositioning and a turnaround is needed, a comprehensive approach is needed.

CEs discussed the challenges of taking ministers with them while working to a timetable. Restructuring within current resources rather than with special funding is a special challenge – if anything goes wrong the money isn't there for alternative strategies. As far as possible, the aim is to 'create certainty for people so they know the process. The worst thing is that it all suddenly goes into a hole and then you get destabilised people.' One CE commented that 'at the end of most change processes most people will say we should have done that more quickly. There is something about how you make the decisions carefully but "execute" well and quickly.'

The HR focus group was strongly in favour of 'constant, small changes' unless there was a 'genuine shift in strategy'. Commented one: 'having just done massive restructuring I believe organic change delivers the best results'.

How is Restructuring Evaluated?

Restructuring is very specific to context, but some clear trends emerged from the role-based focus groups, particularly the pragmatism of CEs, the uneasiness of human resource specialists and the reaction to management initiative response of unionists.

For CEs, the 'longer-term performance gains from a large shift in internal culture are considerable', and there can be impressive 'efficiency/effectiveness benefits from carefully executed small/incremental restructures'. An issue for CEs was whether sufficient time was given for the benefits to be derived – 'or will the new CE want to start over!!'

For the human resource group, restructuring works if 'there is genuine reason for change and follow through to achieve real outcomes'. Implemented with 'strong and early staff involvement', restructuring can be very effective. While that might be the mainstream theoretical view, the human resource focus group was strongly sceptical about restructuring. The statement 'I have yet to see a well-executed restructure in the public service' summed up the concerns. Instead, their views were that restructures tend to create 'nervous, wary staff', a 'loss of engagement', 'inertia' and 'reduced work outputs'. A restructuring can paralyse an organisation for a year and distract from ongoing business. Too often CEs are forced into restructuring, not because it is the right thing to do. Ironically, in the view of the human resource group, the real 'dead wood' seldom is restructured out – 'because dead wood is smart in hiding'. Overall, restructuring 'costs a lot and promises more than it actually delivers'.

The union focus group had the view that 'the loss of staff in a restructuring adds significant pressure to the staff remaining as they struggle to pick up the extra load', and 'restructuring creates an environment of mistrust and fear' that is often not erased until any long-term benefits are realised. Staff are fearful 'with their noses down and bums up, towing the party line and trying not to be noticed as a non-performer'.

How Could Restructuring Processes be Improved?

In reviewing the input of the different groups, a striking trend emerged: only CEs provided comments about ways in which restructuring might be improved. In part this was because the human resource and union groups were asked to comment on other public sector issues, but their negative experiences and perceptions of restructuring so dominated discussion that improvements were not identified. CEs agreed with the approach of Christopher Blake (in Annex A) that 'sureness of execution is a critical issue'.

Central agencies, in the view of chief executives, should be 'exemplars of best practice', ready to share experience and knowledge and provide a 'professional change capability' rather than stand on the side line. For new chief executives, referrals to CEs who had successfully restructured could be helpful. Measurable success indicators should be set for the objectives of a restructure, and later evaluated. The state sector system overall – not just individual agencies – needs a clearer end-state.

Discussion of Research Findings

Restructuring is a fact of life for public sector organisations, whether a result of changes in political mandate, tightening budgets or a CE who seeks to anticipate change. Restructuring is a human resource management strategy that illustrates the diversity of theoretical perspectives that can be used to inform organisational change decisions (Wright and McMahan, 1992). Chief executives in focus groups were aware of their political power and how fleeting that power could be if they failed to deliver on government agendas or to the expectations of the direct employer of public service chief executives, the State Services Commission. Political, economic and financial considerations drove their perspectives. By contrast, human resource managers tended to view restructuring through the people-focused disciplines of psychology and sociology – the impact of structural change on individuals and teams. The comments of chief executives came from the 'hard'-edged perspectives shown in the 7S diagram (Figure 9.1), i.e., strategy, structure and systems. The perspectives of the human resource personnel came from the 'soft' S factors of shared values, skills, staff and style. Such differing perspectives are part of the checks and balances of organisational performance.

This study opens a debate and highlights the diversity of perspectives rather than provides 'evidence' about the impact of restructuring. It challenges the extent to which the metaphor of 'machinery of government' still dominates in an era when governments are less like factories and more like networks of professional services. The capabilities of those professionals are often in the nature of 'insurance policies' for the public and a container for particular skills available in the event of emergencies, as demonstrated with the emergency services response to the Christchurch earthquake of February 2011. The lens of restructuring and the image of 'machinery of government' narrow the focus to the 'hard swords', restricting the debate to disciplines such as economics, accounting and strategy that specialise in those perspectives. When large-scale restructuring of the New Zealand public sector first occurred in the mid-1980s, much of this was driven by the efficiency and effectiveness gains to be achieved by moving from paper-based and people-intensive filing systems to computer storage and retrieval. Most, if not all, of such opportunities to make major productivity gains through such restructuring have long since been achieved.

Instead, the current challenge of productivity is captured in the observation of Schick (1996) that the focus on 'purchase', or the measurement around delivery of outputs, tends to dominate consideration of 'ownership', or the government's interest in the capability of its staff. Restructures fundamentally challenge the 'ownership' or 'soft' elements of organisational capability such as loyalty and commitment. Restructuring, however gently handled, sends a political message to staff that they are dispensable – hired hands rather than members of a community. The psychology of this message is well captured in the term 'fired', the hard-edged and colloquial description of organisational exit. The term 'fired' is an echo of the tradition of villages in medieval Europe to expel unwanted community members by setting fire to their thatched cottages. 'Restructured' is the more neutral current jargon for the equivalent expulsion from an organisational community. The risk for organisational performance is that restructuring can narrow the preoccupations of staff to personal economic survival. The most mobile staff may leave first, and those with fewer options because of family and geographic ties have little option but to feign loyalty to the new order, and may hoard their knowledge as a way of making themselves indispensible and protecting their employment.

The risks of restructuring are well captured in this quotation that circulated widely in the New Zealand public sector during earlier periods of restructuring:

> Every time we were beginning to form up into teams, we would be reorganised. I was to learn later in life that we tend to meet any new situation by reorganisation . . . and a wonderful method it can be for creating the illusion of progress while producing confusion, inefficiency, and demoralisation. (Attributed to Petronius Arbitor, 210 BC, in Downs and Larkey, 1986: 184)

Sadly, the reference cannot actually be traced to 210 BC and is most likely an urban legend created in the 1970s, but the questions about the extent to which rhetoric lives up to reality are fundamental to the process of restructuring.

Restructures are just one possible response to external and internal pressure for organisational change. They are what Burns and Stalker (1961) categorise as a mechanistic response, one most associated with organisations working in stable environments, where change is infrequent. Organisations that change continuously work in what Burns and Stalker term an 'organic' way, adjusting work roles to match changes in the environment. The 'responsible restructurers' described by Cascio (2002), with their focus on preserving employment security, are 'organic' in their change strategies.

Conclusions

Available data show restructuring in the New Zealand public sector is high by international standards and a product of the 'freedom to manage' approach adopted in the late 1980s. Compared with other jurisdictions, most restructuring is initiated by chief executives rather than driven by cabinet political considerations. The majority of new chief executives initiate restructuring in their first year in the role and an increasing number of outgoing chief executives initiate changes in their last year. Restructuring is sometimes characterised as a lever of control, which in the authors' view is a comparison that has been overused: to use the analogy we opened with, it is more like a hammer that has redefined too many organisational performance challenges as nails.

It is not surprising that CEs use the technique of restructuring almost as a matter of course. They perceive that their own careers are dependent on making changes that will be noticed by their arm's-length employer, the State Services Commission or, in the wider state sector, a board with a changing membership. Restructuring creates a perception of being decisive and in charge. It has an immediate benefit for a chief executive, of making it possible to assemble a management team compatible with that CE's working style. Restructuring offers a way of tackling performance issues that is faster and less subject to legal challenge than a formal process of performance management. Ultimately the initiation of restructuring is a declaration about power – in the New Zealand public sector, a CE has that power, at least for the term of a five-year contract. The use of fixed terms almost means that any CE is now seen as unusual if he or she does not restructure within the first twelve months of appointment. Most CEs have been appointed from outside their organisations, meaning they have little or no existing loyalty to staff in the organisation, but are there to take a task-focused approach to the expectations of government and their employer. The dynamic is a predictable and inevitable result of the accountability system that has dominated the New Zealand public sector during the past 25 years. In terms of the McKinsey 7S model, New Zealand is using the 'hard S' approach, focusing on strategy, systems and structure. The soft S factors of organisational life – staff, shared values, style and skills – are undervalued.

Restructuring has a simplicity as a metaphor – one that fits with a 'machinery of government' perspective in which the building blocks of government are like pieces of meccano (a toy of an earlier era) or Lego: interchangeable parts to be moved around in pursuit of the perfect combination. Its limitations as a metaphor are well captured by the question of 'what is the difference between a frog and a bicycle?' (Mant, 1997: 40–51). Pull the bicycle apart and you can reassemble it. Pull the frog apart and it dies. The 'pull it apart' mechanics are increasingly harmful for an era in which most public service is dependent on in-depth know-how and relationships. Restructuring prompts senior managers and staff to focus on generic, transferrable know-how rather than in-depth expertise, which in many functions of government has few potential employers other than the current one. It damages the relationships of trust that can speed the cross-organisational networking necessary for economic and social issues that do not fit within the boundaries of any one government agency.

The decisions of an individual CE to restructure can affect multiple agencies. The opening chapter of this volume, the summary of the Future State report (see also Ryan in chapter 3), discusses how inter-agency working is going to be increasingly common, but that working in this way takes sustained effort to build the shared commitment and responsibility required to work effectively across boundaries. Research on working across government agencies has identified frequent restructuring as one of the major systemic barriers to more effective inter-agency working (Eppel, Gill, Lips and Ryan, 2008).

In the view of the authors, restructuring should be subject to the same scrutiny as major investment decisions on infrastructure such as roads, information technology systems and buildings. Managerial independence has been taken too far in New Zealand. In too many cases the result is the loss of institutional capacity, and the undermining of the ability of public organisations to work effectively on cross-cutting issues. The CEs in our sample were those who might be termed 'responsible restructurers', reflecting on their practice and using restructuring sparingly. The sample of human resource specialists, on the other hand, came from a spectrum of organisations and experienced first hand the negative consequences of over-reliance on the hammer of restructuring as a change tool.

We conclude that the New Zealand public sector system needs an institutional safeguard that gives 'pause for thought' in the interests of the whole system, just as the Treasury forces a pause for thought before major capital expenditure is approved. Departmental chief executives need to act more like stewards of their organisations and less like owners. The burden of proof needs to be reversed so that, rather than being rewarded for action, CEs are rewarded for stewarding and building the capability of the organisation. Just as any spending proposal for cabinet is required to have a Treasury report, any restructuring proposal should be required to have an SSC report and should include the requirement for independent evaluation.

Annex One

Personal Reflections on Restructuring

Christopher Blake
Chief Executive, Department of Labour

It's true that I'm an inveterate practitioner of large restructuring, generally as the instigator, and have been so in each of the four departments I've led to date.

At the Ministry of Cultural Affairs in the early 1990s it was a start-up situation with a new public management system driver, in this case creating an organisation with 'simple and clear purposes' focused on the cultural sector and acquiring related activities from other parts of government. This was a cabinet-mandated exercise.

At the National Library it was a reorganisation driven by a new strategy supported by new technology that couldn't be delivered by the existing frameworks because there were new functions and activities – it was literally a new era. The reasons here for reorganisation were around fundamental changes to the business and the mandate was the chief executive's.

Moving on to Internal Affairs, the focus was on performance – arresting a decline and putting resources together in a way that would enable the department to lift its performance, again CE-mandated but supported by a cabinet seeking better results.

Today at the Department of Labour the reorganisations have had a CE mandate and have been driven by a need to resolve performance problems, the better and more efficient application of scarce and declining resources, and a clearer alignment of functions and responsibilities.

As a group of reorganisation stories they are fairly unremarkable and, in fact, fairly typical. Whether they amount to unnecessary or overuse of restructuring as a management tool is debatable.

Each is characterised by an imperative to organise work properly within a particular operating environment, and to make choices about how that's to be done by selecting the most optimal arrangements. The real issue about restructuring that emerges from these examples is that this is the only real tool for organising and re-organising work when there are large shifts in the operating environment to be addressed.

If I look at the results of these change examples, I would say that I was pleased with the outcomes. They broadly achieved their purposes in responding to the changes in the operating environment. The first three were durable for a reasonable period of time, until the next set of shifts in the environment required a larger response to be made.

So this is an argument that endorses the use of restructuring as a management tool and sanctions its use as a legitimate part of our management and leadership equipment. It also provides a different perspective on restructuring from the backgrounder to this session.

But all is not sweetness and light. Restructuring has a dark side. Its success ultimately depends on the validity of its drivers and the sureness of execution.

There is a common pattern of top-tier restructuring on appointment that bears some scrutiny. We need to ask how many of us have done this and how many of us have paused to consider the possibility of an unconscious and deep-seated motivation to build affiliation and allegiances through creating conditions that enable us to appoint our own team – a suggestion that you are welcome to contest!

To what extent does the configuration of the New Zealand public service context drive this behaviour?

Five-year contracts can typically mean you need to establish credentials according to a particular timetable if you seek renewal or new posts. In years one and two you restructure and appoint. In years three and four you consolidate, display and exploit benefits. In year five you execute your reappointment strategy. If you factor in the three-year election cycle and changes of regime and ministers, the five-year sequence I've outlined might in fact become a three-year sequence. Again, you are welcome to disagree.

That's a point about the validity of drivers. Sureness of execution is a critical issue. Big change done well can be a powerful builder of higher performance, a conducive and productive culture, excitement and commitment. If not done well then the damage is deep-seated and lingering. In my experience any particular change also has a particular rhythm to it. If you do it fast, à la Roger Douglas, the productivity dip is deep and steep and the recovery is long and slow. Well-managed change is characterised by minute attention to detail, a focus on the individual, the maintenance and provision of tools and training to enable all parts of the organisation to play their part, and a practical timeframe that invests time upfront to ensure a low productivity dip and a rapid approach to the desired end state. In any event, fast or slow, the achievement of the end state cannot be hurried, but the measured approach is always the most likely to succeed and produce benefits earlier.

Do we follow mechanistic or organic strategies in the public service? I would argue that the dictates of the State Sector Act will generally require a responsible, organic approach.

Is restructuring overused? Probably not, but it may well be misused from time to time.

10

Skills and People Capability in the Future State: Needs, Barriers and Opportunities

Geoff Plimmer, Richard Norman and Derek Gill

Introduction

Chapter 1 of this volume describes several powerful new trends beginning to impact on public sector management including limited funding, rising public expectations and more complex problems in a less stable and predictable environment. But what are the implications of these trends on human resource management (HRM) within the New Zealand public sector? What ideas are emerging within the HRM literature, and how do these relate to the perspectives of practitioners – human resource managers, CEOs and senior executives, and staff – in New Zealand's public sector organisations?

The formal system in New Zealand, focused on improvement of pre-specified and auditable outputs monitored through detailed agency performance plans, may no longer be sufficient for the public sector environment of the future. Instead, new individual and collective capabilities may be needed. Current state servants have been selected, developed and rewarded in an environment that has emphasised stability, control, linear accountability and outputs. In contrast, we will argue that the emerging environment requires adaptability and the ability to work across public, private and non-profit public sector boundaries, locally and internationally. Bottom-line accountability for the efficient operations of a tightly defined functional task is fundamentally different from the messiness of managing public sector responses to shifting social and economic challenges that have no easily defined finish lines.

We begin this chapter with an overview of the current state of skills and people capability in the New Zealand public sector, including employee commitment and engagement, and the impact of the new wave of reforms over the last decade. We then identify several emerging ideas about the future of public sector HRM, including the need to develop better leaders, encourage innovation and collaboration, and make a longer-term, more intense effort in capability development. These ideas were explored with practitioners in a series of focus groups in April and May 2011. In this chapter, we discuss the results of the focus groups, in which we found general agreement with many of the ideas tabled for discussion but some key differences in perspective between human resource managers, CEOs and senior executives, and staff. We conclude this chapter with a discussion of the future of public sector HRM in New Zealand.

The Current State of Skills and People Capability

Human resource management is extremely decentralised in the New Zealand state sector. The State Services Commission's core business is chief executive performance management. The Commissioner does, however, have a leadership role on ethics and integrity in the wider state sector that balances the decentralisation underlying the New Zealand model. Within the public service, SSC responsibilities include promoting and developing policies and standards for personnel administration, senior leadership and management capability, and integrity and conduct (SSC, 2011). On human resource development, the SSC in recent years has interpreted its role in a narrow way rather than taking a broader developmental role.

Scott (2001) noted that insufficient attention was paid to ownership issues, including personnel capability and the intellectual property residing in the workforce. Schick (2001) noted that purchase issues dominated ownership issues because of the immediacy and tangibility of outputs. Ten years later, despite some changes, existing performance management arrangements are still far from perfect, with frequent poor management behaviours apparently persisting over a number of years (Francis, 2011).

Other identified shortfalls in the current state sector include a short-term focus and accompanying lack of strategic capacity, as well as fragmentation, lack of evaluation, and gaps between what services are required to do and what they do. The need for more integrated service delivery and an improved public service culture has been recognised for a decade now.

The task- and mission-focused formula of the New Zealand system has also had a predictable 'shadow' side in limited employee commitment and engagement, both of which are sources of organisational innovation and contribution beyond the job description (Bélanger, Giles and Murray, 2002).

Employee Commitment and Engagement

In their drive to achieve targets, have managers who have thrived on delivering outputs undermined the adaptive capabilities of the public sector system? An employee survey commissioned using the Gallup Engagement Scale found relatively few public organisations with high staff engagement and many with low engagement compared with international benchmarks (SSC, 2010b). Surveys about issues of integrity and conduct commissioned by the SSC in 2006 and 2010 identified that state servants are, by and large, satisfied with the organisation they work for (SSC, 2010c). In 2010, 74 per cent agreed or strongly agreed that they were satisfied, in general, with their organisation, and the majority responded that the organisation kept them adequately informed. The same survey, however, found that 38 per cent of staff had witnessed abusive or intimidating behaviour toward other staff, improper use of the internet or email, or lying to other employees in the previous year (SSC, 2010c). In other research, 43 per cent of New Zealand women state sector survey respondents reported either workplace bullying or discrimination (Donnelly, Proctor-Thomson and Plimmer, in press).

The disparity of these findings will partly reflect measurement issues, but they share a common theme that, while most responses were generally positive, about one-third of responses were negative (dissatisfaction with the organisation they work for, or reports of intimidation or abuse). Thus, it may be that where most work environments are 'satisfactory', many are not; and where on balance employees are generally satisfied (perhaps partly through adjusting expectations), there are some problems around over-controlling leadership, abuse and intimidation.

Workplace incivility, such as that reported in these surveys, negatively affects productivity by undermining motivation and the trust needed for innovation; the effects extend beyond those most directly involved (Estes, 2008). Process innovations and 'good ideas' tend not to deliver the expected payoffs unless managers explicitly encourage innovations, and workers can exercise discretion and are allowed to feel responsible (Baer and Frese, 2003). Discretionary behaviours are important to innovation and collaboration because they encourage the use and sharing of tacit knowledge – a feature of more complex, knowledge-based work (Bélanger et al., 2002). In addition, workplace incivility can result in unresolved conflicts that make it more likely that employees will pursue private interests that are contrary to organisational interests (McGregor and Cutcher-Gershenfeld, 2006).

Lack of employee commitment and engagement can also be the result of negative management styles. Research by Human Synergistics about the effect of leadership styles on the cultures of New Zealand public organisations found they tend to be unconstructive, with an emphasis on control, power and covert criticism whereby 'Security is then achieved by retreating into conventions and procedures' (McCarthy, 2008: 295). While many state sector managers record that they would like a supportive work environment, McCarthy's sample of public organisations shows staff commonly rate government workplaces as aggressive and defensive.

Such a culture has not gone unnoticed by the ministers of state. Political concern about a risk-averse public sector has been raised by the Minister of Finance, Bill English, who comments that 'the culture of caution and risk

management in the public sector has been deeply embedded in the last 10 years.
. . . officials were not encouraged to think or speak freely, or to take risks'
(English, 2010).

The New Zealand and International Evolution of Public Sector Reform

Early on in the New Zealand reform process, human resource management
responsibilities were delegated to state sector organisations on the logic that they
were best suited to develop policies in response to the imperatives they faced,
and that more ready access to the labour market would develop HR capability.
By the late 1990s a new breed of hard-driving managers had emerged who were
good at pursuing outputs but poor at capacity building. They assumed that all
skills could be purchased in the market (Schick, 2001).

Internationally, at the start of the millennium, a new wave of reforms sought
more joined-up government and a stronger focus on relationships (Lindorff,
2009). While the reforms allowed the introduction of soft people-management
practices like engagement and empowerment, in practice the international
evidence is that the rise of managerialism has led to more control, monitoring,
rigidity and gaming (Diffenbach, 2009).

Despite these well-established characteristics, the New Zealand system
shows some signs of evolution. As the Future State (Stage 1) report pointed
out, collaborative rather than control-based approaches are emerging (see also
chapters 1 and 3, this volume), but are constrained and at times deliberately
made invisible because of the control orientation within agencies, and output
(rather than outcome) accountability between principals and agencies. However,
reforms have been half-hearted and treated symptoms rather than causes,
possibly a result of reform weariness and rigid mindsets (Christensen and
Lægreid, 2007b). Government reform processes seem 'stuck', with considerable
problem definition and limited solution-finding. Lindquist (this volume) queries
whether current debates about reform can move past sense-making to genuine
change. Overload and scarcity, uncertainty about what is critical and the role of
unique organisational contexts all represent barriers to moving beyond knowing
what should happen, to being able to make it happen.

In sum, long-standing ownership problems persist, reflected in limited people
capability. Risk aversion and tolerance of staff victimisation are two markers of
these problems. The current state sector environments and management models
have valued control, competition and continuity to deliver pre-determined
outputs. These problems are becoming less tolerable in a more financially
constrained environment with rising public demands, instability, harder-to-
define problems and harder-to-find solutions.

The Future of Public Sector HRM: Emerging Ideas

According to the emerging New Zealand and international research on high performance workplaces, people management does make a difference to organisational performance. The difference can be large, and New Zealand is something of a laggard (Birdi et al., 2008; Fabling and Grimes, 2010; Green and Agarwal, 2011). While it is important to get the basics right – like hiring the right staff – bundles of practices that encourage staff autonomy, development, rewards and teamwork seem to have meaningful positive impacts on organisational level outcomes (Fabling and Grimes, 2009; Gould-Williams, 2003). The actions and capabilities of middle managers are particularly crucial in turning formal practices into actual behaviours (Becker and Huselid, 2006; Guest, 2011). Now, new conditions are emerging that make the issues even sharper.

The conditions reflect changes in wider society (and the world), and the evolution of the state sector since the distant days of major reform. They in turn require new state sector guiding values and capabilities. All these changes have HR implications. In many ways, the current model has been effective, so shifts are likely to supplement rather than replace existing models. Reforms are likely to be 'and' rather than 'or'.

Environment is Now Less Stable and Predictable

Future State 1 identified that the environment was becoming increasingly unstable and diverse. It is also becoming less predictable. As stakeholders require improved and often more customisable solutions, more discretion and judgement by staff near the coal-face are likely to be necessary. These shifts challenge the competencies of staff themselves and their managers. This will happen in environments where success (and failure) will be hard to measure, and plans will likely be more emergent than pre-ordained.

Shift from Competition to Collaboration

One consequence of these changes is the need for increased collaboration, to construct bundles of services and manage the complexity of issues in uncertain environments. A 'one-stop-shop' cuts across the pursuit of quantifiable outputs, and the competition between agencies that has characterised the system to date. Collaboration has not always been encouraged by the new breed of hard-driving managers. Relational skills, still capable of assertion and getting results, will likely be needed.

Shift from Control to Flexibility

There are tensions between innovation and flexibility within a public sector with strong control and accountability systems (Norman, 2008a). Idiosyncratic amalgamations of different styles, cultures, structures and management can sometimes co-exist, but they require attention and testing rather than default assumptions. Arguably, a focus on control and accountability makes innovation and flexibility difficult as:

- staff avoid taking risks;
- compliance becomes more important than innovation; and
- staff who are good at control and accountability get ahead, and others do not.

Shift from Continuity to Creativity

In a similar vein, as organisational services and products need adaptation, rather than continuity of service, they are likely to require creativity, which inherently involves risk-taking. Continuity of service can clash with adaptability of service.

Continuing Pre-specified Outputs While Focusing on Broader Outcomes From Networks

A revised system would need to supplement rather than replace existing arrangements and their achievements. Clearer and stronger accountabilities for people capabilities and a more transparent and networked system would build both a common state sector platform of values and leadership, and allow more differentiation and innovation in both service delivery and people management.

Shift From Hierarchy and Accountability to Delegation, Development and Transparency

The current approach to people management has emphasised hierarchy and accountability for outputs. Management layers have (in many organisations) increased after an initial fashion for flat structures, and technical delivery skills have been valued more than leadership skills. HRM practices lack transparency. Pay systems are kept confidential. A revised state sector model would address incentives concerning people capability (currently neglected), provide information to enable better decisions, and also champion the means to change and develop.

Innovation and Flexibility Skills Are in Tension with Control and Accountability Skills

The tightly focused, compliance and efficiency-oriented hierarchies that have emerged in the current public sector management model serve to reinforce control and accountability. They can, however, be tunnel-visioned, and unable to detect environment changes fast enough to adapt. A more balanced and flexible mix of culture, structures and management styles will need to co-exist. The current model of contracting can force changes in delivery patterns and put a focus on costs, but it is less likely to foster anticipatory thinking and cross-boundary work, as the staff involved seek only to provide specified outputs.

Shift from Control to Soft Skills Such as Dealing With Ambiguity, Managing Vision and Purpose

The SSC's capability toolkit uses the Lominger framework to posit that future state sector leaders will need 'mental, people, change and results agility' (SSC, 2008b: 25). However, there is little or no mention of the 'coping with ambiguity' competencies that the future state seems likely to need equally, but which are more challenging to incumbent operating styles (Lombardo and Eichinger, 2004). Furthermore, although these creative, agile and social competencies have been identified, it is unclear how common they are currently, and whether there is sufficient impetus to make them more widespread. Doubts about whether 'human factors' really make a difference, and belief that current techniques are adequate for the task, may be some of the reasons why capability development has been so half-hearted. A focus on employees as the consumers of human resource practices would help drive the needed productivity change (Paauwe, 2009).

Shift From Management to Leadership

Better leadership skills (as opposed to hard transactional skills) might help avoid the rigid and unadaptive interpretation of rules common in traditional control environments, but a focused mindset and an analytical orientation will still be needed (Mastracci, Newman and Guy, 2010). One shift likely to be needed is from management, concerned with technical delivery, to leadership, which is more concerned with the social system. If formalised, control-based systems that encourage standardisation and continuity are to be loosened (to get innovation, creativity and collaboration), a greater emphasis on soft leadership systems will be needed. Although ways of organising production vary widely across the state sector, a common base of effective leaders and meaningful ground rules around acceptable behaviours will be needed. Regardless of whether organisations or business units are regulatory in orientation and consequently require tight process control, or conduct service design and delivery and maybe require innovation, or do cognitively demanding and contentious policy analysis, leadership skills will need to be high to attract, retain and develop good workers. Clearer differentiation between how production is managed (formal processes, often control oriented) and how work is organised (social processes, such as leadership, teamwork and the sharing of tacit knowledge) will need to be high to manage down the cost of turnover, cope with uncertainty, and build the skills of innovatation and collaboration (Bélanger et al., 2002).

Shift From Performance Appraisal to Coaching

New skill levels will also be required from staff. They will often be highly contextual, and best taught through on-the-job development and reflection, rather than offsite, event-based training. Appraisals will still need to take place, but coaching-type skills will be required of managers to ensure new forms of work organisation emerge, and that both individual and collective skills evolve.

Shift to Group Performance and Less Emphasis on Individual Performance

The more complex requirements of government will often require collaboration. Often, but not always, they will need team work and consequent feedback to the level where production takes place, rather than the current focus on the individual as the unit of production regardless of how production is organised. More transparent feedback to groups will be needed. Engagement surveys are an embryonic form of this.

Feedback From Practitioner Focus Groups

Three focus groups of practitioners were run in April and May 2011 to help define the people capability challenge in more depth.

To encourage a considered conversation, all participants were sent, in advance, a three-page summary of the emergent ideas outlined earlier in this chapter, and summarised in Figure 10.1. To get past the pro-forma, rehearsed positions that sometimes characterise public management discussions, practitioners met in a computer suite and used decision-making software that enabled them quickly to contribute ideas anonymously and then to vote on those ideas.[1] Three focus groups were held – one with 18 senior human resource managers, one with 14 workplace representatives and Public Service Association organisers, and a

---

1   WIQ software, from <http://www.gowiq.com/WIQ/servlet/WIQ?REQ=FRONT&SESS IONID=&GROUPID=&OTHER=0.95059884035653840.27619015057994633&MEE TINGID=&EXERCISEID=>.

third with two senior central agency executives and three chief executives (this group is referred to later as 'senior executives'). Sampling was as follows: CEOs and senior executives were recruited via a professional forum, senior human resources managers by referrals, and worker and union representatives from nominations from the union.

In this section we provide an overview of the results, with a general discussion of differences between and within the different participant groups. We then discuss in more depth seven themes that emerged from the discussions:

Theme 1 – Managing the tensions between control and flexibility
Theme 2 – The relationship between risk aversion, ambiguity and success
Theme 3 – Impact of ministerial demands on people capability
Theme 4 – Leadership and the role of central agencies
Theme 5 – Leadership skills within agencies
Theme 6 – Restructuring as a substitute for people capability development
Theme 7 – The strategic role of human resource managers

We conclude the discussion of the focus group results with participants' answers to the question: what is to be done?

Overview of Results

Participants' ratings of their agreement or disagreement with key ideas from the background paper are shown in Figure 10.1. As can be seen, agreement with the ideas was consistently high.

There was a high degree of consensus *within* groups, with standard deviations less than one.

There was slightly less consensus *between* the groups on the need for change. Although all three stakeholder groups converged on the propositions that the environment is now less stable, senior executives saw the least need for the type of change suggested in the background paper. An exception was the strong endorsement for continued delivery of pre-specified outputs while focused on broader outcomes delivered by networks. Human resource managers and worker representatives were in general agreement about many of the changes sought, including the need for soft skills, collaboration, performance coaching and group performance. The largest divergence was between senior executives and human resource managers, and concerned the belief that innovation and flexibility were in tension with control and hierarchy. Human resource managers believed in this tension most strongly.

The worker representatives sought a greater emphasis on innovation directly, while human resource managers sought a greater emphasis on management skill to enable innovation.

Figure 10.1. Implications for HR Practices of Environmental Shifts

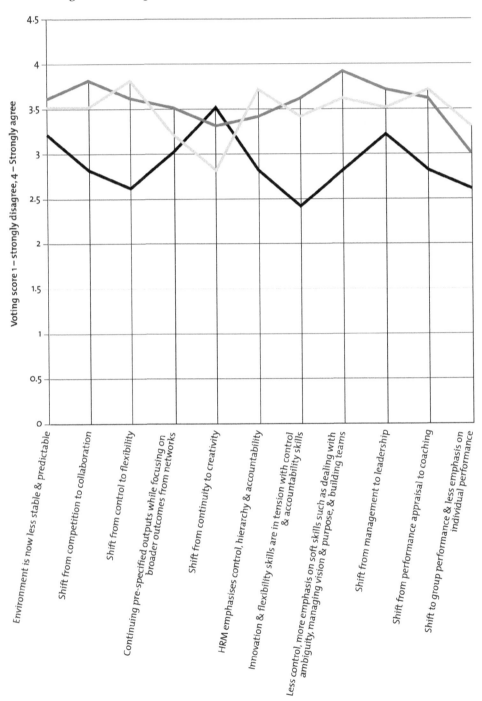

Environmental shifts and implications for values, capabilities and HRM practices

CEOs ━━━ N= HRM ╍╍╍ PSA

Participants' contributions are discussed in more detail under the following themes.

Theme 1 – Managing the Tensions Between Control and Flexibility

The first theme explored how tensions are managed between flexibility and control and the implications for skills and capabilities.

Senior executives focused on the configuration of accountability/control with innovation/flexibility systems. Senior executives mentioned the government's strategy for dealing with illegal methamphetamine (known as 'P') supply and use in New Zealand, as an exemplar for setting accountability for results, and providing a mandate to come up with new and innovative (cross-agency) solutions. In contrast, a debate about education highlighted a sector that was seen by this group as unsuccessful in managing innovation.

> In the education sector, there is little accountability and huge scope for innovation – but there has been little impact on improving learning outcomes over the last two decades since the devolved system was introduced. I would argue the lack of accountability means there is little incentive to focus on/specify desired performance.

Another participant responded:

> I agree. We run the risk of confusing accountability with overt control. They are very different, at times opposite concepts.

Such views reflect the fact that creating innovating environments is difficult and often unpredictable, and that it is easy to look in familiar, but wrong, places for improvement. Accountability and control are easily confused – one does not lead to the other. Moreover, enabling innovation does not necessarily lead to improved performance.

The reference to the education sector warrants further discussion. An evidence-based approach to education reform might have instead seen teacher quality, rather than structural reform, as more critical to improving performance, enabled by an environment where error is welcomed as a learning opportunity (Hattie, 2009). Policy and structural changes in education create the appearance of change (and can mediate it) but they often do not reach the practices of teachers in the classroom. A parallel argument, applied to the wider state sector, would be that structural reform may be necessary and provide some benefit, but the marginal return diminishes quickly. In the education sector, a revised configuration might have earlier focused on teacher's capability and skills, as well as structural change.

In the case of the generally successful 'P strategy', people capability implications included co-ordination between agencies and training (DPMC,

2011b). The 'P strategy', documented partly through indicators and progress reports, is also notable for its cross-sector co-ordination, its extensive but cautious use of data, and its use of data as a performance dashboard for tracking outcomes and learning. Its central co-ordination by the Department of the Prime Minister and Cabinet may be one reason for its success as an example of 'joined-up government'. Its outcomes, however, are still very unclear.

Complicated social problems will require more networked approaches such as that used with P, which will in turn require feedback information that is essential *and* ambiguous *and* accountability enhancing. Both cross-agency collaboration *and* intra-agency delivery will be needed; or, in the language of the Lominger competency framework, required skills include coping with ambiguity, influencing through others and structured but reflective learning (Lombardo and Eichinger, 2004).

Theme 2 – The Relationship Between Risk Aversion, Ambiguity and Success

A second theme concerned the relationship between risk aversion and ambiguity and how success might be described. All three stakeholder focus groups supported the propositions about the need to balance conflicting imperatives. Risk aversion was seen as a constraint on change, and an inhibitor of flexibility and innovation. Senior executives mentioned limited political (ministerial) accountability for outcomes, and the need for ministers to champion innovations in order for them to make headway. This suggests a mix of incentives that makes agencies dependent on ministers to innovate but leaves agencies responsible when things go wrong.

Further down the chain, senior executives saw incentives for middle managers to encourage risk aversion rather than innovation. Human resource managers also saw poor incentives for managers as barriers to innovation, and resource constraints as forcing a focus on business as usual. Worker representatives saw human resource management systems as focused on reducing risks and accountability to the business by using set formulae that worked poorly for employee well-being. Remuneration and performance management were seen as controlling rather than developing.

Lack of managerial interaction with staff in service design and a lack of stretch assignments were seen as innovation barriers. The low value attached to enhancing skills was seen as a barrier to more risky stretch assignments. Rigid application and over application of out-dated HR practices in the state sector were also mentioned by HRM practitioners as constraints on reconfiguring innovation/consistency dilemmas. Human resource managers attributed the durability of dated practices to the organisation and its managers. While private sector managers were seen as quickly grabbing ideas from elsewhere and applying them, by contrast, in the words of one participant, 'in the public sector HR people might get really excited but nothing happens'. Instead, old practices were followed in laborious detail. Other reported 'institutional constraints' on people capability development were insufficient credit for risks but heavy penalties for failure, a perception that productivity gains equated to cost cutting and organisational designs that focused on strongly specified structures that discouraged team work.

Although the New Zealand system may have evolved into a control-oriented system, arguably this mirrors the rise of managerial control in the private sector identified by Mintzberg (2009). The practice of selecting CEOs as a 'safe pair of hands' permeates down the organisation, and may discourage innovation. A senior executive wrote:

> Some of the lack of innovation I think reflects senior public servants' views of their role, i.e. implementing ministers' wishes once the minister has said what s/he wants versus giving frank advice. In agencies dominated by the former view, a censorship process tends to operate – closing down ideas that the minister has not yet raised herself/himself.

Senior executives were sanguine about the real level of risk that was politically tolerable, but acknowledged the need for ideas to be voiced and rewarded, even if in practice few would be adopted. One recent innovation was that some 'CEs are actively encouraging fast failure and exploration cultures within parameters of risk determined by the executive team. Managers were seen as poor at articulating what success looked like. A senior executive wrote:

> Managers often do not have the people capability to articulate or communicate what success looks like – either in output or process terms, so the HR tools largely go unused.

Ambiguity about what success looks like (and consequently what measures mean) can combine to create office politics where performance information is used (or not used) as power plays rather than as performance improvement exercises (Courpasson, 2000). This in turn leads to a concentration and centralisation of power and influence, which presumably also means a lack of employee participation and voice. New Zealand workers generally have higher levels of participation and influence in workplaces than elsewhere, but managers often lack the skills to capitalise on these characteristics (Haynes, Boxall and Macky, 2005). In Lominger terms, enhanced people capability would include better management of vision and purpose to clarify what success looks like (Lombardo and Eichinger, 2004). Strategic agility and managerial courage to deal with both risk aversion and self- and organisational censorship might also help.

Theme 3 – Impact of Ministerial Demands on People Capability

The third theme concerned the impact of ministerial demands on people capability building.

The convention embodied in the *Cabinet Office Manual* (2008: para 3.5) is that ministers are responsible for policy and priorities for departments but 'should not be involved in their departments' day to day operations'. The reality is more complex and messy than that (see Hitchener and Gill, 2011a).

In practice, short-term and even day-to-day demands from ministers shape both skill needs and skill requirements. CEO participants reported risk aversion restricting more creative, flexible arrangements; they referred to the need to 'bring ministers along' and the ministers' need for control, as well as resistance on the part of ministers to collaborate with other agencies (and other ministers). Worker representatives commented that 'political risk to the minister is taken as a very serious guiding factor in assessing whether to proceed with a decision, even if the risk is negligible. This is stifling innovation.'

Others commented that although ministerial control inhibited innovation, the public service responded if a minister promoted a particular initiative. Some ministers supported long-term people capability building, whereas others were focused on a few discreet successes during their time with the portfolio.

One senior executive commented that few innovations came from central government, where ministerial control was strongest. Most innovations came from parts of government that had very strong focused goals and were distant from ministers, allowing more flexibility. A human resource manager commented that 'ministers are more focused on being able to allocate blame – there is no mechanism for holding ministers to agreements they have reached with their CE'. The State Sector Act and the Public Finance Act make the chief executive responsible for the delivery of outputs but the minister lacks a similar responsibility for outcomes (see also Di Francesco and Eppel, this volume). We note, however, that the political outcomes (ultimately, but by no means only, at the ballot box) for ministers who fail to deliver outcomes are traditionally seen as providing this accountability.

The need to 'keep ministers happy' was seen to have downstream impacts on leadership development. Ministers were reported as often being reluctant to invest for future ministers. Human resource managers inferred that the ability to influence ministers (managing up) may crowd out the presence of people with leadership (managing down) skills. In one discussion of the SSC, a human resource manager pointed out that demand for a particular skill profile came from the political level too:

> the commission actually wants a chief policy adviser. At Cabinet the issue is –
> will I be happy about this adviser. It is never about CE competencies at that level
> – always about policy . . . [this] is about being honest about the core requirements.

Theme 4 – Leadership and the Role of Central Agencies

The fourth theme that emerged was the role of the central agencies[2] and the need for sustained leadership on people capability building.

The SSC was mentioned extensively by both senior executives and human resource managers, but less frequently by employee representatives (who are less likely to have interaction with this employer of chief executives or to use the HR practices guides issued by the SSC). Criticisms clustered around leadership, lack of credibility within the HRM community, and the behaviours it encouraged. One senior executive commented:

> When 'keeping ministers happy' is the only objective, it's hard to develop and lift organisational performance. SSC puts too much weight on this as an overriding basis for assessing CE performance.

The SSC's own practices were criticised for focusing on short-term accountability for outputs rather than accountability for results. These were then reflected in its expectations of the system. Similarly, workers' representatives saw the focus on 'widgets' rather than 'outcomes'. Senior executives saw vertical accountabilities as hindering the allocation of resources to shared work, and the SSC's short time horizon as limiting the attention that could be given to building people capability. Senior executives agreed that the formal accountability model did not encourage across-system sharing and learning, and that informal arrangements were inadequate.

Human resource managers saw the need for more system-wide leadership. They were critical of the SSC for not promoting a coherent vision of public sector management, and being compliance focused rather than leading the way. There was a strong consensus around comments that there was 'no overall vision for future organisational development and a human resource approach from the SSC'; in other words, that there was no or little recognition of the need for 'leaders rather than technical experts to manage people', that the 'SSC had lost its leadership of public sector HR' and that it 'lacked credibility with HR practitioners'.

More specific criticisms of the State Services Commission included low attention to culture, creativity and innovation in CE performance reviews (because they are harder to measure), lack of workforce planning, and a tendency to request information but not to provide useful information in return. Human resource managers commented that the fixed-term nature of CE appointments[3] was seen as limiting their independence and ability to innovate and narrowing the time horizon for people capability building. Suggested improvements included

---

2 The central agencies are the Treasury, the State Services Commission, and Department of the Prime Minister and Cabinet for policy co-ordination.

3 New Zealand chief executives are generally appointed for an initial term of five years with the option of a contract for a further three years.

more purposive leadership development, with more active cross-government career development; and more 'explicit prioritisation of the outcomes that really matter and transparency about what is being done, who is accountable and the progress that is being made'. One senior executive suggested:

> In the core public sector, leadership is very weak on communicating direction and strategies for achieving them. Review of policy expenditure has a very short term focus, keeping ministers happy and one step in front as opposed to how to really lift performance.

Theme 5 – Leadership Skills Within Agencies

The fifth theme concerned the need to balance conflicting imperatives.

Poor senior executive leadership skills were identified by human resource managers as a constraint on more effective configurations of innovation/flexibility and control/accountability. Managers were described as the 'checkers in the organisation', who were often unrewarded for innovation and, paradoxically, sometimes lacking in real accountability despite the plethora of control. Worker representatives identified line managers as critical bottlenecks in managing tensions between control/accountability and innovation/flexibility. Mismanagement of the tension included managers being reluctant to involve staff in decision-making, not updating processes and systems in response to change, and having weak and unclear guidelines within which discretion could be exercised.

Human resource managers used different language, referring to limited real accountability of managers, limited skill sets, lack of communication with staff, as well as poor self and collective reflection. Senior executives commented on the need to promote and recognise innovative leaders in a risk-averse environment where there was often a 'pressure to first do no harm'. Moreover:

> we tend to replicate ourselves and this sameness is not conducive to diversity of thought and innovation – and reflects a view that there is a 'right' way forward.

This 'cloning' process means that skill and people capability weaknesses can persist in the face of failure. A narrow range of skills can be hired, developed and rewarded because they are similar to those of current managers, even if they are not what jobs and situations require. Developing and managing diverse teams takes effort and a complex mix of competencies.

Theme 6 – Restructuring as a Substitute for People Capability Development

Restructuring is endemic in the New Zealand public sector, with around two-thirds of staff reporting being involved in restructuring in the last two years (SSC, 2010c; see also Gill and Norman, this volume). Restructuring quickly emerged as a key theme affecting people capability development. As a result, focus groups explored the people capability implications.

Restructuring was seen as a substitute for people capability development, and reflected behaviours at the top. Senior executives saw management expectations of staff as reflections of ministers having low appetites for ideas that were not their own. Restructuring was sometimes needed to drive deep change including attitude change, the development of softer skills and a focus on what counts. It was seen, however, to take place in environments characterised by poor and destructive people management – environments that were harmful to innovators, trust and people capability growth. A worker representative commented, 'major restructuring can be indicative of the failure of an organisation to adapt to change on an on-going basis'.

Both human resource managers and worker representatives agreed that restructuring could be effective when it was well planned and implemented with 'strong and early staff involvement'. The effectiveness of restructurings are rarely evaluated, and even if they are well managed in terms of avoiding personal grievances, the ability to convey vision, purpose and a rationale for restructuring was seen as poor. It was regarded as a substitute for longer- term and deeper investment in people and organisations.

Both human resource managers and senior executives reported that major drivers of restructuring were second-tier performance problems and the need to address them quickly. Restructuring was also seen as an over-used technique that was expensive and prone to under-delivering. Skill and people capability implications included increased pressure on staff to pick up extra workloads, a distraction from ongoing organisational business, and an avoidance of underlying culture and performance issues by those who have done well in the current system:

> Soft skills are not soft – when will people get this? . . . Someone from a government agency said it was really hard to focus on outside and inside stuff at the same time. You won't get the outside stuff unless you build the inside people capability. We manage things down, don't take risks.

Theme 7 – The Strategic Role of Human Resource Managers

Senior executives saw human resource managers as followers rather than as strategy leaders. Human resource managers were aware of this and discussed the need to express HRM benefits in terms of financial outcomes, move from being 'process queens' to organisational developers, identify needed capabilities and focus on those, be more systematic, talk in business language rather than HR language, and deliver organisational outcomes.

Excluded from a strategic role, their functional, development and leadership expertise was limited by poor clarity about what leadership means in the state sector and what success looks like. Both human resource managers and worker representatives saw line managers as over-dependent on human resource staff. This over-dependence by line managers, plus a limited political, strategic and change agent role, and an instinctive siding with those in power (as reported by worker representatives) limited the credibility of human resource managers.

Worker representatives saw HR groups as bloated and representing an offloading by executives of workforce issues. HR people were seen as having limited freedom to contribute, with their advice often ignored by managers who face 'no sanction for poor judgement'. Incentives to develop and measure talent were said to be poor. Very poor line management behaviours are also sometimes tolerated with impunity, which further damages human resource managers' credibility:

> HR managers need to recognise bullying in the worksite rather than sweeping issues under the table. . . . Managers must receive guidelines and training to identify examples of this and also realise the enterprise does not condone it. Many managers who display such stuff again and again are never challenged and this perpetuates the issue.

> At XXX we had two different parts of HR working in different ways with a manager – one to help correct the poor behaviour and the other enabling it. Which do you think won? Yep, the enabler.

On a more positive note, a CE of a large operational department commented that the most important priorities for HR were leadership support and development. Through leaders, a strong, positive culture could be built, and:

> these are the key challenges in times of big change . . . we still have to get the basic HR practices done well, but we do know that stuff reasonably well now.

Systemic problems identified by human resource managers included patch protection, selection focused solely on a 'safe pair of hands', control mechanisms being seen by staff as a lack of trust, and a perception that productivity enhancements equalled cost cutting.

Each of the workshops did, however, report a culture shift in recent years toward collaboration (particularly in sector groupings), but vertical accountability and weak incentives constrained its extent. HRM has been reshaped in recent years by growing awareness of the critical role it can play in high performance, a desired elevation in the stature of HRM from process managers to strategic partners, and growing awareness of the role of line managers in implementing HR policies because they are where the 'rubber meets the road'.

What Needs to Happen?

Workshops concluded with a session on 'what needs to be done'. Most suggestions for change are embedded in the criticisms made previously. There was some cynicism about the extent of change possible, indicated by the scope of suggested changes. That said, participants, particularly HR managers, recognised that there had been a shift to capabilities clustered around flexibility, innovation and ambiguity in recent years.

Senior executives identified the following opportunities for improvement:

- more focused development of rising stars;
- interchange between public and private sectors;
- explicit prioritisation of outcomes;
- transparency of progress and accountability; and
- stronger central agency leadership.

Senior executives emphasised configurations of control and innovation rather than either/or choice. They identified the need to reframe accountability as a return-on-investment and a decision-making tool, rather than as a means to hold individuals to account.

The need to focus on outcomes rather than control of processes was also mentioned by senior executives. Poor feedback loops were seen as another problem, with consequent higher spending but deteriorating outcomes (e.g., the sector's response to domestic violence). Strong, focused goals were also regarded as helping innovation.

Ministers were seen by senior executives to influence both public sector dynamics and consequent skill and people capability implications. A clearer distinction between ministers' rights to determine spending directions, and public servants' freedom to manage, innovate, and give free and frank advice to ministers was called for. Ministerial championing was portrayed as effective, but central government was seen as a poor environment for innovation. Innovations were more likely to occur away from central government, where there was more flexibility.

Skill and people capability implications included larger-scale engagement with staff, toolkits for managers, role clarification and helping HRM initiatives to cascade downwards. One senior executive mentioned that co-ordinated initiatives across large numbers of managers were needed. Capabilities and leadership in the core public sector were 'weak on communicating direction and strategies for achieving them'.

HR managers sought a clearer end state for the overall system, with the central agencies providing better oversight and modelling best practice. Stronger people capability within the sector, through sharing of information and centralised expertise, was suggested. HR managers saw technology as a means of outsourcing transactional activities, thus freeing HR managers up for strategic activities. HR managers suggested a compelling vision for the state sector: a better selected, more skilled and more divergent crop of CEOs and second-tier managers; tighter reward–performance links for desired behaviours; and more HR manager influence.

Worker representatives sought improved interactive processes for change and development, the sharing of agency innovations, a fundamental rethink of workplace culture, and greater voice in decision-making and planning for the union. More coherent sector-wide training and development, and increased availability of stretch assignments, were also sought.

Worker representatives identified the Christchurch earthquake response as an example of state sector innovation, although it had mixed results. Positives concerned collaboration, whereas minuses concerned poor consultation.

Current people capability management practices sit within a state sector system characterised by strong ministerial influence, and by short-term delivery rather than longer-term people capability development. Within organisations, low management skills and the demand for output delivery have created a cycle of control orientation with low tolerance of ambiguity despite changing external environments. These characteristics may be embedded in the authorising environment and are certainly reinforced by the New Zealand state sector's contractualism. In other countries, recognition that public sector employees have lower participation, management information and voice than private sector comparators, and that public restructuring and change management are less effective than those in the private sector, have added to disillusionment with the contractualist approach, and sparked a search for new, more balanced and better-configured approaches (Lindorff, 2009). Locally, the search for solutions is characterised by formalised, repetitive position-taking, focused on structures and contracts. A relatively small number of influential voices continues to tinker with worn out tools.

System-wide People Capability Challenges

Across the New Zealand state sector, change is currently constrained because of risk aversion and inherent dilemmas and tensions in the authorising environment and the public management system. System-wide changes that are most needed include a rebalancing of:

- sector/organisational coherence *and* the ability to choose and assemble more idiosyncratic and experimental configurations of skills and capabilities at different levels;
- soft *and* technical skills, i.e., greater valuing and demonstration of soft skills, and less tolerance of failings in those areas;
- ambiguity *and* goal directedness, i.e., the ability to set a clear direction, with less prescription about the means to reach goals.

The New Zealand state sector's dependence on restructuring as a substitute for performance management and people capability development rests on the assumption that the next restructuring will be better than the last, that the underlying problem will be solved, or that the problem is unsolvable and that restructuring is the best stopgap. When public sector reform was introduced in New Zealand over 20 years ago, a position-based merit system open to lateral entry was envisaged in which it was assumed leaders would be tested under fire and, if unsuccessful, not be reappointed. The behaviours that have emerged from this approach are not always positive.

The Influence of the SSC

The State Services Commission was commented on widely in this study. A longer-term, and more meaningful, people capability orientation would more actively counterbalance the downsides of short-term demands from 'purchasers' (ministers), focus on selecting and developing a diverse range of leaders, improve information flows within internal labour markets and strengthen the role of HR managers as strategic people capability managers rather than transaction managers. More transparency and feedback about people capability and 'people issues' would help. This is not a new recommendation, but current processes are still clearly inadequate (Scott, 2001). Currently, people capabilities do exist in accountability frameworks, but in practice are often confined to exhortations and soft tools.

Those looking for change levers could consider a greater focus on, and valuing of, long-term ownership issues at the state sector system level, supported by a coherent people capability framework to evaluate HRM and its consequences. There are several models available, of which the Harvard model of commitment, competence, cost-effectiveness and congruence with goals might be useful because of its durability and configurability to diverse situations (Beer et al., 1985). Solutions are likely to be contextual.

Collaboration between state agencies and other non-state sector agencies may be one of the most important areas of desired change. Although there are circumstances where collaboration works well, factors such as risk aversion, ambiguity about what success looks like, disturbance from restructuring and weak leadership could all be possible causes of limited people capability in this area.

Isomorphism

Conformity or 'isomorphism' poses another set of people capability challenges and stands in contrast to the market innovations sought in the original New Zealand system reforms. Central agencies, such as the SSC, the Treasury, Department of Prime Minister and Cabinet, and Office of the Auditor General[4]

---

4   Strictly speaking, the Controller and Auditor General is an Office of Parliament, not a central agency, but for the current purposes they perform as part of the centre.

act to encourage uniformity of practice in the state sector by 'soft' methods such as promulgating norms or peer imitation.

The tendency for convergence of practice is surprising, considering that New Zealand is characterised by a relatively weak centre in comparison with similar jurisdictions such as Canada, the UK and Australia (at both their federal and state levels) (Norman, 2008a). The centre does, however, have teeth. For instance, it conducts CE performance appraisals, and chooses whether or not to reappoint CEs after the standard five-year term. However, in using these levers it apparently amplifies rather than manages ministers' concerns, and pays little attention to outcomes but considerable attention to organisational actions such as restructuring. The tendency for isomorphic behaviours emerges originally from an authorising environment that discourages risk-taking and learning and encourages risk minimisation, providing strong incentives to stay close to the norm. The current authorising environment appears to fit that description.

Poor Information Flows

Poor information flows might also be a problem where lack of knowledge about both inputs and outcomes conceals the true level of quality. The SSC's recently introduced Performance Improvement Framework, and the evaluations that accompany it, are a much-needed step in the right direction (SSC, 2010a).

Organisational Level Capability Challenges

Organisations and business units will need a wider and deeper toolkit with which to make and implement change where values must co-exist in a state of tension. Organisations will need the ability to choose and assemble more idiosyncratic and experimental configurations of skills and capabilities between business units, teams and hierarchies. Localised adaptations that are configured to business unit drivers, and performance management and pay systems that are more discriminating, risk-taking and accountable, are examples of the complexity of change needed. Team appraisals for development, more nuanced blends of hard and soft HR, and development activities that integrate into working life are other examples of possible people capability building approaches. However, these approaches are time-consuming, not always practical and need to be done well.

In particular, selection, training and development, performance management and rewards will need to value wider and deeper skill mixes within both individuals and teams. Collective as well as individual competencies may require more focus. Workers will need to know the 'rules of the game' to exercise discretion wisely within hierarchies, and will have to have new skills and tools to work more autonomously.

The supplementation of hierarchies with network systems implies reconfigured accountability and feedback systems that are more reciprocal, systemic and transparent, and less hierarchical. The inclusion of learning and performance goals at business unit and agency levels may be another avenue for change, particularly in managing the tensions within public management. Generalisations are difficult, but evolution of the public management system has been accompanied by aspects of market cultures and hierarchies (with hard-driving but under-skilled managers, and an emphasis on control) (Schick, 2001). A shift to more 'clan' elements may encourage the staff development and commitment needed. Care, however, will be needed as to which unit of the 'clan' is developed – to ensure horizontal clans (such as senior managers) do not self-protect and are open to feedback, and that vertical clans (organisations) are able to collaborate with each other. The innovation and agility of network approaches is appealing but unlikely to be entirely realistic across the whole of the state sector.

HR Manager Capability Challenges

For the state sector to evolve, HR managers will need to manage more complex mixes of risk management and innovation and to juggle different roles including strategic partner, change agent, administrator and manager of employee contribution (Ulrich and Brockbank, 2005). Within organisations, elevation of HRM to 'people capability management', both in hierarchical rank and in scope, would assist. HR managers may need to be more sophisticated, activist, business oriented and generally 'strategic', as it is defined in the literature. Clearer processes, and possibly ethics, around bullying and victimisation issues would enhance their credibility.

Table 10.1. Ulrich and Brockbank's Revised Typology of Human Resource Manager Roles

Strategic partner	Change agent, business expert, planner and knowledge manager
Functional expert	Admin efficiency policy and intervention design
Employee advocate	Needs of current workforce
Human capital developer	Preparing employees to meet future challenges
Leader	Leadership of HR function, collaborate with other areas, effective in other 4 roles.

Source: Ulrich and Brockbank (2005).

Growing confidence in the effectiveness of HRM has already occurred, alongside a deepening and widening of the role of HR managers in organisations. They are moving from process managers to people capability developers. Ulrich and Brockbank's (2005) revised typology of human resource manager roles differs sharply from HRM's traditional process management function, as Table 10.1 indicates.

Line Manager Capability Challenges

Managers will need new skills to convey and manage the shifting levels of discretion required in different business units and between different job tasks among workers. The system (including line managers) may resist change. In many ways the current system has performed well, and decision makers have often done well under current arrangements. As line managers are critical to high performance and to organisational credibility with staff, the selection, development and performance management of line managers are likely to be fruitful areas for change (Boxall and Macky, 2009).

Many senior managers are strong on technical policy, but poor at integrating and executing internal and external strategy. Managers are crucial links between formalised strategy and actual practice so a shift in skill and mindsets will be needed (Becker and Huselid, 2006; Guest and Conway, 2011). Better integration of strategies, culture and HRM might be useful starting points. Feedback loops will be crucial to address shortcomings in the information flows that internal labour markets need, and the tendency of hierarchies to cut themselves off from what they most need to know. The existing tools are a good starting point, but how organisations use them determines their impact. Current incentives are to turn a blind eye. More transparency might help, such as more open information about good and poor places to work, and the underlying reasons.

The advocated reforms might also reduce the need for restructuring, if performance problems at the tier-two management level are indeed a driver for restructuring. As others have commented, a shift in mindset from short to long term and from being 'architects to gardeners' is likely to be difficult because of the entrenched mindsets of senior public servants (Gregory, 2006). Incentives will need to change. Drawing from the emerging recognition of the capacity for mixed cultures and values, and from the sector's need for formalised processes as a necessary means to drive change, the following practical recommendations might help:

- a re-articulation of a public sector ethos beyond servicing ministers;
- stronger weight toward ownership and capability issues in CEO performance expectations;

- elevated consideration of human resource management issues, and elevating HR managers from process operators to positions of influence;
- better measurement, and more transparent, accessible and reciprocal information about agency people capability issues;
- more sustained commitment to senior management selection and development; and
- better processes for victimisation complaints.

Conclusion

The results of this research suggest there is room for more systematic and less tentative development in skill and people capability, and that some bad habits need to be 'unlearned'. The New Zealand model of bottom line efficiency and pre-specified results is insufficient for developing organisations for the future. The culture of caution, risk management and limited innovation in the public sector is likely to remain if the state sector continues with its current recipe of control, reviews and restructurings.

11

Past, Present and the Promise:
Rekindling the Spirit of Reform

Bill Ryan and Derek Gill

From the late 1980s, New Zealand burst onto the firmament of public administration, lighting up the night sky.[1] This country put in place a programme of radical public sector reform that made it a recognised world leader. Officials took up the mantle with energy and a spirit of reform drove a wave of public sector improvement in the 1980s and 1990s.

Several factors drove the reforms, including a burning platform for change and ministerial urgency, the capability inside the public sector to pick up new ideas and develop them – and a powerful sense that traditional public administration, the basis on which the New Zealand public sector was organised, no longer provided a progressive agenda to meet the challenges of the future. New Zealand's economic and fiscal position relative to the rest of the world was poor and getting worse. Bureaucracy and public administration had developed, as Hughes points out, 'at a particular point in industrial development: its systems and technology were suited to an earlier age' (2003: 43). Like all ideas of the past that continue into the present, at some point in time, usually triggered by some new set of circumstances, they suddenly and decisively lose their relevance. In the eyes of public servants in the mid-to-late 1980s, traditional public administration lost its legitimacy and they turned elsewhere for ideas. In New Zealand, a group of economists and accountants based in the Treasury reached into new institutional economics and theories of management and organisation. They proposed a new vision of how governing might be conducted that drew heavily on markets and contracting (Treasury, 1987). After the State Services Commission's unsuccessful last stand on state-owned enterprises in the mid-1980s, apart from the weakened public service unions, no-one was left to defend the old regime. The majority of public servants put down their arms and allowed the wall between public and private sector, between state and economy, to be dismantled.

These reforms were not reforms for reform's sake, and nor indeed were they intended to just improve the performance of the public sector. The public sector reforms were part of a much more wide-ranging programme

---

1   A remark reportedly made in the early 2000s by the Secretary of the British Cabinet Office.

of social and economic reforms. Indeed, apart from state-owned enterprise reform, public sector reforms generally lagged behind the rest of a structural adjustment programme that had already commenced. Treasury (1987: 96) had argued:

> Very substantial amounts of New Zealand resources are controlled by state and local authority trading activities. The process of recent economic policy reform has exposed the internationally traded goods sector increasingly to international competition. This has, in turn, highlighted the importance of the efficiency and pricing policies of the non-traded sector of the economy in determining the overall competitiveness and productivity of the New Zealand economy.

Accelerating the reforms of the sheltered or non-tradeables sector[2] (of which government is a significant part) was required to ease and share the burden of adjustment. In other words, there was a strategic imperative rather than just a fiscal imperative to get improved public sector performance. This also provided the political imperative for change. It fired up a spirit of reform that flowed through the leadership to the rest of the public sector.

Our argument is that the spirit of reform in the 1980s and 1990s was driven by a combination of that strategic imperative, a collection of available ideas, ministerial leadership, and a capable bureaucracy with the ability to pick up new concepts and turn them into a reform programme. In 2011, the same conditions apply and the spirit of reform needs to be rekindled. There are again powerful economic, fiscal and political imperatives – different from those of the 1980s, but no less demanding. Public management ideas that became established in New Zealand (and Britain, Australia, Canada and the United States) in the 1980s and 1990s have recently started losing their currency and legitimacy. New ideas regarding governing in the future are emerging internationally – but have so far impacted only slightly in New Zealand and then quietly and in unremarked ways. At the senior levels of the public sector the view seems to be that what is required is 'continuing evolution rather than a fundamental change of direction' (Treasury, 2008: 16; see also Whitehead, 2008). We have a different view. We suggest that the time has come for ministers and officials to seize the moment and pursue these new ideas even if they lead to fundamental changes as they probably will.

A parallel is worth observing in the situation confronting the software company Microsoft in the mid-2000s. For years it had achieved immense success with the Windows desktop operating system. As time went by, it preserved the core of Windows to retain its market-share and maintain backwards compatibility. As new technological software developments (including open

2 Non-tradeables are services or goods produced and used within a country that are not exposed to competition from world production

source), customer demands and competition emerged, and as viruses and malware designed to exploit the system's weaknesses surfaced, Microsoft needed to adapt the Windows kernel but felt it should not do so. Instead, it was patched, fixed and added to. It became, as software developers say, a jumbled mess of over-layered code. Eventually, the pressures for change could be ignored no longer. Parts of the kernel had to be discarded and other parts rewritten. The new Windows (Vista) was not a widespread success but, with further work, the next version (Windows 7) was, enabling Microsoft to look to the future.

We argue that the challenges facing the New Zealand public sector management model are akin to the challenges facing Microsoft in the mid-2000s. As we enter the second decade of the twenty-first century, it still seems to have some strengths but increasingly also several weaknesses. The model of public management articulated in legislation, circulars and guidelines, patched-up and added to in the light of recent developments, has been preserved. But present circumstances and the future look different to those of the late 1980s and early 1990s. The model now seems unprepared for the years ahead. It is time to recognise the need for change, to redesign significant parts of it by mapping backwards from the future, creating a system that will enable the promise to emerge. But in order for this to happen, the 'spirit of reform' once attributed to the New Zealand public sector (Schick 1996) again needs to soar. In our view, that spirit was alive and well throughout the late 1980s and early 1990s, re-emerged weakly for several years in the early twenty-first century but then faded away. Possibilities exist at present for its resurgence. In this final chapter, it is worth taking a brief look back over recent history to see why and how the present is as it is in order to grasp fully the opportunities for the future in the present.

The public sector reforms introduced in New Zealand in the late 1980s, designed to transcend traditional public administration, were based on several interconnected changes:

- Market principles were widely applied to significant parts across the public sector, particularly commercialisation, corporatisation and in some cases privatisation;
- Budgetary appropriations were based on outputs and no longer inputs, with outputs made the basis of management;
- Generally accepted accounting practice and accrual accounting were adopted for present and future financial and budgetary management (including forward estimates and full fiscal disclosure);
- Large conglomerate organisations were broken up into smaller, single-purpose organisations, many of them created by statute, designed to operate at arm's length from government;

- Chief executives were given the authority to manage finance and people resources and made accountable for organisational performance (single-organisation accountability) against priorities or goals agreed with the minister;
- Chief executives were employed by the State Services Commissioner but worked for the minister; staff were made accountable to the chief executive as their employer (vertical accountability), with skills and competencies relative to corporate performance expectations; and performance contracts and performance pay were made the basis of employment; and
- Policy and delivery were separated, with delivery often organised around competitive tendering and contract management (also known as contracting out).

These changes were designed, developed and implemented with zeal and brought momentous changes to the ways in which day-to-day governing was carried out in New Zealand. There is still debate over whether or not NPM represented the inappropriate application of economic and managerial ideas in the political realm (e.g., Denhardt and Denhardt, 2007; Pollitt, 1993; Ranson and Stewart, 1994; cf. also Scott, 2001). This is a valid debate but, for the purposes of the following discussion, we take the view that the reforms were led by professional and capable public officials fulfilling certain roles who defined the problem in particular ways and who drew upon their knowledge of emerging ideas that seemed most likely to meet the challenges of the future confronting them. As we will note shortly, some of these changes have brought lasting benefits. Others have not. Some subsequent changes have been made. We therefore interpret the last 30 years as a long-run learning process about how best to govern a modern country in the changing, often complex, economic, social and political circumstances in which ministers and officials find themselves. Our interest is in the present state of understanding and the capacity and willingness once again to learn our way into the future.

The public sector reforms brought significant improvements to the ways in which contemporary liberal democracies were governed, particularly in New Zealand, Australia, Britain, Canada and, to a lesser degree (since it was a less enthusiastic reformer), the United States. In general it:

- broke up the traditional bureaucratic approach, rigidities and rule-boundedness;
- loosened the sector-wide administrative framework (more flexibility);
- strengthened budgetary and financial management (previously historical and input-based);

- improved transparency of government finances (present and future, and results orientation); and
- clarified vertical (managerial) accountability.

The era of public management is said to have superseded that of public administration (Hughes 2003) but there were continuities as well as discontinuities. The 'spirit of service', the ethics and values of public service, and traditions of a non-partisan, non-corrupt public service continue into the present. Elements of the 1912 bargain struck between ministers and officials including (in today's terminology) the independent role of the State Services Commissioner were retained and are still intact (Lodge and Gill 2011). The Westminster conventions relating to minister–official relationships were maintained although redefined in technocratic ways to strip out the oft-remarked ambiguities – the shadowy, multi-dimensional partnership between ministers and officials within a system of ministerial responsibility was reconstituted as a tangible and instrumental one wherein ministers were charged with responsibility for outcomes and chief executives for outputs. Policy advice to government thereafter would be contestable (which the increasingly important role of ministerial offices reinforced). In short, whatever its other influences in economic theory, the model of public management adopted in this country also retained an emphasis on vertical accountability and the role of hierarchy in asserting control.

The comprehensiveness and speed of the implementation of the State-Owned Enterprises Act enacted in 1986, the State Sector Act 1988, the Public Finance Act 1989 and the Fiscal Responsibility Act 1994 helped anchor the changes. By the mid-1990s, the structures, practices, norms and values of the New Zealand model of public management had become deeply embedded in the everyday routines of the public sector. However, awareness was growing of its limits as well as it strengths. Reviews such as that conducted by Schick (1996) – whose term 'the spirit of reform' we have borrowed – applauded several aspects of the New Zealand reforms, pointing particularly to the recognised improvements as already noted. Weaknesses, however, were also becoming apparent. Schick argued there was too much focus on outputs and not enough attention paid to outcomes, that the very strong emphasis on accountability had in some places become an exercise in compliance, that there was a lack of attention to strategic management, and doubts were arising as to whether the strategic capability of the public sector was being maintained. In this respect, he was critical not just of chief executives and senior managers but also of ministers not attending to their 'ownership' interests.

Following Schick, the central agencies continued with some developments particularly around outcomes and strategic management, but not at the same rate or with the same vigour as in previous years. Some senior officials were concerned they might detract from the coherence, purpose and perceived success of the original design. As Boston, Martin, Pallot and Walsh (1996) note, no systematic evaluation had been conducted but officials were generally staunch in their belief in what they were doing.

The years 1999 to 2000 brought a new round of developments and, once again, ministers (but this time new ministers) and officials settled on a reform agenda – a somewhat different one – that seemed to move things forward. The newly elected Labour government was critical of some aspects of the marketisation agenda, wanting in essence to return relationships between citizens and the state to their more conventional political form ('citizens not customers') (Mallard 2003; see also Boston and Eichbaum, 2007; Chapman and Duncan, 2007). It set up the Advisory Group on the Review of the Centre (RoC) under the direction of the ministers of finance and state services, requiring it to report within only a few months (Ministerial Advisory Group, 2001). This group combined selected public figures with the heads of the central agencies, working with a secretariat composed largely of central agency personnel. The RoC's recommendations proved to be cautious although significant, revolving around the need to reduce fragmentation and improve alignment in the public sector, make service delivery more connected, and improve the capability and culture of the public sector. Follow-up work streams created during 2002 focusing on service delivery, regional networks, and people and capability were at first pursued enthusiastically but by 2004 the impetus was fading.

In a separate but interconnected move, cabinet also signed off on 'managing for outcomes' (MFO) at the end of 2001. As one of us has previously argued (Ryan, 2004), the introduction of MFO was one of the most important developments in public management in countries like New Zealand since the early 1990s. Efficiency had been a strong focus in New Zealand, and turning attention to outcomes promised to bring an equal focus on effectiveness. 'Public management' ultimately is the organisation and conduct of everyday processes of governing, of how systems, resources and policies are brought together in ways intended to improve the collective well-being of citizens and society. Ensuring this is done effectively is just as important as ensuring it is done efficiently. From 2002, the implementation of MFO proceeded apace, eventually being extended to 'shared outcomes', which itself later led to work on 'co-ordination', but then started to languish. In 2003, cabinet signed off on the fourth component of the MFO cycle, namely, 'evaluative activity', although this did not progress far either. Eventually, following extensive parliamentary debate, some of developments arising out of the RoC and MFO were realised in the 2004 amendments to the Public Finance Act, the State Sector Act and the creation of the Crown Entities Act. (Mention should also be made of the

Local Government Act of 2002, in which territorial authorities in New Zealand were given a power of general competence, thereby recognising the increasing importance of local government in the whole governance picture.) However, in subsequent years, MFO seemed to flounder because of the inability of the central agencies to implement the required changes successfully. It certainly disappeared off the radar of central agencies (Gill, 2008b) – although, not as we will see shortly, that of line agencies.

In short, the purpose and energy that marked the first years of reform returned in the period 2001–5. Initiatives continued to emerge periodically[3] but the drive was fading. Some maintenance-oriented initiatives emerged during 2005–9 (e.g., the Review of Accountability Documents) but nothing significant. The Review of the Centre had opened up new and significant possibilities for new directions for public management in New Zealand and hinted at a vision for the future, but any enduring 'spirit of reform' faded in following years. Equally, few ministers of the period showed interest in ongoing system development; leadership from a capable bureaucracy is necessary for effective change but instigating and pursuing ongoing development crucially depends on ministerial expectation and leadership.

During this same period, unresolved issues were coming to the surface. Some emerged because public management was not being implemented as the original reformers had hoped. Learning to manage for outcomes was difficult enough and the original model had always intended that, eventually, outcomes would become a management focus, but some of the barriers to MFO seemed to come from the existing system. Others were arising out of unintended consequences of reforms that otherwise worked well. In other respects, a particular focus had been taken too far and was distorting behaviour. For example, Schick had already noticed that accountability and control processes could lead to a 'checklist' compliance mentality. In performance management and reporting processes throughout the public sector, a heavy emphasis on standard operating procedures and monitoring targets and outputs ('widgets') was leading to the recreation of an 'iron cage' wherein corporate control mechanisms were crowding out frontline attempts at innovation and managing for outcomes (e.g., Ryan, Gill and Dormer, 2011; Gill, Kengmana and Laking, 2011; see also Gill, 2011, more generally). A preoccupation with outputs was creating organisational silos that restricted performance to pre-specified actions and a single-organisation focus that limited innovation and collaboration in finding new ways of achieving government objectives (Gill, Pride, Gilbert and Norman, 2010: 32).

---

3 Initiatives over this period included senior management and leadership development and e-government. A new State Services Commissioner released a new code of practice and a set of State Sector Development Goals but the latter did not survive his departure.

Tensions were emerging where new developments were in conflict with the 1980s model of public management. Norman (2006), for example, identified several dilemmas confronting decision makers such as partnership or arm's-length deliverers, performance or capability, single-organisational focus or collaboration, central control or autonomy in decision-making, outputs or outcomes, responsiveness or frank advice, and clients or citizens. In private discussions (rarely on paper), practitioners were concerned about too much command and control and not enough enablement; too much focus on risk (and risk elimination rather than risk management) and not enough pursuit of opportunity or strategy; too much accountability as mistake detection and blame and not enough on deliberation, experimentation and learning; and so on. Also widely noted was that the complex, interdependent Westminster partnership between ministers and officials[4] had become one more like simple obedience of the latter to the former (although whether ministers demanded this or whether it was self-imposed by officials in the light of an imagined response was not clear) (see also James, 2002) – a culture that had its parallel in the command and control styles of some hard-driving public managers and their relationships with staff.

It seems that by the middle years of the past decade, the central agencies held the view that such issues were of no great consequence – worth attending to but not decisive. For example, a background paper from Treasury (2008) notes the public management developments since the late 1990s such as MFO but sees them as ongoing refinement and additions that 'have sought to reinforce rather than change the high-level system settings that were determined in the 1980s' (Treasury, 2008: 5). This paper then proceeds to identify a range of significant recent changes in society and the polity including the altered relationship between the executive and the legislature as a result of MMP, the complexity of policy questions and the need for cross-agency, whole-of-government solutions, increasing expectations of citizens regarding service quality and their desire to be consulted on matters that affect them. The paper notes: 'These trends have also been seen internationally, with increased importance given to the involvement of citizens in government, and changing demands as a result of more participative democracy' (Treasury, 2008: 6). The Future State 1 researchers, of course, noted the same or similar shifts and concluded that the time has come

---

4   Strangely, despite the reliance on these conventions in New Zealand, there is relatively little discussion of them – especially so since the advent of MMP. This may account for the highly pragmatic but philosophically reduced version that is conventionally maintained (e.g., the introduction by Keith to the *Cabinet Manual*: Cabinet Office, 2008; also Prebble, 2010). The nuances have been discussed in much greater detail in Australia and have been for some time (e.g., for classic accounts, see the selection of papers in Weller and Jaensch, 1980, especially that by R.W. Cole).

for a step change in the manner in which public management in New Zealand is conducted. Treasury's conclusions were quite different:

> There are areas of the public management system that we need to protect, build on and enhance, just as there are areas of weakness that we can and must remedy. There are also areas where the system needs to be reconsidered in the light of experiences over the last 20 years. None of these necessarily involves a fundamental rethink or significant change of direction. (Treasury, 2008: 16)

The Treasury secretary at the time made similar remarks in an address a few weeks later (Whitehead, 2008).

This view would explain why the spirit of reform – the ongoing attempt to ensure that the public management system is appropriate for the society it serves and which adapts in accord with emerging trends in the society – had faded among the leadership of the public service.

In fact, however, the spirit of reform had not faded. It had – and has – relocated. The realisation that society had changed and that the old ways of managing in the public sector would no longer work had already occurred elsewhere in government. Some line agencies, especially those involved in direct delivery to citizens, were not holding back in developing their public management practice. The RoC and MFO had given them permission to manage for outcomes. Obliged by the 2004 amendments to the Public Finance Act to show connections between outputs and outcomes, line agencies started on the journey even if, at first, they were puzzled about how to do so. In the manner discussed by Eppel, Turner and Wolf (this volume), they began making sense of outcomes, what they meant, what they were hoping to achieve, how they would do it and the evidence they would need to demonstrate success. Signs started appearing in planning documents and annual Statements of Intent, often fragmentary and far from perfect, but they showed that the movement had started. By 2008–9, outcome-oriented management frameworks, indicators and funding arrangements were starting to take shape in several organisations (e.g., for Road Safety, see Laking, 2011; the Department of Conservation, see Ryan, 2011c; and Work and Income, see Gill and Dormer, 2011).

Equally telling, pockets of practitioners, dotted throughout many organisations and driven by the new conditions confronting them that were emanating from society – the kinds of changes noted in Future State 1, the implications of which are discussed in several chapters of this volume – were starting to act differently. These offered new opportunities for innovative state employees to invent new procedures and processes. In particular, officials at the interface of government and citizens were finding that standard operating procedures were inadequate to the task and that new ways of working based on networking, collaboration and co-production had to be created. Cases could be found in many places across the public sector, among senior officials and at the frontline, in central and local government, where emergent forms of practice were being created in and through relationships between organisations and with providers and clients, organised in networks, and with a heavy emphasis on action learning (Eppel, Gill, Lips and Ryan, 2008). Public entrepreneurs and their fellow travellers (including their counterparts in civil society) were learning their way forward, being inventive (by bending rules where necessary) to ensure that clients were treated holistically and that the actual outcomes were what government policy wanted.

But they often had to work under the radar and in spite of the system under which they operate. They were also fragile unless protected by a guardian angel, and often subject to staffing restructures and transfers, so continuity was often punctuated. In other words, these officials were not behaving like the output-focused, single-organisation, output- and control-oriented personnel presumed by the prescribed, formal public management system. They were precisely like the people facilitating and leading the community-like (or governance) approaches described in chapter 3 of this volume. It was they who were creating the necessary step change, or the new form of public management required to take this country into the future. Quietly and unheralded, unlike the fanfare that accompanied reform in the 1980s and 1990s, these officials were getting on with initiating the next necessary stage of reform of the New Zealand public sector – as they continue to do so now. As such, it is clear that the 'spirit of reform' still soars in the New Zealand public sector, but in a different place compared with 30 years ago, at a different pace, for different reasons, with different ends in mind and enacted by different people.

The implication we take from this narrative is that parts of the public sector have recognised that society is changing and that the conduct of governing must change accordingly. In the face of these shifts, it is tempting to want to defend the past and continue to refine and adjust it. But tweaking is no longer enough. As the Future State 1 report pointed out, a step change is required – in the same way that Microsoft realised in the mid-2000s.

The chapters in this book offer some pointers for directions forward, some elements that might comprise that step change. They identify known trends and project them into the future as scenarios. Together they deal with possibilities but not all of them; some important ones such as the role of Māori and tino rangatiratanga in the New Zealand version of public management are not covered here. Out of them, certain principles can be identified that practitioners can take forward, work through and make real, following where they lead. Expressed in the simplest of terms, we offer the following as a minimum list.

- The changes to the public management system to support twenty-first century public services will be different from the changes of the late 1980s. Rather than altering the architecture of government – although some of this is required to remove barriers to emerging developments – the important changes will be significant and multi-faceted modifications to the mental models, practices and leadership styles used in the public sector. Overturning some taken-for-granted assumptions to allow what is new and emergent to be fully explored should be expected.

- A major challenge for government processes built on rational methods, hierarchy and command is that in a range of circumstances, major new goals and objectives or the strategies to achieve them will not be explicable in advance via technical, expert means – the same applies to pre-formed theories devised by academics and others. Given the nature of complexity, the most effective answers in some fields will be found through practice, experimentation and learning by doing (with constant monitoring and evaluation). This will mean (re)integrating development and implementation. Learning to recognise, support and reward critical adaptations when they emerge will be essential.

- The future state will not be built on a single 'big idea' – one particular theory or model of public management, universally applied. In terms of competing frameworks, 'both–and' will apply more than 'either–or'. Multiplicity and context-dependency will prevail. Across government as a whole, different settings will require different approaches to organisation and management. In some, hierarchical forms will be most appropriate. In others, market forms will be best. Community forms of public management will predominate in others. The public management framework embedded in legislation must enable each approach to function fully.

- Top-down governing through bounded, established institutions governed by rules or contract will no longer work in many important settings. Some significant aspects of government will be built around extensive networks that connect the polity, economy and civil society. Enablement will be more important than control, with collaboration and partnership more important in some settings than command or competition. Citizens will expect to participate in matters that affect them and to be engaged in co-design and co-production. Many of these shifts towards networked governance will be enabled by the new information and communication technologies.

- Ministers must understand that they do not sit outside these new demands. They too have an obligation to recognise the coming changes and change their practice accordingly. They do not hold a sanctified position. Seeing themselves atop a pyramid of power and 'in charge' will no longer work. They must understand the interdependency they have with others and others with them. This will require new forms of leadership, working with officials (and others) as partners. In this respect, the Westminster-derived bargain with public sector employees will need to be renegotiated.

- Single-point, vertically aligned accountability will not work in many settings in the future state. Responsibility will be as important as accountability. Both will be shared and more diffuse, and new forms of joint arrangements will need to be developed. Collective deliberation, consensus formation and a willingness to accept failure when experimenting will become more important than blame and scapegoating. Again, Westminster-based conventions of individual and collective ministerial responsibility will have to change as will the relationship between the executive and the legislature.

- Tools such as organisational restructuring to achieve short-term performance improvements will no longer work. Organisations of the future will need to be flexible, adaptable and creative and, as they became more porous and unbounded when intersecting with networks, their capability and human capital will need to be preserved, built and expanded – a critical role for executives of the future. Equally, officials will need new kinds of skills and capabilities to create the constituent conditions of the future state, and future-focused strategic human resource management will be a fundamental requirement.

Presented here baldly, these principles seem radical and idealistic. We would suggest, however, that they are not any more so than proposals for a professional, apolitical public service would have seemed in the face of the patronage system of civil service in the nineteenth century, or arguments for market-based solutions to the problems of over-bureaucratised government one hundred years later. Besides, history does not hold still and some of these trends are already emerging. Signs of the future are already here suggesting these proposals are less extreme than they might otherwise appear. Moreover, as the contributors to this volume make clear, most of the ideas they discuss already have a significant presence in theory and practice in countries such as Australia, Britain and Canada, but only a few of them appear in official discourse in this country and then only to a limited degree. New Zealand may have held back too long in recognising the need for change.

There are many signs that the ideas and trends discussed in this book and others like them will be part of the future state. The task for ministers and officials today is to avoid reverting to the safety of the familiar, but to find opportunities for pushing ahead and enabling them to emerge, for exploring the future and allowing the interplay of theory and practice in doing so. They need to make creative space for this to happen; to give permission to themselves and others with whom they are engaged to pick up these ideas, especially ideas emerging from practice; and to work with them and bring them to reality – not try to control them but to enable them, wherever they may lead. Some officials are saying they sense that we are on the cusp of change. It is time to grab the moment and act. New Zealand's public sector once showed it could make dramatic adaptations to changing circumstances. We believe that time is once again upon us and that it is time to reignite that spirit of reform. We hope this book contributes.

References

6, P., Leat, D., Seltzer, K. and Stoker, G. (2002) *Towards Holistic Governance: The New Reform Agenda*. New York, Palgrave.

Aberbach, J., Putnam, R. and Rockman, B. (1981) *Bureaucrats and Politicians in Western Democracies*. Cambridge, M.A., Harvard University Press.

Advisory Group on Reform of Australian Government Administration (2010) *Ahead of the Game: Blueprint for the Reform of Australian Government Administration*. Canberra, Commonwealth of Australia.

Agranoff, R. (2006) Inside Collaborative Networks: Ten Lessons for Public Managers. *Public Administration Review* 66(S1): 56–65.

Aiginger, K. (2004) The Economic Agenda: A View from Europe. *Review of International Economics* 12(2): 187–206.

___ (2005) Towards a New European Model of a Reformed Welfare State: An Alternative to the United States Model. *Economic Surveys of Europe* 1: 105–14.

Alford, J. (2008) The Limits to Public Administration, or Rescuing Public Value from Misrepresentation. *Australian Journal of Public Administration* 67(3): 357–66.

___ (2009) *Engaging Public Sector Clients: From Service-delivery to Co-production*. London, Palgrave Macmillan.

Allen, P.M., Strathern, M. and Baldwin, J.S. (2006) Evolutionary Drive: New Understandings of Change in Socio-Economic Systems. *Emergence: Complexity and Organization* 8(2): 2–20.

Allison, G.T. (1971) *Essence of Decision: Explaining the Cuban Missile Crisis*. Boston, Little-Brown.

Alvesson, M. and Skoldberg, K. (2000) *Reflexive Methodology: New Vistas for Qualitative Research*. London, Sage.

Alvesson, M. and Sveningsson, S. (2008) *Changing Organisational Cultures: Cultural Change Work in Progress*. London, Routledge.

ANAO (2007) *Application of the Outputs and Outcomes Framework: 2006–07 Performance Audit Report No 23*. Canberra, Australian National Audit Office.

Anderson, B. and Dovey, L. (2003) *Whither Accountability*. Wellington, State Services Commission, Working Paper No. 18.

Anderson, P. (1999) Complexity Theory and Organisation Science. *Organization Science* 10: 216–32.

APSC (2006) *Supporting Ministers, Upholding Values*. Canberra, Australian Public Service Commission.

___ (2009) *Delivering Performance and Accountability*. Canberra, Australian Public Service Commission.

___ (2010) *State of the Service Report 2009–10*. Canberra, Australian Public Service Commission.

Armstrong, J. and Lenihan, G. (1999) *From Controlling to Collaborating: When Governments Want to be Partners, A Report on the Collaborative Partnerships Project New Directions – Number 3*. Toronto, Institute of Public Administration of Canada.

Askim, J. (2009) The Demand Side of Performance Measurement: Explaining Councillors' Utilization of Performance Information in Policymaking. *International Public Management Journal* 12(1): 24–47.

Atkinson, M.M. and Coleman, W.D. (1989) *The State, Business, and Industrial Change in Canada*. Toronto, University of Toronto Press.

Aucoin, P. (1990) Administrative Reform in Public Management: Paradigms, Principles, Paradoxes and Pendulums. *Governance* 3(2): 115–37.

___ (1995) *The New Public Management: Canada in Comparative Perspective.* Montreal, Institute for Research on Public Policy.

Australian Government (2010) *Standards of Ministerial Ethics.* Canberra, Australian Government.

Australian Public Service Commission (2007) *Tackling Wicked Problems: A Public Policy Perspective.* Canberra, Commonwealth of Australia.

Ayer, A.J. (1936) *Language, Truth, and Logic.* London, Gollancz.

Baer, M. and Frese, M. (2003) Innovation is Not Enough: Climates for Initiative and Psychological Safety, Process Innovations, and Firm Performance. *Journal of Organisational Behavior,* 24(1), 45–68.

Baerenholdt, J.O., Büscher, M., Scheuer, J.D. and Simonsen, J. (2010) Perspectives on Design Research. In Simonsen, J., Baerenholdt, J.O., Büscher, M. and Scheuer, J.D. (Eds) *Design Research: Synergies from Interdisciplinary Perspectives.* London, Routledge: 1–15.

Banks, G. (2009) *Challenges of Evidence-Based Policy Making.* Canberra, Australian Government Productivity Commission.

Barber, B. (1984). *Strong Democracy: Participatory Politics for a New Age.* Berkeley, University of California Press.

Bardach, E. (2005) *A Practical Guide for Policy Analysis: The Eightfold Path to More Effective Problem Solving* (2nd edn). Washington, D.C., CQ Press.

Barrett, S.M. (2004) Implementation Studies: Time for a Revival? Personal Reflections on 20 Years of Implementation Studies. *Public Administration* 82(2): 249–62.

Barzelay, M. (2001) *The New Public Management: Improving Research and Policy Dialogue.* Berkeley, University of California Press.

Barzelay, M. and Gallego, R. (2006) From New Institutionalism to Institutional Processualism: Advancing Knowledge about Public Management Policy Change. *Governance* 19(4): 531–57.

Barzelay, M. and Thompson, F. (2010) Back to the Future: Making Public Administration a Design Science. *Public Administration Review* 70(Supplement): 295–97.

Bason, C. (2011) Public Design: How Do Public Managers Use Design Thinking? Paper for Work in Progress (WIP) Seminar, 21 January. Copenhagen, MindLab.

Battaglio, R. and Condrey, S. (2009) Reforming Public Management: Analyzing the Impact of Public Service Reform on Organizational and Managerial Trust. *Journal of Public Administration Research and Theory* 19(4): 689–707.

BBC (2004) *Building Public Value: Renewing the BBC for a Digital World.* London, British Broadcasting Corporation.

Becker, B.E. and Huselid, M.A. (2006) Strategic Human Resources Management: Where Do We Go From Here? *Journal of Management* 32(6): 898–925.

Beer, M., Spector B., Lawrence P., Quinn Mills, D. and Walton, R. (1985) *Human Resource Management: A General Manager's Perspective.* Glencoe, Ill., Free Press.

Bélanger, P., Giles, A. and Murray, G. (2002) Towards a New Production Model: Potentialities, Tensions and Contradictions. In Murray, G., Bélanger, J., Giles, A. and Lapointe, P. (Eds) *Work and Employment Relations in the High-Performance Workplace.* London, Continuum.

Bellamy, C. and Taylor, J.A. (1998) *Governing in the Information Age.* Buckingham, Open University Press.

Bennington, J. and Moore, M. (2011) Public Value in Complex and Changing Times. In Bennington, J. and Moore, M. (Eds) *Public Value: Theory and Practice.* Basingstoke Hampshire, Palgrave Macmillan.

Berlinski, S., Dewan, T. and Dowding, K. (2010) The Impact of Individual and Collective Performance on Ministerial Tenure. *The Journal of Politics* 72(2): 559–71.

Biesta, G. (2010) Pragmatism and the Philosophical Foundations of Mixed Methods Research. In Tashakkori, A. and Teddlie, C. (Eds) *SAGE Handbook of Mixed Methods in Social and Behavioral Research.* Los Angeles, Sage.

Biesta, G. and Burbules, N.C. (2003) *Pragmatism and Educational Research*. Lanham, M.D., Rowman & Littlefield.

Birdi, K., Clegg, C., Patterson, M., Robinson, A., Stride, C.B., Wall, T.D., et al (2008) The Impact of Human Resource and Operational Management Practices on Company Productivity: A Longitudinal Study. *Personnel Psychology* 61(3): 467–501.

Bishop, P. and Davis, G. (2002) Mapping Public Participation in Policy Choices. *Australian Journal of Public Administration* 61(1): 14–29.

Bisley, A. (2010) *The Land and Water Forum: Making Progress*. Paper presented at the Environmental Defence Society Conference, Auckland, 2 June.

Blackmore, S. (2005) *Conversations on Consciousness*. Oxford, Oxford University Press.

Blaikie, N. (1993) *Approaches to Social Enquiry*. Cambridge, Polity Press.

Blond, P. (2010) *Red Tory: How Left and Right have Broken Britain and How We Can Fix It*. London, Faber and Faber.

Bogason, P. (2007) Postmodern Public Administration. In Ferlie, E., Lynn, L. and Pollitt, C. (Eds) *The Oxford Handbook of Public Management*. Oxford, Oxford University Press.

Bogdanor, V. (Ed.) (2005) *Joined-Up Government*. Oxford, British Academy and Oxford University Press.

Bohm, D. and Hiley, B.J. (1993) *Undivided Universe: An Ontological Interpretation of Quantum Theory*. London, Routledge.

Boisot, M.H. and Child, J. (1999) Organizations as Adaptive Systems in Complex Environments: The Case of China. *Organization Science* 10(3): 237–52.

Bolman, L. and Deal, T. (1997) *Reframing Organisations: Artistry, Choice and Leadership* (2nd edn). San Francisco, Jossey-Bass Publishers.

Borchert, J. and Zeiss, J. (Eds) (2003) *The Political Class in Advanced Democracies: A Comparative Handbook*. Oxford, Oxford University Press.

Borins, S., Kernaghan, K., Brown, D., Bontis, N., 6, P. and Thompson, F. (2007) *Digital State: At the Leading Edge*. Toronto, University of Toronto Press.

Boston, J. (1991) Corporate Management: The New Zealand Experience. In Davis, G., Weller, P. and Lewis, C. (Eds) *Corporate Management in Australian Government*. South Melbourne, Macmillan.

___ (1992) Assessing the Performance of Departmental Chief Executives: Perspectives from New Zealand. *Public Administration* 70(3): 405–28.

___ (2000) The Challenge of Evaluating Systemic Change: The Case of Public Management Reform. *International Public Management Journal* 3(1): 23–46.

Boston, J. and Eichbaum, C. (2007) State Sector Reform and Renewal in New Zealand: Lessons for Governance. In Caiden, G. and Su, T. (Eds) *The Repositioning of Public Governance: Global Experience and Challenges*. Taipei, Best-Wise Publishing.

Boston, J. and Halligan, J. (2009) Political Management and the New Political Governance: Reconciling Political Responsiveness and Neutral Competence. Paper presented at *A Symposium in Honour of Peter Aucoin*, Dalhouise University, Halifax, Nova Scotia, 11–13 November.

Boston, J., Levine, S., McLeay, E. and Roberts, N. (1996) *New Zealand under MMP: A New Politics?* Auckland, Auckland University Press.

Boston, J., Martin, J., Pallot, J. and Walsh, P. (Eds) (1991) *Reshaping the State: New Zealand's Bureaucratic Revolution*. Auckland, Oxford University Press.

Boston, J., Martin, J., Pallot, J. and Walsh, P. (1996) *Public Management: The New Zealand Model*. Auckland, Oxford University Press.

Boston, J. and Pallot, J. (1997) Linking Strategy and Performance Developments in the New Zealand Public Sector. *Journal of Policy Analysis and Management* 16(3): 382–404.

Bouckaert, G. and Halligan, J. (2008) *Managing Performance: International Comparisons*. New York, Routledge.

Boulding, K.E. (1956) General Systems Theory – The Skeleton of Science. *Management Science* 2: 197–208.

Bourgon, J. (2007) Responsive, Responsible and Respected Government: Towards a New Public Administration Theory. *International Review of Administrative Sciences* 73(1): 7–26.

___ (2008) The Future of Public Service: A Search For a New Balance. *Australian Journal of Public Administration* 67(4): 390–404.

___ (2009a) New Directions in Public Administration: Serving Beyond the Predictable. *Public Policy and Administration* 24(3): 309–30.

___ (2009b) New Governance and Public Administration: Towards a Dynamic Synthesis. Public lecture hosted by the Australian Department of the Prime Minister and Cabinet, Canberra, 24 February.

___ (2009c) Serving Beyond the Predictable. Keynote address to the CISCO Public Services Summit, Stockholm, 9–10 December.

___ (2010) The History and Future of Nation-building? Building Capacity for Public Results. *International Review of Administrative Sciences* 76(2): 198–218.

Bourgon, J., et al. (2009). *Literature Review No 1: On the Need for a New Synthesis in Public Administration.* Available at <http://www.ns6newsynthesis.com/documents> (accessed 10 December 2009).

Bourgon, J., with Milley, P. (2010) *The New Frontiers of Public Administration: The New Synthesis Project.* Ottawa, Public Governance International.

Bovaird, T. (2007) Beyond Engagement and Participation: User and Community Coproduction of Public Services. *Public Administration Review* 67(5): 846–60.

___ (2008) Emergent Strategic Management and Planning Mechanisms in Complex Adaptive Systems. *Public Management Review* 10(3): 319–40.

Bovens, M. (2007) Public Accountability. In Ferlie, E., Lynn, L.E. Jr. and Pollitt, C. (Eds) *The Oxford Handbook of Public Management.* Oxford, Oxford University Press.

Boyle, D. and Harris, M. (2009) *The Challenge of Co-production: How Equal Partnerships Between Professionals and the Public Are Crucial to Improving Public Services.* London, NEF, The Lab and National Endowment for Science, Technology and the Arts (NESTA).

Boyle, D., Slay, J. and Stephens, L. (2010) *Public Services Inside Out: Putting Co-production into Practice.* London, NEF, The Lab and NESTA.

Boxall, P. and Macky, K. (2009) Research and Theory on High Performance Work Systems: Progressing the High Involvement Stream. *Human Resource Management Journal* 19(1): 3–23.

Brandsen, T. and Pestoff, V. (2006) Co-production, the Third Sector and the Delivery of Public Services. *Public Management Review* 8(4): 493–501.

Briggs, L. (2007) Public Service Secretaries and their Independence from Political Influence: The View of the Public Service Commissioner. *Australian Journal of Public Administration* 66(4): 501–6.

Bromley, D.W. (2008) Volitional Pragmatism. *Ecological Economics* 68(1): 1–13.

Brudney, J. and England, R. (1983) Toward a Definition of the Co-production Concept. *Public Administration Review* 43(2): 59–65.

Bryson J., Crosby, B. and Stone, M. (2006) The Design and Implementation of Cross-sector Collaborations: Propositions from the Literature. *Public Administration Review* (Special Issue): 44–55.

Buchanan, J. and Musgrave, R. (1999) *Public Finance and Public Choice: Two Contrasting Visions of the State.* Cambridge, M.A., The MIT Press.

Buchanan, J. and Tollison, R. (Eds) (1981) *Theory of Public Choice: Political Applications of Economics.* Michigan, University of Michigan Press.

Bunt, L., Harris, M. and Westlake, S. (2010) *Schumpeter Comes to Whitehall: Cuts and Innovation in Public Services.* London, National Endowment for Science, Technology and Arts.

Burns, T. and Stalker, G. (1961) *The Management of Innovation.* London, Tavistock.

Butler, M.J.R. and Allen, P.M. (2008) Understanding Policy Implementation Processes as Self-Organizing Systems. *Public Management Review* 10(3): 421–40.

Byrne, D.S. (1998) *Complexity Theory and the Social Sciences: An Introduction*. London, Routledge.

Cabinet Office, New Zealand (2008) *Cabinet Manual 2008*. Wellington, Department of the Prime Minister and Cabinet.

Cabinet Office, United Kingdom (2009) *Capability Reviews: An Overview of Progress and Next Steps*. London, Cabinet Office, United Kingdom.

Cabinet Office, United Kingdom (2010) *Enhanced Departmental Boards: Protocol*. Available at <http://www.cabinetoffice.gov.uk/content/enhanced-departmental-boards-protocol> (accessed 22 September 2011).

Caiden, G.E. and Su, T. (Eds) (2007) *The Repositioning of Public Governance: Global Experience and Challenges*. Taipei, Best-Wise Publishing.

Cameron, K.S. and Quinn, R.E. (2006) *Diagnosing and Changing Organizational Culture: Based on the Competing Values Framework* (revised edn). San Francisco, Jossey-Bass.

Cameron, K.S., Quinn, R.E., Degraff, J. and Thakor, A.V. (2006) *Competing Values Leadership: Creating Value in Organizations*. Cheltenham, Edward Elgar.

Camp, L.J. (2003) *Identity in Digital Government*. A Research Report of the Digital Government Civic Scenario Workshop. Cambridge, Kennedy School of Government, Harvard University.

Cascio, W.F. (2002) *Responsible Restructuring: Creative and Profitable Alternative to Layoffs*. San Francisco, Berrett-Koehler.

Castells, M. (1996) *The Rise of the Network Society: The Information Age: Economy, Society and Culture, Volume 1*. Oxford, Blackwell Publishers.

CCNZ (2010) *Regional Cancer Networks Evaluation Report*. Wellington, Cancer Control New Zealand.

Chapman, J. and Duncan, G. (2007) Is There Now a New 'New Zealand Model'? *Public Management Review* 9(1): 1–25.

Chisholm, D. (1992) *Coordination Without Hierarchy: Informal Structures in Multiorganizational Systems*. Berkeley, University of California Press.

Christensen, T. and Laegreid, P. (Eds) (2002) *The New Public Management: The Transformation of Ideas and Practice*. Burlington, V.T., Ashgate.

___ (Eds) (2006) *Autonomy and Regulation: Coping with Agencies in the Modern State*. Burlington, V.T., Ashgate.

___ (Eds) (2007a) *Transcending New Public Management: The Transformation of Public Sector Reforms*. Burlington, V.T., Ashgate.

___ (2007b) The Whole of Government Approach to Public Sector Reform. *Public Administration Review*, 67(6), 1059–66.

Cilliers, P. (1998) *Complexity and Postmodernism: Understanding Complex Systems*. London, Routledge.

Cleary, H. and Reeves, R. (2009) *The 'Culture of Churn' for UK Ministers and the Price We All Pay*. London, Demos.

COAG National Reform Initiative Working Group (2006) *Human Capital Reform: Report by the COAG National Reform Initiative Working Group*. Canberra, Council of Australian Governments.

Cohen, J. and Arato, A. (1994) *Civil Society and Political Theory*. Cambridge, M.A, The MIT Press.

Considine, M. (2002) The End of the Line? Accountable Governance in the Age of Networks, Partnerships and Joined-up Services. *Governance* 15(1): 21–40.

Cooper, T., Bryer, T. and Meek, J. (2006) Citizen-Centered Collaborative Public Management. *Public Administration Review* 66(S1): 76–88.

Courpasson, D. (2000) Managerial Strategies of Domination: Power in Soft Bureaucracies. *Organization Studies* 21(1): 141.

Cribb, J. (2006) Agents or Stewards? Contracting with Voluntary Organisations. *Policy Quarterly* 2(2): 11–17.

Crowley, K. (2009) Can Deliberative Democracy be Practiced? A Subnational Policy Pathway'. *Politics & Policy* 37(5): 995–1021.

Davis, G. (1995) *A Government of Routines: Executive Coordination in an Australian State.* South Melbourne, Macmillan.

Davis, G. and Gardiner, M. (1995) Who Signs the Contract? Applying Agency Theory to Politicians. In Boston, J. (Ed.) *The State Under Contract.* Wellington, Bridget Williams Books.

DeHue, T. (2001) Establishing the Experimenting Society: The Historical Origin of Social Experimentation According to the Randomised Controlled Design. *American Journal of Psychology* 114(2): 283–302.

Denhardt, J.V. and Denhardt, R.B. (2007) *The New Public Service: Serving, Not Steering* (expanded edn). Armonk, N.Y., Sharpe.

Denis, J-L., Langley, A. and Rouleau, L. (2007) Rethinking Leadership in Public Organisations. In Ferlie, E., Lynn, L. and Pollitt, C. (Eds) *The Oxford Handbook of Public Management.* Oxford, Oxford University Press.

Dennard, L., Richardson, K.A. and Morçöl, G. (2008) *Complexity and Policy Analysis: Tools and Concepts for Designing Robust Policies in a Complex World.* Goodyear, A.Z., ICSE Publishing.

Diffenbach, T. (2009) New Public Management in Public Sector Organizations: The Dark Sides of Managerialistic Enlightenment. *Public Administration* 87(4): 892–909.

DoL (2010) *Final Evaluation Report of the Recognised Seasonal Employer Project 2007–2009.* Wellington, Department of Labour.

Dollery, B. (2009) The Influence of Economic Theories of Government Failure on Public Management Reform. In Goldfinch, S. and Wallis, J. (Eds) *International Handbook of Public Management Reform.* Cheltenham, Edward Elgar.

Donnelly, N., Proctor-Thomson S.B. and Plimmer, G. (in press) *Women's 'Voice' in Matters of 'Choice': Flexible Work Outcomes For Women in the New Zealand Public Services.* Victoria Management School Working paper Series. Wellington.

Dormer, R. (2010) *Missing Links.* Unpublished PhD Thesis, Victoria University of Wellington.

Douglas, M. (1986) *How Organisations Think.* London, Routledge and Kegan Paul.

Douglas, R. (1990) Speech to the Australian Education Council Conference, Adelaide, 6 December (reported in the *Evening Post*, 24 October 1991).

Downs, G.W. and Larkey, P.D. (1986) *The Search for Government Efficiency: From Hubris to Helplessness.* Philadelphia, Temple University Press.

DPMC (2009) *Cabinet Handbook* (6th edn). Canberra, Department of the Prime Minister and Cabinet.

___ (2011a) *A Modern Business Model for Government.* Wellington, Department of the Prime Minister and Cabinet, Treasury & State Services Commission. Available at <http://www.dpmc.govt.nz/better_public_services/documents/ssr-2141821.pdf> (accessed 1 October 2011).

___ (2011b) *Tackling Methamphetamine: Indicators and Progress Report.* Wellington, Department of the Prime Minister and Cabinet.

du Gay, P. (2002) How Responsible is "Responsive" Government? *Economy and Society* 31(3): 461–82.

Duncan, G. and Chapman, J. (2010) New Millennium, New Public Management and the New Zealand Model. *The Australian Journal of Public Administration* 69(3): 301–13

Duncan, I. and Bollard, A.E. (1992) *Corporatization and Privatization: Lessons from New Zealand.* Auckland, Oxford University Press.

Dunleavy, P., Margetts, H., Bastow, S. and Tinkler, J. (2006a) New Public Management is Dead: Long Live Digital-era Governance. *Journal of Public Administration Research and Theory* 16(3): 467–94.

___ (2006b) *Digital-Era Governance: IT Corporations, the State, and E-Government.* Oxford, Oxford University Press.

Dunleavy, P. and Rhodes, R. (1990) Core Executive Studies in Britain. *Public Administration* 68(1): 29–60.

Dunn, W.N. (1998) The Experimenting Society: Essays in Honor of Donald T. Campbell. *Policy Studies Review Annual* 11.

___ (2008) *Public Policy Analysis: An Introduction*. Upper Saddle River, N.J., Pearson Education.

Durie, M. (2004) Public Sector Reform, Indigeneity, and the Goals of Māori Development. Paper presented to the Commonwealth Advanced Seminar, Wellington, 17 February.

Edwards, M. and Clough, R. (2005) *Corporate Governance and Performance: An Exploration of the Connection in a Public Sector Context*. University of Canberra Corporate Governance Project, Issues Series Paper No. 1.

Eichbaum, C. and Shaw, R. (2009) Purchase Advisers and the Public Service: Who Pays the Bill? *Public Sector* 32(2): 16–17.

___ (Eds) (2010) *Partisan Appointees and Public Servants: An International Analysis of the Role of the Political Adviser*. Cheltenham, Edward Elgar.

Elliott, E. and Kiel, L.D. (1997) Nonlinear Dynamics, Complexity and Public Policy: Use, Misuse and Applications. In Eve, R.A., Horsfall, S. and Lee, M.E. (Eds) *Chaos, Complexity and Sociology: Myths, Models and Theories*. Thousand Oaks, C.A., Sage.

English, B. (2010) How to Make Public Sector Reforms Last. Presentation to the Australia and New Zealand Annual Conference on *Delivering Policy Reform: Making it Happen, Making it Stick*, Melbourne, 11–12 August.

___ (2011a) The 'New Responsibility Model' for New Zealand Public Sector CEOs. In Lindquist, E., Vincent, S., and Wanna, J. (Eds) *Delivering Policy Reform: Anchoring Significant Reforms in Turbulent Times*. Canberra, ANU ePress.

___ (2011b) Speech to the Institute of Public Administration New Zealand, Wellington, 29 March. Available at <http://www.beehive.govt.nz/speech/speech-institute-public-administration-new-zealand> (accessed 26 September 2011).

English, B. and Ryall, T. (2011) Government Reviews More State Agencies. Press release, 31 May. Available at <http://www.beehive.govt.nz/release/government-reviews-more-state-agencies> (accessed 26 September 2011).

English, L. and Skellern, M. (2005) Public–Private Partnerships and Public Sector Management Reform: A Comparative Analysis. *International Journal of Public Policy* 1(2): 1–21.

Eppel, E. (2010) The Contribution of Complexity Theory to Understanding and Explaining Policy Processes: A Study of Tertiary Education Policy Processes in New Zealand. Unpublished PhD Thesis, Victoria University of Wellington. Available at <http://researcharchive.vuw.ac.nz/handle/10063/1202> (accessed 26 September 2011).

___ (2011a) *Land and Water (Protection and Use) Forum: Illustrative Case*. Wellington, Institute of Policy Studies.

___ (2011b) Campaign for Prevention of Family Violence and the Community Study: Illustrative Case. Wellington, Institute of Policy Studies.

Eppel, E., Gill, D., Lips, M. and Ryan, B. (2008) *Better Connected Services for Kiwis: A Discussion Document for Managers and Front-line Staff*. Wellington, Institute of Policy Studies.

Eppel, E., Lips. M. and Wolf, A. (2011) Understanding Complexity in Public Policy Processes: The Case of Establishing New Zealand's Tertiary Education Commission. Manuscript submitted for publication.

Estes, B. (2008) Integrative Literature Review: Workplace Incivility: Impacts on Individual and Organizational Performance. *Human Resource Development Review* 7(2): 218–40.

Ethics Resource Centre (2007) *New Zealand State Services Ethics and Conduct Survey, Summary of Findings*. Wellington, State Services Commission. Available at <http://www.ssc.govt.nz/upload/downloadable_files/IntegrityandConduct_Survey.pdf> (accessed 1 October 2011).

Eve, R.A., Horsfall, S. and Lee, M.E. (1997) *Chaos, Complexity and Sociology: Myths, Models and Theories*. Thousand Oaks, C.A., Sage.

Fabling, R. and Grimes, A. (2010) HR Practices and New Zealand Firm Performance: What Matters and Who Does It? *The International Journal of Human Resource Management* 21(4): 488–508.

FACS (2010) *Strong Families Connected Communities 2010*. Wellington, Family and Community Services.

Feilzer, M.Y. (2010) Doing Mixed Methods Research Pragmatically: Implications for the Rediscovery of Pragmatism as a Research Paradigm. *Journal of Mixed Methods Research* 4(1): 6–16.

Flinders, M. and Buller, J. (2006) Depoliticization: Principles, Tactics and Tools. *British Politics* 1(3): 293–318.

Floyd, S. and Wooldridge, B. (2000) *Building Strategy from the Middle: Reconceptualizing Strategy Process*. London, Sage.

Fonberg, R. (2006) Top-down Approaches and the Alternatives. In Benington, J (Ed.) *Reforming Public Services*. London, National School of Government.

Fountain, J.E. (2001) *Building the Virtual State. Information Technology and Institutional Change*. Washington, D.C., Brookings Institution Press.

Francis, C. (2011) *Inquiry into Alleged Abuse by Boss*. Stuff (Online) 8 July. Available at <http://www.stuff.co.nz/dominion-post/news/politics/5252969/Inquiry-into-alleged-abuse-by-boss> (accessed 22 September 2011).

Frederickson, H. (2007) Whatever Happened to Public Administration? Governance, Governance Everywhere. In Ferlie, E., Lynn, L. and Pollitt, C. (Eds) *The Oxford Handbook of Public Management*. Oxford, Oxford University Press.

Freeman, C. (2007) The ICT Paradigm. In Mansell, R., Avgerou, C., Quah, D. and Silverstone, R. (Eds) *The Oxford Handbook of Information and Communication Technologies*. Oxford, Oxford University Press.

Gauld, R. and Goldfinch, S. (2006) *Dangerous Enthusiasms: E-government, Computer Failure and Information System Development*. Dunedin, Otago University Press.

Gerrits, L. (2010) Public Decision-Making as Co-Evolution. *Emergence: Complexity and Organisation* 12(1): 19–28.

Gerrits, L., Marks, P. and van Buuren, A. (2009) Coevolution: A Constant in Non-Linearity. In Teisman, G., van Buuren, A., and Gerrits, L. (Eds) *Managing Complex Governance Systems*. New York, Routledge.

Giddens, A. (1984) *The Social Constitution of Society*. Cambridge, Polity Press.

___ (1994) *The Third Way*. Cambridge, Polity Press.

Gill, D. (2008a) By Accident or Design – Changes in the Structure of the State of New Zealand. *Policy Quarterly* 4(2): 27–32.

___ (2008b) Managing for Performance in New Zealand – The Search for the "Holy Grail"? In KPMG, *Holy Grail or Achievable Quest? International Perspectives on Public Sector Performance Management*. Canada, KPMG, CAPAM, IPAA, IPAC.

___(Ed.) (2011) *The Iron Cage Recreated: The Performance Management of State Organisations in New Zealand*. Wellington, Institute of Policy Studies.

Gill, D. and Hitchener, S. (2011a) Achieving a Step Change. In Gill, D. (Ed) *The Iron Cage Recreated: The Performance Management of State Organisations in New Zealand*. Wellington, Institute of Policy Studies.

___ (2011b) Achieving a Step Change: The Holy Grail of Outcomes-Based Management. *Policy Quarterly* 7(3): 28–35.

Gill, D., Pride, S., Gilbert, H. and Norman, R. (2010) *The Future State*. Institute of Policy Studies Working Paper 10/08. Wellington, Institute of Policy Studies.

Gill, D., Pride, S., Gilbert, H., Norman R. and Mladenovic, A. (2010) The Future State Project: Meeting the Challenges of the 21st Century. *Policy Quarterly* 6(3): 31–39.

Gillinson, S., Horne, M. and Baeck, P. (2010) *Radical Efficiency: Different, Better, Lower Cost Public Services.* London, The Innovation Unit, The Lab and NESTA.

Gore, A. (1993) *From Red Tape to Results: Creating a Government That Works Better and Costs Less. Report of the National Performance Review.* Washington, D.C., US Government Printing Office.

Gore, A. and Peters, T. (1993) *Creating a Government That Works Better and Costs Less: The Report of the National Performance Review.* New York, Plume.

Gould-Williams, J. (2003) The Importance of HR Practices and Workplace Trust in Achieving Superior Performance: A Study of Public-sector Organizations. *The International Journal of Human Resource Management* 14(1): 28–54.

Government of South Australia (2007) *South Australia's Strategic Plan 2007.* Adelaide, Government of South Australia.

Granovetter, M. (1985) Economic Action and Social Structure: The Problem of Embeddedness. *American Journal of Sociology* 91(3): 481–510.

Gray, A. and Jenkins, W. (1985) *Administrative Politics in British Government.* Brighton, Harvester Press.

Green, R. and Agarwal, R. (2011) *Management Matters in New Zealand: How Does Manufacturing Measure Up?* Occasional Papers. Wellington, Ministry of Economic Development.

Greene, J.C. and Hall, J.N. (2010) Dialectics and Pragmatism: Being of Consequence. In Tashakkori, A. and Teddlie, C. (Eds) *SAGE Handbook of Mixed Methods in Social and Behavioral Research* (2nd edn). Los Angeles, Sage.

Gregory, R. (1995a) Bureaucratic 'Psychopathology' and Technocratic Governance: Whither Responsibility? *Hong Kong Public Administration* 4: 17–36.

___ (1995b) Accountability, Responsibility and Corruption: Managing the 'Public Production Process'. In Boston, J. (Ed.) *The State Under Contract.* Wellington, Bridget Williams Books.

___ (1996) Tragedy at Cave Creek: Political Responsibility for 'Careful Incompetence'. Paper presented at a conference of the Structure and Organisation of Government Research Committee of the International Political Science Association, University of Canberra, 1–3 August.

___ (2003a) All the King's Horses and All the King's Men: Putting New Zealand's Public Sector Back Together Again. *International Public Management Review* 4(2): 41–58.

___ (2003b) Accountability in Modern Government. In Peters, G. and Pierre, J. (Eds) *Handbook of Public Administration.* London, Sage.

___ (2006) Theoretical Faith and Practical Works: De-Autonomizing and Joining-Up in the New Zealand State Sector. In Christensen, T. and Laegreid, P. (Eds) *Autonomy and Regulation: Coping with Agencies in the Modern State.* Burlington, V.T., Ashgate.

Guest, D. and Conway, N. (2011) The Impact of HR Practices, HR Effectiveness and a 'Strong HR System' on Organisational Outcomes: A Stakeholder Perspective. *The International Journal of Human Resource Management* 22(8): 1686–702.

Guest, D.E. (2011) Human Resource Management and Performance: Still Searching for Some Answers. *Human Resource Management Journal* 21(1): 3–13.

Haack, S. (2003) *Defending Science – Within Reason: Between Scientism and Cynicism.* Amherst, N.Y., Prometheus Books.

Hall, D. (2010) *Why We Need Public Spending.* Greenwich, Public Service International Research Unit, University of Greenwich.

Halligan, J. (2000) Public Service Reform Under Howard. In Singleton, G. (Ed.) *The Howard Government: Australian Commonwealth Administration 1996–1998.* Sydney, UNSW Press.

___ (2007) Reform Design and Performance in Australia and New Zealand. In Christenson T. and Laegreid, P. (Eds) *Transcending New Public Management.* Burlington, V.T, Ashgate.

___ (2008) Australian Public Service: Combining the Search for Balance and Effectiveness with Deviations on Fundamentals. In Aulich, C. and Wettenhall, R. (Eds) *Howard's Fourth Government*. Sydney, UNSW Press.

___ (2010a) The Fate of Administrative Tradition in Anglophone Countries During the Reform Era. In Painter, M. and Peters, B. (Eds) *Tradition and Public Administration*. Basingstoke, Palgrave Macmillan.

___ (2010b) The Australian Public Service: New Agendas and Reforms. In Aulich, C. and Evans, M. (Eds) *The Rudd Government: Australian Commonwealth Administration 2007–2010*. Canberra, ANU ePress.

___ (forthcoming) Central Steering in Australia. In Dahlstrom, C., Peters, B.G. and Pierre, J. (Eds) *Steering from the Center: Central Government Offices and their Roles in Governing*. Toronto, University of Toronto Press.

Harrison, A. (2009) A Problem Solver: A Letter to the Editor. *The New Yorker* (April 27): 5.

Hartley, J. (2005) Innovation in Governance and Public Services: Past and Present. *Public Money and Management* 25(1): 27–34.

Hattie, J. (2009) *Visible Learning*. London, Routledge.

Hawke, L. and Wanna, J. (2010) Australia after Budgetary Reform: A Lapsed Pioneer or a Decorative Architect? In Wanna, J., Jensen, L. and de Vries, J. (Eds) *The Reality of Budgetary Reform in OECD Nations: Trajectories and Consequences*. Cheltenham, Edward Elgar.

Haynes, P., Boxall, P. and Macky, K. (2005) Non-union Voice and the Effectiveness of Joint Consultation in New Zealand. *Economic and Industrial Democracy* 26(2): 229–56.

Heady, B. (1974) *British Cabinet Ministers*. London, Routledge.

Held, D. (2006) *Models of Democracy* (3rd edn). Cambridge, Polity Press.

Henman, P. (2010) *Governing Electronically: E-government and the Reconfiguration of Public Administration, Policy and Power*. London, Palgrave Macmillan.

Hill, M. (1997) Implementation Theory: Yesterday's Issue? *Policy and Politics* 25(4): 375–85.

Hill, M. and Hupe, P. (2006) Analysing Policy Processes as Multiple Governance: Accountability in Social Policy. *Policy and Politics* 34(3): 557–73.

___ (2009) *Implementing Public Policy* (2nd edn). London, Sage.

Hill, R., Capper, P., Wilson, K., Whatman, R. and Wong, K. (2007) Workplace Learning in the New Zealand Apple Industry Network: A New Co-design Method for Government 'Practice Making'. *Journal of Workplace Learning* 19(6): 359–76.

Hitchener, S. and Gill, D. (2011a) The Formal System as it Evolved. In Gill, D. (Ed.) *The Iron Cage Recreated: The Performance Management of State Organisations in New Zealand*. Wellington, Institute of Policy Studies.

___ (2011b) Part 2: The Formal System for Organisational Performance Management in the State Sector. In Gill, D. (Ed.) *The Iron Cage Recreated: The Performance Management of State Organisations in New Zealand*. Wellington, Institute of Policy Studies.

HM Treasury (2005) *Corporate Governance in Central Government Departments: Code of Good Practice*. London, HM Treasury.

___ (2010) *Total Place: A Whole Area Approach to Public Services*. London, HM Treasury.

HM Treasury and Cabinet Office (2011) *Corporate Governance in Central Government Departments: Code of Good Practice 2011*. London, HM Treasury.

Hodge, G. (1998) Contracting Public Sector Services: A Meta-Analytic Perspective of the International Evidence. *Australian Journal of Public Administration* 57(4): 98–110.

Hodge, G. and Greve, C. (2007) Public–Private Partnerships: An International Performance Review. *Public Administration Review* 67(3): 545–58.

Holmes, A. (2010) A Reflection on the Bushfire Royal Commission – Blame, Accountability and Responsibility. *Australian Journal of Public Administration* 69(4): 387–91.

Holmes, M. and Shand, D. (1995) Management Reform: Some Practitioner Perspectives on the Past Ten Years. *Governance* 8(4): 551–78.

Homburg, V. (2008) *Understanding E-government: Information Systems in Public Administration*. London and New York, Routledge.

Hood, C. (1990) De-Sir Humphreyfying the Westminster Model of Bureaucracy: A New Style of Governance. *Governance* 3(2): 205–14.

___ (1991) A Public Management For All Seasons? *Public Administration* 69(1): 3–19.

___ (2011) *The Blame Game: Spin, Bureaucracy and Self-Preservation in Government*. Princeton, Princeton University Press.

Hood, C., Emmerson, C. and Dixon, R. (2009) *Public Spending in Hard Times: Lessons from the Past and Implications for the Future*. London, Institute for Fiscal Studies (Economic and Social Research Services).

Hood, C. and Lodge, M. (2006) *The Politics of Public Service Bargains: Reward, Competency, Loyalty and Blame*. Oxford, Oxford University Press.

Hookway, C. (2008) Pragmatism. *The Stanford Encyclopedia of Philosophy*. Available at <plato.stanford.edu/archives/fall2008/entries/pragmatism> (accessed 26 September 2011).

Horner, L. and Hutton, W. (2011) Public Value, Deliberative Democracy and the Role of Public Managers. In Bennington, J. and Moore, M. (Eds) *Public Value Theory and Practice*. Basingstoke Hampshire, Palgrave Macmillan.

Horner, L., Lekhi, R. and Blaug, R. (2006) *Deliberative Democracy and the Role of Public Managers*. London, The Work Foundation.

Howlett, M. and Ramesh, M. (1995) *Studying Public Policy: Policy Cycles and Policy Subsystems*. Oxford, Oxford University Press.

___ (2003) *Studying Public Policy: Policy Cycles and Policy Subsystems* (2nd edn). Toronto, Oxford University Press.

Hughes, O. (2003) *Public Administration and Management* (3rd edn). Basingstoke, Macmillan Press.

Hughes, P. (2011) Public Sector Reform. Speech to the Institute of Public Management of New Zealand (IPANZ), Wellington, 19 July.

Huxham, C. (2000) The Challenge of Collaborative Governance. *Public Management Review* 2(3): 337–58.

Institute for Government (2010) *System Error: Fixing the Flaws in Government IT*. London, Institute for Government.

Jackson, B. and Parry, K. (2008) *A Very Short, Fairly Interesting and Reasonably Cheap Book about Studying Leadership*. London, Sage.

James, C. (2002) *The Tie that Binds: The Relationship Between Ministers and Chief Executives*. Wellington, Institute of Policy Studies.

James, O. (2003) *The Executive Agency Revolution in Whitehall: Public Interest vs. Bureau-shaping Perspectives*. Basingstoke, Palgrave Macmillan.

Jasinski, J. (2001) *Sourcebook on Rhetoric: Key Concepts in Contemporary Rhetorical Studies*. London, Sage Publications.

JCPAA (2002) *Review of the Accrual Budget Documentation: Report 388*. Canberra, Parliament of Australia, Joint Committee of Public Accounts and Audit.

Jessop, B. (2003) Changes in Welfare Regimes and the Search for Flexibility and Employability. In Overbeek, H. (Ed.) *The Political Economy of European Employment*. London, Routledge.

___ (2006) The Third Way: Neo-liberalism with a Human Face? In Berg, S. and Kaiser A. (Eds) New Labour und die Modernisierung Gross Britanniens. Wissener Verlag, Augsberg.

Jones, B.D. and Baumgartner, F.R. (2005) *The Politics of Attention: How Government Prioritises Problems*. Chicago, University of Chicago Press.

Jones, G. and Stewart, J. (2009) New Development: Accountability in Public Partnerships – The Case of Local Strategic Partnerships. *Public Money and Management* 29(1): 59–64.

Jordan, A., Wurzel, R. and Zito, A. (2005) The Rise of 'New' Policy Instruments in Comparative Perspective: Has Governance Eclipsed Government? *Political Studies* 53(3): 477–96.

Jun, J.S. (2009) The Limits of Post-New Public Management and Beyond. *Public Administration Review* 69(1): 161–65.

Kauffman, S.A. (1993) *The Origins of Order: Self Organisation and Selection in Evolution.* New York, Oxford University Press.

___ (1995) *At Home in the Universe: The Search for the Laws of Self-Organization and Complexity.* Oxford, Oxford University Press.

Keating, M. and Holmes, M. (1990) Australia's Budgetary and Financial Management Reforms. *Governance* 3(2): 168–85.

Kelly, G., Mulgan, G. and Muers, S. (2002) *Creating Public Value.* London, UK Prime Minister's Strategy Unit.

Kelly, J., Norman, R. and Bentley, T. (2010) *Shaping a Strategic Centre.* ANZSOG Research Report. Melbourne, Australia and New Zealand School of Government.

Kelman, S. (2005) *Unleashing Change: A Study of Organizational Renewal in Government.* Washington, D.C., Brookings Institution.

___ (2006) Downsizing, Competition, and Organizational Change in Government: Is Necessity the Mother of Invention? *Journal of Policy Analysis and Management* 25(4): 875–95.

Kelsey, J. (1995) *The New Zealand Experiment: A World Model for Structural Adjustment?* Auckland, University of Auckland Press.

Key, J. (2011) Prime Minister's Statement to Parliament 2011, 8 February. Available at <http://www.beehive.govt.nz/gallery/statement-parliament-2011> (accessed 26 September 2011).

Kibblewhite, A. (2011) Role of Public Sector performance in Economic Growth. Speech delivered to the Institute of Policy Studies, Wellington, 1 April. Available at <http://www.treasury.govt.nz/publications/media-speeches/speeches/pubsecperfecongrowth> (accessed 26 September 2011).

Kickert, W. (1997) Public Governance in the Netherlands: An Alternative to Anglo-American 'Managerialism'. *Public Administration* 75(4): 731–52.

___ (2003) Beyond Public Management. *Public Management Review* 5(3) 377–99.

Kickert, W.J., Klijn, E. and Koppenjan, J. (Eds) (1997) *Managing Complex Networks: Strategies for the Public Sector.* London, Sage.

Kingdon, J.W. (1995) *Agendas, Alternatives and Public Policies* (2nd edn). New York, Addison-Wesley Educational Publishers.

Klijn, E-H. and Koppenjan, J. (2000) Public Management and Policy Networks: Foundations of a Network Approach to Governance. *Public Management* 2(2): 135–58.

___ (2004) *Managing Uncertainties in Networks: A Network Approach to Problems and Decision Making.* London, Routledge.

Kooiman, J. (1999) Social-Political Governance: Overview, Reflections and Design. *Public Management: An International Journal of Research and Theory* 1(1): 67–92.

___ (2003) *Governing as Governance.* London, Sage.

Kuhn, T. (1962) *The Structure of Scientific Revolutions.* Chicago, University of Chicago Press.

Kurtz, C. and Snowden, D. (2003). The New Dynamics of Strategy: Sense-making in a Complex and Complicated World. *IBM Systems Journal* 42(3): 462–83.

Land and Water Forum (2010) *Report of the Land and Water Forum: A Fresh Start for Fresh Water.* Available at <http://www.landandwater.org.nz/> (accessed 26 September 2011).

Landau, M. (1969) Redundancy, Rationality and the Problem of Duplication and Overlap. *Public Administration Review* 29: 346–58.

Lenihan, D. (2009) *Rethinking the Public Policy Process: A Public Engagement Framework.* Ottawa, Public Policy Forum.

Lenk, K. (2007) Reconstructing Public Administration Theory from Below. *Information Polity* 12(4): 207–12.

Lerner, A.W. (1986) There is More Than One Way to be Redundant: A Comparison of Alternatives for the Design and Use of Redundancy in Organizations. *Administration and Society* 18(3) 334–59.

Lindblom, C.E. (1979) Still Muddling, Not Yet Through. *Public Administration Review* 6: 517–26.

Lindorff, M. (2009) We're Not all Happy Yet: Attitudes to Work, Leadership, and High Performance Work Practices among Managers in the Public Sector. *Australian Journal of Public Administration* 68(4): 429–45.

Lindquist, E.A. (1992) Public Managers and Policy Communities: Learning to Meet New Challenges. *Canadian Public Administration* 35(2): 127–59.

___ (1999) Efficiency, Reliability, or Innovation: Managing Overlap and Complexity in Canada's Federal System of Governance. In Young, R.A. (Ed.) *Stretching the Federation: The Art of the State.* Kingston, Queen's University, Institute of Intergovernmental Relations.

___ (2009a) Waiting for the Next Wave: Trajectories, Narratives, and Conveying the State of Public Sector Reform. *Policy Quarterly* 5(1): 44–52.

___ (2009b) How Ottawa Assesses Department/Agency Performance: Treasury Board's Management Accountability Framework. In Maslove, A.M. (Ed.) *How Ottawa Spends 2009–2010: Economic Upheaval and Political Dysfunction.* Montreal and Kingston, McGill–Queen's University Press.

___ (2010) From Rhetoric to Blueprint: The Moran Review as Concerted, Comprehensive and Emergent Strategy for Public Service Reform. *Australian Journal of Public Administration* 69(2): 115–51.

___ (2011a) Surveying the World(s) of Visualization. Background paper prepared for the HC Coombs Policy Forum, Australian National University, 24 July.

___ (2011b) Grappling with Complex Policy Challenges: Exploring the Potential of Visualization for Analysis, Advising and Engagement. Discussion paper prepared for the HC Coombs Policy Forum Roundtables, Australian National University, 24 July.

Lindquist, E. and Wanna, J. (2010a) Co-Production is Not Alone: Parallel Traditions and Implications for Public Management and Governance. Paper prepared for Australia New Zealand School of Government, Australia Public Service Commission, and Victoria State Services Authority for the 'New Synthesis' Project, 11 November.

___ (2010b) Collaborative Governance and the New Synthesis; Antecedents, Perspectives, Possibilities, Implications. Discussion Paper. Canberra, Australia New Zealand School of Government and Australian Public Service Commission.

Lips, A.M.B., Eppel, E.A., Cunningham, A. and Hopkins-Burns, V. (2010) *Public Attitudes to the Sharing of Personal Information in the Course of Online Public Service Provision.* Final research report. Wellington, Victoria University of Wellington.

Lips, A.M.B., Taylor, J.A. and Organ, J. (2009) Managing Citizen Identity Information in e-Government Service Relationships in the UK: The Emergence of a Surveillance State or Service State? *Public Management Review* 11(6): 833–56.

Lipsky, M. (1980) *Street-Level Bureaucracy: Dilemmas of the Individuals in Public Services.* New York, Russell Sage Foundation.

Lister, R. (2004) *Poverty.* Cambridge, Polity Press.

Lodge, M. and Gill, D. (2011) Toward a New Era of Administrative Reform? The Myth of Post-NPM in New Zealand. *Governance* 24(1): 141–66.

Lombardo, M.M. and Eichinger, R.W. (2004) *FYI: For Your Improvement.* Greensboro, N.C., Center for Creative Leadership.

London School of Economics (2005) *The Identity Project: An Assessment of the UK Identity Cards Bill and its Implications.* The LSE Identity Project Final Report. London, London School of Economics.

Lyon, D. (2001) *Surveillance Society: Monitoring Everyday Life.* Buckingham, Open University Press.

MacDermott, K. (2008) *Whatever Happened to Frank and Fearless? The Impact of New Public Management on the Australian Public Service.* Canberra, ANZSOG and ANU ePress.

MacIntosh, R. and MacLean, D. (1999) Conditioned Emergence: A Dissipative Structures Approach to Transformation. *Strategic Management Journal* 20(4): 297.

MacKenzie, D.A. and Wajcman, J. (Eds) (1985) *The Social Shaping of Technology: How the Refrigerator Got Its Hum*. Milton Keynes, Open University Press.

Maclure, M. (2009) Explaining Pragmatic Trials to Pragmatic Policy Makers, *Canadian Medical Association Journal* 180(10): 1001–3.

Management Advisory Committee (2004) *Connected Government: Whole of Government Responses to Australia's Challenges*. Canberra, Commonwealth of Australia.

Mant, A. (1997) *Intelligent Leadership*. St Leonards (NSW), Allen & Unwin.

March, J.G. and Olsen, J.P. (1984) The New Institutionalism: Organizational Factors in Political Life. *The American Political Science Review* 78(3): 734–49.

Marks, M. and Mirvis, P. (2001) Making Mergers and Acquisitions Work: Strategic and Psychological Preparation. *Academy of Management Executive* 15(2): 80–92.

Marsh, D., Richards, D. and Smith, M. (2000) Re-assessing the Role of Departmental Cabinet Ministers. *Public Administration* 78(2): 305–26.

Martin, J. (1996) Ministerial Responsibility: Anachronism or Pillar of Democracy. Paper presented at the Australasian Study of Parliament Group Conference, Wellington, 25–26 October.

Marx, G.T. (2004) What is New about the "New Surveillance"? Classifying for Change and Continuity. *Knowledge, Technology, and Policy* 17(1): 18–37.

Mascarenhas, R.C. (1991) State-owned Enterprises. In Boston, J., Martin, J., Pallot, J. and Walsh, P. (Eds) *Reshaping the State: New Zealand's Bureaucratic Revolution*. Auckland, Oxford University Press.

Maslow, A. (1966) *The Psychology of Science*. Chicago, Regnery.

Mastracci, S.H., Newman, M.A. and Guy, M.E. (2010) Emotional Labor: Why and How to Teach It. *Journal of Public Affairs Education* 16(2): 123–41.

May, P.J. (2003) Policy Design and Implementation. In Peters, B.G. and Pierre, J. (Eds) *Handbook of Public Administration*. Thousand Oaks, C.A., Sage.

McCarthy, S. (2008) *Transforming Leadership and Culture: The State of the Nations*. Wellington, Human Synergistics.

McClorey, J., Quinlan, V. and Gruhn, Z. (2011) *All Aboard? Whitehall's New Governance Challenge: Summary Document*. London, Institute for Government.

McConnell, A. (2010) Policy Success, Policy Failure and Grey Areas in Between. *Journal of Public Policy* 30(3): 345–62.

McGregor, D. and Cutcher-Gershenfeld, J. (2006) *The Human Side of Enterprise*. New York, McGraw-Hill.

McLaren, F. and Stone, G. (2010) *Supporting Complex Initiatives with Research and Evaluation: The Campaign for Action on Family Violence and the Community Study Approach*. Paper presented at the Australasian Evaluation Conference, Wellington, 1–3 September.

McLeay, E. (1995) *The Cabinet and Political Power in New Zealand*. Auckland, Oxford University Press.

___ (1996) Who Do We Blame? Some Problems of Democratic Accountability. Paper presented at the New Zealand Political Studies Association Conference, University of Auckland, 8–10 July.

Meek, J.W., De Ladurantey, J. and Newell, W.H. (2007) Complex Systems, Governance and Policy Administration Consequences. *Emergence: Complexity and Organization* 9(1/2): 24–36.

Meijer, A. (2007) Why Don't They Listen to Us? Reasserting the Role of ICT in Public Administration. *Information Polity* 12(4): 233–42.

Midgley, G. (2000) *Systemic Intervention: Philosophy, Methodology and Practice*. New York, Kluwer Academic/Plenum Publishers.

Ministerial Advisory Group (2001) *Review of the Centre*. Wellington, Minister for State Services.

Ministerial Advisory Group on a Maori Perspective for the Department of Social Welfare (1988; reprinted 2001) *Puao-te-ata-tu*. Wellington, Department of Social Welfare.

Ministerial Review Group (2009) *Meeting the Challenge*. Wellington, Ministry of Health.

Ministry of Defence (2010) *Defence White Paper 2010*. Wellington, Ministry of Defence.

MSD (2011) *Statement of Intent 2011–2014*. Wellington, Ministry of Social Development.

Mintzberg, H. (2009) *Managing*. N.J., Prentice Hall.

Mintzberg, H. and Jorgensen, J. (1987) Emergent Strategy for Public Policy. *Canadian Public Administration* 30(2): 214–29.

Mitleton-Kelly, E. (Ed.) (2003) *Complex Systems and Evolutionary Perspectives on Organisations: The Application of Complexity Theory to Organisations*. Oxford, Elsevier Science.

Moore, M. (1995) *Creating Public Value: Strategic Management in Government*. Cambridge, M.A., Harvard University Press.

Morçöl, G. (2010) Issues in Reconceptualising Public Policy from the Perspective of Complexity Theory. *Emergence: Complexity and Organisation* 12(1): 52–60.

Morgan, G. (2006) *Images of Organization*. California, Sage.

Mulgan, R. (1991) Accountability and Responsibility. Unpublished paper.

___ (1994) *Politics in New Zealand*. Auckland, Auckland University Press.

___ (2003) *Holding Power to Account: Accountability in Modern Democracies*. Basingstoke, Palgrave.

___ (2004) *Politics in New Zealand* (4th edn). Auckland, Auckland University Press.

___ (2008a) The Accountability Priorities of Australian Parliamentarians. *Australian Journal of Public Administration* 67(4): 457–69.

___ (2008b) How much Responsiveness is Too Much or Too Little. *Australian Journal of Public Administration* 67(3): 345–56.

___ (2010) Where Have All the Ministers Gone? *Australian Journal of Public Administration* 69(3): 289–300.

Mumford, P. (2010) Enhancing Performance-based Regulation: Lessons from New Zealand's Building Control System. Unpublished PhD Thesis, Victoria University of Wellington.

___ (2011) *Enhancing Performance-Based Regulation: Lessons from New Zealand's Building Control System*. Wellington, Institute of Policy Studies.

Murakami-Wood, D., Ball, K., Lyon, D., Norris, C. and Raab, C.D. (2006) *A Report on the Surveillance Society*. For the Information Commissioner by the Surveillance Studies Network, Full Report. Available at <http://www.ico.gov.uk/upload/documents/library/data_protection/practical_application/surveillance_society_full_report_2006.pdf> (accessed 28 September 2011).

Nabatchi, T. (2010) Addressing the Citizenship and Democratic Deficits: The Potential of Deliberative Democracy for Public Administration. *American Review of Public Administration* 40(4): 376– 99.

National Audit Office, United Kingdom (2001) *Modern Policy-Making: Ensuring Policies Deliver Value for Money*. London, NAO.

Newman, J. and McKee, B. (2005) Beyond the New Public Management? Public Services and the Social Investment State. *Policy & Politics* 33(4): 657–73.

New Zealand Cabinet (2009) Cabinet Paper (09) 31/5. Wellington, New Zealand Government.

NHS Croydon and Croydon Council (2010) *Child: Family: Place: Radical Efficiency to Improve Outcomes for Young Children*. Croydon, NHS Croydon and Croydon Council.

Noble, G.S. (1995) *Report of the Commission of Inquiry into the Collapse of a Viewing Platform at Cave Creek*. Wellington, Department of Internal Affairs.

Norman, R. (2003) *Obedient Servants? Management Freedoms and Accountabilities in the New Zealand Public Sector*. Wellington, Victoria University Press.

___ (2008a) At the Centre or in Control? Central Agencies in Search of New Identities. *Policy Quarterly* 4(2): 33–38.

___(2008b) Managing Performance – New Challenges for Central Agencies: The Case of New Zealand. In KPMG International (Ed.) *Holy Grail or Achievable Quest? International Perspectives on Public Sector Performance Management.* Switzerland, KPMG International.

___ (2009) New Zealand Public Management: Tensions of a Model from the 1980s. Paper Prepared for the Emerging Issues Programme: Future State Project. Wellington, Institute of Policy Studies.

NSW Government (2006) *State Plan: A New Direction for NSW.* Sydney, NSW Premier's Department.

NZCTU (2010) *Alternative Economic Strategy: An Economy that Works for Everyone.* Wellington, New Zealand Council of Trade Unions.

O'Donnell, G. (1998) Horizontal Accountability in New Democracies. *Journal of Democracy* 9(3): 112–26.

OECD (2000) *Government of the Future.* Paris, Organisation for Economic Co-operation and Development.

___ (2001a) *Government for the 21st Century.* Paris, Organisation for Economic Co-operation and Development.

___ (2001b) *Citizens as Partners: Information, Consultation and Public Participation in Policy-Making.* Paris, Organisation for Economic Co-operation and Development.

___ (2001c) *Public Sector Leadership for the 21st Century.* Paris, Organisation for Economic Co-operation and Development.

___ (2003) *The e-Government Imperative,* Paris, Organisation for Economic Cooperation and Development.

___ (2005a) *Modernising Government: The Way Forward.* Paris, Organisation for Economic Cooperation and Development.

___ (2005b) *Enhancing the Performance of the Services Sector.* Paris, Organisation for Economic Co-operation and Development.

___ (2009a) *Focus on Citizens: Public Engagement for Better Policy and Services.* Paris, Organisation for Economic Cooperation and Development.

___ (2009b) *Measuring Government Activity.* Paris, Organisation for Economic Co-operation and Development.

___ (2009c) *Rethinking e-Government Services: User-Centred Approaches,* Paris, Organisation for Economic Co-operation and Development.

___ (2011) *Government at a Glance 2011.* Paris, Organisation for Economic Co-operation and Development.

O'Neill, R.R. (2009) E-government: Transformation of Public Governance in New Zealand? Unpublished PhD Thesis, Victoria University of Wellington.

Orlikowski, W.J. and Barley, S.R. (2001) Technology and Institutions: What Can Research on Information Technology and Research on Organizations Learn From Each Other? *MIS Quarterly* 25(2): 145–65.

Osborne, D. and Gaebler, T. (1992) *Reinventing Government: How the Entrepreneurial Spirit is Transforming the Public Sector.* Reading, M.A., Addison Wesley.

Ostrom, E. (2007) Institutional Rational Choice: An Assessment of the Institutional Analysis and Development Framework. In Sabatier, P.A. (Ed.) *Theories of the Policy Process.* Boulder, C.O., Westview Press.

Oxman, A.D., Lombard, C., Treweek, S., Gagnier, J.J., Maclure, M. and Zwarenstein, M. (2009a) A Pragmatic Resolution. *Journal of Clinical Epidemiology* 62(5): 495–98.

___ (2009b) Why We Will Remain Pragmatists: Four Problems with the Impractical Mechanistic Framework and a Better Solution. *Journal of Clinical Epidemiology* 62(5): 485–88.

Paauwe, J. (2009) HRM and Performance: Achievements, Methodological Issues and Prospects. *Journal of Management Studies* 46(1): 129–42.

Palmer, G. (1987) *Unbridled Power: An Interpretation of New Zealand's Constitution and Government*. Auckland, Oxford University Press.

Pandey, S. (2010) Cutback Management and the Paradox of Publicness. *Public Administration Review* 70(4): 564–76.

Parker, R.S. (1993) Statesmen in Disguise. In Parker, R.S. (Ed.) *The Administrative Vocation: Selected Essays of RS Parker*. Sydney, Hale & Iremonger.

Pateman, C. (1970) *Participation and Democratic Theory*. Cambridge, Cambridge University Press.

Patton, M.Q. (2011) *Developmental Evaluation: Applying Complexity Concepts to Enhance Innovation and Use*. New York, Guilford Press.

Pawson, R. (2006) *Evidence-Based Policy: A Realist Perspective*. London, Sage.

Pestoff, V. (2006) Citizens and Co-production of Welfare Services. *Public Management Review* 8(4): 503–19.

Peters, G. and Pierre, J. (Eds) (2001) *Politicians, Bureaucrats and Administrative Reform*. London, Routledge.

Peters, T.J. and Waterman, R.H. (1982) *In Search of Excellence: Lessons from America's Best-run Companies*. New York, Harper & Row.

Podger, A. (2007) What Really Happens: Departmental Secretary Appointments, Contracts and Performance Pay in the Australian Public Service. *Australian Journal of Public Administration* 66(2): 131–47.

___ (2009) *The Role of Departmental Secretaries: Personal Reflections on the Breadth of Responsibilities Today*. Canberra, ANU ePress.

Polidano, C. (1998) Why Bureaucrats Can't Always Do What Ministers Want: Multiple Accountabilities in Westminster Systems. *Public Policy and Administration* 13(1): 35–50.

Pollitt, C. (2003a) *The Essential Public Manager*. London, Open University Press.

___ (2003b) Joined-up Government: A Survey. *Political Studies Review* 1(1): 34–49.

___ (2006a) Performance Information for Democracy: The Missing Link? *Evaluation* 12(1): 38–55.

___ (2006b) Performance Management in Practice: A Comparative Study of Executive Agencies. *Journal of Public Administration Research and Theory* 16(1): 25–44.

___ (2010) *Public Management Reform During Financial Austerity*. Stockholm, Statskontoret (Swedish Agency for Public Management).

___ (2011) Cutbacks and Innovation: Public Management Reform in an Age of Austerity. Presentation to the KSAP (Polish National School of Public Administration), Warsaw, 27 April.

Pollitt, C. and Bouckaert, G. (2004) *Public Management Reform: A Comparative Analysis* (2nd edn). London, Oxford University Press.

Pomeroy, A. (2007) Changing the Culture of Contracting: Funding for Outcomes. *Social Policy Journal of New Zealand* 31 (July): 158–69.

Powell, W. (1991) Neither Markets Nor Hierarchy: Network Forms of Organisation. *Research in Organizational Behavior* 12: 295–336.

Prebble, M. (2010) *With Respect: Parliamentarians, Officials and Judges Too*. Wellington, Institute of Policy Studies.

Prentice, S. (2006) Childcare, Co-production and the Third Sector in Canada. *Public Management Review* 8(4): 521–36.

Pressman, J.L. and Wildavsky, A.B. (1973) *Implementation: How Great Expectations in Washington are Dashed in Oakland*. Berkeley, University of California Press.

Pride, S. and Meek, N. (November 2009) *A Question of Voice: Secondary Futures as an Experiment in Democratising Education Design*. Seminar Series (Centre for Strategic Education (Vic.); no.109.

Prigogine, I. (1987) Exploring Complexity. In Midgley, G. (Ed.) *Systems Thinking*. London, Sage.

Prigogine, I. and Stengers, I. (1984) *Order Out of Chaos: Man's New Dialogue with Nature.* Toronto, Bantam Books.

Provan, K. and Kenis, D. (2008) Modes of Network Governance: Structure, Management, and Effectiveness. *Journal of Public Administration Theory and Research* 18(2): 229–52.

Public Administration Review (2010) The Future of Public Administration in 2020. *Public Administration Review* 70(S1).

Quinn, R.E. (1988) *Beyond Rational Management: Mastering the Paradoxes and Competing Demands of High Performance.* San Francisco, Jossey-Bass.

___(2004) *Building the Bridge As You Walk On It: A Guide for Leading Change.* San Francisco, Jossey-Bass.

Quinn, R.E., Faerman, S.R., Thompson, M.P., McGrath, M. and St Clair, L. (2006) *Becoming a Master Manager: A Competing Values Approach* (4th edn). New York: Wiley.

Ranson, S. and Stewart J. (1994) *Management in the Public Domain.* London, Palgrave Macmillan.

Review of Expenditure on Policy Advice (2010) *Improving the Quality and Value of Policy Advice.* Wellington: New Zealand Government.

Reynolds, P. (2011) Biophysical Limits and Their Policy Implications: The Nature of the Problem. *Policy Quarterly* 7: 3–7.

Rhodes, M.L. and Murray, J. (2007) Collaborative Decision Making in Urban Regeneration: A Complex Adaptive Systems Perspective. *International Public Management Journal* 10(1): 79–101.

Rhodes R. (1997) *Understanding Governance: Policy Networks, Governance, Reflexivity and Accountability.* London, Open University Press.

Rhodes, R. (2005) Everyday Life in a Ministry: Public Administration as Anthropology. *American Review of Public Administration* 35(1): 3–25.

___(2007) The Everyday Life of a Minister: A Confessional and Impressionist Tale. In Rhodes, R.A.W., t'Hart, P. and Noordegraaf, M. (Eds) *Observing Government Elites: Up Close and Personal.* Basingstoke, Palgrave Macmillan.

___(2011) *Everyday Life in British Government.* Oxford, Oxford University Press.

Rhodes, R. and Wanna, J. (2007) The Limits to Public Value, or Rescuing Responsible Government from the Platonic Guardians. *Australian Journal of Public Administration* 66(4): 406–21.

___(2009) Bringing the Politics Back In: Public Value in Westminster Parliamentary Government. *Australian Journal of Public Administration* 87(2): 161–83.

Rhodes, R., Wanna, J. and Weller, P. (2009) *Comparing Westminster.* Oxford, Oxford University Press.

Rhodes, R. and Weller, P. (Eds) (2001) *The Changing World of Top Officials: Mandarins or Valets?* Buckingham, Open University Press.

Richardson, K.A. (2008) Managing Complex Organizations: Complexity Thinking and the Science and Art of Management. *Emergence: Complexity and Organization* 10(2): 13–27.

Riddell, P., Gruhn, Z. and Carolan, L. (2011) *The Challenge of Being a Minister: Defining and Developing Ministerial Effectiveness.* London, Institute for Government.

Rittel, H. and Webber, M. (1973) Dilemmas in a General Theory of Planning. *Policy Sciences* 4: 155–69.

Roland, M. and Torgerson, D.T. (1998) Understanding Controlled Trials: What are Pragmatic Trials? *British Medical Journal* 316(7127): 285.

Roy, J. (2008) Beyond Westminster Governance: Bringing Politics and Public Service into the Networked Era. *Canadian Public Administration* 51(4): 541–68.

Ryan, B. (2004) *Learning MFO: Developments in Managing for Outcomes.* Brisbane, Institute of Public Administration Australia.

___ (2006) Beyond Westminster: Thinking the Aotearoa/New Zealand Way of Governing. *Policy Quarterly* 2(3): 40–47.

___ (2010) Public Management in the 21st Century: The Public Sphere Redux. Seminar, School of Government and Institute of Policy Studies, Victoria University, Wellington, 20 August.

___ (2011a) Getting in the Road: Why Outcome-oriented Performance Monitoring is Underdeveloped in New Zealand. In Gill, D. (Ed.) *The Iron Cage Recreated: The Performance Management of State Organisations in New Zealand*. Wellington, Institute of Policy Studies.

___ (2011b) Public Management in Difficult Economic Times. *Policy Quarterly* 7(3): 20–27.

Sabatier, P.A. (Ed.) (2007) *Theories of the Policy Process*. Cambridge, M.A., Westview Press.

Sabatier, P.A. and Jenkins-Smith, H. (1993) *Policy Change and Learning: An Advocacy Coalition Approach*. Boulder, C.O., Westview Press.

Sabatier, P.A. and Weible, C.M. (2007) The Advocacy Coalition Framework. In Sabatier, P.A. (Ed.) *Theories of the Policy Process*. Cambridge, M.A., Westview Press.

Salamon, L. (Ed.) (2002) *The Tools of Government: A Guide to the New Governance*. Oxford, Oxford University Press.

Saleebey, D. (2008) (Ed.) *The Strengths Perspective in Social Work Practice* (5th edn). London, Allyn and Bacon.

Sanderson, I. (2009) Intelligent Policy Making for a Complex World: Pragmatism, Evidence and Learning. *Political Studies* 57: 699–719.

Savoie, D.J. (2006) The Canadian Public Service has a Personality. *Canadian Public Administration* 49(3): 261–81.

Schick, A. (1996) *The Spirit of Reform: Managing the New Zealand State Sector in a Time of Change*. Wellington, State Services Commission and The Treasury.

___ (2001) *Reflections on the New Zealand model*. Lecture notes based on a lecture at the New Zealand Treasury in August.

Schön, D.A. and Rein, M. (1994) *Frame Reflection: Toward the Resolution of Intractable Policy Controversies*. New York, Basic Books.

Schumpeter, J.A. (1943) *Capitalism, Socialism and Democracy*. London and New York, Routledge.

Scott, C. and Baehler, K.J. (2010) *Adding Value to Policy Analysis and Advice*. Sydney, University of New South Wales Press.

Scott, G. (2001) *Public Sector Management in New Zealand: Lessons and Challenges*. Canberra, Centre for Law and Economics, Australian National University.

Scott, G., Bushnell, P. and Sallee, N. (1990) Reform of the Core Public Sector: The New Zealand Experience. *Governance* 3: 138–66.

Scott, W.R. (2008) *Institutions and Organisations: Ideas and Interests* (3rd edn). Los Angeles, Sage.

Shergold, P. (2007) What Really Happens in the Australian Public Service: An Alternative View. *Australian Journal of Public Administration* 67(3): 367–70.

Smith, M. (1999) *The Core Executive in Britain*. Basingstoke, Palgrave Macmillan.

Smith, M. (2000) Prime Ministers, Ministers and Civil Servants in the Core Executive. In Rhodes, R.A.W. (Ed.) *Transforming British Government. Volume 1: Changing Institutions*. Basingstoke, Palgrave Macmillan.

Smith, P., Smith, N., Sherman, K., Goodwin, I., Crothers, C., Billot, J. and Bell, A. (2010) *The Internet in New Zealand 2009*. Auckland, Institute of Culture, Discourse and Communication, AUT University.

Smyth, P. (2007) *Social Investment in Human Capital: Revisioning Australian Social Policy*. Social Policy Working Paper No. 8. Melbourne, Brotherhood of St Lawrence.

Snellen, I.Th.M. and Van de Donk, W.B.H.J. (Eds) (1998) *Public Administration in an Information Age: A Handbook*. Amsterdam, IOS Press.

Snider, K.F. (2000) Rethinking Public Administration's Roots in Pragmatism: The Case of Charles A. Beard. *American Review of Public Administration* 30(2): 123–45.

SSC (1995) *Report of the Commission of Inquiry into the Collapse of a Viewing Platform at Cave Creek – State Sector Reform Issues*. Wellington, State Services Commission.

___ (1997) *Responsibility and Accountability: Standards Expected of Public Service Chief Executives: Key Documents*. Wellington, State Services Commission.

___ (2000) *Declining Government Performance? Why Citizens Don't Trust Government*. Working Paper No. 9. Wellington, State Services Commission.

___ (2001) *Annual Report of the State Services Commission for the year ending 30 June 2001, Including the Annual Report of the State Services Commissioner*. Wellington, State Services Commission.

___ (2003) Lessons Learned from Leading Organisational Change: Establishing the Ministry of Social Development. Wellington, State Services Commission. Available at <http://www.ssc.govt.nz/publications-and-resources/2739/all-pages> (accessed 1 October 2011).

___ (2004) *Getting Better at Managing for Shared Outcomes: A Resource for Agency Leaders*. Wellington, State Services Commission.

___ (2006) *Enabling Transformation: A Strategy for E-Government 2006*. Wellington, State Services Commission.

___ (2008a) *Factors for Successful Coordination – A Framework to Help State Agencies Coordinate Effectively*. Wellington: State Services Commission.

___ (2008b) *The Capability Toolkit: A Tool to Promote and Inform Capability Management*. Wellington, State Services Commission.

___ (2010a) *Performance Improvement Framework*. Wellington, State Services Commission, The Treasury and Department of the Prime Minister and Cabinet.

___ (2010b) Employee Engagement in the State Sector. State Services Commission. Available at <http://www.ssc.govt.nz/employee-engagement-2008-09> (accessed 20 October2010).

___ (2010c) *Integrity and Conduct Survey*. Wellington, State Services Commission.

___ (2011) *State Services Commissioner – role and functions*. State Services Commission. Available at <http://www.ssc.govt.nz/sscer> (accessed 21 October 2011).

SSC, Treasury, and Department of the Prime Minister and Cabinet (2009) *Performance Improvement Framework Agency Formal Assessment: The Performance Improvement Framework in Detail*. Wellington, State Services Commission, Treasury, and Department of the Prime Minister and Cabinet.

SSCFPA (2007) *Transparency and Accountability of Commonwealth Funding and Expenditure*. Canberra, Parliament of Australia, Senate Standing Committee on Finance and Public Administration.

Stacey, R.D. (2003) *Strategic Management and Organisational Dynamics: The Challenge of Complexity* (4th edn). Harlow, Pearson Education/Prentice Hall.

Stanyer, J. (1974) Divided Responsibilities: Accountability in Decentralised Government. *Public Administration Bulletin* 17(December): 14–30.

State Sector Reform Secretariat (2011) *Draft Issues Paper: Best-Sourcing Public Services*. Wellington, State Sector Reform Secretariat.

Stewart, A.F. (1997) *Elements of Knowledge: Pragmatism, Logic, and Inquiry*. Nashville, T.N., Vanderbilt University Press.

Stewart, J. (2009) *The Dilemmas of Engagement: The Role of Consultation in Governance*. Canberra, ANU ePress.

Stiglitz, J., Sen, A. and Fitoussi, J-P. (2008) *Report by the Commission on the Measurement of Economic Performance and Social Progress*. Paris, Government of France.

Stoker, G. and John, P. (2009) Design Experiments: Engaging Policy Makers in the Search for Evidence about What Works. *Political Studies* 57: 356–73.

Stone, B. (1995) Administrative Accountability in the 'Westminster' Democracies: Towards a New Conceptual Framework. *Governance* 8(4): 505–26.

Surowiecki, J. (2004) *The Wisdom of Crowds*. New York, Random House.

Tashakkori, A. and Teddlie, C. (Eds) (2009) *Foundations of Mixed Methods Research*. Thousand Oaks, C.A., Sage.

Task Force on Management Improvement (1992) *The Australian Public Service Reformed: An Evaluation of a Decade of Management Reform.* Canberra, AGPS.

Taylor, J.A. (1998) Informatization as X-ray: What is Public Administration for the Information Age? In Snellen, I.Th.M., and Van de Donk, W.B.H.J. (Eds) *Public Administration in an Information Age: A Handbook.* Amsterdam, IOS Press.

Taylor, J.A. and Lips, A.M.B. (2008) The Citizen in the Information Polity: Exposing the limits of the e-government paradigm. *Information Polity* 13(3-4): 139–52.

Taylor, J.A., Lips, A.M.B. and Organ, J. (2009) Identification Practices in Government: Citizen Surveillance and the Quest for Public Service Improvement. *Identity in the Information Society* 1(1): 135–54.

Teisman, G., van Buuren, A. and Gerrits, L. (Eds) (2009) *Managing Complex Governance Systems.* New York, Routledge.

Ter Bogt, H. (2004) Politicians in Search of Performance Information? Survey Research on Dutch Aldermen's Use of Performance Information. *Financial Accountability and Management* 20(3): 221–52.

Thaler, R.H. and Sunstein, C.R. (2008) *Nudge: The Gentle Power of Choice Architecture.* New Haven, Yale University Press.

Thomas, P.G. (2009) Parliament Scrutiny of Government Performance in Australia. *Australian Journal of Public Administration* 68(4): 373–98.

Thompson, G., Frances, J., Levačić, R. and Mitchell, J. (Eds) (1991) *Markets, Hierarchies and Networks: The Coordination of Social Life.* London, Open University Press.

Thorpe, K.E., Zwarenstein, M., Oxman, A.D., Treweek, S., Furberg, C.D., Altman, D.G., et al. (2009) A Pragmatic-Explanatory Continuum Indicator Summary (PRECIS): A Tool to Help Trial Designers. *Journal of Clinical Epidemiology* 62: 464–75.

Tiernan, A. and Weller, P. (2010) *Learning to be a Minister: Heroic Expectations, Practical Realities.* Carlton, Melbourne University Press.

Treasury (1987) *Government Management: Briefing to the Incoming Government.* Wellington, The Treasury.

___ (2005) *A Guide to the Public Finance Act.* Wellington, The Treasury.

___ (2007) Treasury Circular 2007/05. Wellington, The Treasury.

___ (2011a) *Fiscal Strategy Report 2011 Budget.* Wellington, The Treasury.

___ (2011b) Budget 2011 Information Release. Release document, June. Available at <http://www.treasury.govt.nz/publications/informationreleases/budget/2011> (accessed 26 September 2011).

___ (2011c) Working Towards Higher Living Standards for New Zealanders. Wellington, The Treasury.

Turnbull, L. and Aucoin, P. (2006) *Fostering Canadians' Role in Public Policy: A Strategy for Institutionalizing Public Involvement in Policy.* Ottawa, Canadian Policy Research Networks.

Uhr, J. (1998) *Deliberative Democracy in Australia: The Changing Place of Parliament.* Cambridge, Cambridge University Press.

___ (2005a) *Terms of Trust: Arguments Over Ethics in Australian Government.* Sydney, UNSW Press.

___ (2005b) Professional Ethics for Politicians. *International Public Management Journal* 8(2): 247–61.

___ (2008) Distributed Authority in a Democracy: The Lattice of Leadership Revisited. In t'Hart, P., and Uhr, J. (Eds) *Public Leadership: Perspectives and Practice.* Canberra, ANU ePress.

UK Audit Office (2006) *Achieving Innovation in Central Government Organisations.* Report by the Comptroller and Auditor General, HC 1447-I, July. London, The Stationery Office.

Ulrich, D. and Brockbank, W. (2005) *The HR Value Proposition.* Boston, Harvard Business Press.

Varney, D. (2006) *Service Transformation: A Better Service For Citizens and Businesses, a Better Deal For the Taxpayer*. London, HSMO.

von Bertalanffy, L. (1972) The History and Status of General Systems Theory. *Academy of Management Journal* 15(4): 407–26.

Waitangi Tribunal (2011) *Ko Aotearoa Tenei: A Report into Claims Affecting Māori Culture and Identity, Waitangi Tribunal Report 262*. Wellington, Waitangi Tribunal.

Waldrop, M.M. (1992) *The Emerging Science at the Edge of Order and Chaos*. New York, Simon and Schuster.

Wanna, J. (2006) From Afterthought to Afterburner: Australia's Cabinet Implementation Unit. *Journal of Comparative Policy Analysis* 8(4): 347–69.

Wanna, J., Kelly, J. and Forster, J. (2000) *Managing Public Expenditure in Australia*. Sydney, Allen & Unwin.

Wanna, J. and O'Flynn, J. (Eds) (2008) *Collaborative Governance*. Canberra, ANU ePress.

Wamsley, G. (1990) The Agency Perspective: Public Administrators as Agential Leaders. In Wamsley, G., Bacher, R.N., Goodsell, C.T., Kronenberg, P.S., Rohr, J. A., Stivers, C.M., White, O.F. and Wolf, J.F. (Eds) *Refounding Public Administration*. New York, Sage.

Watzlawick, P. (Ed.) (1984) *The Invented Reality*. New York, W.W. Norton.

Weber, M. (1948) *From Max Weber: Essays in Sociology*. Translated, edited, with an Introduction by Gerth, H.H. and Wright Mills, C. London, Routledge and Kegan Paul.

___ (2004) Politics as a Vocation. In Owen, D. and Strong, T. (Eds) trans. by Livingstone, R. *Max Weber: The Vocation Lectures*. Indianapolis, Hackett Publishing.

Weber, E. and Khademian, K. (2008) Managing Collaborative Processes: Common Practices, Uncommon Circumstances. *Administration & Society* 40(5): 431–64.

Weick, K.E. (1979) *The Social Psychology of Organizing* (2nd edn). New York, McGraw-Hill.

___ (1995) *Sense Making in Organisations*. London, Sage.

___ (2001) *Making Sense of the Organization*. Malden, M.A., Blackwell.

Weimer, D.L., and Vining, A.R. (1999) *Policy Analysis: Concepts and Practice*. Upper Saddle River, N.J., Prentice Hall.

Weller, P. (2001) *Australia's Mandarins: The Frank and the Fearless*. Sydney, Allen & Unwin.

Weller, P. and Grattan, M. (1981) *Can Ministers Cope? Australian Federal Ministers at Work*. Melbourne, Hutchinson.

Weller, P., Scott, J. and Stevens, B. (2011) *From Postbox to Powerhouse: A Centenary History of the Department of the Prime Minister and Cabinet*. Sydney, Allen & Unwin.

Whitcombe, J. (1990) *The Accountability Relationship between Chief Executive and Minister Under the State Sector Act 1988*. Wellington, Institute of Policy Studies.

___ (2008) Policy, Service Delivery and Institutional Design: The Case of New Zealand's Social Sector Government Agencies, 1984–2007. Unpublished PhD Thesis, Victoria University of Wellington.

White, A. and Dunleavy, P. (2010) *Making and Breaking Whitehall Departments: A Guide to Machinery of Government Changes*. London, U.K., Institute for Government; LSE Public Policy Group. Available at <http://www.instituteforgovernment.org.uk/publications/10/making-and-breaking-whitehall-departments> (accessed 1 October 2011).

Whitehead, J. (2008) *Continuity and Change: The Ongoing Pursuit of State Sector Performance*. Institute of Public Administration and Victoria University School of Government Symposium, Wellington, 28th February.

Wilks, S. (2007) Boardization and Corporate Governance in the UK as a Response to Depoliticization and Failing Accountability. *Public Policy and Administration* 22(4): 443–60.

Williams, P. (2002) The Competent Boundary Spanner. *Public Administration* 80(1): 103–24.

Wright, P.M. and McMahan, G.C. (1992) Theoretical Perspectives for Strategic Human Resource Management. *Journal of Management* 8(2): 295–320.

Wyn, H. (2007) *Organisational Culture Change: The Centrality of Bureaucratic-Ministerial Relationships.* Unpublished Master of Public Management Thesis, Victoria University of Wellington.

Young Foundation (2010) *Communities in the Big Society: Shaping, Managing, Running Services.* London, Young Foundation.

Young, B. and Hazell, R. (2011) *Putting Goats Among the Wolves: Appointing Ministers From Outside Parliament.* London, The Constitution Unit, University College London.

Young, R.D. (2005) *An Overview: Oregon Shines II and Oregon Benchmarks.* South Carolina Indicators Project Publication. Columbia, Institute for Public Service and Policy Research, University of South Carolina.

Index